THE MADONNA DI SAN SISTO.
(Virgin and Child with St. Barbara and Pope Sixtus II.)
Raphael.
(Dresden Gallery.)

APOLLO

AN ILLUSTRATED MANUAL OF
THE HISTORY OF ART THROUGHOUT THE AGES

By S. REINACH

Member of the Institute of France

From the French by FLORENCE SIMMONDS

With Six Hundred Illustrations

NEW EDITION, REVISED BY THE AUTHOR

New York: CHARLES SCRIBNER'S SONS
London: WILLIAM HEINEMANN

FUNERAL OF RICHARD II. IN LONDON.
(Miniature from a French MS. of 1480 at Breslau.)

PREFACE

With the exception of the last, which I have altered and re-written several times, all these lectures appear more or less exactly as given by me at the Ecole du Louvre in 1902-1903. I claim it as a merit for them, that they have stood the test of oral delivery. The dissent and approval of an audience, some echo of which always reaches the lecturer, are the most instructive of guides to him; I have taken them into account in revising these lessons for publication, just as I took note of them when lecturing.

Every science requires not only special works of erudition, but synthetic exposition, written and spoken. In such exposition, general ideas are necessarily of the first and facts of the second importance, whereas in erudite instruction, every hour of synthesis should, as Fustel de Coulanges has said, be based on a year of analysis. This hour does not come to all men; but when it comes, it is well to profit by it, and, better still, to make others profit.

At the Ecole du Louvre, I finished each of my lessons with a few words of bibliography, restricting myself to the mention of three or four recent and indispensable works. In publishing these lectures I have thought it well to develop this feature more especially. I have been very moderate with regard to antique art, because there are many accessible books of reference; I myself have published one or

PREFACE

two. But there is scarcely anything touching the Middle Ages and modern times even in the largest works. I have had to build up a complete bibliography, and I am sure it will prove useful. After careful consideration, I deliberately excluded all works bearing rather upon archæology than on art-history. I have also excluded, with few exceptions, all books and articles published before 1880, and more especially large and expensive volumes, only to be found in important libraries. On the other hand, I have freely quoted good popular works and articles in reviews, particularly those of the *Gazette des Beaux-Arts*, which has a wide circulation, may be purchased in single numbers, and has excellent illustrations.[1] If my text appeals primarily to beginners and to the leisured classes, I may hope that even the most highly educated will be able to glean in the bibliographies; they will also find there references to many works and artists which I have omitted to mention, or have only mentioned in passing in the text, being anxious to avoid a monotonous enumeration of proper names.

The title *Apollo* reminds my readers that this book is intended to be a companion volume to *Minerva*, an introduction to the Greek and Latin classics published by me in 1889, and still maintaining its popularity after four large editions. I hope that *Apollo* may share the good fortune of his sister, and that by disseminating the principles of art-history, he may gain new adherents for that antique Wisdom, that Minerva of the Acropolis, which, far from teaching us to neglect, the study of mediæval and modern art will help us to enjoy more perfectly.

S. REINACH.

ROMAN ALTAR OF THE FIRST CENTURY.
(Museum, Arles.)

[1] A chronological list of the principal articles which have appeared in the Gazette appears in 1909, I., p. 13. A complete general index has been published covering the years 1910-1915.

CONTENTS

CONTENTS

BAS-RELIEF, THE ACROPOLIS, ATHENS.
Fourth Century B.C.

I

THE ORIGIN OF ART

Art a Social Phenomenon.—The Art of the Savage and of the Child akin.—Primitive Manifestations of the Artistic Instinct.—Art in the Quaternary Period.—The Art of the Reindeer Hunters.—Prehistoric Paintings in Cave Dwellings.—The Caves of Périgord and of the Pyrenees.—The Magic Element in Primitive Works of Art.

HUMAN industry is the outcome of need, or as the proverb has it, necessity is the mother of invention. From the first dawn of humanity, man was obliged to fashion tools, weapons, and clothing, to provide himself with shelter against the fury of the elements and the attacks of wild beasts. He was industrious of necessity before he became an artist by choice.

A work of art differs in one essential characteristic from those products of human activity which supply the immediate wants of life. Let us consider a palace, a picture. The palace might be merely a very large house, and yet provide a satisfactory shelter. Here, the element of art is *superadded* to that of utility. In a statue, a picture, utility is no longer apparent. The element of art is *isolated*.

This element, sometimes accessory, sometimes isolated, is itself a product of human activity, but of an activity peculiarly free and disinterested, the object of which is not to satisfy an immediate need,

1

but to evoke a sentiment, a lively emotion—admiration, pleasure, curiosity, sometimes even terror.

Art, in whatever degree it may manifest itself, appears to us under the dual aspect of a luxury and a diversion.

Its object being the evocation of sentiment in others, art is primarily a *social* phenomenon. Man fashions a tool for his own use, but he decorates it to please his fellow-men, or to excite their admiration.

No society, however rudimentary, has altogether ignored art. It is to be found in embryo in the strange tattooed devices that cover the body of the savage, as also in his efforts to give an agreeable shape to the handle of his hatchet or of his knife.

The study of primitive art may be carried on in two ways: by the observation of living savages, or by examination of the relics of primæval savages found buried in the soil. It is interesting to find that the two methods have, on the whole, the same results. Art manifests itself first in the desire for symmetry, which is analogous to the rhythm of poetry and music, and the taste for colour, not so arranged as to produce images, but applied or exhibited to please the eye. It goes on to trace ornaments composed of straight or curved, parallel or broken lines. Man next attempts to reproduce the animals that surround him, first in the round, afterwards in relief and by means of drawing; finally he essays, though timidly, the imitation of the human figure and of vegetation. This suggestion of evolution may be verified by observing children, who, in our civilised society, offer a parallel with primitive savagery. A child delights successively in symmetry, colour, the juxtaposition and inter-lacement of lines. When he begins to draw, his first scrawls are the silhouettes of animals, which interest him much more than his fellow-creatures; it is not until later that he draws men and plants.

A science born in the nineteenth century, prehistoric archæology, has revealed to us the fruits of human industry at a period prodigiously remote, centuries anterior to the building of the pyramids of Egypt and the palaces of the Babylonian kings.

Geologists have given the name *quaternary* period to this epoch, because it was the last of the four great geological periods. The aspect of the earth was very different to that it wears at present. To mention but one or two divergences, France was not then separated from England by the Straits of Dover, nor Sicily from Italy by the Straits of Messina. Sweden, Denmark, and Scotland were buried under a sheet of polar ice; the glaciers of the Alps were of vast extent; one descended as far as Lyons.

In the quaternary period, horses, cattle, and goats already existed both in England and in France, but as wild animals; man had not domesticated them, and, ignorant of agriculture, he lived solely on the fruits of plants and the spoils of hunting and fishing. In addition to the species which still persist, there were others which have disappeared, such as the mammoth and the rhinoceros with divided nostrils; and others again which now exist only in warmer climates than ours, such as the hippopotamus, the hyæna, and the lion, or in colder latitudes, such as

FIG. I.—ENGRAVED BONE.
From the Caverne de la Madeleine, Dordogne.
(British Museum.)

the reindeer. Man, armed with clubs, flint axes, and horn daggers, contrived to nourish himself on the flesh of cattle, horses, and reindeer, which he took in snares, or hunted down in the chase. Armed with a harpoon of bone or horn, he also killed fish, and so varied his diet.

The quaternary period lasted for thousands of years, coming to an end some 10,000 or 12,000 years before the Christian era, according to the most moderate calculations of the geologists. It closed when the climate, the fauna, and the flora of Europe had become much what they are to-day, when the last reindeer of the

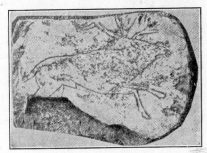

FIG. IA.—REINDEER GALLOPING.
Drawn on a flat stone (Indre).
(Museum, St. Germain.)

Alps and Pyrénées had disappeared after the last mammoth.

We are beginning to acquire some exact knowledge of the phases of this long period: we know that there was an earlier one, when the climate was hot and very damp; a later one, when it was cold and dry.

During the first phase, man, hunter or fisher, lived on the banks of the rivers, then much broader than now. He made flint axes which have been found in thousands deep beneath the sands piled up by rivers in flood; notably at Saint Acheul on the Somme and at Chelles on the Marne. Many of these axes, triangular or oval in shape, are carved with great dexterity by means of small chips flaked off the stone, and show a regularity of outline which testifies to the delight of primitive man in symmetry. It seems probable that the men of this period lived in the open air, or in huts made of the branches of trees; no traces of their habitations have been found.

Our knowledge of the second period is more abundant. The reindeer, non-existent in the earlier phase, became as numerous as horses or kine, furnishing man not only with succulent meat, but with horn, bone, and tendons, which lent themselves to the first essays of industry and art. Daggers, harpoons, stilettoes, and various implements made of reindeer horn have been unearthed; and also carved reindeer horns and bones, covered with reliefs and drawings.

FIG. 2 —MAMMOTH ENGRAVED ON WALL.
(Cave of Combarelles, Dordogne.)

The man who lived on reindeer's flesh had remarked the chromatic qualities of certain earths, more particularly of ochre. He was fond of vivid colours, and it is probable that like the savages of our own times he painted his body. But he did much more than this. On the walls and roofs of the caves where he sought shelter from the cold (which at that period obtained for nine months of the year), he amused himself by engraving and painting animals with extraordinary dexterity. During the last few years, prehistoric paintings of the highest interest have been discovered in many of the caves of Périgord and the Pyrénées.

In those caves of France, where it has been possible to observe the superposition of the various strata of civilisation, it has been found that figures in the round, carved in stone, or in the bones of mammoth and reindeer, lay buried more deeply, and are consequently earlier, than those carved in relief or drawn. Drawings made with a style, the products of this art in its greatest perfection, are contemporary with paintings, which show the same characteristics, and deserve no less admiration.

Of these characteristics, the most striking is realism. Fancy

4

seems to be absolutely excluded; whether represented alone or in groups, the animals are depicted with a correctness to which we find no parallel in the art of the modern savage. The next character-istic is sobriety. There are no useless details; certain animal forms of this period, either engraved or painted, will bear comparison with the fine animal-studies of modern artists. Finally—and this is perhaps the most extraordin-ary trait of all—the artist of the reindeer age is in love with life and movement; he likes to represent his animals in lively and picturesque atti-tudes; he seizes and repro-duces their movements with extraordinary precision.

FIG. 3.—BISON ENGRAVED AND PAINTED ON A WALL.
(Cave of Fond de Gaume, Dordogne.)
Revue de l'École d'Anthropologie, July, 1902.
Félix Alcan, Paris.

It must, of course, be under-stood that these eulogies do not apply to all the works of art of the cave-dwellers. They apply to perhaps thirty or forty specimens, carved, engraved, or painted, among the hundreds that have been collected and reproduced. Then, as always, there were gifted artists and mediocre artists. But in this rapid sketch of the art of all ages, I must confine myself to the mention of masterpieces, and the mas-terpieces of the reindeer period are worthy of the name.

How and where was this art developed? It is evident that its finest productions were the final outcome of a long progression. The man of the quaternary period, like the modern man, was per-haps born with the artistic instinct, but he was not born an artist. Many generations had to pass before he had learnt to draw the outline of an animal correctly with his sharpened flint, before his first essays, his first scrawls, took on the dignity of true works of art. Our knowledge of this period is as yet far too restricted to enable us to trace the stages of this development. It is indeed possible, and even probable, that it began in another part of Europe, for the reindeer, which did not exist in France in the warm phase of the quaternary period, must then have abounded in the more northern regions, and there is every reason to suppose that the ancestors of the reindeer hunters of Périgord and the Pyrénées flourished to-gether with their favourite game. The evolution of art, however, cannot have made much progress in this primitive field; and, no doubt, it was in the basin of the Garonne that it was accelerated and accomplished. When the cold period came to an end, the reindeer disappeared almost suddenly, and was replaced by the stag. At this epoch, which marks the close of the quaternary period, the drawings become rare and finally disappear altogether. The civilisation of the reindeer-hunters seems to have died out, or to have migrated with the reindeer towards the north of Europe. But, so far, no trace of it has come to light, nor has it been possible to establish any definite connection between the art of the reindeer-hunters and that of civilisations of great antiquity, though certainly more recent than theirs, such as those of Egypt and Babylonia.

Thus we find that the art of quaternary France forms a clearly defined phase in the very genesis of art history. We may trace the successive apparition of the desire for symmetry, of sculpture, bas-relief, engraving, and painting; of all the loftier forms of art, architecture alone is absent.

The masterpiece of this phase of art is perhaps the group of stags (Fig. 4) engraved on an antler discovered in the cave of Lorthet (H. Pyrénées). First we see the hind feet of a stag which is galloping away. Next comes another galloping stag, in an attitude first revealed to us in modern times by instantaneous photography as applied to the analysis of rapid movement. An artist of our own day, Aimé Morot, first made use of the knowledge gleaned from photographs, and reproduced this action in his horses.

FIG. 4.—ENGRAVED STAG BONE.
Grotte de Lorthet, Hautes Pyrénées.
(Museum, St. Germain.)

L'Anthropologie, 1894. (Masson, Paris.)

It was unknown to all the artists of intermediate ages. The second stag is followed by a doe, turning her head to bell and call her fawn; her action again is like that of the deer in front of her. Between the animals the artist drew some salmon, as if to fill up the empty spaces; above the last stag, he placed two pointed lozenges. It has been suggested that these constitute a signature. But what is the meaning of the salmon? This association of the great river-fish with the stag is doubtless due to some religious idea; the artist combined the two species which

FIG. 5.—A HORSE GALLOPING.
(From instantaneous photographs.)

formed the principal nourishment of his tribe or clan. It is, in fact, to be noted that all the animals represented by quaternary art are of the comestible kinds, which savages engraved or painted in order to attract them by a sort of magic sympathy. Civilised man makes hyperbolic use of the expression "the magic of art." The primitives actually believed in it.

In a cave in the department of the Indre, a slab of schist was recently discovered, decorated with a galloping reindeer, another example of the taste for movement, combined with precision and sobriety of outline, which

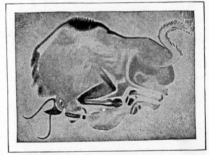

FIG. 6.—BISON PAINTED ON THE ROCK.
Cave of Altamira (Spain).
L'Anthropologie, 1904 (Masson, Paris.)

characterised the best artists of this period.

Of their paintings, the finest, those in the cave of Altamira near Santander in Spain, have been copied (Fig. 6). Other specimens found in the caves of Périgord (Figs. 2, 3), as well as a group of figures in the round sculp-

FIG. 6A.—GROUP OF TWO BISONS.
Cavern of Tuc d'Audoubert (Ariège).

7

tured in clay, found in a cave of the Ariège (Fig. 6a), are also of the deepest interest.

In a cave of Périgord was found a stone lamp, ornamented with a beautiful incised representation of an ibex. The artists of the period must have made use of such lamps when graving and painting their decorations, for the ornamented portions of the caves are quite dark, even in broad daylight.

/ Among all these surprising discoveries, this seems to be the most amazing! These paintings, consisting sometimes of over a hundred animals of large dimensions, could only have been executed, and were only visible, by artificial light! Why then did their authors take the trouble to execute them? Was it only to please the eye of the reindeer-hunter, when, retiring to his cavern at nightfall, he made his evening meal on the spoils of the chase, by the dim light of smoking lamps filled with oil from the fat of deer?

It is impossible to accept such an hypothesis. I have already spoken of the magic element in the works of art carved, engraved, or painted by primitive man. They show us the first steps of humanity in the path which led to the worship of animals (as in Egypt), then to that of idols in human shape (as in Greece), and finally to that of divinity as a purely spiritual conception. The study of the birth of religion is interwoven with that of the origin of art. Born simultaneously, art and religion were closely connected for long ages; their affinity is still evident enough to the thinking mind. /

BIBLIOGRAPHY OF CHAPTER I.

Alex. Betrand, *La Gaule avant les Gaulois*, 2nd ed., Paris, 1891 (with an Appendix by E. Piette on the Reindeer Age and the Pyrenean caverns explored by him); G. and A. de Mortillet, *Le Musée Préhistorique*, 2nd ed., Paris, 1903 (copiously illustrated); S. Reinach, *Alluvions et Cavernes*, Paris, 1889; *Repertoire de l'art quatenaire*, Paris, 1913; M. Boule, *Les hommes fossiles*, Paris, 1921; H. F. Osborn, *Men of the Old Stone Age*, 3rd ed., New York, 1918; E. Piette, *L'Anthropologie*, 1904, p. 130.

For the paintings recently discovered in the caves by Messrs. Rivière, Capitan, Breuil, and Cartailhac, see the *Revue Mensuelle de l'Ecole d'Anthropologie*, 1902, and *L'Anthropologie*, 1902-1904; Cartailhac and Breuil, *Altamira Monaco*, 1908 (*L'Anthropologie*, 1904, p. 625). For an explanation of these works, cf. S. Reinach, *L'Art et la Magie* (*L'Anthropologie*, 1903, p. 257).

On primitive Art in general: E. Grosse, *Les Débuts de l'Art*, French translation, Paris, 1902.

On the Art of the Child: J. Sully, *Studies of Childhood*, London, 1903.

On the idea of Art and Æsthetics: E. Véron, *L'Esthétique*, Paris, 1876; English ed., London, 1877; V. Cherbuliez, *L'Art et la Nature*, 2nd ed., Paris, 1892; G. Séailles, *Essai sur le Génie dans l'Art*, 2nd ed., Paris, 1897; M. Guyau, *L'Art au point de vue Sociologique*, 5th ed., Paris, 1901; A Fouillée, *La Morale, l'Art et la Religion d'après Guyau*, 3rd ed., Paris, 1901; K. Lange, *Das Wesen der Kunst*, 2 vols., Berlin, 1901; M. Vauthier, *Le plaisir esthétique* (*Rev. Univ.*, Bruxelles, 1909, p. 481).

On Method in Art History: C. Bertaux, *L'Histoire de l'Art et les Œuvres d'Art* (*Revue de Synthèse historique*, 1902).

II

ART IN THE POLISHED STONE AND BRONZE AGES

The Extinction of the Art of the Reindeer Hunters.—Primitive Dwellings, Rude Flint Implements.—Lacustrine Dwellings and Polished Stone Implements.—Dolmens, Menhirs, Cromlechs.—Domestication of Animals and Culture of Cereals.—First Use of Metals.—The Bronze Age.—Tumuli of Gavrinis, Morbihan, and New Grange, Ireland.—The Absence of Animal Forms in the Decoration of the Bronze Age.—High Degree of Excellence in Linear Decoration of this Period.—Stonehenge.—The Second Stone Age in Egypt.—Pre-Pharaonic Art: Painted Vases discovered at Abydos and Negadah (Upper Egypt).—Primitive Art in the Grecian Archipelago.—Babylon and Egypt the Precursors of Classic Art.

THE extinction of the civilisation of the reindeer-hunters seems to have been brought about by a change of climate. Some geological phenomenon hitherto unexplained caused a cessation of the cold, which was succeeded by torrential rains and damp warmth. The reindeer, for which the present climate of St. Petersburg is too hot, disappeared or migrated; the caves, invaded by streams of water, and often swept by the rivers in flood, became uninhabitable; vast plains were transformed into swamps. The population of France was not, indeed, annihilated, but it certainly diminished very greatly, the reduction being brought about partly by the change of climate, partly by emigration. The civilisation of the reindeer age disappeared. When we find traces of a new civilisation in France, it is marked by a poverty and coarseness that reveal the catastrophes among which it was brought forth. A new humanity may almost be said to have come into being; and if that of the quaternary age had required thousands of years to evolve true works of art, some thirty or forty centuries had again to pass before works of art worthy of the name were produced in Western Europe.

The first buildings of the present period (using the term in its geological sense) are the camps or remains of villages, where the chief evidences of human activity are the flint implements of a primitive type known as celts, and fragments of coarse pottery with incised ornaments. These latter mark an industrial progress, for the artists of the reindeer age knew nothing of pottery. To a later epoch, some 4,000 or 3,000 years before Christ, belong the first traces of those encampments built upon piles on the banks of lakes

FIG. 7.—DOLMEN OF KORKONNO.
(Morbihan, Brittany.)

in Switzerland and France, and known as lacustrine dwellings. These were used as places of refuge and as workshops. The civilisation of the lake-dwellers is familiar to us, for thousands of objects fashioned by them have been discovered embedded in the mud. Among these, in addition to hand‑made pottery, are hatchets of polished stone, sometimes very elegant in shape, arms, tools, and pendants; but not a single work of art has come to light.

This polished stone period to which the lake-dwellings belong, was also the age when in other regions of Europe, notably in Brittany, the Cevennes, England, Denmark and Sweden, men began to raise those huge tombs of undressed stone known as dolmens (Fig. 7), the obelisks known as menhirs, the circles of rough stone known as cromlechs, and long lines of massive blocks such as those of Carnac (Fig. 8). The dolmens are indubitably of the same period as the most ancient of the lacustrine dwellings, for in both polished stone axes have been discovered, whereas there is scarcely a trace of metals.

The phase of human history on which we are now touching is marked by two innovations of the highest importance: the culture of cereals and the domestication of animals. Carbonised cereals

FIG. 8.—ROWS OF STONE BLOCKS AT CARNAC.
(Morbihan, Brittany.)

and heaps of manure have been found in the mud of the lake-dwellings, and it is more than probable that the civilisation of the dolmen-builders was analogous to that of the lake-dwellers. We cannot now inquire into the question how man first conceived the idea of domesticating animals, sowing corn, barley, millet, and flax; it will be sufficient to point out that these immense advances in civilisation were made before the discovery of metals.

The construction of lake-dwellings and of dolmens continued even after man had begun to make use of gold and copper, the first two metals he knew. A little later the dis-covery of tin, and some happy incident which led to the idea of fusing tin and copper, placed a new metal, bronze, at man's disposal, and thus gave a considerable impetus to material civilisation.

FIG. 9.—CARVED MENHIR. PRIMITIVE STATUE. (Saint Sernin, Aveyron.)

Lake-dwellings of the age of bronze have been discovered, the axes, swords, and metal ornaments of which bear witness to the advanced stage of technical proficiency reached by their inhabitants. But in the dolmens, only very simple bronze objects, such as beads, buttons, and knives have been found; the practice of burying the dead in dolmens must therefore have been discontinued before the abandonment of the lake-dwellings (B.C. 1000?).

The total absence of pure works of art at this period is a subject of much sur-prise to archæologists. If we except a few wretched figures in terra cotta, a few menhirs rudely carved into a semblance of the human form (Fig. 9), there are no images either of men or animals. But, on the other hand, linear decoration is very highly developed. On the little island of Gavrinis, off the coast of Morbihan,

FIG. 10.—ENGRAVED GRANITE BLOCKS IN THE COVERED ALLEY, GAVRINIS. (Morbihan, Brittany.)

rises one of those huge mounds of earth called tumuli. Inside the tumulus is a dolmen, approached by a long alley bordered with enormous blocks of granite. These blocks are covered with elaborate designs, carved with flint implements, works which must have cost their authors an infinity of time and trouble (Fig. 10). We find a few axes introduced among the ornament, but nothing resembling any living creature. There is a similar monument in Ireland, at New Grange, near Dublin. Here the walls are covered with designs very like those at Gavrinis, and perhaps older. In Denmark, Sweden, Spain, and Portugal there are other large dolmens, in all of which representations of human and animal life are likewise conspicuous by their absence.

The existence of art in the age of bronze is manifested by the graceful form of such objects as spears, daggers, swords, bracelets, vases, etc., and also by the purely linear ornament with which they are embellished. This ornament consists of dog-toothing, triangles, zigzags, rectangles, dotted bands, and concentric circles, showing a variety and ingenuity of combination that bear witness to the decorative instinct of the potters and bronze-workers of the age (Fig. 11). But the decoration is invariably and exclusively linear, as if some religious law, some fear of maleficent sorcery, had forbidden the representation of men and animals. In Western Europe

FIG. 11.—BRONZE BRACELET.
Found at Reallon, Hautes Alpes.
(Museum. St. Germain.)

this was the case for centuries, with some unimportant exceptions, even after the introduction of iron tools and weapons. The utmost achieved by the Gauls before Cæsar's conquest of Gaul was the execution of a few animals in bronze, and of a few more or less shapeless figures on coins. Before a new plastic art arose among them. the Gauls, who excelled alike as workers in metal and in enamel, had to become the pupils of Roman artists, themselves disciples of the Greeks. In Great Britain, as in the regions now included in the German Empire, it was also Roman conquest or Roman commerce which led to the tardy adoption of figure-ornament. Sweden and Denmark only began to produce it towards the period of the downfall of the Empire, though the inhabitants of these countries had continuously manufactured weapons, ornaments, and vases of metal, decorated with an astonishing variety of linear motives (Fig. 12). All this was art, for it was in the nature of luxury and amusement; but it was incomplete art, for the imitation of living nature had no place in it.

Dolmens and menhirs mark the beginnings of architecture, but of architecture scarcely worthy of the name, for decoration plays hardly any part in

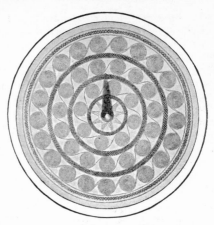

FIG. 12.—BRONZE PLAQUE.
Found in Sweden. (Stockholm Museum.)

it, and the elements of construction can claim no excellence other than that of a massive solidity. The only monument of this nature which has any artistic character is the circle of triliths, each consisting of two uprights with a lintel, at Stonehenge on Salisbury Plain, but the blocks of stone are hewn, and Stonehenge does not apparently date from a more remote period than the bronze age (Fig. 13). After this age, the only stone buildings of Western Europe were walls of defence; the dwellings and even the temples were of wood. It was the Roman Conquest, again, which gave the Gauls the principles and the first models of architecture.

FIG. 13.—STONEHENGE.
(Photo. by Spooner.)

Thus we see that the genius of the arts, after having flourished in France for several thousands of years before the Christian era, underwent a long eclipse of at least forty centuries, giving place to a decorative sentiment that excluded the representation of living things.

This was, happily, not the case on the eastern shores of the Mediterranean. Stone axes like those of Saint-Acheul have been discovered in Egypt and on the coast of Asia; but so far, we have no evidences that art had developed there in the quaternary age, nor do we find there traces of anything analogous to the marvellous drawings of the reindeer hunters. On the other hand, the second stone age in Egypt was marked by a civilisation no less consummate than rapidly achieved. Of the corresponding period in Babylon we know little as yet; but thanks to the recent researches of Messrs. Morgan, Amélineau, and Flinders Petrie in Egypt, we know that the Egyptians, before they had begun to use bronze and iron, produced thousands of fictile vases decorated with paintings, large flint knives most admirably worked, articles of luxury, and personal ornaments of hippopotamus-ivory and schist, and vases of hard stone. Before the epoch of the Pharaohs, which was also that of introduction of metals, Egypt, though destitute of architecture, boasted a very flourishing industry, which did not hesitate to essay the representation of human figures, animals, and plants, in painting, in terra cotta, in ivory, and in schist. It is true that these essays are extremely rude, and that the personages drawn or engraved by the Egyptians of the stone age resemble the sketches of savages; but the Egyptian savage possessed a manual dexterity superior to that of his western contemporaries, and, for him, art was not confined to linear decoration.

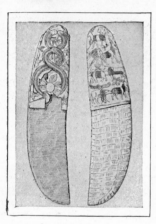

FIG. 14.—FLINT KNIFE WITH A GOLD SHEATH.

(Museum, Cairo.)

Morgan, *Recherches sur les Origines de l'Égypte*, vol. i. (Leroux, Paris.)

Let us examine the flint-knife, ornamented with a sheet of engraved gold, in the Museum of Cairo. Gold, which is found in its raw state, was known in the later stone age; it was, perhaps, this

metal which suggested the discovery and employment of others.
The style of the engraved animals—serpents, lions, and antelopes—
is totally different from that which obtained in the Egypt of the
Pharaohs; but it is already a style which aims at the suggestion of
life (Fig. 14).

This object, however, is exceptional in quality. To get a general
idea of primitive Egyptian art, we must study the painted vases
which have been discovered in large numbers in the burial-places of
Abydos and Negadah (Upper Egypt). Some of these are decorated
with paintings of ostriches, and of Nile boats, with flags fore and

aft; there are also human
figures in attitudes expressive
of adoration or distress. Other
examples of these gestures are
to be seen in the terra cotta
figures at Negadah, which
appear to be tattooed all over.
From the same necropolis we
have little figures in ivory and
in schist, dating, no doubt,
from about the year 4000 B.C.

In the deeper strata of the
city of Troy, excavated by

FIG. 15.—PAINTINGS ON PRIMITIVE EGYPTIAN
VASES.

(Museum, Cairo.)

Morgan, *Recherches sur les Origines de
l'Égypte*, vol. ii. (Leroux, Paris.)

Schliemann, as also in the more archaic tombs of the Archipelago, vases and primitive figurines have been discovered which
may be compared to those found in Egypt, though they are
not in any sense imitations. Here, also, the civilisation of the
stone age, though not strictly speaking artistic, reveals elements
other than those of the purely decorative style. On the other hand,
the eastern shores of the Mediterranean did not, during the bronze
age, show a development of geometric decoration equal to that
achieved in the west and north of Europe. A parallel may be
found in the fact that Mussulman art, which refrained from the
representation of the human figure, reached a higher stage of
development in the science of ornament than the western art of the
Middle Ages.

We have now come to the period verging on the year 4000 B.C.
At this epoch, Babylon and Egypt took the lead in civilisation, and
prepared the way for the splendour of classic art. From about the
year 2500 B.C. a new centre of activity was formed in the Archipelago, and developed with extraordinary rapidity. After a temporary eclipse about the year 1000 B.C. Greece entered upon her

triumphal progress towards the art of Phidias and Praxiteles. Greece had to submit to Rome, and Rome to conquer part of the ancient world, before Italy and the west of Europe at last participated in the radiance of this manifestation. It was destined to die out in Greece, as it had already died out in Egypt and Assyria, and to dawn again, after a fresh eclipse, in Western Europe, which, from the year 1000 A.D., became and has remained the home of art. This rapid survey will have indicated the divisions of my subject, and prepared my readers for the developments I propose to trace.

BIBLIOGRAPHY OF CHAPTER II.

Works by J. Déchelette and G. de Mortillet, given in bibliography of Chap. I. (lacustrine dwellings, dolmens, menhirs, cromlechs). For the carved menhirs (Aveyron), see Hermet, *Bulletin du Comité*, 1898, p. 500.

For the Bronze Age in Western and Northern Europe: O. Montelius, *Chronologie der aeltesten Bronzezeit*, Brunswick, 1900, and *Les Temps préhistoriques en Suède*, French translation by S. Reinach, Paris, 1895; *La Chronologie préhistorique en France* (*L'Anthropologie*, 1901, p. 609); *Orient und Europa*, 1901; *Die aelteren Kulturperioden im Orient und in Europa*, vol. i., Stockholm, 1903; M. Hoernes, *Urgeschichte der bildenden Kunst in Europa*, Vienna, 1898; J. Romilly Allen, *Celtic Art*, London, 1904.

For Prehistoric Egypt: J. de Morgan, *Recherches sur les Origines de l'Egypte*, 2 vols., Paris, 1896, 1897; W. Budge, *Egypt in the Neolithic and Archaic Periods*, London, 1902; J. Capart, *Primitive Art in Egypt*, London, 1905; S. Reinach, *L'Anthropologie*, 1897, p. 327; A. J. Reinach, *L'Egypte préhistorique*, Paris, 1908.

For the Prehistoric Civilisation of the Archipelago: Perrot and Chipiez, *Histoire de l'Art*, vol. vi., Paris, 1894; S. Reinach, *L'Anthropologie*, 1899, p. 513; W. Ridgway, *The Early Age of Greece*, vol. i., Cambridge, 1901; E. Meyer, *Geschichte des altertums*, 2nd ed., vol. i., Berlin, 1909 (French translation, Paris, 1912); R. Dussaud, *Civilisations préhelleniques dans la mer Egée*, 2nd ed., Paris, 1904.

III

EGYPT, CHALDÆA, AND PERSIA

Art in Egypt under the Pharaohs.—The Saite Revival.—The Characteristics of Egyptian Art.—Egyptian Temples.—Karnak.—Egyptian Statues, Figurines, Bas-reliefs, and Paintings in Tombs.—The Scribe in the Louvre.—Conventions of Egyptian Art.—Lange's "Law of Frontality."—Egyptian Decorative Motives.—The Idea of Duration dominant in Egyptian Art.—Chaldæan Art: The Monuments of Tello, near Bassorah.—Assyrian Art: The Bas-reliefs of the Palace of Nineveh.—Assyrian Palaces.—Type of Assyrian Temples.—Persian Art: The Palaces of Susa and Persepolis.—The Frieze of Archers in the Louvre.—Hittite Art based on that of Assyria.—The Phœnicians: Purely Industrial Character of their Art.—Jewish Art derived from that of Assyria.—The Antiquity of Indian and Chinese Art a Delusion.—Both derived from Greece.

THE art of historic Egypt, the Egypt of the Pharaohs, began about the year 4000 B.C. The so-called *Ancient Empire* lasted from about this date to the year 3000 B.C.; the *Middle Empire*, destroyed by the incursion of the shepherds of the desert, or Hycsos, from 3000 to 2000 B.C. and the *New Empire* from 1700 to 1100. This was succeeded by a long period of decadence, only temporarily arrested, from 720 to 525 B.C. by a brilliant Renaissance under the Pharaohs of Saïs (Saïte period). In 525, Egypt was conquered by the Persians, in 332 by Alexander, and then successively by the Romans, the Arabs, the Turks, the French and the English. She has never regained her independence since 525 B.C. But in our own times she has achieved a prosperity almost equal to that of her period of ancient splendour.

FIG. 16.—HYPOSTYLE OR COLUMNED HALL OF THE TEMPLE OF KARNAK.

(Reconstructed by Ch. Chipiez.)

The history of Egyptian art which we are able to trace in existing monuments, is marked by certain invariable characteristics; on the one hand, a technical skill that has remained unsurpassed throughout the ages; on the other, an absolute incapacity to throw aside archaic conventions and rise to liberty and beauty.

First among the nations of the earth, the Egyptians raised great

17

buildings of stone, with vast halls upheld by columns, lighted laterally from above. Such is the great hall of the temple of Karnak at

FIG. 17.—PYRAMID OF CHEOPS, WITH THE GREAT SPHINX.
(Near Cairo.)

Thebes (Fig. 16), with its 134 columns, some of them nearly 70 feet high (New Empire). Egypt boasted many temples more imposing than the Athenian Parthenon; but these massive buildings are only impressive because of their bulk; they are decorated without taste or sobriety. The most obvious defect of the Egyptian temple is that it is too long for its height and that the exterior shows too much wall and too few apertures. In this respect the Egyptian temple is the antithesis of the Gothic church; in the one we have an excess of massive surface, in the other an excess of empty space; Greek and Renaissance art found the just mean and kept to it.

Diodorus Siculus, a Greek historian who flourished towards the Christian era, says that the Egyptians looked upon their houses as mere places of passage, and on their tombs as their permanent dwellings. So true is this, that our knowledge of Egyptian art is

FIG. 18.—EGYPTIAN BAS-RELIEF AT ABYDOS.
Jackal-headed Anubis and Falcon-headed Heros.

derived mainly from the enormous pyramids of stone and brick destined for royalty, or the chapels built above the ground, and the sepulchres hewn in the rocks. The tombs of the rich are adorned inside with sculpture, paintings, and bas-reliefs. They are, in fact, temples, of which the dead were the divinities.

Thousands of Egyptian statues have come down to us, statues in stone, bronze, and terra-cotta, from the colossal Sphinx adjoining the great Pyramids (Fig. 17) and the royal statues of Ipsamboul, some 60 feet high, to the tiny figurines which fill the glass cases of our museums.

18

These statues represent gods and goddesses, often with the animal heads ascribed to them by Egyptian mythology, men, women, and children, singly, and in groups, and animals, both real and fantastic. The bas-reliefs and paintings are even more varied in subject. The majority represent the Pharaonic victories, the interminable ceremonial of religious worship, scenes of daily life, or of the soul's journey to the land of the dead (Fig. 18). Landscape backgrounds are very frequent; but as the Egyptians had no knowledge of perspective, their views of country or of gardens appear in the guise of maps on the vertical surfaces, without foreshortening or differentiation of planes.

FIG. 19.—WOODEN STATUE KNOWN AS THE CHEIK EL BELED (MAYOR OF THE DISTRICT).

(Museum, Cairo.)

On first entering an Egyptian museum, we are struck by the apparent resemblance between all the figures, and we wonder that the art of a nation should have remained so uniform for centuries. But a more careful examination, such as may be adequately carried on at the British Museum or the Louvre, at once reveals essential differences. Under the Ancient Empire, the figures are shorter and sturdier, and are more directly inspired by nature (Fig. 19); the admirable *Scribe* in the Louvre, in limestone painted red, would be a masterpiece, had the artist, who showed such skill in rendering the human form, been able to give an expression of intellectual life to the vigorous head (Fig. 20). From the rise of the Middle Empire, the figures begin to lengthen, the modelling to become more flaccid; a superficial elegance is the accepted ideal, and the results, though occasionally charming (Fig. 21), are more superficial and frigid. These tendencies were still more pronounced under the New Empire, the academic period of Egyptian art, a period

FIG. 20.—THE SCRIBE.
(The Louvre.)

19

FIG. 21.—TAKOUSHIT, AN EGYPTIAN LADY.

(Bronze in the Museum, Athens.)

characterised by extraordinary technical skill, subservient to a conventional style destitute of character. In the Saïte epoch, the traditions of the Ancient Empire again prevailed, encouraged by a national reaction against exotic influences. At this period, Egyptian art produced masterpieces such as the basalt head in the Louvre (Fig. 22), which, in the realistic perfection of its modelling, is comparable to the finest Flemish portraits of the fifteenth century, Van Eyck's *Man with the Pink* and *Canon Van de Paele.*

Nevertheless, the visitor's first impression of monotonous uniformity finds at least a partial justification. Throughout its long career, Egyptian art never succeeded in casting off the trammels of certain conventions. Conspicuous among these is what the Danish archæologist, Lange, called the *law of frontality.* All the figures, standing or sitting, walking or motionless, confront the spectator; the top of the head, the junction of neck and shoulders, and the centre of the body are on the same vertical plane; all deviations from the vertical column, or, in other words, any inclination to the right or to the left, is forbidden. When several figures are grouped on the same pedestal, the vertical axes of their bodies are exactly parallel (Fig. 23). Secondly, all the figures, whether motionless or walking, rest all their weight on the soles of their feet; no Egyptian ever represented a person resting his weight on one leg, and touching the ground lightly with the disengaged foot. The male figures are nearly always walking, with the left foot advanced; but the women and children are generally in repose, their legs pressed together. In the reliefs and paintings, with very few exceptions, the figures are in profile, but strange to say, the eyes and the shoulders are

FIG. 22.—BASALT HEAD. SAÏTE PERIOD. (The Louvre.)

turned to the front (Fig. 18). Such a disregard for realities is striking enough, but it does not end here. Painting, whether applied to statues and reliefs, or executed on a flat surface, is mere colouring, without gradation or fusion of tones, and without chiaroscuro. Perspective is so absolutely ignored, that when two persons are supposed to be side by side, the second is generally drawn on top of the first. Thus Egyptian compositions, whether carved or painted, hardly deserve this name, for they lack any attempt at arrangement and symmetry; they consist of a medley of motives, which bear the same relation to

FIG. 23.—EGYPTIAN GROUP IN LIMESTONE. (The Louvre.)

the grouping of Greek art as does the driest of chronicles to history.

After monumental architecture, of which they set the example, the greatest gift of the Egyptians to art was their system of decoration. Of all the sculptural types they created, one only, that of the Sphinx, or lion with a human head, has persisted down to our own times (Fig. 24) ; but we have retained, with very slight modification, the decorative motives borrowed by the Egyptians from the flora of the Nile, notably from their two favourite plants, the lotus and the papyrus. We feel ourselves strangely out of touch with a collection of Egyptian statues and bas-reliefs, but we greet a group of Egyptian ornaments almost as familiar objects (Fig. 25). This is why our modern goldsmiths and jewellers are able to draw inspiration from the admirable jewels of ancient Egypt, without any unduly archaistic effort.

FIG. 24.—EGYPTIAN SPHINX OF PINK GRANITE. (The Louvre.)

Summing up the character of Egyptian art in a word, we might say that it represents, above all things, the idea of *duration*. Nature has decreed that all things should persist in Egypt, from the imperishable granite of her monuments to the most fragile objects of wood and stuff, preserved by the dryness of her climate. But the

FIG. 25.—EGYPTIAN DECORATION.

Egyptian himself was in love with the idea of duration. He built gigantic tombs like the Pyramids, impervious to the action of long ages, and temples with columns massive and manifold, and sloping walls like earthworks. He embalmed his dead for eternity, placing beside them in the tomb statues and statuettes of rare material, to serve them as companions, and in case of need, to replace them, should their mummies disappear; he carved and painted on the walls of tombs and temples historic, religious, and domestic scenes, destined to perpetuate the memory of the history of the gods, of the mighty deeds of kings, of the ritual and familiar life of his day. This idea of duration naturally engendered a respect for the past and for tradition. Egyptian art was not immobile, for no living thing is without motion, but it was fettered by conventions and formulæ. It achieved liberty only by the accident of individual inspiration, and even when it came in contact with Greek art, it persevered in the narrow path it had marked out for itself.

Did primitive Egypt exercise any influence upon Chaldæa, or was she herself influenced by the latter? The question is open to controversy. Perhaps neither influenced the other. It is unquestionably the fact that the most ancient of the works of art discovered since 1877 by M. de Sarzec at Tello, not far from Bassorah in Lower Chaldæa, examples dating from between 4000 and 2500 B.C., show no trace of Egyptian feeling, but contain all the qualities and defects of Assyrian art in embryo.

Up to the present time, the art of the valleys of the Tigris and the Euphrates is known to us mainly by two groups of monuments: those of Tello, which date from very remote antiquity, and those of Nineveh, the capital of the Assyrian kings, which date from the eighth and seventh centuries before Christ. The former are known as Babylonian or Chaldæan. There are further great numbers of small objects, notably cylindrical seals in hard stone (called cylinders) on which are engraved mythological or religious scenes, which reveal the art of Chaldæa and Assyria at every period of their history, under the kings of Babylon and those of Nineveh.

FIG. 26.—THE ARCHITECT OF TELLO.
(The Louvre.)

The chief monuments of Chaldæan art, discovered at the palaces of Tello and Susa, are all in the Louvre. They are bas-reliefs, such as the famous Stela of the Vultures, which represents Eannadou, king of Sirpourla, exulting over enemies whom vultures are devouring, and the great statues of black diorite, eight of which bear the name of Goudea, Prince of Sirpourla (Fig. 26). The statues are not only astonishing by virtue of their workmanship, to which technical difficulties seem mere child's play; they reveal a particular conception of the human form, directly opposed to that of the Egyptians. Whereas the Egyptian sculptor loved to attenuate details, to soften his modelling, to elongate his figures, the Chaldæan artist preferred sturdy, robust types, with salient muscles and broad shoulders. The bas-reliefs of the palace of Nineveh, though later by fifteen centuries than these Chaldæan sculptures, are a continuation of the same art. As M. Heuzey has remarked: " the muscular forms of Assyrian art, standing out from the body like pieces of mail, and generally carved in relief in the soft stone, represent a systematic exaggeration of those qualities of strength and power which Chaldæan sculpture drew directly from nature."

FIG. 27.—HEAD.
Discovered at Tello, Babylon.
(The Louvre.)

To get some idea of the characteristics of this art, realistic

23

FIG. 28.—ASSYRIAN HER-
CULES.
(The Louvre.)

and almost brutal, yet refined by its striving after expressive modelling, we have but to study one of the statues in the Louvre, *The Architect with the Rule* (Fig. 26). As a fact, it represents, not an architect, but one of the princes of the land in the character of a constructor; on his knees is a rule, the length of a Babylonian foot (about 10½ inches) subdivided into sixteen equal parts. The modelling of the arm and of the foot sufficiently indicates the tendencies of Chaldæan art; we find nothing akin to it in Egypt, save perhaps the heads of the Saïte school, later by some 2000 years. Even in Greece it would be difficult to point to sculpture showing the same exaggeration of muscular energy.

A head, in very excellent preservation, was discovered at the same place (Fig. 27). It represents a fat man with a shaven face, wearing a sort of turban with swathed folds in relief. The thick eyebrows and widely-opened eyes are features common to all Chaldæan and Assyrian art. The square structure of the face, and the prominent cheek-bones, bear the same stamp of physical vigour we have already noted in *The Architect with the Rule*. The expression has no touch of benevolence, not the shadow of a smile; the folks of Tello must have been unpleasant neighbours.

The glorification of brute-force, and a delight in cruel spectacles characterise the long series of alabaster bas-reliefs dating from about 800 —600 B.C. which Botta and Layard discovered at Nineveh, and brought home to the Louvre and the British Museum. They formed the interior decoration of palaces, and commemorated the victories and diversions of the Assyrian kings. Whereas in Egyptian art the gods are the protagonists, in that of Assyria the kings take their

FIG. 20.—ASSYRIAN WINGED BULL.
(The Louvre.)

place, kings eager for military fame, glorying in the recollection of bloody victories. The bas-reliefs show scenes of revolting carnage, of horrible tortures inflicted on the vanquished in the presence of the conqueror. The cuneiform inscriptions that accompany the bas-reliefs celebrate the most hideous butcheries as high exploits. Representations

FIG. 30.—ASSYRIAN BAS-RELIEF.
(British Museum.) (Photo. by Mansell.)

of tutelary divinities are not, however, altogether lacking. The Louvre owns a colossal figure of a bearded god, probably Gilgames, the Assyrian Hercules, gripping a lion to his breast (Fig. 28). Elsewhere, Assyrian sculptures show winged genii, sometimes mighty bulls with human faces, guarding the entrances of palaces (Fig. 29), sometimes eagle-headed monsters performing some sort of ritual on either side of a sacred tree. The goddesses who figure so frequently on the cylinders never appear in the bas-reliefs; indeed, the Assyrian sculptors did not portray women, save in a few instances as queens or captives.

Another favourite theme is a royal hunting party. The representation of animals (horses, dogs, and lions) is the triumph of Assyrian art (Fig. 30). Greek antiquity produced nothing finer than the wounded lion and lioness in the British Museum (Fig. 31); the realism of these studies is startling. The men, with their hard, bony faces, their square, symmetrically curled beards, their exaggerated muscularity, are at once less elegant and less natural than the animals.

FIG. 31.—ASSYRIAN BAS-RELIEF. A WOUNDED
LION.
(British Museum.)

Yet the drawing is more correct here than in the Egyptian bas-reliefs; and if the eyes are still shown looking to the front in profile figures, the shoulders do not confront the spectator, as do those of the Egyptian sculptures.

Assyrian art has left us but very few figures in the round. Its essential object was the decoration of surfaces, which were also faced with painted stuccoes, enamelled bricks, and figured bronzes. A party of German explorers has recently discovered at Babylon a colossal lion in enamelled bricks, very similar to the great friezes in the Louvre, brought by M. Dieulafoy from Susa; but the exploration of the temples and palaces of Babylon has only just begun.

The Assyrians had no building stone. They used bricks for the construction of their vast palaces, composed of rectangular halls and long corridors surrounding a series of interior courts, and decorated their immense surfaces with paintings and sculptures. We know very little about their temples, save that they were in the shape of a pyramid with steps, surmounted by a chapel containing the image of the god (Fig. 32). This was the traditional type of the famous *Tower of Babel*, a temple dedicated to the god Bel, built at Babylon by Nebuchadnezzar about the year 600 B.C.

FIG. 32.—CHALDÆAN TEMPLE.
(Reconstructed by Ch. Chipiez.)

The most interesting feature of Assyrian architecture is the importance given to the vault. The Egyptians were not altogether ignorant of it, but they made only a very restricted use of it, whereas the Assyrians built not only vaults, but cupolas of brick, rising boldly above their square halls. It is a mistake, therefore, to attribute this oriental invention to the Romans, an invention which Greek art of the perfect period did not adopt, but which seems to have passed from Assyria to the Lydians, from the Lydians to the Etruscans, from Etruria to Rome, and thence to Byzantine and modern art.

Indeed, the influence of Chaldæan and Assyrian art was very much more extensive and far-reaching than that of the art of Egypt; it made itself felt on the one hand in Persia, on the other over a great part of Asia Minor. Persian art is, strictly speaking, only the official art of the dynasty of the Achæmenides, which began with Cyrus and ended with Darius Codoman; it lasted for barely two centuries (550-330 B.C.). Its most important relics are the ruins of the palaces of Susa and Persepolis. The architecture of these palaces is thoroughly impregnated with the influences of Ionian Greece, in other words, of the Greeks of the Asiatic coasts; the decoration—bas-reliefs and friezes of enamelled bricks—is derived from Assyrian art. The master-piece of Persian art, the Frieze of Archers in the Louvre (Fig. 33), reveals not only an Assyrian origin, but a delicacy of drawing and a sobriety of motive due to the proximity, if not to the direct intervention, of Greek artificers.

FIG. 33.—ARCHERS FROM THE PALACE AT SUSA.
(Frieze of enamelled brick, in the Louvre.)

Bas-reliefs, statues, and jewels of a peculiar style, bearing inscriptions as yet indecipher-able, have been discovered in the vast region lying between Northern Syria and Armenia (Fig. 34). These objects have been attri-buted to the Hittites, a people mentioned in the Bible, who maintained relations alter-nately peaceful and hostile with the Egyp-tians and Assyrians, and who seem to have founded an empire in Asia between 1600 and 600 B.C. Hittite art is saturated with Assyrian influences; those of Egypt are much less perceptible. It lacked vitality as it lacked originality, and hardly deserves mention in such a rapid survey as the present.

The coast of Syria, with which the neighbouring island of Cyprus was closely connected, was inhabited by the Phœnicians. Attempts have been made to show that the Phœnicians, a race of skilful traders, were the masters of the Greeks; an art founded on that of Assyria and of Egypt has been attributed to them, and of this art, it has been main-tained, traces have been found, not only in Greece, but in Italy, in Central Europe, and even in Gaul.

FIG. 34.—HITTITE LION.
(Museum, Constantinople.)

The whole assumption is baseless. A brisk trade in decorative objects was undoubtedly carried on by the Phœnicians; but for the last hundred years, students have vainly sought any traces of that

Phœnician art, the existence of which was first suggested to them at the beginning of this period. Both in Phœnicia and Cyprus, the Phœnicians of B.C. 1000 were mediocre imitators of the Assyrians; about the period of the Egyptian renaissance under the Saïte dynasty, they imitated the Egyptians, while at the same time they imitated the Greeks. We may allow that they showed a certain skill in the manufacture of coloured glass and of engraved metal cups; but these industrial products, the designs of which were inspired by foreign models, are not sufficient to constitute a national art.

The Biblical descriptions of the Temple of Jerusalem and Solomon's palace show that these monuments were Assyrian in character; prominent among the decorative motives were the *Kherubim*, which are identical with the winged bulls of Assyria. The word *cherub*, which is now used to signify an angel, a winged child, is an Assyrian term which passed into the Hebrew tongue, and thence into all modern languages. It was likewise from Assyria, or rather from Chaldæa, that modern art received at the hands of the Greeks those winged figures of men and animals of which it still makes so liberal a use, especially in decoration.

Thus, if we set aside the primæval art of the reindeer-hunters, we see that before the fruition of Hellenic genius only two great schools of art had flourished in the world, those of Egypt and of Chaldæa. The first gave expression mainly to the idea of duration, the second to that of strength; it was reserved to Greek art to realise the idea of beauty.

If I pass over the art of India and of China, it is because the great antiquity attributed to these is a delusion. India had no art before the period of Alexander the Great, and as to Chinese art, it first began to produce masterpieces during the mediæval ages in Europe. The most ancient Chinese sculptures of ascertained date were executed about the year 130 of our era. They show the influences of a bastard form of Greek art, which had spread from the shores of the Black Sea towards Siberia and Central Asia.

BIBLIOGRAPHY OF CHAPTER III.

G. Perrot and Ch. Chipiez, *Histoire de l'Art dans l'Antiquité* (vols. i.–v., Paris, 1882–1890): Egypt, Assyria, Phœnicia, Cyprus, Judæa, Asia Minor, Phrygia, Lydia, Persia; M. Jastrow, *Babylonia and Assyria*, London, 1915; E. Babelon, *Manuel d'Archéologie Orientale*, Paris, no date; G. Maspero, *Histoire ancienne des Peuples de l'Orient*, 3 vols., Paris, 1895–1899; *L'Archéologie Egyptienne*, new ed., Paris, 1906; *Causeries d'Egypte*, Paris, 1908; *Egypt* (Ars Una Series), 1912; A. Choisy, *L'Art de bâtir chez les Egyptiens*, Paris, 1904; W. Spiegelberg, *Geschichte der ägyptischen Kunst*, Leipzig, 1903; Em. Vernier, *La Bijouterie et la joaillerie égyptiennes*, Paris, 1907; H. Schaeffer, *Aegyptische Goldschmiedekunst*, Berlin, 1910; L. Heuzey, *Catalogue des Antiquités Chaldéennes du Louvre*, Paris, 1902; C. Bezold, *Niniveh und Babylon*, Bielefeld, 1903.

On the Law of Frontality, see Lechat, *Une Loi de la Statuaire primitive*, in the *Revue des Universités du Midi*, vol. i. (1895), p. 1, and Perrot, *Histoire de l'Art*, vol. viii, p. 689. Lange's work, written in Danish, has been translated into German.

Short notices: G. Bénédite, *Statuette de la Dame Toui, xx. Dynastie* (*Monuments Piot*, vol. ii., p. 29); Berthelot, *Sur les Métaux Egyptiens* (*ibid.*, vol. vii., p. 121); G. Maspero, *Le Scribe accroupi de Gizeh* (*ibid.*, vol. i., p. 1); L. Heuzey, *Le Vase d'Argent d'Entéména* (*ibid.*, vol. ii., p. 1); E. Pottier, *Les Antiquités de Suse, Mission Dieulafoy* (*Gazette des Beaux-Arts*, 1886, ii., p. 353); *Les Fouilles de Suse, Mission de Morgan* (*ibid.*, 1902, i., p. 17; 1906, i., p. 5); *Le Lotus dans l'Architecture Egyptienne* (*ibid.*, 1898, i., p. 77, after a work by G. Foucart); *Le roi Akhouniaton* (*ibid.*, vol. xiii., p. 1); *Le Mastaba* (*Tombe de la v*ᵉ *Dynastie*) *du Louvre* (*ibid.*, 1905, i., p. 177); A. Moret, *Autour des pyramides* (*Revue de Paris*, Sept. 15, 1907); S. Reinach, *Le Mirage Oriental* (*Chroniques d'Orient*, Paris, 1896, vol. ii., p. 509); V. A. Smith, *History of Art in India*, London, 1911; *Le Déblaiement du grand Sphinx, Les Fouilles de Suse*, etc. (*Esquisses archéologiques*, Paris, 1886); A. Foucher, *Sculptures gréco-bouddhiques* (*Monuments Piot*, vol. vii., p. 39); *L'Art gréco-bouddhique*, vol. i., Paris, 1905; *La Madone Bouddhique* (*Monuments Piot*, vol. vii., p. 39); H. Focillon, *L'Art bouddhique*, Paris, 1921; E. Chavannes, *La Sculpture sur pierre en Chine*, Paris, 1893 (cf. *Revue Archéologique*, 1901, i., p. 224).

IV

ÆGEAN, MINOAN, AND MYCENÆAN ART: TROY, CRETE, AND MYCENÆ

THE islands and the coast of the Ægean Sea (the Archipelago) were the seat of a very ancient civilisation which had become a mere brilliant memory by the time of Homer (about 850 years before Christ). It was not until our own day that the evidences of this civilisation were brought to light.

As early as 3000 B.C. the hardy mariners of these regions were familiar with copper, the first metal commonly used by man. It was found in abundance in the island of Cyprus, from which, no doubt, its name was derived (Κυπρος). Many vestiges of primitive industry have been discovered in this island, of a much earlier date than the imitations of Assyrian works; similar discoveries have been made in Crete, at Amorgos, and at Thera (Santorin), and in certain districts on the coast of Asia and in Northern Greece (Thrace, the modern Roumelia). The products of this industry have one marked characteristic; the tendency to represent, more or less rudely, the human form. They consist for the most part of coarse sculptures, feminine idols in white marble, which, contrary to the usage of Egypt and Chaldæa, are always nude. Even the clay jars found often affect the form of the body, with paunches, shoulders and necks, surmounted by indications of eyes and of a pointed nose.

From the year 1870 onwards, Heinrich Schliemann, a German who had made a fortune in America, undertook a series of important excavations at Hissarlik, on the Dardanelles, the supposed site of legendary Troy. Beneath the Greek city of Ilium he found six small towns, one beneath the other; the most ancient of these contained but a few objects made of copper, with a number of stone implements. The four towns above this first contained bronze tools, and vases with incised ornament, unpainted. The town sixth in

FIG. 35.—MYCENÆAN DAGGER.
(Museum, Athens.)

order from the base yielded many fragments of painted vases, similar to those Schliemann afterwards discovered at Mycenæ. This town was the Troy of Priam, destroyed by the Achæans under Agamemnon. Thus it may fairly be said that the discoveries of archæology confirmed the Homeric tradition in its main lines.

Schliemann's excavations at Troy brought to light a vast number of objects of all kinds, among others a treasure of golden vases and ornaments, clay jars in the shape of human figures, weights ornamented with incisions which mark a first step towards written characters, a little leaden figure of a nude woman, etc. But all these discoveries were eclipsed by those Schliemann himself made at Mycenæ and Tiryns in 1876 and 1884. In these two ancient cities mentioned by Homer, he found relics of an advanced civilisation, which bore testimony to a very original artistic taste, absolutely independent of that of Egypt and Assyria.

At Mycenæ, where tombs built of stone in the form of cupolas were already known to exist, Schliemann excavated royal tombs of extraordinary splendour under the great public place of the ancient city. The faces of several skeletons were covered with mask-like sheets of gold; there were also vases of gold and silver, delicately-wrought ornaments, bronze daggers, incised with hunting-scenes inlaid with fillets of gold and silver (Fig. 35), and a gold ring engraved with a religious subject.

FIG. 36.—MYCENÆAN VASE.
(Museum, Marseilles.)

At Tiryns, Schliemann unearthed a palace ornamented with mural paintings, the best preserved of which represents an acrobat or a hunter bounding over a galloping bull.

Both at Mycenæ and at Tiryns, the explorer found hundreds of fragments of painted pottery of a very original character, decorated with plants, leaves, and marine animals (cuttle fish, octopuses, etc.), that is to say, with objects drawn from organic nature (Fig. 36). Nothing of the sort occurs in Chaldæa or Egypt, or in central and western Europe, where geometrical decoration prevails. He also found a great many seals of hard stone, on which fantastic figures of men and animals were engraved in a precise and vigorous style, which recalls that of the Chaldæan cylinders, but shows no likeness to that of Egypt.

In 1886, a learned Greek, M. Tsountas, explored a large tomb at Vaphio, not far from Sparta. It contained, besides engraved stones

FIG. 37.—RELIEFS ON ONE OF THE GOLDEN VASES OF VAPHIO.
(Museum, Athens.)

and other objects, two admirable golden goblets, decorated with scenes representing the capture of wild bulls (Fig. 37). These vases are celebrated, and the bulls of Vaphio are as life-like and as well-drawn as the finest productions of the Assyrian animal-sculptors.

Lastly, since the year 1900, Mr. Arthur Evans has excavated at Cnossus, in the island of Crete, the ancient palace which the Greek legend described as the habitation of King Minos, and called the Labyrinth. This word, which is still used to signify a complicated arrangement of paths and passages, originally meant, according to Mr. Evans, "The Palace of the Axe," and was derived from the old word, *labrys*, which signifies axe in one of the dialects spoken on the Asiatic coast. Now the Palace of Cnossus was certainly the Palace of the Axe, for throughout it a two-edged axe, a religious symbol, is outlined on the walls, and it is also a labyrinth in the modern sense, as it is difficult not to lose one's way in it, for, like the Assyrian palaces, it shows a most perplexing tangle of corridors.

This palace was decorated with a profusion of plaster bas-reliefs and paintings. These latter are amazing in their variety and freedom of style (Figs. 38, 39). Interspersed among the life-size figures there are little scenes with numerous personages, among others a group of elaborately adorned women in low-cut gowns, assembled on a balcony. A woman's face in profile is so modern in treatment that we should hesitate to attribute it to the sixteenth century before Christ, if there were any room for doubt in the matter (Fig. 39). There are also hunting scenes, landscapes, a view of a town, in short a whole series of picturesque subjects, which have come as a revelation to the art-historian. Two other palaces similar to that of Cnossus were discovered at another point on the island of Crete, Phæstus, and successfully explored by an Italian scholar, Halbherr. Together with a number of mural paintings, he found a vase of steatite, decorated with very spirited reliefs, representing a procession of reapers (Fig. 40).

FIG. 38.—A CUP-BEARER.
From a Fresco in the Palace of Cnossus.
(Museum, Candia.)

Modern archæologists indicate three periods in the distant past of pre-Homeric Greece: 1st. The Ægean Period, of little marble idols (from about 3000 to 2000 years before Christ); 2nd. The Minoan Period (that of Minos), or Cretan Period, of which the Island of Crete seems to have been the principal centre, characterised by a rapid advance in the arts of design and of work in metal, first towards realism and afterwards towards elegance; Egyptian influences appeared in this development, without inducing servile imitation (2000-1500 B.C.). 3rd. The Mycenæan Period, the only one known to Schliemann, which seems, in certain respects, to have been the age of the Minoan decadence; it is characterised by a very original style of painted pottery, decorated with plants and animals (B.C. 1500-1100). These civilisations, forming a continuous development, are reflected in the poems ascribed to Homer, which received their present form towards the year 800 B.C. In the interval between the Mycenæan civilisation and Homer, a catastrophe had come about, analogous

FIG. 39.—YOUNG CRETAN GIRL.
Fresco from the Palace of Cnossus (Crete).
(Museum, Candia.)

to the ruin of the Roman Empire by the Barbarians. Certain warlike tribes from northern Greece, the Dorians among others, destroyed the Mycenæan civilisation and plunged Greece once more into barbarism, about 1100 B.C., a few years after the Trojan war. But civilisation did not utterly perish. Several tribes, flying before the invaders, took refuge in the islands, notably at Chios and Cyprus, on the coast of Asia Minor and of Syria; these places inherited a part of the Mycenæan civilisation, and preserved the memory thereof. The isle of Chios was doubtless the birthplace of the Homeric poems, which celebrated the vanished glory of the ancient royal houses of Greece. The day came when the descendants or heirs of the exiled Mycenæans presented themselves as the educators of a Greece that had relapsed into barbarism, and gave her back some sparks of the genius their ancestors had received from her. We see here a phenomenon similar to that which manifested itself in the fourteenth century, at the close of the Christian Middle Ages, when the learned men of Constantinople, remote heirs of Roman civilisation, came to carry on its tradition on Italian soil, and prepared the way for the Renaissance in Florence and in Rome.

The term *Hellenic Middle Ages* (in contradistinction to that of Christian Middle Ages) is applied to the period of about three centuries which elapsed between the downfall of the Mycenæans, and the first dawn of the Renaissance in Greece. Before Schliemann's excavations, our knowledge was confined to the beginnings of this Renaissance; we therefore owe him an immense increase in our knowledge. The energetic explorer has added more than six centuries to the glorious history of Greek art.

Mycenæ, Tiryns, and other ancient towns of Greece, Italy, and Asia Minor, are surrounded by walls composed of enormous blocks of stone, irregular or polygonal in shape, sometimes 18 or 20 feet

FIG. 40.—CARVED RELIEF.
On the so-called Vase of Reapers, discovered at Phæstus, Crete.
(Museum, Candia.)

long. These walls are called *Cyclopean*, because the Greeks believed them to be the work of the giants of mythology called Cyclops. At Mycenæ the wall is interrupted by a huge gate, crowned by two lionesses, one on either side of a column (Fig. 41). This sculpture forms a single triangular block, probably much later in date than the wall. Indeed, the so-called Cyclopean walls are older than the Mycenæan civilisation, and point to an initial occupation of the district

FIG. 41.—GATE OF THE LIONS AT MYCENÆ.

by a military or sacerdotal aristocracy. They show a certain affinity with the dolmens of Western Europe, and bear witness to the existence of an analogous social order, in which thousands of men obeyed the commands of a small number of chieftains, and worked in their interest and for their glory. The fact that similar walls are found from Italy to Asia proves that the invasion of the tribes among whom the Mycenæan civilisation was evolved, about the year 2000 B.C., was not confined to the Balkan peninsula, but extended east and west of this region.

No Minoan or Mycenæan temples have been unearthed; the buildings discovered are all palaces. It seems probable therefore that the palace was also the temple, and that the dwelling of the god was comprised in that of the king. The palaces are very slight in construction, and wood was used more freely than stone in building them. They had wooden columns, which, like the legs of our modern chairs and tables, taper from top to bottom. When these wooden columns were imitated in stone, as, for instance, in the Gate of the Lions at Mycenæ, their characteristic form was retained, a form only found in Mycenæan art. The capitals which surmount the columns show the first essays in the constitution of the two orders, the Doric and Ionic, which played such a brilliant part in Greek architecture, and are still used at the present day.

The Minoans and Mycenæans have left us no large statues in the round, but a great number of their bas-reliefs in alabaster, plaster, and metal, figurines in terra cotta, ivory, and bronze, and specimens of chased and *repoussé* metal-work have come down to us. Both at Cnossus and Mycenæ there is a strange difference in quality between works excavated at the same level, and belonging, no doubt, to the same period; the explanation is, that a popular art, as yet rude and imperfect, existed side by side with the official art, which was perhaps the monopoly of certain corporations, and produced its masterpieces only for the great.

To say that Greek art before the year 1000 B.C. realised the ideal of beauty would be a manifest exaggeration. Even in works as remarkable as the goblets of Vaphio, probably made at Cnossus, the human figures with their wasp-like proportions and their long thin legs, are still far indeed from the masterpieces of classic art. But if Assyrian art expresses the idea of strength, Minoan art may be said to embody that of life. It has no trace of the cold elegance of the Egyptian art of the new Empire, which flourished at the same time. Objects of Egyptian manufacture have been found in the Minoan and Mycenæan towns, and Mycenæan vases have been unearthed in Egypt; the Egyptians, Minoans, and Mycenæans knew each other, and traded together; but these Greeks were in no sense tributary to Egypt, and all they borrowed from the latter were certain technical processes and an occasional decorative motive.[1]

The love of the Minoan artist for life and movement manifests itself most strongly in his admirable renderings of animals; in this respect there is a certain likeness between his art and that of the reindeer-hunters. It would be interesting to trace a connection, a historic link between these two arts, in spite of the interval of some sixty centuries that lies between them. Who shall say we may not some day discover that the art of the reindeer-hunters, which disappeared from France some thousands of years before the glories of Cnossus and Mycenæ, was preserved in some unexplored corner of Europe, and finally introduced into Greece in one of the numerous invasions of the northern tribes, who were incessantly pouring down from Central Europe to the Mediterranean?

Be this as it may, the future will no doubt reveal what is now an unsolved mystery—the origin of that extraordinary manifestation of plastic genius which it was reserved to our own age to discover.

[1] Writing was an art known to the Minoans; thousands of tablets bearing inscriptions have been discovered in Crete; but these inscriptions, which have not yet been deciphered, have hardly anything in common with the Egyptian hieroglyphs.

BIBLIOGRAPHY OF CHAPTER IV.

W. Doerpfeld, *Troja und Ilion*, 2 vols., Athens, 1902; E. Pottier, *Catalogue des Vases du Louvre*, Paris, 1896, vol. i., pp. 173–211; A. Furtwängler, *Die antiken Gemmen*, Leipzig, 1900, vols. iii., pp. 13–67 (Mycenæan Epoch and Hellenic Middle Ages); F. Poulsen, *Der Orient und die frühgriechische Kunst*, Leipzig, 1912.

On the recent discoveries in Crete there are various articles by Mr. Arthur Evans (*Annual of the British School of Athens*, vols. vi.-x., London, 1899–1904; *Journal of Hellenic Studies*, vol. xxi., London, 1901); R. M. Burrows, *The Discoveries in Crete*, London, 1907. See also for the Italian excavations, *Monumenti antichi dei Lincei*, vols. xii-xiv., Milan, 1902–1905; R. Weill, *Le Vase de Phaestos* (*Revue Archéologique*, 1904, i., p. 52). Summaries of these works in French have been published by E. Pottier, *Revue de Paris*, and *Revue de l'Art ancien et moderne*, 1902, and by S. Reinach, in *L'Anthropologie*, 1902, pp. 1–39; 1903, pp. 110–193; 1904, p. 257. P. La Grange, *Revue Biblique*, 1907, p. 163; Collignon, *La Peinture préhellenique* (*Gazette*, 1909, ii., p. 5); Fougères, *La Grèce* (*Guide Joanne*), Paris, 1909.

V

GREEK ART BEFORE PHIDIAS

The Abundance of Marble a Determining Factor in the Tendencies of Greek Art.—The Rationalistic Cast of the Greek Intellect.—The Rapid Development of Greek Art.—Archaic Statues.—The Artemis of Delos, the Hera of Samos, and the Statue of Chares.—The Treasury of the Cnidians.—The Chian Sculptors and their Invention of the Winged Victory.—The Dawn of Expression in Sculpture.—The Orantes of the Acropolis.—Archaic Apollos and Athletes.—The Type replaced by the Individual.—The Impetus given to Art by the Greek Victories over the Persians.—The Pediments of the Temple of Aphaia at Ægina.—The Pediments of the Temple of Zeus at Olympia.—Myron and the Statue of the Discobolus.—Polyclitus and the Statue of the Doryphorus.—The Creation of the Type of the Amazon.—Phidias, Myron, and Polyclitus the Supreme Masters of the First Great Period.—The Eternal Progression of Art.

MANY of the islands of the Archipelago, notably Paros, are merely enormous blocks of marble; this material is also very abundant in Attica—where were the famous quarries of Pentelicus and of Hymettus—in northern Greece, and on the coast of Asia. The Greeks had this great advantage over the Assyrians and the Egyptians: they had at their disposal an admirable material, less hard than granite, less soft than alabaster, agreeable to the sight, and comparatively easy to work. Nor was this all; still more important was the fact that as yet they had never felt the yoke of despotism and superstition. As soon as they appeared in history, the Greeks presented a striking contrast to all other peoples: they had the instinct of liberty, they loved novelty, and were eager for progress. The Greeks were never bound to the past by the chains of a tyrannical tradition. Even their religion was but a slight restraint on their liberty. At a very early period we find among them a tendency of which there is no trace in any Oriental nation, the habit of considering human things as purely human, of reasoning upon them as if they were concerned solely with reason. This tendency is what is known as *Rationalism*. Together with their love of liberty and their taste for the beautiful, rationalism is a precious gift made by Greece to humanity.

FIG. 42.—ARCHAIC STATUE OF ARTEMIS.

Found at Delos.

(Museum, Athens)

The progress of the Greeks in the domain of art was extraordinarily rapid; barely two centuries and a half elapsed between the origin of sculpture in marble

FIG. 43.—ARCHAIC STATUE OF HERA.
Found at Samos.
(The Louvre.)

and its apogee. This would seem inexplicable and altogether phenomenal had not Asiatic or Ionian Greece, the legatee of Mycenæan art, influenced by the art of Egypt and Assyria, played a part it would be unjust to ignore in the education of Greece proper. But we must hasten to add that no genius was ever less prone to servile imitation than that of the Greeks; what they knew of Oriental art only incited them to rise above it.

One of the most ancient marble statues discovered in Greece is an Artemis, excavated by M. Homolle at Delos; it dates from about the year 620 B.C. (Fig. 42). It might almost be taken for a pillar or a tree-trunk, with summary indications of a head, hair, arms, and a girdle; it is more primitive than the Egyptian art of the period of the Pyramids. The Greeks called these figures *xoana* (from *xeein*, to scrape wood), that is to say, images carved in wood, which seems to have been the material first used for large statues. Another feminine type, the *Hera* of Samos (Fig. 43), now in the Louvre, is about thirty or forty years later in date (580 B.C.). The general aspect is still that of a column, but if we observe the shawl in which the goddess is draped, we shall note folds that were studied from nature, a severe grace, a dawning freedom. By the middle of the 6th century B.C., we get the seated statue of King Chares, discovered at Branchidæ, near Miletus, in Asia Minor, and preserved in the British Museum (Fig. 44). It is a typical example of Greek art in Asia, or Ionian art; it shows a tendency to squatness in the forms, but the lines of the body are already indicated under the draperies, which are cast with a certain boldness. A similar heaviness of form,

FIG. 44.—STATUE OF CHARES.
(British Museum.)

combined with great delicacy of execution, characterises the Caryatides and friezes of the little temple known as the *Treasury of the Cnidians* (Fig. 45) dating from 530 B.C., which was excavated at Delphi by M. Homolle, and reconstructed in plaster at the Louvre, to the left of the *Victory* of Samothrace.

About the year 550, a family of sculptors, mentioned by two ancient writers, were working in the isle of Chios. One of them, Archermos, invented a new type, that of a winged goddess, Victory or Gorgon, advancing with a rapid movement. A statue of this school was discovered in the isle of Delos (Fig. 46). This figure marks an important innovation in sculpture. Remember that Egyptian art had hardly ever essayed to represent a woman, save with her legs pressed together as in a sheath, and that Assyrian art rarely represented her at all; here, barely 150 years after the first lispings of Greek art, we have a woman who is running, displaying the upper part of a muscular leg, and even smiling, a greater innovation than all the rest. It is true that the smile lacks sweetness, that it is somewhat of a grimace, that the mouth is harsh, the cheek bones too prominent: but the smile is there, and this is the first time we meet with it in art (Fig. 47). The Egyptian and Assyrian divinities have too little of humanity to smile; they either grimace or look out stolidly at the spectator. In the Niké of Delos, we see an art

FIG. 45.—FAÇADE OF THE TREASURY OF THE CNIDIANS AT DELPHI.

(Reconstruction in the Louvre.)
(Photo. by Giraudon.)

FIG. 46.—RECONSTRUCTION OF AN ARCHAIC STATUE OF NIKÉ.
Found at Delos.
(Museum, Athens.)

39

FIG. 47.—HEAD OF THE NIKÉ OF DELOS.
(Museum, Athens.)

which is no longer content to imitate forms; it is seeking after, and beginning to express, sentiment, spiritual life. This was a great discovery, heralding a new art.

The Chian sculptures were brought to Athens, and soon found imitators. Thanks to the excavations made on the Acropolis in 1886, in the stratum of *débris* accumulated by the Persians in 480 B.C., we possess a whole series of statues of this school. As they represent neither Gorgons nor Victories, but Orantes, they are closely veiled, and are not running; but occasionally they smile delightfully, with an evident desire to please (Fig. 48). Stiff and rigid in their long tunics, they are nevertheless living, and no one who has seen them can forget them. This appearance of life was enhanced by vivid colouring, of which, happily, considerable traces still remain, a proof that Greek archaic sculptors were not content to carve the marble, but that they also painted it.

FIG. 48.—ARCHAIC STATUE.

Found on the Acropolis.
(Museum. Athens.)

A male type akin to this, that of a nude man, standing, his arms against his body, was probably created in the isle of Crete before the year 600 A.D., and developed in the sixth century, notably in Attica. It was the type first applied to Apollo and to victorious athletes (Fig. 49). A series of examples has survived in which we may trace the gradual progress of art. Here it was the form of the body, the indication of the muscles, with which the sculptor was primarily occupied. Just as the school of Chios developed the expression of faces and the rendering of draperies, that of the Athletes, as we may call it, first taught the treatment of what are known as " academies," *i.e.*, studies from nude models.

These statues of men and women, in spite of dawning qualities of drawing and expression, have the grave defect of being mere abstract types, distinguished by no individuality of action. It was in vain that the sculptor bestowed attributes on his personages; they seem to take no sort of interest in these, which appear merely as labels. The momentous progress which was accomplished towards the close of the sixth century, consisted in breaking the mould in which these *types* had been cast, and essaying the representation of *individuals*, in all the diversity of their occupations and attitudes.

This progress was achieved rapidly, but not all at once. It is probable that painting, always a freer vehicle of expression than sculpture, contributed largely to the result. In default of the frescoes of this period, which have perished, we have the last vases with

FIG. 40.—ARCHAIC STATUE OF APOLLO.

(Museum, Athens.)

black figures, and the first vases with red figures, in which the rupture with traditional motives is very marked. The habit of representing the victorious athletes of the public games in sculpture must also have exercised a salutary influence, for it was necessary to differentiate these images, and to make them commemorative of the various exploits of strength and skill by which the victors had distinguished themselves.

The great historic events of 490 to 479 B.C.[1] gave an immense impetus to all the forces of Hellenic genius, by revealing to it the full extent of its powers, and its superiority to the servile civilisations of Asia. To this beneficent crisis we owe the master-pieces of Greek poetry, the odes of Pindar and the

FIG. 50.—WOUNDED WARRIOR.

Figure from the eastern pediment of the Temple of Aphaia at Ægina.

(Munich. Photo. by Bruckmann.)

tragedies of Æschylus. But after Salamis and Mycale, there were not only pæans to sing, but ruins to rebuild. The Persians had destroyed the majority of the Greek temples, and all those in Athens. Rich with the spoils taken from the invaders, the Greeks

[1] The invasion of Greece by the armies of Darius and of Xerxes (the so-called Persian Wars).

FIG. 51.—CENTRAL PART OF THE WESTERN PEDIMENT OF
THE TEMPLE OF ZEUS AT OLYMPIA.
(Reconstruction by Treu.)

were able to restore what their enemies had sacked or demolished. They set themselves to the task, and new born classic art found an exceptional opportunity of expressing itself in many ways at once.

The first works which presage the perfect emancipation of Greek genius were produced between 480 and 470 B.C. These were the pediments of the temple of Aphaia at Ægina (now at Munich).[1]

The sculptured groups represent combats between the Greeks and the Trojans, an allusion to the recent struggle between Hellas and Asia; the Greek warriors are protected by Pallas Athene. The heads are more archaic than the bodies, as if the emancipation of art in dealing with these, being more recent, was for that very reason more complete. The body of a fallen warrior on the eastern pediment is almost equal to the masterpieces of the perfect period (Fig. 50).

The pediments of the temple of Zeus at Olympia, discovered during the German excavations of 1875 to 1880, are some fifteen years later, and date from about 460 B.C. (Figs. 51, 52). The eastern pediment represents the preparation for the race in which Pelops and Œnomaus were to compete; that of the west depicts

FIG. 52.—HEAD OF A WOMAN OF THE
LAPITHÆ.
Western pediment of the Temple of Zeus at
Olympia.

[1] It was discovered in 1901 that the temple was dedicated to the local goddess, Aphaia (*Comptes rendus de l'Académie des Inscriptions*, 1901, p. 523).

42

the battle of the Centaurs and Lapithæ, in which Apollo appears as the protector of the Lapithæ, for whom Theseus and Pirithoös were fighting (Fig. 51). Some fine metopes from this temple, excavated by the French explorers in the Morea, are in the Louvre; other fragments, discovered since, are at Olympia (Fig. 53). They are vigorous works, marked by a certain rudeness; their robust simplicity has been not inaptly compared to that of the tragedies of Æschylus, which were being performed at Athens about the time when the sculptures were executed.

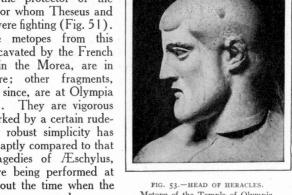

FIG. 53.—HEAD OF HERACLES.
Metope of the Temple of Olympia.
(Museum, Olympia.)

They have a quality more novel in the history of art than the knowledge of form, and this is the excellence of their composition. The Egyptians and the Assyrians brought figures together and juxtaposed them; they never thought of arranging them round a central figure as if to balance it.

FIG. 54.—THE NIKÉ OF PÆONIOS.
(Restoration at Dresden.)
(Museum, Olympia.)

FIG. 55.—COPY OF MYRON'S
DISCOBOLUS.
(Palazzo Lancelotti. Rome.)

43

FIG. 56.—HEAD, COPY OF MYRON'S DISCOBOLUS.

(Palazzo Lancelotti, Rome.)

Composition, as understood by the Greeks of the fifth century B.C., was not a rigorous symmetry, which would have been a servitude for art, but that artistic symmetry which reveals the perfection of liberty, combining both order and freedom.

The eastern pediment contains only figures in repose; in the western pediment, they are nearly all in motion. Pausanias, who described the temple of Olympia, attributed the eastern pediment to Pæonios of Mende (Thrace), and the western pediment to Alcamenes, who is said in some texts to have been the pupil, in others the rival of Phidias. It is probable that there were two artists of the name, and that the Olympian pediment was the work of the elder, further known to us by good copies of his *Head of Hermes* (c. 450 B.C.). A Niké by Pæonios, dedicated and signed about 454 B.C., has also been discovered at Olympia. It is a powerful figure, no doubt a work of the artist's maturity (Fig. 54); the eastern pediment, a little hard and stiff in its vigour, may have been executed in his youth.

I have spoken, in dealing with Egyptian art, of that law of *frontality* pointed out by Lange, which, in all primitive art, condemned the human figure to move on a vertical plane. Greek art of the first half of the fifth century freed itself from these bonds. The sculptor who distinguished himself most by this emancipation was the Athenian, Myron, famous for his statues of athletes. One of these, the *Discobolus*, is known to us from a fine copy preserved at Rome; it

FIG. 57.—COPY OF POLYCLITUS' DORYPHORUS.

(Museum, Naples.)

(Photo. by Alinari.)

represents a young man, who is bending with a vigorous gesture to hurl the discus (Fig. 55). His body is thrown violently towards the left, by a twisting action which calls every muscle into play. But whereas the whole torso is full of life and expression, the head is still cold; it seems quite unmoved by the energetic action of the body (Fig. 56). This was a characteristic of Greek archaism which lingered later than any other; isolated examples are to be found after the time of Phidias.

FIG. 58.—AMAZON, AFTER POLYCLITUS (?)
(The Vatican.)
(Photo by Alinari.)

Polyclitus of Argos, who, with Myron and Phidias, makes up the triad of great Greek sculptors, was the author of a colossal statue of Hera, which we do not know, and of several bronze statues, copies of which have come down to us—the so-called *Doryphorus,* a youth carrying a lance, and the *Diadumemus,* an athlete passing a fillet around his head. The *Doryphorus* was called by the ancients the *Canon,* or Rule, because the right proportions of the human body seemed to have been more exactly observed in it than in any other work. The head, a bronze replica of which was found at Herculaneum, seems somewhat expressionless to us; but it is one of the oldest examples of that classic perfection of the Greek type in which strength and beauty are equally mated (Fig. 57).

The ancients noted as a distinguishing characteristic of Polyclitus' statues that they supported the weight of the body on a single foot. This again marks an emancipation, the credit of which belongs to the Greek art of the fifth century. In Egypt, in Assyria, in primitive Greek art, all figures in the round or in relief plant both feet on the ground; the tradition is still observed in the pediments of Ægina. This heavy attitude was first discarded in the treatment of figures in motion, like Myron's *Discobolus;* but it was Polyclitus who seems to have introduced the attitude we may describe as "standing with one foot free." The most beautiful example we can point to is the bronze figure of an Amazon, formerly at Ephesus, of which there are several copies in marble (Fig. 58). The type of these masculine heroines was a favourite one with Greek artists of the fifth century, because of the old legends which represented them as coming from Asia to measure themselves against the Greeks; the combats of the Greeks and the Amazons were a transparent allusion to the great struggle of the Greeks against the Persians. In addition to this, the Amazon was the feminine pendant of the Athlete, a type which permitted the Greek artist to create a purely human ideal of female vigour side by side with that of goddesses. This ideal was realised with such perfection by Polyclitus that, down to the end of the classic period, all the statues of Amazons are more or less derived from his; he did for the Amazon what Phidias did for Jupiter.

Polyclitus and Myron were contemporary with Phidias; if I have spoken of them before him, it is because they seem to have retained more of the archaic tradition, notably in that lingering coldness on which I have insisted. Phidias himself never cast off its trammels altogether; his glory lies in having been its highest expression, just as the genius of Raphael was the most complete expression of the Renaissance. The evolution of art is never complete; to speak of perfection in art is a dangerous error, for, by implication, it condemns artists to an eternal reproduction of the same models, to the renunciation of progress. The function of men of genius is rather to prepare the way for new tendencies by giving adequate and definite expression to those of their own times.

BIBLIOGRAPHY OF CHAPTER V.

M. Collignon, *Histoire de la Sculpture Grecque*, vol. i. (to the building of the Parthenon), Paris, 1892, E. Gardner, *Handbook of Greek Sculpture*, 2nd ed., London, 1906; G. Perrot, *Histoire de l'Art*, vols. viii., ix., Paris, 1903, 1912 (to the Persian Wars); E. Loewy, *Griechische Plastik*, 2 vols., Leipzig, 1911; J. Klein, *Geschichte der griechische Kunst*, 3 vols., Leipzig, 1904–7; H. Lechat, *Au Musée de l'Acropole*, Lyons, 1903; *La Sculpture Attique avant Phidias*, Paris, 1905 (cf. Collignon, *Journal des Savants*, 1906, p. 121); A. Joubin, *La Sculpture Grecque entre les Guerres Médiques et l'Epoque de Péricles*, Paris, 1901; A. Furtwängler, *Masterpieces of Greek Sculpture*, translated by E. Sellers, London, 1895; *Die Antiken Gemmen*, vol. iii., Leipzig, 1900; *Aegina*, 2 vols., Munich, 1906; A Mahler, *Polyklet*, Leipzig, 1902; F. Studniczka, *Kalamis*, Leipzig, 1907; S. Reinach, *Têtes antiques idéales ou idéalisées*, Paris, 1903 (the notes to this work refer to most of the important articles on the history of art before Phidias); *Répertoire de la Statuaire*, vols. i.–iii., Paris, 1897–1904 (reproductions in outline of Greek statues, with references to all the best publications, and a complete bibliography of Greek sculpture); *Répertoire de reliefs*, 3 vols., Paris, 1909–1912.

For the *Hermes* of Alcamenes, a copy of which, with an inscription, has been discovered at Pergamum, see *Alterthümer von Pergamon*, Berlin, 1908, vol. vii., p. 48.

For the excavations of the French School of Athens at Delphi, see Th. Homolle, *Gazette des Beaux-Arts*, 1894, ii., p. 441; *Bulletin de Corresp. hellénique*, 1900, pp. 427, 616; *L'Aurige de Delphes* (*Monuments Piot*, vol. iv., p. 169); G. Perrot, *Histoire de l'Art*, vol. viii., pp. 336–392 (for the *Treasury of the Cnidians*, described above, p. 39); F. Poulsen, *Delphi*, L., 1920; *Les ruines de Delphes*, P., 1914.

VI

PHIDIAS AND THE PARTHENON

The Embellishment of Athens under Pericles.—Phidias, Ictinus, and Callicrates.—The Building of the Parthenon and of the Erechtheum.—The Structure of Greek Temples.—The Three Orders.—The Technical Perfection of the Parthenon.—The Propylæa, the Erechtheum, and the Temple of Niké Apteros.—The Sculptures of the Parthenon.—The Chryselephantine Statues of Athene and of Zeus.—Furtwängler's Reconstruction of the Lemnian Athene.—The Venus of Milo.

FROM about 460 to 435 B.C. Pericles was the head of the Athenian democracy, and the master of all the resources of the Athenian State. His dictatorship may be described as one of persuasion. Admirable in spite of certain grave defects of character, he had a passion for the beautiful, and to his initiative we owe one of the most exquisite things in the world, the Parthenon (Figs. 59-61).

FIG. 59.—RECONSTRUCTED VIEW OF THE ACROPOLIS AT ATHENS.

From R to L.: Erechtheum, Colossal Statue of Athene Promachos by Phidias, Parthenon, Propylæa, Temples of Athene Ergane and Niké Apteros.

(Springer and Michaelis, *Kunstgeschichte*. Seemann, Leipzig.)

Phidias, the sculptor, was the friend and counsellor of Pericles in all matters relating to the embellishment of Athens. Surrounded by a numerous band of artists, some of whom, such as Ictinus and Callicrates, were men of superior talents, Phidias directed and superintended all the work. His position was much like that of Raphael in the court of Leo X. during the decoration of the *Stanze* and *Loggie* of the Vatican. Like Raphael, he was not the sole author of the works he conceived or inspired; but he left the sovereign impress of his genius upon them all.

FIG. 6c.—VIEW OF THE PARTHENON.

47

The tutelary *guardian* divinity of Athens was Athene Parthenos, that is to say, the *Virgin;* the temple which was her dwelling was called the

FIG. 61.—CORNER OF THE PARTHENON.
From a drawing by Niemann.
(Springer and Michaelis, *Kunstgeschichte.*
Seemann, Leipzig.)

Parthenon. The ancient stone Parthenon on the Acropolis had been destroyed by the Persians in 480 B.C., and Pericles determined to build another, larger and more sumptuous. For twenty years, the quarries of Attica yielded their most beautiful marbles to thousands of artists and workmen. Their labours, favoured by a period of comparative peace, were completed in 435 B.C. Soon afterwards, they began to rebuild in marble the little temple of Poseidon and Erechtheus, called the Erechtheum, to the north of the Parthenon; it was not finished until 408, twenty years after the death of Pericles. The Peloponnesian war had already begun, casting a shadow of mourning over the close of the century.

Parisians, and visitors to Paris, having seen the church of the Madeleine, have some general idea of the form of a Greek temple. It is essentially a rectangular building, with doors, but without windows, surrounded on all sides by a single or double row of columns which, while supporting the roof, seem to mount guard round the dwelling of the god (*cella*). On the two shorter sides of the temple, the roof forms a triangle called the *pediment,* which is sometimes

FIG. 62.—THE PORTICO OF THE CARYATIDES, THE ERECHTHEUM, ATHENS.

decorated with statues. The upper part of the wall is adorned with bas-reliefs, forming the *frieze.* When the temple is of the Doric order, like the Parthenon, the upper part of the architrave supported by the columns is composed of slabs with three vertical grooves called *triglyphs*, alternating with other slabs, sometimes plain, sometimes ornamented with reliefs known as *metopes* (Fig. 61).

Greek architecture made use of three *orders*, that is to say, three principal types of columnar construction. The most ancient, to which belong the Parthenon, the temple of Zeus at Olympia, the temple of Aphaia at Ægina, the temples of Sicily and Southern Italy (Pæstum, Selinus,

FIG. 63.—TEMPLE OF NIKÉ APTEROS, ON THE ACROPOLIS.
Lateral view.

and Agrigentum), is called Doric, because the ancients believed it was invented by the Dorians. In the Doric order the column was not very lofty; it was crowned by a simple capital, composed of a part that formed an expanding curve and was called the *echinus*, and of a square slab called the *abacus*. In the Ionic order, the great examples of which are in Asia Minor, at Ephesus, and Priene, though there is also a beautiful

FIG. 64.—GROUP OF THE FATES.
From the eastern pediment of the Parthenon.
(British Museum.)
(Photo. by Mansell.)

specimen on the Athenian Acropolis (Fig. 63), the column is more slender, and it is crowned by a capital which is like a cushion with volutes. Finally, the Corinthian order, which was chiefly used in the Roman period, as also during the Renaissance and in our own times, is characterised by a capital which reproduces a cluster of acanthus leaves.

Both the Doric and the

FIG. 65.—PROCESSION OF ATHENIAN MAIDENS.
From the Frieze of the Parthenon.
(British Museum.)

Ionic orders are derived from the forms used in timber construction. The column was evolved from the wooden post which upheld a beam. The shaft was strengthened at the top to receive the beam, by the addition of a cube or slab, and this expansion was the origin of the capital. The Corinthian capital was adopted at a period when Greek artists had forgotten the exigencies of timber construction, or they would hardly have proposed to support a burden on a bunch of leaves.

FIG. 66.—HORSEMEN.
From the Frieze of the Parthenon.
(British Museum.)
(Photo. by Mansell.)

The Doric order is marked by a solidity, a virile robustness which contrasts with the somewhat frail and feminine elegance of the Ionic order. The Corinthian order suggests luxury and splendour. One of the most striking proofs of the genius of the Greeks is the fact that neither the Renaissance nor modern art has created a new order; our architecture continues to rely upon the wealth of the Greek orders, which lend themselves to the most varied combinations.

The most admirable feature of the Parthenon is, perhaps, its perfection of proportion. The relation between the height of the columns, their thickness, the height of the pediments, and the dimensions of the temple, was determined with such unerring judgment that the whole is neither too light nor too heavy, that the

FIG. 67.—ZEUS, APOLLO, AND PEITHO.
From the Frieze of the Parthenon, at Athens.

lines harmonise in such a manner as to give the impression at once of strength and grace. The technical perfection of the construction is no less amazing. The great blocks of marble, the drums of the columns, are joined and adjusted without cement, as exactly as the most delicate piece of goldsmith's work. Modern architecture, which makes such a lavish use of cement, has never been able to compete with the workmen directed by Ictinus.

The Parthenon is now a ruin. The Byzantines used it as a church; it was gutted by an explosion in 1687; in 1803, Lord Elgin carried off the greater part of the sculptures, which are now the pride of the British Museum. But the wreck remains a masterpiece and a place of pilgrimage for all humanity.

A magnificent portico, the Propylæa, gave access to the Parthenon from the side nearest the sea; it was decorated

FIG. 68.—HEAD OF PEITHO.
From the Frieze of the Parthenon.
(Museum, Athens.)

with paintings which have disappeared. The little temple of Poseidon and Erechtheus, to the north of the Parthenon, is better preserved; it is flanked by a portico, where, in place of columns, the architect introduced female figures, to which the ancients gave the name of Caryatides (Fig. 62), because they supposed them to represent young maidens carried away captive from the city of Caryæ in Laconia. Another little Ionic temple, that of the Wingless Victory (Niké Apteros), was restored after 1830 with fragments found in a Turkish bastion. It stands in front of the Propylæa (Fig. 63).

FIG. 69.—REDUCED COPY OF THE ATHENE PARTHENOS OF PHIDIAS.
(Museum, Athens.)

The pediments of the Parthenon represented the birth of Athene, and the dispute between Athene and Poseidon for the possession of Attica (Fig. 64). On the metopes were carved the battles of the Centaurs and the Lapithæ. The subject of the frieze was the procession of the Panathenæa, the principal festival of the goddess, on which occasion the young girls of the noblest families, clad in the long chiton falling in vertical folds, came to offer Athene a new veil woven for her. These young girls, bearing different objects, walk in an imposing *cortège* of old men, matrons, soldiers, horsemen, and men leading the sacrificial beasts. They advance towards a group representing the gods in the centre of the eastern front: this part of the frieze is, fortunately, one of the best preserved portions of the whole (Figs. 65, 66, 67).

Inside the temple was a *chryselephantine* statue (*i.e.* a statue of gold and ivory) of Athene, standing. This and the seated Zeus, also of gold and ivory, in the temple of Olympia, were, according to the ancients, the masterpieces of Phidias. Both have disappeared; but we can form some idea of the Athene Parthenos from a little marble copy discovered at Athens in 1880, near a modern school called the Varvakeion (Fig. 69). No copy of the Zeus has come down to us; but it is probable that a beautiful marble head in the Ny-Carlsberg collection in Denmark reproduces the majestic features of the god with sufficient accuracy (Fig. 70).

FIG. 70.—HEAD OF ZEUS, STYLE OF PHIDIAS.

(Ny-Carlsberg Gallery, near Copenhagen.)

FIG. 72.—COPY OF AN ATHENE ATTRIBUTED TO PHIDIAS.

(Museum, Dresden; the head at Bologna.)

(Furtwängler, *Masterpieces of Greek Sculpture.* Heinemann, London.)

FIG. 71.—STATUETTE OF ATHENE PROMACHOS.

(Museum, Boston.)

Another Athene by Phidias, a colossal bronze, about 30 feet high, stood in front of the Parthenon on the north west. It was called the Athene Promachos, that is to say, the *Guardian.* I think I discovered a copy of it in a little statuette of very fine quality, now at Boston; it came from the neighbourhood of Coblentz, where a legion known as the *Minervia* was stationed under the Roman Empire (Fig. 71).

Lastly, by combining a head at Bologna with a torso at Dresden, Herr Furtwängler has reconstituted an admirable statue, the marble copy of a bronze original, which, in common with various other experts, he pronounces to have been an Athene by Phidias, the one executed by the master for the Athenian settlers on the isle of Lemnos (Fig. 72).

Classic writers have not asserted in so many words that the sculptures of the Parthenon were by Phidias himself; but it is certain that they were executed under his direction. To form any idea of this series of masterpieces, we must study the casts in the Louvre, the École des Beaux-Arts, or British Museum. I would call particular attention to the group of the three goddesses, generally called the Three Fates, from the eastern pediment, whose draperies are indescribably beautiful, and to some fragments of the frieze, the despair of all artists who have striven to imitate their noble composition, their serene majesty, and infinite variety (Figs. 64-68).

FIG. 73.—HEAD OF ARTEMIS.
From the eastern pediment of the Parthenon, British Museum.
(Laborde Collection, Paris.)
(Photograph by Giraudon.)

In a head of Artemis of the east pediment of the Parthenon (now belonging to the Marquis de Laborde in Paris) we are struck by the vigorous mould and the robust oval of the face, characterised by a certain squareness of outline. That head presents two traits which appear in all of them alike: the short distance between the eyebrow and the eyelid, and the strong protuberance of the eyeballs. These are relics of the archaic style. The general im-

FIG. 74.—HEAD OF A STATUE OF APOLLO
(PERHAPS AFTER PHIDIAS).

(Museum of the Thermæ, Rome.)

FIG. 75.—VENUS OF MILO
(APHRODITE OF MELOS).
(The Louvre.)
(Photograph by Giraudon.)

pression they produce is that of a serene and self-reliant strength, a quality that breathes from all the art of Phidias (Fig. 74). But there are other things in human nature besides strength, serenity, and beauty; enthusiasm, for instance, and reverie, and passion, and suffering, clamant or discreet. These were the things that remained to be expressed in marble after Phidias; we shall see how his successors carried out the task.

I cannot turn from the work of Phidias, whose pupils (Agoracritus, Alcamenes) continued to work during the first decades of the fourth century, without speaking of the masterpiece in the Louvre, the statue discovered in 1820 in the island of Melos (Figs. 75, 76). Though the majority of modern archæologists pronounce it to be a work dating from about 100 B. C., I am convinced that it is some 250 years older than this; and I believe it to be a masterpiece of the school of Phidias, representing, not Venus, but the goddess of the sea, Amphitrite, holding a trident in her extended left arm. One reason I give for this belief is, that we find in it all the qualities that go to make up the genius of Phidias, and nothing that is alien to it. The Venus of Milo is neither elegant, nor dreamy, nor nervous, nor impassioned; she is strong and serene. Her beauty is all noble simplicity and calm dignity, like that of the Parthenon and its sculptures. Is not this the reason the statue has become and has remained so popular, in spite

FIG. 76.—HEAD OF THE VENUS OF MILO.
(The Louvre.)

of the mystery of the much-discussed attitude? Agitated and feverish generations see in it the highest expression of the quality they
most lack, that serenity which is not apathy, but the equanimity of
mental and bodily health.

BIBLIOGRAPHY OF CHAPTER VI.

M. Collignon, *Histoire de la Sculpture Grecque*, vols. i. and ii., Paris, 1892, 1897; *Le Parthénon*, Paris, 1912 (Phot. of all sculptures); G. Periot and Ch. Chipiez, *Histoire de l'Art*, vol. vii., Paris, 1898 (the Greek orders, elements of architecture); R. Kekulé, *Die Griechische Skulptur*, Berlin, 1907; A. Choisy, *Histoire de l'Architecture*, vol. i., Paris, 1899; F. Benoît, *L'Architecture*, vol. i., Paris, 1911; H. Lechat, *Le Temple Grec*, Paris, 1902; E. Gardner, *Handbook of Greek Sculpture*, London, 1896; Fougères and Hulot, *Sélinante*, Paris, 1909; A. Furtwängler, *Masterpieces of Greek Sculpture*, London, 1895; A. Michaelis, *Der Parthenon*, Leipzig, 1870–1871 (with a volume of plates); A. Michaelis and A. Springer, *Handbuch der Kunstgeschichte*, 9th ed., vol. i., Leipzig, 1909; H. Lechat, *Phidias et la Sculpture du ve Siècle*, Paris, 1906; Bruno Sauer, *Der Laborde'sche Kopf*, Giessen, 1903; and *Das sogenannte Theseion*, Leipzig, 1899; S. Reinach, *Répertoire de la Statuaire*, Paris, 1897–1910; *Répertoire des Reliefs*, Paris, 1909–12; *Têtes Antiques*, Paris, 1903; W. Deonna, *L'Archéologie et ses méthodes*, Paris, 1911–12. For the controversies concerning the *Venus of Milo*, see the *Revue Archéologique*, 1906, i., p. 199, which gives all the recent bibliography; for the date, *Revue des Etudes grecques*, 1908, p. 13.

Shorter Studies: H. Lechat, *L'Acropole d'Athènes* (*Gaz. des Beaux-Arts*, 1892, ii., p. 89); E. Michon, *Tête d'Athlète (de Bénévent) au Louvre* (*Monuments Piot*, vol. i., p. 77); E. Pottier, *La Tête au Cécryphale* (*Bullet. de Correspondance hellénique*, vol. xx., 1896, p. 445; study on the feminine type of Phidias); S. Reinach, *Têtes de l'Ecole de Phidias* (*Gazette des Beaux-Arts*, 1902, ii., p. 449; *Le Blessé défaillant de Crésilas* (*ibid.*, i., p. 193); Eug. Strong, *La tête Humphry Ward* (*Gazette*, 1909, i., p. 52); Amelung, *Athena des Phidias* (*Oesterreiche Jahreshefte*, 1908, p. 169; against Furtwängler's reconstruction of the Lemnian *Athena*).

VII

PRAXITELES, SCOPAS, AND LYSIPPUS

The Modification of the Athenian Temperament brought about by the Peloponnesian War.—The Psychological Art of Scopas and Praxiteles.—The Irene and Plutus of Cephisodotus.—The Hermes with the Infant Dionysus of Praxiteles.—Other Works by the Master.—Lord Leconfield's Head of Aphrodite.—The Sculptures of the Temple of Tegæa.—Passion the Characteristic of Scopas' Art.—Lysippus and his Work in Bronze.—The Apoxyomenus.—The Borghese Warrior.—The Woman of Herculaneum at Dresden.—The Mausoleum of Halicarnassus.—The Group of Niobe and her Children.—The Victory of Samothrace.—The Demeter of Cnidus.—Funereal Stelæ.—The Ceramicus at Athens.

FIG. 77.—IRENE AND PLUTUS.

Copy of a group by Cephisodotus.

(Museum, Munich.)

THE Peloponnesian War, undertaken by Pericles in 432 B.C., came to an end in 404 B.C. with the capture of Athens. These disasters brought about a religious and political reaction, the most illustrious victim of which was Socrates (399 B.C.). Meanwhile Athens, though conquered and humiliated by Sparta, never ceased to be the intellectual capital of Hellas; it might even be said that her sovereignty became more extensive and firmly rooted in the fourth century. But her character, ripened by adversity, had changed. In addition to this, the school of philosophy founded by Socrates and carried on by Plato, bore fruit; it inculcated reflection, self-examination, and fostered depth and subtlety of thought. To the serene art of the fifth century B.C. succeeded a meditative art, the most illustrious exponents of which were Praxiteles and Scopas.

Praxiteles' master, Cephisodotus, is known to us by a statue of *Irene* (Peace), carrying the infant *Plutus* (Riches); there

FIG. 78.—HERMES, BY PRAXITELES.

(Museum, Olympia.)

56

is a good antique copy of the work at Munich (Fig. 77). The goddess bends her dreamy head over the child with an air of tender solicitude. In the proportions and the cast of the draperies, this group shows its close affinity to the school of Phidias; but the sentiment that pervades it is identical with that which informs the work of Praxiteles. The *Irene* dates probably from the year 380 B.C.

By Praxiteles, who was born about 385 B.C., we possess one original work, which was found in 1877 in the temple of Hera at Olympia, in the very spot where Pausanias had noted its presence. It is a group repre-

FIG. 79.—HEAD OF THE HERMES BY PRAXITELES.

(Museum, Olympia.)

senting Hermes carrying the youthful Dionysus, whom Zeus had confided to his care (Figs. 78, 79). The analogy of the conception with that of Cephisodotus' group has often been pointed out. But the *Hermes* shows a greater independence of the Phidian tradition

FIG. 80.—SILENUS AND INFANT DIONYSUS.

(Upper part of a group in the Louvre, perhaps after Praxiteles.)

than the *Irene*. It is characterised by a sinuous, almost feminine, grace and an intensity of spiritual life, which is a new phenomenon in art. The execution has a beauty of which neither photographs nor casts can give an adequate idea. A careful examination of the head reveals two characteristics which distinguish it from all others of the fifth century: first, the hair, treated with a picturesque freedom, and a determination to emphasise the contrast between its furrowed surface and the polished smoothness of the flesh; and secondly, the overhanging brow and deep-set eye, the material indications of reflection.

57

FIG. 81.—ARTEMIS,
KNOWN AS THE DIANA
OF GABII.
Perhaps after Praxiteles.
(The Louvre.)

Numerous copies of the Roman period have preserved other works by Praxiteles for us, at least in their general features: a Silenus (Fig. 80), a Satyr, two figures of Eros, and two of Dionysus, a Zeus, an Apollo, and perhaps an Artemis (Fig. 81), The most famous of his works among the ancients was a nude figure of Aphrodite about to enter the sea, which was long admired in the temple of the goddess at Cnidus. Unfortunately, the copies that have come down to us are very mediocre (Fig. 82). But in Lord Leconfield's London house there is a head of Aphrodite, so marvellously supple in execution and so exquisitely suave in expression that we may fairly accept it as the work, if not of Praxiteles himself, then of one of his immediate pupils (Fig. 83). The characteristics of the feminine ideal as conceived by this great and fascinating genius are all clearly defined in this head. The form of the face, hitherto round, has become oval; the eyes, instead of being fully opened, are half closed, and have that particular expression which the ancients described as " liquid," the eyebrows are but slightly marked, and the attenuation of the eyelids is such, that they melt, by almost insensible gradations, into the adjoining planes. The hair, like that of the Hermes, is freely modelled; and finally, the whole reveals a preoccupation with effects of chiaroscuro, of a subdued play of light and shadow, which precludes any lingering vestiges of harshness and angularity. It is here that we note the influence of painting upon sculpture. The great achievements of Attic painting are entirely unknown to us; but as the ancients extolled them as

FIG. 82.—HEAD OF AN ANTIQUE COPY OF
THE APHRODITE OF CNIDUS BY PRAXITELES.
(The Vatican.) (Photo. by Alinari.)

equal to the sculptures, we may believe that they were indeed masterpieces. The most renowned painter of the fifth century, Polygnotus, was, we are told, less pre-eminent as a colourist than as a draughtsman, whereas those of the fourth century, Parrhasius, Zeuxis, and Apelles, were above all colourists. If their pictures had been preserved to us, we should perhaps have found them more akin to Correggio than to Mantegna, or Bellini. The suavity of a head like Lord Leconfield's *Aphrodite* does, as a fact, recall Correggio; we recognise in it that essentially pictorial quality which the Italian critics call *sfumato*, meaning a vaporous gradation of tones, a melting of one tint into another.

FIG. 83.—HEAD OF APHRODITE.
(Lord Leconfield's Collection, London.)

Scopas survives for us in certain heads from the pediment of the temple of Tegæa (about 360 B.C.). The study of these fragments has enabled us to recognise the same style in a number of Roman marbles, copies of works by Scopas. We may form some idea of it from two heads, one that of a warrior from the pediment of Tegæa, the other a beardless Heracles (Fig. 84). The oval of the face is less pronounced than with Praxiteles, but the eyes are more deeply set, and the eyebrow forms a strong projection, casting a semicircle of shadow above the eye. This peculiarity, combined with the marked undulation of the lips, gives an impassioned and almost suffering expression to Scopas' heads; we seem to divine in them the intensity of a struggle against desire, the anguish of unsatisfied aspirations.

FIG. 84.—HEADS OF THE SCHOOL OF SCOPAS.
(Athens and Florence.)

Here lay the originality of Scopas. Praxiteles expressed a languorous reverie in his marbles, Scopas gave utterance in his to passion.

FIG. 85.—COPY OF THE
APOXYOMENUS OF LY-
SIPPUS.
(The Vatican.)
(Photo. by Anderson.)

The third great artist of the fourth century,
Lysippus, was younger than the two others.
He was the accredited sculptor of Alexander
the Great, and worked principally in bronze,
whereas Praxiteles and Scopas won renown
mainly by their works in marble. Lysippus
was born at Sicyon, a town in the Peloponnesus; he declared that his sole teachers had
been Nature and Polyclitus' *Doryphorus*, that
figure of an athlete which was known as the
Canon. Polyclitus,
as I have said, was
a native of Argos.
Thus the art of
Lysippus presents
itself as a kind of
Doric reaction
against Attic art,
which tended to lay
an increasing stress on sentiment, and
might be thought to incline to effeminacy
and sensuality. Lysippus modified the
Canon of Polyclitus, that is to say, the
classic tradition of the
fifth century,
by a more
marked tendency to
elegance,

FIG. 86.—HEAD OF THE
APOXYOMENUS.
(The Vatican.)

FIG. 87.—THE BORGHESE WARRIOR.
(The Louvre.)

making his bodies nearly *eight* times the
length of the head (instead of seven
times), and emphasising the joints and
muscles at the expense of their fleshy
covering. His heads express neither
reverie nor passion; they are content to
be merely nervous and refined. There
is in the Vatican a good copy of his best
statue of an athlete, the *Apoxyomenus*,
rubbing his arm with a strigil to remove
the oil and dust of the palestra (Figs. 85,
86). It is probable that the famous

FIG. 88.—VENUS DE'
MEDICI.
(Florence, Uffizi.)
(Photo. by Alinari,
Florence.)

Borghese *Warrior* in the Louvre, another athlete, also reproduces a bronze original by Lysippus; the artist who has signed his name on this fine, but somewhat frigid study of the nude, Agasias of Ephesus, was obviously only the copyist (Fig. 87). A statue of an athlete, discovered at Delphi, is believed to be a free copy of a lost bronze by Lysippus. Lastly, there are several statues of Heracles and of Alexander the Great, derived from originals by the master, and we further owe him some fine female statues, of which there are various

FIG. 89.—COPY OF
THE MNEMOSYNE (?)
OF LYSIPPUS.
(Museum, Dresden.)

replicas, among them the so-called *Venus de' Medici* at Florence (Fig. 88), and a draped figure discovered at Herculaneum (Figs.

FIG. 90.—HEAD, COPY OF THE
MNEMOSYNE (?) OF LYSIPPUS.
(Museum, Dresden.)

FIG. 91.—ARTEMISIA AND MAUSOLUS.
Statues from the Mausoleum at
Halicarnassus.
(British Museum.) (Photo. by Lévy.)

FIG. 92.—COMBAT OF GREEKS AND AMAZONS.

Bas-relief from the Frieze of the Mausoleum at
Halicarnassus.

(British Museum.)

89, 90). This feminine type, the head of which shows analogies with that of the *Apoxyomenus*, is certainly one of the most beautiful creations of antique art; her draperies have such simplicity and grandeur that they still find many imitators.

Four sculptors, Scopas, Bryaxis, Leochares, and Timotheus, worked about the year 340 B.C. on the decorations of the Mausoleum at Halicarnassus, raised by Artemisia, Queen of Caria, to the memory of her husband Mausolus. Thanks to Newton's excavations in 1857, the British Museum possesses a series of statues and bas-reliefs which formerly decorated this mausoleum. Two fine statues, representing Mausolus and Artemisia crowned the structure (Fig. 91). The statue of Mausolus is one of the most ancient Greek portraits known to us, and is all the more remarkable in that the face of the model was not that of

FIG. 93.—NIOBE AND HER YOUNGEST DAUGHTER.

(Uffizi, Florence.)

FIG. 94.—NIKÉ (VICTORY) OF
SAMOTHRACE.

(The Louvre.)

a Hellene, but of a Carian, that is to say, a semi-barbarian. The draperies, modelled with a perfect comprehension of the play of light and shadow, mark a stage in the progress that led up to the masterpiece of classic drapery, the *Victory* of Samothrace.

The bas-reliefs of the Mausoleum

represent a battle of Greeks and Amazons; it is very instructive to compare these with the frieze of the Parthenon. We find in them all the characteristics of the new art, a taste for lively and sudden movement, for the picturesque and the effective, an elegance which does not preclude vigour, but which sometimes verges on excessive refinement (Fig. 92).

Even in classic times it seems to have been an open question whether Scopas or Praxiteles should be credited with the authorship of the famous group of Niobe and her children, struck down by the arrows of Apollo and Artemis. Antique copies of several figures of the composition, varying a good deal in quality, are preserved in

FIG. 95.—DEMETER OF CNIDUS.
(British Museum.)

Florence, Rome, Paris (the Louvre), and elsewhere. To judge by these copies, the originals must have been works of the school of Scopas. In the centre was Niobe with her youngest daughter, a group of which there is a copy at Florence (Fig. 93). The deeply pathetic motive, that of a mother who sees her daughter killed before her eyes, is treated with noble simplicity; we find as yet no trace of the physical anguish, the painful contortions of the Laocoön. The child, pressed closely to the mother, is an admirable conception. Her transparent tunic, clinging to her young body, and gathered into innumerable little pleats, bears witness to the influence of painting upon sculpture. We shall find a diaphanous pleated tunic of the same sort draping the *Victory* of Samothrace. We are again reminded of this *Victory* by another fine figure from the Niobid group, known to us by an excellent copy in the Vatican.

FIG. 96.—STELA OF HEGESO.
(Museum, Athens.)
(Photo. by Giraudon.)

63

FIG. 97.—FRAGMENT OF AN ATTIC TOMBSTONE.
(Museum, Athens.)

Here the analogy is most evident in the movement, and in the picturesque cast of the drapery.

The *Victory* of Samothrace (Fig. 94), which the Louvre is fortunate enough to possess, in which the figure stands on the prow of a galley, blowing a trumpet, was carved to commemorate a naval victory gained in 306 B.C. by Demetrius Poliorcetes over the Egyptian General Ptolemy, off the island of Cyprus. The precise date is now a matter of dispute, but this is correct within fifty years. Two influences were at that time predominant in Greek sculpture, that of Lysippus, and that of the school of Scopas; it was the latter which inspired the *Victory*. The irresistible energy, the victorious swing of the body, the quivering life that seems to animate the marble, the happy contrast afforded by the flutter of the wind-swept mantle and the adherence of the closely-fitting tunic to the torso, combine to make the statue the most exquisite expression of movement left to us by antique art. The sculptor has not only translated muscular strength and triumphant grace into marble; he has also suggested the intensity of the sea-breeze, that breeze the breath of which Sully-Prud'homme, too, has caught in a verse winged like the *Victory* herself:—

"Un peu du grand zéphir qui souffle à Salamine."

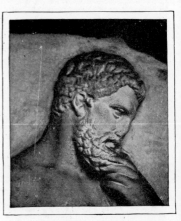

FIG. 98.—FRAGMENT OF AN ATTIC TOMBSTONE.
(Museum, Athens.)

A life-size statue of Demeter, seated, and mourning for her daughter Persephone, carried off by Pluto, was discovered by Newton at

Cnidus, and is now in the British Museum (Fig. 95). It is a work dating from about 340 B.C. and betrays the double influence of Praxiteles and Scopas. It has often been compared to those figures of the Mater Dolorosa so frequent in the art of the Renaissance. But if we examine it closely, we shall see that the differences are more profound than the analogies. The grief of the heathen mother is reticent and subdued; it is suggested rather than proclaimed. We shall see that after the fourth century the ancients did not shrink from realistic expression of the most intense physical suffering; but they expressed moral suffering only in a contained and chastened form. A figure like Roger van der Weyden's *Mater Dolorosa* is entirely alien to classic genius.

This expression of reserved sorrow gives charm to a great number of funereal *stelæ*, by anonymous artists, which are among the purest and most delicate productions of Attic art in the fourth century (Figs. 96—98). The regret of survivors is expressed in these with so much reserve that their significance has not always been understood, and they have been supposed to represent the dead reunited to the members of their family in the Elysium of the blest. Despair is never suggested in these compositions; gestures and countenances are alike placid; a slight inclination of the head is all that reveals the pensive intention of the sculptor. One of the most beautiful of these monuments is the Athenian *stela* which represents a dead woman, seated, taking a jewel from a casket held by an attendant (Fig. 96). The deceased is shown engaged in one of the familiar occupations of her earthly life. We must not look here for any mystic meaning, any promise of a happy life beyond the tomb. But the veil of sadness that obscures the charming faces is woven with true Attic subtlety. How noble is this tearless sorrow which conceals itself with a certain modesty, and, over a newly-made grave, recalls a smile of the lost one! Fortunately for us, we have many means of entering into the secrets of the classical mind. We can read Euripides and Plato, Xenophon and Isocrates, the fragments of Menander, we can study hundreds of statues and painted vases. But nothing, not even the most beautiful of Plato's pages, can so familiarise us with antiquity, can make us so appreciate its delicate taste and the infinite refinement of its grace as a walk through the Ceramicus of Athens, the quarter of Tombs, where amidst the spring scents of mint and thyme, we breathe another perfume, that of the unique and immortal flower of human genius we call Atticism.

APOLLO

BIBLIOGRAPHY OF CHAPTER VII.

M. Collignon, *Histoire de la Sculpture grecque*, vol. ii., Paris, 1897 (descriptions of the Mausoleum of Halicarnassus, the *Niobe and her children*, etc.); *Statues funéraires*, Paris, 1911; E. Gardner and S. Reinach, works quoted on p. 55; Klein, *Praxiteles*, Leipzig, 1898, and *Praxitelische Studien*, Leipzig, 1899; G. Perrot, *Praxitèle*, Paris, 1905; B. Graef, *Römische Mittheilungen*, vol. iv., 1889, p. 189 (on Scopas); G. Mendel, *Fouilles de Tégée* (*Bulletin de Correspondance hellénique*, 1901, vol. xxv., p. 241); Th. Homolle, *Lysippe et l'ex-voto de Daochos* (Delphi) (*Bulletin*, 1899, vol. xxiii., p. 421); M. Collignon, *Lysippe*, Paris, 1905; W. Hyde, *Lysippus* (*American Journal*, 1907, p. 396); S. Reinach, *Strongylion* (*Revue Archéologique*, 1904, i., p. 28); *Le Type féminin de Lysippe* (*ibid.*, 1900, ii., p. 380; on the Herculanean statue at Dresden); A. Mahler, *La Vénus de Médicis* (*C. R. de l'Acad.*, 1905, p. 623); O. Rayet, *Monuments de l'Art Antique*, vol. ii., pl. 64 (the *Borghese Warrior*); C. B. Stark, *Niobe und die Niobiden*, Leipzig, 1863; A. Furtwängler, *Masterpieces*, London, 1895 (reviewed, *Revue critique*, 1894, i., p. 97); A. Furtwängler and H. L. Urlichs, *Denkmäler griechischer und römischer Skulptur*, 2nd ed., Munich, 1904; P. Gardner, *Sculptured Tombs of Hellas*, London, 1896.

On the influence of Painting: S. Girard, *La Peinture Antique*, Paris, no date; A. Michaelis, *Von griechischer Malerei* (*Deutsche Revue*, 1903, p. 210).

VIII

GREEK ART AFTER ALEXANDER THE GREAT

The Conquests of Alexander and their Influence on Greek Art.—The Rise of Alexandria, Antioch, and Pergamum.—The Hellenistic Epoch.—The Schools of Rhodes and Pergamum. —The First Representation of the Barbarian and of Nature in Art.—The Dying Gaul, formerly known as the Dying Gladiator.—The Altar of Zeus at Pergamum.—The Laocoön.— The Belvedere Apollo.—The Pourtalès Apollo.—The Centaur and Eros.—The so-called Sarcophagus of Alexander.

IN the year 336 B.C. Alexander of Macedon succeeded his father Philip; he was but twenty years old. After consolidating his father's work in Greece, by taking and laying waste Thebes, and subduing Athens, he conquered successively Asia Minor, Syria, Egypt, Persia, Bactriana, and the north of India, and died at Babylon in 323 B.C. His generals divided his vast empire among them, and established Greek civilisation from the banks of the Nile to those of the Oxus and the Indus. India, which had perhaps received the rudiments of her art from Persia, thus became the pupil of Greece, but she remained a capricious pupil, whose temperament, recalcitrant to every kind of rule and measure, was destined to produce a totally different style.

The consequences of Alexander's victories were momentous for Hellenism and for Greek art. Athens ceased to be the centre of the latter; her intellectual supremacy passed to the Alexandria of the Ptolemies in Egypt, to the Antioch of the Seleucidæ in Syria, and the Pergamum of the Attalidæ in Asia Minor. Thus uprooted and internationalised, Hellenism lost in purity what it gained in extent. Its political organisation underwent a complete change. The small Greek states with their free cities, were supplanted by Oriental monarchies, with hereditary sovereigns wielding almost absolute power. Art worked primarily for these

FIG. 99.—GAUL KILLING HIMSELF AFTER KILLING HIS WIFE.

Formerly in the Ludovici Collection. (Museum of the Thermæ, Rome.)

67

sovereigns and the new capitals they sought to beautify; its aim was to dazzle by material greatness and splendour, and it strove after grandiose effects rather than perfection of form and workmanship.

The term *Hellenistic Epoch* is applied to the period comprised between the death of Alexander (323 B.C.) and the conquest of Egypt by the Romans (30 B.C.), to distinguish it from the *Hellenic Epoch*. During this period art made a rapid evolution, and underwent a complete transformation, which cannot, however, be described as decadence, for amidst these changes were born and developed new elements, the destined heritage of modern art. After serene strength (Phidias), languorous grace (Praxiteles), passion (Scopas), and nervous elegance (Lysippus), art had yet to express physical suffering, anguish, the tumult and disorder of the soul and the body, and this was admirably done by the schools of Rhodes and Pergamum.

FIG. 100.—THE DYING GAUL.
(Museum of the Capitol, Rome.)
(Photo. by Anderson.)

But this was not all. After having fixed the types of gods and heroes, and sculptured amazons and athletes, art had still to render the individual man, to create portraiture; it had further to admit into its sphere beings who were neither gods nor Greeks, to represent, with a due regard for reality and picturesqueness, barbarians such as the Ethiopian and the Gaul. This was accomplished mainly at Pergamum and Alexandria. Genre sculpture, the familiar treatment of familiar themes, scarcely existed; the Alexandrians

FIG. 101.—ATHENE SLAYING A YOUNG GIANT.
Fragment from the Pergamene Frieze.
(Berlin Museum.)
(Photo. by Lévy and Son.)

68

developed it, following the example set them in the art of ancient Egypt.

Finally, in addition to gods and men, there was nature, hitherto neglected. The Hellenistic artists taught the art of landscape to the world; rural scenes, in all their rustic simplicity, made their appearance not only in painting, but in statuary and bas-reliefs. All this progress, all these interesting innovations, were brought about in less than two centuries. The period that witnessed them is one of the great epochs of the human mind.

Among the Hellenistic capitals, Pergamum, to the north of Smyrna, is the one of which we know most. About 240 B.C. King Attalus repulsed the Gauls who had invaded Asia Minor after devastating Delphi in 279 B.C. To commemorate his victory, he made votive offerings of bronze statues representing vanquished Gauls. Marble copies of several of these were found in Rome early in the 16th century; the two most important are, a Gaul killing himself after having slain his wife (Fig. 99), and the famous statue, erroneously called the *Dying Gladiator* (Fig. 100). The so-called gladiator is clearly a Gaul, for his neck is encircled by a torque, and his physical type, his shield and his trumpet, have nothing Greek in their character. The *Dying Gladiator*

FIG. 102.—LAOCOÖN AND HIS SONS.
(Museum of the Vatican.)

is a work at once realistic and pathetic; the Greek sculptor—he was called Epigonus—was interested in the brave and robust barbarian, who had met his death so far from his own land, a victim to his adventurous spirit. The treatment of the marble recalls that of the *Warrior* in the Louvre, and allows us to ascribe the statue to the school of Lysippus.

At a later date, about 166 B.C., another king of Pergamum, Eumenes II, commemorated other military successes by the erection of a colossal altar in white marble, dedicated to Zeus, on the Acropolis of Pergamum. The remains of this were brought to light by a German archæological mission. The base was decorated with a frieze in high relief representing the contest between the Gods and the Giants. The Hellenes saw in this frieze an allusion to con-

FIG. 103.—STATUE KNOWN AS THE
APOLLO BELVEDERE.
(Museum of the Vatican.)

temporary events: the Giants of the fable were the Gauls, the Gods were the Greeks of Asia.

Some three hundred feet of this frieze, the figures on which are six feet high, were excavated between 1880 and 1890 and taken to the Berlin Museum. As a complete decorative composition, this is the most imposing achievement that has come down to us from antiquity; the first impression made on the spectator by these colossal sculptures is dazzling. On closer examination defects become apparent; there is a tendency to exaggeration, a certain monotony of violence and agitation; but, on the other hand, what a profusion of admirable episodes, what wealth of motive, what a mastery of the chisel! If we look about in modern art for anything to compare with it, we find only isolated groups or figures, such as Puget's *Milo of Crotona*, and Rude's *Marseillaise;* neither the Renaissance nor the nineteenth century offers any parallel in the shape of a sustained and continuous composition. No artist has imagined a mightier figure than that of the warring Zeus, a more moving one than that of the vanquished giant, for whom his mother Gæa (The Earth) intercedes, emerging from the ground to arrest the arm of Athene (Fig. 101). It is one of the glories of the art of Pergamum that it could celebrate victories without refusing sympathy to the vanquished.

FIG. 104.—HEAD OF APOLLO.
Formerly belonging to the Comte de Pourtalès. (British Museum.)

This eloquence of physical suffering, so touchingly rendered in the head of the young giant, is carried still farther in the famous *Laocoön* group in the Vatican, the work of three Rhodian sculptors, who executed it about the year 50 B.C. (Fig. 102). Now that the marvels of the great period of Attic art have been revealed to us, the *Laocoön* is no longer for us what it was to Lessing and his contemporaries, the highest expression of Greek genius; but it is undoubtedly the most pathetic and the most moving. The Trojan priest, enveloped in the folds of the serpents, sees his two sons dying beside him, and breathes out his own life in a supreme cry of anguish. A purely physical anguish, it has been objected, and the superficial subtlety of this criticism has made its fortune. But in the *Laocoön*, is not the agony of the dying man complicated by the pangs of the father? And why should the sufferings of *Laocoön* be less interesting than those of the martyrs, whose tortures are so fre-

quently set forth in modern art? To decry Greek art after Phidias and Italian art after Raphael is a very common form of intellectual snobbishness; of those addicted to it, it may be said that the most venial of their faults is a total mis-apprehension of the evolution of art. If Greek art had made no further developments after producing the pediments of the Parthenon, it would have been as incomplete in its way as that of Assyria or of Egypt; we cannot appreciate its incomparable grandeur unless we can admire at once the productions of its youth, its adolescence, and its maturity.

FIG. 105.—CENTAUR AND EROS.
(The Louvre.)
(Photo. by Giraudon.)

Since the middle of the nineteenth century the prejudices of an intolerant æstheticism have, in like manner, tended to belittle the famous *Apollo* in the Belvedere of the Vatican (Fig. 103). It is a copy of a bronze statue which must have been executed a few years after the death of Alexander; the original has been attributed, on no very sufficient evidence, to Leochares, one of the artists who worked upon the Mausoleum under the direction of Scopas. The body of Apollo offers a complete contrast to those of the gods and giants of the frieze of Pergamum. In the latter, the muscles are all strongly emphasised; the artist seems to take pleasure in insisting upon them; in the *Apollo*, the skeleton is enveloped in flesh and skin; elegance has been achieved at the expense of vigour. The head of the

Belvedere *Apollo* has characteristics which connect it with the school of Scopas. The god has just hurled a dart, and his expression

FIG. 106.—FRAGMENT OF THE SO-CALLED SARCOPHAGUS OF THE WEEPERS.
(Museum, Constantinople.)

is wrathful; but he is at the same time passionate and uneasy. In Hellenistic art. the gods have lost their Olympian calm; even when victorious and triumphant, they are agitated.

This characteristic is still more strongly marked in a beautiful head of Apollo, formerly in Paris, which passed from the Pourtalès Collection to the British Museum, and bears a sort of family likeness to the *Apollo Belvedere* (Fig. 104). Why does the Pourtalès Apollo seem to suffer? Is it a musical frenzy that agitates him, as has been suggested? The question has not yet received a satisfactory answer. But how remote is this pain or disquietude which shows itself in the drawn features of a beautiful face from the discreet sadness of the Demeter of Cnidus! Here Greek art touches the limit of pagan æsthetics, a limit Christian art will not hesitate to overstep when it represents the Virgin and St. John sobbing at the foot of the cross.

The head of an old man with a suffering expression in the Barracco Collection at Rome would no doubt have provoked a lively controversy, if it had not been recognised as a replica of the head of a Centaur tormented by Eros, a Hellenistic group, of which there is a fine copy in the

FIG. 107.—THREE HEADS FROM THE SARCOPHAGUS OF ALEXANDER.

Louvre (Fig. 105). But Eros inflicts no material torture on the Centaur; he is but the symbol of the pangs of love. Thus an unhappy or unsatisfied passion may set its stigmata on the face just as do the fangs of the serpents in the *Laocoön*. Excelling in the rendering of vivid and painful emotions, Hellenistic art sought motives for such representations even in episodes of mythologic love-lore, finding in them a medium for the display of its mastery and opportunities of interesting by exciting sympathy.

The Hellenistic epoch witnessed the building of a great number of temples, larger and more ornate than the Parthenon, though hastier in workmanship and less pure in style. Unfortunately, but few fragments have survived of the statues and bas-reliefs with which they were ornamented. To get some idea of the great compositions in relief of this period, we may examine the magnificent sarcophagus in the museum at Constantinople, discovered at Sidon in 1888 (Fig. 107). This shrine of Attic marble, which dates from about the year 300 B.C., is decorated with episodes from the history of Alexander, and no doubt contained the body of one of his comrades, whom his favour had enriched and exalted. The work is already eclectic, in so far as we recognise in it not only the predominant influence of Scopas, but also that of Lysippus and of others; yet the genius and individuality of the great artist who conceived and executed these scenes are never for a moment obscured. Not only is the so-called Sarcophagus of Alexander one of the masterpieces of Greek Art, but of all these masterpieces it is the one which is most intact, both as regards the modelling of the figures, which might date from yesterday, and the delicate charm of the polychromatic colouring. Hellenistic art is there, though the period it characterises has but just begun. Hellenistic art rich with the promise of all its ulterior developments: life, movement, emotion, realism in costume and accessories. We know not which should move us to wonder most, the genius which produced such a work, or the strange caprice of the military chieftain who thrust it away, as soon as it was finished, into a dark and inaccessible cavern, where the chance of a fortunate exploration brought it to light, together with several others (Fig. 106), for the joy of the student and the glory of Greek art.

BIBLIOGRAPHY OF CHAPTER VIII.

M. Collignon, E. Gardner, Kekulé, Loewy, Klein, S. Reinach, *op. cit.*, p. 49; M. Collignon and E. Pontremoli, *Pergame*, Paris, 1900; H. Winnefeld, *Peragmon, Friese*, Berlin, 1910 (very costly); Furtwängler, *Masterpieces*, London, 1895 (The Apollo Belvedere); W. Amelung, *L'Artémis de Versailles et l'Apollon du Belvedère* (*Revue archéol.*, 1904, ii., p. 325); S. Reinach, *Les Gaulois dans l'Art antique*, Paris, 1889 (cf. *Revue Critique*, 1909, i., p. 281); R. Förster, *Laokoon* (*Jahrb. des Instit.*, 1906, p. 1); Hamdi-Bey and Th. Reinach, *Une Nécropole royale à Sidon*, Paris, 1892; Th. Reinach, *Les Sarcophages de Sidon* (*Gazette des Beaux-Arts*, 1892, i., p. 89); Fr. Hauser, *Die neu-attischen Reliefs*, Stuttgart, 1899; Th. Schreiber, *Die Wiener Brunnenreliefs aus Palazzo Grimani, eine Studie über das hellenistische Relief-bild*, Leipzig, 1888; *Das Bildniss Alexanders des Grossen*, Leipzig, 1903; J. J. Bernoulli, *Griechische Ikonographie*, 3 vols., Munich, 1901–1905; E. Courbaud, *Le Bas-relief romain*, Paris, 1899.

Greek Origin of Hindu Art (Buddhist): J. Darmesteter, *Revue critique*, 1885, i., p. 6; Sylvain Lévi, *Revue des Etudes grecques*, vol. iv., p. 41 (1891); A. Grünwedel, *Handbuch der buddhistischen Kunst*, 2nd ed., Berlin, 1900; A. Foucher, *L'Art gréco-bouddhique*, vol. i., Paris, 1905; S. Reinach, *Cultes*, Paris, 1912 (vol. iv., p. 63).

IX

THE MINOR ARTS IN GREECE

THE Greek artisan had a natural inclination to work in the manner of an artist. When he had to decorate a vase, a tripod, a mirror, to model a terra-cotta figurine, to engrave a seal or a coin, he carried out his work with an instinctive desire to please the taste and rejoice the eye. Even in the humblest crafts, he showed himself the imitator, and sometimes even the rival of the great masters of his time. We may say, indeed, that there was no essential difference in Greece between high art and industrial art, for artists and artisans sought inspiration from the same sources, and displayed the same unerring taste.

FIG. 108.—SILVER VASE.
Found at Alesia (Côte d'Or).
(Museum, St. Germain.)

Examples of great Greek art are, unfortunately, few in number, and nearly all mutilated. Exposed to the elements and to accidents of various kinds, they have been, for the most part, destroyed or damaged. Barely fifty antique bronze statues have come down to us—I mean life-size statues—and of these only some fifteen belong to the Greek epoch. But the productions of the minor arts were often buried with the dead; and they are to be found in great numbers in tombs, often in exactly the same state as when they were laid in the grave by the ancients. To give but a few examples, the great tombs of the Crimæa and of Etruria have yielded gold ornaments extraordinarily beautiful in workmanship; the burial places of

74

Asia Minor, Greece, Southern Russia, Etruria and Cyrenaica have restored to us thousands of painted vases, terra-cotta figurines, glass vessels, and en-graved stones which were used as seals. In the same way, the smaller bronzes have been better able to escape the destructive forces that threaten pre-cious objects than the larger statues.

FIG. 109.—THE ALDOBRANDINI MARRIAGE.
(Antique painting in the Museum of the Vatican.)

These minor works, statuettes or reliefs, have made us familiar with many motives of sculpture which would have remained unknown to us but for them. But the great majority of them are not reduced copies of more important works; they were specially designed for execution on a small scale. Finally, engraved stones or gems, thanks to their durability, and coins, thanks to their number and their relatively small size, have survived in thousands, and furnish materials no less precise than abundant for the history of art.

FIG. 110.—ACHILLES AMONG THE DAUGHTERS OF SCYROS.
(Painting at Pompeii.)

Besides the ornaments—necklaces, bracelets, and earrings—taken from tombs, our museums guard magnificent chased and *repoussé* silver vases, which chance has preserved from the greed of man. In some cases they were buried in the centre of huge tumuli very difficult to explore (like the Crimean vases in the Hermitage at St. Petersburg); in others they formed the treasure of some temple or of some private individual, and were carefully concealed by their guardians or their owners at the time of the barbaric invasions (like the Treasure of Hildesheim, Hanover, now in the Berlin Museum, and the Treasure of Bernay, Eure, now in the Cabinet des Médailles in Paris); while in others, again, they were lost in the stress of battle (Fig. 108). A splendid collection of silver vases and other objects presented by M. Edmond de Rothschild to the Louvre, was discovered under the ashes of Vesuvius, at Boscoreale, near Pompei. Antique metal vases were often decorated with plaques in relief, cast and chased separately, and some of these, better able to resist chemical action than the vases themselves, have come down to us, though the vessels they decorated have disappeared.

The great works of the classic painters have all perished. Polygnotus, Zeuxis, Parrhasius, Apelles, are but names to us. The best fresco that has survived, the nuptial scene known as the *Nozze Aldobrandini* in the Vatican (Fig. 109), so much admired by Poussin, makes us divine the greatness of our loss, though it is but the shadow of a beautiful work.[1] The same may be said of the mosaics, somewhat coarse imitations of painting, executed with many-coloured cubes of stone, which were used to decorate pavements and occasionally walls, notably in the Roman period. One of the finest mosaics known is at Naples. It represents the battle of Issus, and like many other works of the same class, it seems to be the copy of a painting executed at Alexandria.

The numerous frescoes discovered at Pompei, Herculaneum, Rome, and Egypt are, for the most part, decorative works of slight importance, all of later date than the Greek period (Figs. 110, 111). Egypt has given us a series of good realistic portraits, dating from the first centuries of the Roman Empire, which are very valuable specimens of encaustic painting. Eleven of these are in the National Gallery, London.

Failing the actual works of Polygnotus and Zeuxis, we have the

---

[1] In the centre is the bride conversing with the goddess of Persuasion (Peitho); both are crowned with garlands; the bridegroom is seated on the threshold. A third woman holds a patera with oil for the libations. To the left, attendants prepare the bath; on the right, others offer a sacrifice. This painting was discovered at Rome in 1606, and belonged at first to Cardinal Aldobrandini, whence its name.

painted vases of their period, inspired by their style and by the motives they created. The Louvre and the British Museum own the largest and perhaps the best arranged collections of these in the world. A few words will suffice to classify them roughly.

I have already mentioned the Mycenæan vases (1600 to 1100 B.C.), the ornament of which is characterised by a sort of aversion from the straight line, and a preference for plant forms and those of marine creatures. From 1100 to about 750 B.C. the geometric style[1] obtained, or rather reappeared; in this style the decoration is composed of single or concentric circles, and of lines, broken, parallel, crossed, or interlaced in various combinations. On

FIG. 112.—VASE.
Found in the Dipylon, Athens.
(Museum, Athens.)

vases of this type even the figures and animals are conventionalised; the varied and sinuous lines of nature are approximated to those of geometrical design. The most interesting series of these vases, a series painted with naval battles and funeral processions, comes from the Athenian cemetery of the Dipylon (the double gate), whence the name *Dipylon* Vases by which they are distinguished. (Fig. 112). About 750 B.C. a new style appeared, characterised by an ornamentation in zones, recalling that of Oriental carpets; the vases so treated are called Corinthian (Fig. 113). The ground is light yellow, the figures reddish-brown, heightened with white, black, and violet. Finally, about the year 600 B.C. began the period of Greek pottery, with black figures on

FIG. 113.—CORINTHIAN VASE.
(Museum, Munich.)
(From Woermann's *Geschichte der Malerei*, vol. i., Seemann, Leipzig.)

[1] Pottery decorated with geometric designs was made before the Mycenæan period, not only in Greece but throughout Europe, where this style persisted until the epoch of the Roman Empire and even later.

a red ground, which lasted till about the year 500 B.C., when a fresh type of decoration was gradually evolved, that of red ornament on

FIG. 114.—ATHENE ON HER CAR.
Greek Vase with Black Figures.
(Museum, Wurzburg)

a black ground. These two kinds of vases are often called Etruscan, because great numbers of them have been found in the tombs of Etruria; but the term is inaccurate, for it seems certain that nearly all the vases were made in Athens, at least in the fifth century, and that *all the finer vases* discovered in Etruria are of Athenian origin.

The style of the vases with black figures is archaic, but already shows a remarkable precision of draughtsmanship (Fig. 114). Among the vases with red figures produced in great quantities at Athens from 500 to 400 B.C., and still manufactured in the fourth century (Fig. 115), there are masterpieces signed by the potters or painters to whom we owe them; three of these names at least, Euphronios, Douris, and Brygos, deserve to be generally known.

The lecythi are a peculiarly interesting class of Athenian vases. They were made especially to deposit in tombs, and are ornamented with polychrome figures on a white ground. The motives deal for the most part with the worship of the dead. Among them are designs which may be reckoned among the most exquisite of all ages, as, for instance, that in which Hypnos (Sleep) and Thanatos (Death) gently bear a young woman to the tomb in the presence of Hermes (Fig. 116).

FIG. 115.—ŒDIPUS AND THE SPHINX.
Bottom of a Cup painted with Figures in Red.
(Museum of the Vatican.)

After the Peloponnesian War, Athens ceased to be the exclusive centre of the manufacture of vases. Important potteries were established in Southern Italy. Here were modelled and painted those enormous vases which first attract the visitor's attention in museums, though the decoration is often mediocre. The specimen reproduced in Fig. 117 is very fine. It adorns a large amphora in the Munich Museum, and represents the infernal regions, a subject frequently treated at this period (about 350 B.C.), though rarely in the great period of art.

FIG. 116.—ATHENIAN LECYTHUS.
(Museum, Athens.)

The manufacture of vases with red figures ceased, even in Italy, about the year 280 B.C. They were replaced by vases decorated with reliefs of bright red glaze, imitations of metal vases. As the reliefs were made by the help of moulds, it was easy to multiply specimens; but this was industry in the modern sense of the word rather than art. In the whole of Greek ceramic art, as known to us, there are perhaps no two painted vases absolutely identical; Athenian workmen had a horror of servile copies, and did not even work from patterns or tracings.

The types of Greek vases are very varied; our illustration shows the chief of these (Fig. 118). The classic names for many of them are unknown to us. In special works on ceramics they are indicated by numbers.

FIG. 117.—AMPHORA OF CANOSSA, WITH PAINTING OF THE INFERNAL REGIONS.
(Museum, Munich.)

The study of terra-cotta figurines is even more seductive than that of vases. The Greeks never ceased to model these from the Mycenæan times onward. They have left us a whole world of statuettes representing gods and goddesses, heroes and genii, men and women engaged in the pursuits and pleasures of familiar life, caricatures, animals, reduced copies of famous statues. Together with these figurines we may study the bas-reliefs, often used for the decoration of temples and houses. Nearly all the towns and many of the antique burial grounds have furnished

FIG. 118.—TYPES OF GREEK VASES.
(The Louvre.)

Above, from left to right : Hydria, Lecythus, Amphora, Œnochoe, Crater.
below : Cantharus, Aryballus, Kylix, Rhyton, Aryballisc Lecythus.

specimens of terra-cotta; they were the least costly among works of
art, and, at the same time, the most in vogue as ex-voto offerings to the gods, and as objects to be deposited with the dead in their tombs. The most famous burial-places in this connection are those of Tanagra in Bœotia, and of Myrina in Asia Minor (between Smyrna and Pergamum). At Tanagra there are figurines of every period, but the finest, dating from the close of the fourth century B.C., reveal the influence of Praxiteles. The chief types are draped female figures, often with hats and fans, characterised by the most delicious grace and coquetry (Fig. 119). At Myrina, the finest statuettes date from after the period of Alexander, and are quite different in character. This necropolis

FIG. 119.—TANAGRA STATUETTE.
(The Louvre.)

has furnished a large number of figures representing women and youths, both draped and naked, playing, frolicking, and indulging in a variety of animated move-ments (Fig. 120). We note an echo here of those Asiatic schools of sculpture which loved mobility and exuberant life, the schools to which we owe the frieze of the great altar of Pergamum. Alex-andrian art, too, with its taste for familiar scenes and carica-ture, obviously influenced the brilliant modellers of Myrina.

FIG. 120.—TERRA-COTTAS FROM MYRINA.
(The Louvre.)
(*Nécropole de Myrina*, Fontemoing, Paris.)

Antique terra-cottas may be studied exhaustively in the Louvre and the British Mu-seum, where specimens from Smyrna, Cyprus, Rhodes, Italy, and Cyrenaica, as well as from Tanagra and Myrina, are to be found in large numbers.

From the Mycenæan period onward, engraving on hard stones was practised throughout the Greek world. Hundreds of engraved gems of the Mycenæan type have survived; they have been discovered chiefly in the islands of the Archipelago. They served as seals, and impressions from them have been found on terra-cotta tablets. Stones on which the design is hollowed out are called *intaglios;* they are not to be confused with *cameos,* which were not seals, but ornaments, adorned with a design in relief.

Of all antique objects, en-graved gems are the only ones which have come down to us for the most part in exactly the state in which they were used by the ancients. We have intaglios of nearly all the periods of art, in which we can trace the successive styles, and the influence of the great schools of sculpture. Among the

FIG. 121.—THE TRIUMPH OF AUGUSTUS, THE VICTOR OF ACTIUM.
(Intaglio in the Boston Museum; more than twice the actual size.)

FIG. 122.—PTOLEMY PHILADELPHUS AND QUEEN
ARSINOË. CAMEO.
(Museum, Vienna.)

many gems which are masterpieces it is difficult to choose a typical example. Our Fig. 121 reproduces an intaglio, now at Boston, which represents the triumph of Augustus at Actium; though its length is little over an inch, it has all the delicacy and breadth of style of a historical bas-relief.

The vogue of cameos cut in sardonyx of several strata began with the Alexandrine epoch and lasted till the last century of the Roman Empire. The largest known cameo, representing the Apotheosis of Tiberius, is in the Cabinet des Médailles, Paris. The two most beautiful, on each of which are cut the portraits of Ptolemy Philadelphus and his queen, belong respectively to the Museums of Vienna and of St. Petersburg (Fig. 122). These marvellous cameos certainly date from the third century before Christ. They rank among the most perfect achievements of art, and have never been equalled by the moderns.

If the art of engraving precious stones is very ancient, that of striking coins is comparatively recent; it was unknown in Assyria and in Egypt. The oldest Greek coins date from the seventh century B.C., and were made upon the coast of Asia. It was not until the fifth century that they became veritable works of art, under the influence of the school of Phidias. In this case Athens is no longer supreme. The finest coins were produced in Sicily, where certain engravers of genius, such as Evenetus and Cimon, occasionally signed their works. The incomparable Sicilian coins of the second half of the

FIG. 123.—SILVER COIN OF
SYRACUSE.
(Face and reverse.)

THE MINOR ARTS IN GREECE

fifth century attest the superiority of Greek art no less eloquently than the Hermes of Praxiteles and the Venus of Milo; the profile of the nymph Arethusa is, indeed, perhaps the most exquisite Greek head known to us (Fig. 123). Fine coins have certainly been produced in modern times, as, for instance, the English sovereign with the St. George and the Dragon, and Roty's charming *Sower*, but the superiority of the Greeks in this art is incontestable, and is partly to be explained by a purely material cause. The modern minted coins, intended to be piled one upon the other, are necessarily flat; those of the ancients were always more or less globular, which made it possible to give greater definition and relief to the image upon them.

It is not within the scope of this work to pass in review all the infinite variety of Greek industrial products. I wish only to point out their great interest in connection with the general history of art. Those who are convinced of this truth will find in museums information and satisfactions which escape others; they will recognise that the material and the dimensions of works are of little importance, that style is the essential element, and that the Greek genius set its stamp upon everything which the hand of a Greek artificer fashioned.

BIBLIOGRAPHY OF CHAPTER IX.

M. Collignon, *Manuel d'Archéologie grecque*, new ed., Paris, 1906.

E. Babelon et A. Blanchet, *Catalogue des Bronzes antiques de la Bibliothèque Nationale*, Paris, 1895; H. B. Walters, *Catalogue of the Bronzes in the British Museum*, London, 1899; S. Reinach, *Bronzes figurés de la Gaule romaine*, Paris, 1894; A. de Ridder, *Catalogue des bronzes d'Athènes*, 2 vols., Paris, 1894, 1896; *Miroirs grecs à reliefs* (*Monuments Piot*, vol. iv., p. 77); A. Dumont and E. Pottier, *Miroirs grecs ornés de figures au trait* (*Les Céramiques de la Grèce propre*, vol. ii., Paris, 1890, p. 167).

H. de Fontenay, *Bijoux anciens et modernes*, Paris, 1887; A. Darcel, *La Technique de la Bijouterie ancienne* (*Gazette des Beaux-Arts*, 1888, i., p. 146); K. Hadaczek, *Der Ohrschmuck der Griechen*, Vienna, 1903.

H. de Villefosse, *Le Trésor de Boscoreale, Monuments Piot*, vol. iv., 1899; E. Pernice and Fr. Winter, *Der Hildesheimer Silberfund*, Berlin, 1902; Konkadoff, Tolstoï, S. Reinach, *Antiquités de la Russie méridionale*, Paris, 1892; P. Girard, *Histoire de la Peinture antique*, Paris, no date; A. Michaelis, *op. cit.* p. 59; U. Wilcken, *Hellenistische Porträts aus El-Faijûm* (*Arch. Anzeiger*, 1889, p. 1); G. Ebers, *Antike Porträts*, Leipzig, 1893; P. Gauckler, article *Musivum opus* in the *Dictionnaire des Antiquités* de Saglio (cf., by the same author, *Monuments Piot*, vol. iii., p. 177; vol. iv., p. 233).

H. B. Walters, *History of Ancient Pottery*, 2 vols., London, 1905; O. Rayet and M. Collignon, *Histoire de la Céramique grecque*, Paris, 1888; E. v. Rohden, art. *Vasenkunde* in Baumeister's *Denkmäler*, vol. iii., Munich, 1888; S. Reinach, *Répertoire des Vases peints grecs et étrusques*, 2 vols., Paris, 1899 (with a complete bibliography of ceramics); E. Pottier, *Catalogue des Vases antiques du Louvre*, 3 vols., Paris, 1896-1904 (with album); *Etude sur les lécythes blancs attiques*, Paris, 1883; *La Peinture industrielle des Grecs*, Paris, 1898; *Le dessin par ombre portée chez les Grecs* (*Revue des Etudes grecques*, 1898, p. 355); origin of painting with black figures); E. Pottier, *Etudes de Céramique grecque* (*Gazette des Beaux-Arts*, 1902, i., p. 19); *Douris*, Paris, 1905; F. Poulsen, *Die Dipylonvasen*, Leipzig, 1905; H. B. Walters [and others], *Catalogue of Vases in the British Museum*, 3 vols., London, 1893 *et seq.*; P. Hartwig, *Die griechischen Meister-schalen*, Stuttgart, 1893; Furtwängler, Hauser, and Reichhold *Griechische Vasenmalerei*, Munich, 1900-1904 (very costly); J. C. Hoppin, *Handbook of Signed Vases* (*Attic*), vol. i., London, 1919; A. Joubin, *De Sarcophagis clazomeniis*, Paris, 1901 (Sarcophagi of painted clay, discovered at Clazomenes); J. Déchelette, *Les vases ornés de la Gaule romaine*, Paris, 1904; F. Winter, *Die antiken Terracotten*, 2 vols., Berlin, 1903 (repertory of types); E. Pottier, *Statuettes de terre cuite*, Paris, 1890; *Les Terres cuites de Myrina* (*Gazette des Beaux-Arts*, 1886, i., p. 261); *Diphilos*, Paris, 1909; *Les Terres cuites de Tanagra* (*ibid.*, 1909, i., p. 21); E. Pottier and S. Reinach, *La Nécropole de Myrina*, 2 vols., Paris, 1887; H. Lechat, *Tanagra* (*Gazette des Beaux-Arts*, 1893, ii., p. 1,); E. Babelon, *La Gravure en pierres fines*, Paris, no date;

APOLLO

Les Camées antiques de la Bibliothèque Nationale (*Gazette des Beaux-Arts*, 1898, i., p. 27); S. Reinach, *Pierres gravées*, Paris, 1895; A. Furtwängler, *Antike Gemmem*, 3 vols., Leipzig, 1900; F. Lenormant, *Monnaies et Médailles*, Paris, no date; R. Weil, art. *Münzkunde* in Baumeister's *Denkmäler*, vol. ii., Munich, 1887; A. Babelon, *Traité des Monnaies grecques et romaines*, vol. i., Paris, 1901; A. Blanchet, *Les Monnaies grecques*, Paris, 1894; *Les Monnaies romaines*, Paris, 1895; Hill, *Handbook of Greek and Roman Coins*, London, 1899; P. Gardner, *Types of Greek Coins*, Cambridge, 1883; G. Macdonald, *Coin Types*, Glasgow, 1905; A. Evans, *Syracusan Medallions*, London, 1892; Barclay Head, *Historia Numorum*, Londo , 2nd ed., 1887; *Coins of the Ancients*, London, 1899; Th. Reinach, *L'Histoire par les Monnaies*, Paris, 1903; W. Froehner, *La Verrerie antique*, Paris, 1879 (Collection Charvet), Le Pecq. 1879; A. Kisa, *Das Glas in Alterthum*, 3 vols., Leipzig, 1908; Morin-Jean, article *Vitrum* in the *Dictionnaire des Antiquités*.

X

ETRUSCAN AND ROMAN ART

The Settlement of Lydian Emigrants in Etruria.—Etruscan Monuments and Decorative Objects.—The so-called Etruscan Vases Chiefly Importations from Athens.—Paintings in the "Tomb of François" at Vulci.—Etruscan Portraits in Terra-Cotta.—Roman Art.—The Invasion of Italy by Greek Art. —The Evolution of an Individual Roman Art.—Its Manifestation in Architecture.—The Coliseum. —The Adoption of the Vault.—The Pantheon and the Basilica of Constantine.—Triumphal Arches —The Archaistic Reaction under Augustus.—Its Decline after Claudius and Revival under Hadrian. —The Antinoüs Type.—Portraits of the Imperial Epoch.—The Orientalised Art of the Roman Decadence.—Frescoes at Pompei.—The Rospigliosi Eros with a Ladder.—Anaylsis of Roman Art.

ABOUT the year 1000 B.C., a band of emigrants coming by sea from Lydia, in Asia Minor, settled in central Italy and, intermingling with the natives, laid the foundations of the Etruscan Confederation.

Etruria was conquered by the Romans in the year 283 B.C. Throughout four centuries before this period, she had developed a flourishing civilisation, important evidences of which have survived in the shape of town walls, ruined temples, vast tombs ornamented with paintings and reliefs, statues, sarcophagi, terra-cottas, bronzes of various kinds, and

FIG. 124.—ACHILLES IMMOLATING PRISONERS.
Etruscan Frescoes in a Tomb at Vulci.

(Woermann, *Geschichte der Malerei*, Seemann, Leipzig.)

golden ornaments. As to the painted vases known as Etruscan, it will be well to repeat that they were, for the most part, imported from Attica.

The original element in this civilisation was the groundwork of Italian ruggedness tempered by Celtic elements that underlay it. In all else, it was but a reflection of that of Greece, primarily of Asiatic Greece, then of Athens. The

FIG. 125.—ETRUSCAN SARCOPHAGUS.
Known as the Lydian Tomb.
(The Louvre.)

FIG. 126.—ROMAN TEMPLE AT NÎMES.
Known as the "Maison Carrée."

Athenians exported thousands of painted vases and artistic objects of all kinds to Etruria, because the Etruscans had not only the taste to appreciate them, but the money to pay for them.

There were, however, local schools in Etruria, and these produced many important works, which, though imitated from Greek models, yet bear the stamp of national individuality, like the astonishing paintings in the so-called "Tomb of François" [1] at Vulci, representing Achilles offering sacrifices of Trojan prisoners to appease the manes of Patroclus (Fig. 124). The subject is Greek, but the treatment is thoroughly Etruscan; the Charon

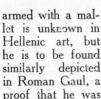

armed with a mallet is unknown in Hellenic art, but he is to be found similarly depicted in Roman Gaul, a proof that he was

FIG. 127.—THE COLISEUM, ROME.

inspired by some old myth peculiar to the West. The style has something of the precision and of the harsh vigour that appear some eighteen centuries later in the frescoes of Mantegna at

[1] The name of a professional excavator, who worked in Etruria during the first half of the nineteenth century.

86

Padua, and of Signorelli at Orvieto.

The same vigour and originality distinguish the numerous Etruscan portraits in terra cotta, some of which are whole length figures (Fig. 125). These are essentially native works, in which the sense of life, the fidelity to the model, the contempt for all that is abstract and typical,

FIG. 128.—RUINS OF THE BASILICA OF CONSTANTINE, ROME.

attest a taste not in the least Hellenic, but racy of the soil.

What we call Roman art is not merely Hellenistic art imported into or copied in Italy, as has been too often asserted. It is true that the imitation of Greek works was an important factor in Roman art. From the third century before Christ onwards, the victorious generals of Rome enriched their city with a quantity of Greek masterpieces from Sicily and Southern Italy; later, after the year 150, the methodical pillage of Greece and Asia Minor began, carried on not only by military leaders and governors, but by

FIG. 129.—THE ARCH OF TITUS, ROME.

influential private persons. On the other hand, the wealth of Rome attracted the Greek artists, who readily found purchasers for their imitations or copies of classic works; the houses, villas, and gardens of wealthy Romans, such as Lucullus or Crassus, were veritable museums. This taste for art became still more general under the Empire. Everyone knows that an eruption of Vesuvius buried Pompei and Herculaneum in A.D. 79, and that more than half of Pompei has been excavated since the year 1753. Now this third-rate town has already yielded up more paintings, statues, and statuettes than could be found to-day in most of our large provincial cities.

At the same time, this invasion of Italy by Hellenism did not interfere with the parallel development of a Roman art, which

FIG. 130.—VIEW OF THE ROMAN AQUEDUCT.
Known as the "Pont du Gard."
(Photo. by Neurdein.)

appears rather as the continuation of the native art of Italy, than as a degenerate form of Greek art.

Roman architecture has covered the earth with great monuments, temples, thermæ, theatres, amphitheatres (or arenas), triumphal arches, and columns, eloquent witnesses to the grandeur of the Empire and its prosperity. The temples and theatres are inspired by Greek models (Fig. 126); but arenas like the Roman Coliseum (Fig. 127) are novelties in the history of art, and the triumphal arches seem to have their prototypes in

FIG. 131. — INTERIOR OF THE SMALL TEMPLE OF BAALBEK, SYRIA.

FIG. 132.—LIONESS AND YOUNG.
Bas-relief in the Vienna Museum.
(Wickhoff, *Roman Art*, Heinemann, London.)

the gates of the Etruscan towns rather than in the commemorative monuments of the Greek world.

The Romans, following the example of the Greeks, made use of the flat roof. But they also constructed great vaults, and domes like that of the Pantheon in Rome, no instance of which is to be found in Greek classic architecture. We have seen that these domes were not unknown to the Assyrians; it is probable that the Etruscans took the principle of them from the east and transmitted it to the Romans.

Within the last few years we have learnt that the vault of the Pantheon was built in the time, not of Augustus, but of Hadrian (A.D. 117—138). This date is of importance in the history of art, for it marks the definite adoption of a system of construction, the further development of which was to produce Byzantine and Romanesque architecture, and less directly, Gothic architecture. From the first century after Christ to the time of the completion of St. Peter's at Rome, the problem of the vault never ceased to occupy architects.

FIG. 133. — FRAGMENT FROM THE ALTAR OF PEACE.
Dedicated at Rome under Augustus.
(Wickhoff, *Roman Art*, Heinemann, London.)

The various solutions they essayed had a powerful influence on the successive styles.

Vaulted architecture was so essentially a Roman product that it continued to develop when sculpture had sunk to uniform mediocrity. Constantine's basilica (Fig. 128), built after 305 A.D., with its three colossal vaults, the central one nearly 120 feet high, with a span of more than 80 feet, marks a great advance on former constructions; it served as a model to the architects of the Renaissance. Bramante, when he conceived the plan of St. Peter's, said that he intended "to raise the Pantheon over the basilica of Constantine."

Among the Roman triumphal

FIG. 134.—AUGUSTUS AS A YOUTH.
Museum of the Vatican.
(Wickhoff, *Roman Art*, Heinemann, London.)

arches, that of Titus (Fig. 129), which commemorates the destruction of Jerusalem (A.D. 70) and that of Beneventum, constructed under

FIG. 135.—BAS-RELIEF ON THE ARCH OF TITUS.
The Emperor's Triumph.

Trajan, show great beauty of execution; the others are chiefly interesting to archæologists. The same may be said of the vast utilitarian works, aqueducts (Fig. 130), bridges, dams, and sewers with which Rome endowed all parts of her Empire. It will be enough here to mention them in passing.

A characteristic of the architecture of the Roman period, which gives it a certain affinity to that of Egypt and Assyria, is its tendency to colossal proportions, as exemplified in the temples of Baalbek and of Palmyra in Syria (Fig. 131). These temples, imitated from Greek models, are primarily remarkable for their size; the decoration is as careless as it is exuberant. But this exuberance, though it offends our taste, does not lack originality; it was in Syria mainly that the new style was elaborated, which gave birth to Byzantine decorative art.

The sculptors of Pergamum and Rhodes had exaggerated the element of pathos. About the year 100 B.C., a reaction set in, the centres of which were Athens and Alexandria; artists returned to the types of the fifth and fourth centuries; they even imitated archaic works; and in their paintings and basreliefs they represented calm, and occasionally idyllic scenes (Fig. 132). This tendency was at its height in the time of Augustus; it is very evident in the beautiful fragments of the Altar of Peace (B.C. 13), the minute workmanship of which suggests the art of the chaser of metal

FIG. 136.—BAS-RELIEF ON THE ARCH OF TITUS.
Spoils from the Temple of Jerusalem carried in Triumph.

(Fig. 133), and in the portraits of the time of Augustus, notably in the charming head of the youthful Octavius in the Vatican

(Fig. 134), a work cold and distinguished as one of Canova's busts. From the reign of Claudius onward, this elegant and some-what timid style gave way before an art far less subservient to the classic tradition, a vigorous, animated, realistic style, good examples of which are the bas-reliefs on the Arch of Titus (Figs. 135, 136), and those on the column set up by Trajan on the Forum A.D. 103, representing the Roman campaigns against the Dacians (Fig. 137). Besides these historic bas-reliefs, others of a more decorative character have come down to us (Fig. 138), showing an innovation in Græco-

FIG. 137.—DACIAN PRISONER BROUGHT BEFORE TRAJAN.

Bas-relief on the Trajan Column at Rome.

Roman art in the form of leaves, flowers, and fruit realistically treated, an abandonment of the conventions that governed plant-form in Greek classic decoration, the chief features of which were the conventionalised palm and acanthus leaf. This picturesque and expressive school also threw off the old trammels in its representation of animals (Fig. 139). From the Alexandrine period onward, occasional signs of an unexpected return to naturalism appear. It was, however, short-lived. To find later examples of decoration based directly upon nature, the student of art must pass over ten centuries and go to Gothic architecture.

FIG. 138.—PILASTER OF THE MONUMENT TO THE HATERII.

(Lateran Museum, Rome.)

(Wickhoff, *Roman Art*, Heinemann, London.)

After the death of Trajan in 117, a fresh Attic and archaistic reaction took place, manifesting itself notably in the reign of Hadrian by the execution of a large number of copies of classic sculpture, and by the creation of the ideal type of Antinoüs, the favourite of Hadrian, a type inspired by the traditions of the fifth and fourth century before Christ

(Figs. 140, 141). The numerous statues erected in honour of Antinoüs, after his early and mysterious death, are frigid imitations of Greek works, and have nothing in common with the realistic portraiture of Roman art.

FIG. 139.—EAGLE.
On a Bas-relief in the Church of the Holy Apostles at Rome.
(Wickhoff, *Roman Art*, Heinemann, London.)

After the middle of the second century, Roman sculpture degenerated in Italy. Though it continued occasionally to produce fine realistic busts of emperors, like that of Caracalla, plastic art fell more and more under the influence of the school that had developed in Asia Minor and Assyria. In these rich provinces, which were never Roman in anything but name, a sort of orientalised Hellenistic art flourished, that had undergone late Persian, *i.e.* Sassanian influences. This art, as yet but little known, was, at least, to some extent, the source of Byzantine art.

In addition to the historic bas-reliefs, the finest examples of which are furnished by the Arch of Titus, and the buildings of Trajan, sculpture of the Imperial Epoch produced a number of admirable portraits, modelled from life, and marked by great individuality. These realistic portraits are inspired not only by Hellenistic influences, but also, and perhaps to a greater degree, by the traditions of antique Italian art. In this connection it is interesting to compare a portrait of Augustus, from a Greek workshop in Rome, with a portrait of Nerva executed a century later,

FIG. 140.—HEAD OF ANTINOÜS.
Crowned with Ivy, as Dionysus.
(Cast in the University of Strasburg, from a lost original.)

in which the realistic tendency is as vigorously asserted as in any portrait by Donatello or by Verrocchio (Fig. 142).

The painting of the Roman period is known to us in the numerous frescoes at Pompei, as well as in the stucco decorations of the walls of houses and tombs in Rome and in the provinces. We also possess the first essays of Christian pictorial art, executed in the catacombs from the second to the fourth century. I pass over the mosaics, very numerous in Italy and more especially in Africa, because they are not, strictly speaking, works of art; but they would play an important part in any study of the evolution of ornament.

Roman painting was not in any sense a mere continuation of Hellenic painting. Here, again, side by side with Greek works, easily recognisable by the vigour of the drawing and the more or less deliberate imitation of bas-reliefs, we find, from the middle of the first century, manifestations of an original style, especially at Pompei. This style is not unlike

FIG 141.—ANTINOÜS AS DIONYSUS.
(Museum of the Vatican.)

that of the modern Impressionists; it is characterised by the use of patches of light and colour, sometimes producing the most charming effect. Certain mural decorations at Pompei, executed in this style, have not been surpassed in our own times. Did it

FIG. 142.—PORTRAITS OF NERVA AND OF AUGUSTUS.
(Museum of the Vatican.)
(Photo. by Anderson.)

originate in Rome or in Alexandria? It is difficult to say; but it is certain that it flourished in Italy, and that no examples of it have survived elsewhere. There is a wonderful specimen in Rome itself, the *Eros with a Ladder*, of the Casino Rospigliosi, a fresco so free in execution that it might easily be attributed to Fragonard (Fig. 143).

APOLLO

Thus we see that the accepted idea of Roman art as a long and monotonous decadence is as contrary to fact as to historic laws. Wholly incontestable, however, is the retrogressive evolution of Hellenic art and classic tradition, which was modified by the intermixture of Oriental elements in Asia, though it still clung to antique types and formulæ, and was finally merged in Byzantine art. But side by side with this obsolescent art sprang up, as early as the first century after Christ, a realism which may fitly be called Roman, since its masterpieces were produced in Rome, a realism which seems to have had its root in Italian soil. Throughout the Middle Ages the two opposing principles were arrayed against each other. Byzantine art lowered for a long time over the western countries like a nightmare; but the day came when Italian realism, brought into touch with the French realism of the fourteenth century, triumphed, and the Renaissance was the result. At the present day, Byzantine art still prevails in Greece, Turkey, and Russia, the ancient religious domain of Byzantium, while the western nations have a wholly different art, akin to the realism of the Romans.

FIG. 143.—EROS WITH A LADDER.
Antique painting in the Casino Rospigliosi at Rome.
(Wickhoff, *Roman Art*, Heinemann, London.)

BIBLIOGRAPHY OF CHAPTER X.

J. Martha, *L'Art étrusque*, Paris, 1899; R. Cagnat and V. Chapot, *Manuel d'archéologie romaine*, Paris, 1899 *et seq.*; A. Choisy, *Histoire de l'Architecture*, vol. i., Paris, 1899; F. Wickhoff, *Roman Art*, translated by Eugénie Strong, London, 1900 (German original, *Wiener Genesis*); Eugénie Strong, *Roman Sculpture*, London, 1907; S Strzygowski, *Orient oder Rom*, Leipzig, 1901 (cf. *Rev. archéol.*, 1903, ii., p. 318); E. Courbaud, *Le Bas-relief romain*, Paris, 1899; M. Collignon, *Style décoratif à Rome au temps d'Auguste* (*Revue de l'Art*, 1897, ii., p. 97); S. Reinach, *Répertoire des reliefs*, vol. i., Paris, 1909 (columns, triumphal arches, etc.); E. Petersen, *Ara Pacis Augustæ*, Vienna, 1903; A. Mau et F. Kelsey, *Pompei, its Life and Art*, London, 1899; P. Gusman, *Pompei*, English translation, London, 1905; *La Villa impériale de Tibur*, Paris, 1904; Thédenat, *Pompei*, 2 vols., Paris, 1906; R. Cagnat, *La Résurrection d'une Ville antique, Timgad*, Paris, 1907 *et seq.*; Alois Riegl, *Die spätrömische Kunstindustrie*, Vienna, 1901 (cf. *Byzantinische Zeitschrift*, 1902, p. 263); J. J. Bernoulli, *Römische Ikonographie*, 4 vols., Stuttgart, 1882–1894; A. Hekler, *Portraits grecs et romains*, Paris, 1912. Many reproductions of buildings are to be found in V. Duruy's *Histoire des Romains* and *Histoire des Grecs*.

XI

CHRISTIAN ART IN THE EAST AND IN THE WEST

The terms Early Christian and Byzantine Art explained.—The Catacombs in Rome: Early Christian Paintings and Symbols.—Early Christian Sarcophagi.—Early Christian Churches built on the Plan of the Roman Basilicas.—St. Paul without the Walls, Rome.—Decorative Mosaics at Rome and at Ravenna.—Sant' Apollinare Nuovo and Sant' Apollinare in Classe.—St. Sophia at Constantinople.—The Iconoclasts.—The Byzantine Renaissance.—Byzantine Ivories, Enamels, Miniatures, and Metal-work.—The Decline of Byzantine Art.—Arab and Moorish Art.—The Mosque of Amrou.—The Alhambra.—The Persistence of the Byzantine Tradition in Russia and Southern Italy.—St. Mark's Church, Venice.—The Byzantine Tradition discarded by Giotto and Duccio.

THE term *Christian Art* was first used in the nineteenth century by the historian Alexis Rio, who died in 1874   Properly speaking, it applies to all manifestations of art in countries where Christianity has prevailed, from the first paintings in the Roman catacombs to the works of our own day.   It is, however, usual to reserve the term *Early Christian Art* for that of the western Christian countries down to the time of Charlemagne, after which the Romanesque epoch begins. The distinctive term Byzantine Art is applied to that of Eastern Christendom, from the time when Byzantium became the capital in 330 A.D. until the taking of Constantinople by the Turks in 1453, and even later.

FIG. 144.—PAINTING IN THE CATACOMBS. ORPHEUS CHARMING THE BEASTS, ETC.

(Woermann, *Geschichte der Malerei*, Seemann, Leipzig.)

Although monuments of each of these arts exist in all the Mediterranean countries, in a rapid survey, such as ours, we must study them mainly in their three principal centres: Rome, Ravenna, and Constantinople.

The Catacombs at Rome are subterranean galleries where the

early Christians buried their dead. They were used for these purposes from the year 100 to about the year 420. When Christianity became the official religion of the Roman Empire the Christians had no longer any need to make these galleries their sepulchres, and they used burial-places above the ground. Individual Christians, however, continued to be buried in the Catacombs occasionally, that their bones might rest beside those of the martyrs.

FIG. 145.

PAINTING IN THE CATACOMBS.

Representing the Virgin and Child, with a Prophet (?).

(Liell. *Marien-Darstellungen*, Herder, Freiburg.)

Early Christian art showed no aversion from imagery, but it was opposed to the representation of God, and that of the crucified Jesus does not appear till the tenth century. Speaking generally, sculpture in the round was repugnant to the early Christians, because the idols of heathen temples were statues. The Catacombs were decorated chiefly with paintings, and with stucco reliefs.

Among these works of art, there are some which set forth incidents in the Old and the New Testament; there are also allegorical figures, like that of the Good Shepherd (Jesus), bringing back the lost sheep to the fold, Orpheus charming the beasts (Fig. 144), a fish, symbolising sometimes the Saviour, and sometimes the faithful, a peacock, typifying eternity. But the examination and exposition of these motives must not detain us; it is a special branch of archæology. Suffice it to say that the art of the Catacombs is only to be distinguished from that of the pagan by the motives it treats, and those it avoids (notably nude figures). In style it is closely akin to the decorative

FIG. 146.—CHRISTIAN SARCOPHAGUS.
(Salona, Dalmatia.)
(From Garrucci's *Storia dell' Arte Cristiana.*)

art of Pompei, and it never succeeded in giving to its personages an expression of purity and beatitude in harmony with the moral and religious ideal of Christianity. To convince ourselves of this, we need but examine the Virgin and Child with a Prophet (Isaiah?), a motive which appears in a Roman painting of the third century (Fig. 145). Here there is nothing Christian but the subject.

At the time when Christianity finally triumphed over Paganism, wealthy pagans often caused themselves to be buried in large marble troughs called sarcophagi, decorated with reliefs inspired by mythology, or dealing with the earthly career of the deceased. The Christians followed the pagan example,

FIG. 147.—INTERIOR OF THE BASILICA OF ST. PAUL WITHOUT-THE-WALLS.

(Lübke, *Architektur*, Seemann, Leipzig.)

save that episodes from the Scriptures replaced those of fable, and the artists who carved these monuments were so accustomed to the introduction of certain decorative motives, that we still see on Christian sarcophagi, Medusa-heads, griffins, and cupids, the primitive pagan sense of which had been forgotten.

As works of art, the Christian sarcophagi are of little interest. They have all the defects of the Roman sculpture of the period, heaviness, crowded composition, incorrect drawing. The interpretation of subjects from sacred history is nearly always prosaic or clumsy. The best examples are those which deal with motives commemorating the life of the deceased, and refer to his faith only by a symbolic figure like that of the Good Shepherd carrying the sheep (Fig. 146).

FIG. 148.—THE EMPRESS THEODORA AND HER COURT.

Mosaic in the Church of San Vitale, at Ravenna.

Architecture was no more successful than painting and sculpture in discovering a new formula, when it was applied to the building of temples for the new faith. The Christian Church is a place for the gathering together

97

of the faithful, thus differing essentially from the pagan temple, which was the abode of the divinity. The first Christian churches were

FIG. 149.—INTERIOR OF SANT' APOLLINARE IN CLASSE, RAVENNA.

accordingly modelled on those enclosed places of assembly known as basilicas. Instead of serving as tribunals or markets, they were used for public worship; here, again, the new wine was put into old bottles.

Among the Roman basilicas, that of St. Paul without-the-Walls, built by Constantine and restored after a fire in 1823, may be cited as a characteristic example (Fig. 147). It consists of a large nave with a horizontal roof, and of two lower side-aisles; the central nave is lighted by windows above the side-aisles. At the end is a gate called the *Triumphal Arch*, behind which is the altar; the end wall is circular and forms the apse. Both apse and triumphal arch are richly decorated with glass mosaics on a blue or gold ground, the splendour of which rivals that of goldsmiths' enamels.

These mosaics ornament the vertical walls and the vaults, instead of forming pavements as in the Roman houses and temples. Specimens of them, very beautiful in colour, and grandiose though frigid in style, are to be seen in Rome, and at Ravenna (Fig. 148), which was the seat of the Roman Court from 404, the residence of Theodoric, King of the Goths, about 500, and an

FIG. 150.—INTERIOR OF SANT' APOLLINARE NUOVO, RAVENNA.
(Photo. by Alinari.)

appanage of Byzantium from 534 to 752. Several churches of the sixth century still exist, as Sant' Apollinare Nuovo, Sant' Apollinare

CHRISTIAN ART IN THE EAST AND IN THE WEST

in Classe (on the ancient port) and San Vitale: the last is a circular domed building, in which Byzantine influences are very apparent; the others are basilicas, the interiors of which are striking and majestic, though their external aspect is neither graceful nor dignified (Figs. 149-151).

FIG. 151.—EXTERIOR OF SANT' APOLLINARE IN CLASSE, RAVENNA.

(Lübke, *Architektur*, Seemann, Leipzig.)

If the architectural type of the basilica, characterised by its rectangular plan and flat roof, predominates in the churches in Italy, those of Constantinople applied and developed the principle of the dome. The great church of Byzantium, St. Sophia (Fig. 152), was built between 532 and 562 under Justinian, by Anthemius of Tralles and Isidorus of Miletus, that is to say, by Asiatic architects. We have seen that the cupola was known to the Assyrians; the tradition had been preserved in Persia, whence it spread into Syria towards the third century after Christ, passing from Syria into Asia Minor in the following centuries. The architects of St. Sophia were probably inspired by Asiatic models, and not by the Roman Pantheon.

As all the world knows, this famous Byzantine temple has been a Turkish mosque since 1453. The mosaics are covered with white-wash, but, as a whole, the building is in good preservation. The superficies of the interior is over 23,000 square feet. Passing through two vast porticoes, we stand beneath a huge vault some 186 feet high and over 100 feet wide. About the middle of the nineteenth century, when some restorations were being carried out in the mosque, permission was given to copy

FIG. 152.—ST. SOPHIA AT CONSTANTINOPLE.

the mosaic figures in water-colours. Although the compositions themselves, dealing with episodes in the history of Justinian, are poor in design and mediocre in conception, the splendour of the mosaics must have added greatly to the grandeur of the general

effect (Fig. 153). Even under present conditions, we are dazzled by walls faced with marble slabs, multi-coloured columns supporting galleries, the sparkle of cubes of mosaic made of gilded glass. The luxury of Byzantine art lay in splendour, in the profusion of colour and gilding. It is a truly Asiatic luxury, which found inspiration in the Persia of the Sassanides, and took as

FIG. 153.—INTERIOR OF ST. SOPHIA AT CONSTANTINOPLE.

its models the carpets of the Orientals, rather than the severe creations of Græco-Roman art. In the sculptured ornament of capitals and friezes, the human figure is conspicuously absent; all is purely geometrical and conventional.

Christian art went through a redoubtable crisis at Byzantium in connection with the ascetic heresy of the image-breakers, called the *Iconoclasts*, who gained the upper hand for a time. During the eighth and part of the ninth century, these fanatics destroyed a great number of works of art, both at Constantinople and in the provinces of the Empire. The Byzantine sculptors and mosaicists had to quit their native land, and some of them came to work at Aix-la-Chapelle, at the Court of Charlemagne. The suppression of this heresy, about the year 850, was the signal for an artistic renaissance that endured throughout the tenth and part of the eleventh century, an epoch of great prosperity and military glory for the Byzantine Empire.

FIG. 154.—VIRGIN AND CHILD.

Byzantine Ivory executed about 1,000 A.D.

(Museum, Utrecht.)

(Schlumberger, *Épopée Byzantine*, Paris.)

It was also, to a certain degree, a period of intellectual renaissance, for the best manuscripts of the Greek writers date from this time; there was even an attempted reaction of liberal philosophy against the theocratic

CHRISTIAN ART IN THE EAST AND IN THE WEST

despotism; but this intellectual movement, checked by the obscurantism of Alexis Comnenus, had no sequel.

Statuary was very little in demand, because of the religious prejudices against idols; but Byzantine mosaics, bas-reliefs in ivory and metal, enamels, paintings on parchment, and specimens of goldsmiths' work have come down to us, executed with great technical skill, and marked by a certain grandeur of style (Figs. 154, 155). A masterpiece of this art is a silver bas-relief (Fig. 156) in the Louvre, which belonged to the Abbey of St. Denis —an angel shows the Saviour's empty tomb to the Magdalen and Mary, the sister of James. With this may be classed a beautiful ivory of the Cabinet des Médailles, Paris, representing a Byzantine emperor and empress of the tenth century crowned by

FIG. 155.—THE BAPTISM OF CHRIST. Byzantine Miniature of the Eleventh Century. (Mount Athos.) (Schlumberger, *Épopée Byzantine*, Paris.)

Christ (Fig. 157). But to understand the somewhat theatrical majesty of Byzantine art, its gloomy gravity and the poverty of its means of expression, we must devote ourselves mainly to the study of the great mosaics of the eleventh century, notably the decoration of the Church of Daphni, mid-way between Athens and Eleusis. Byzantine art shows a very high sense of the monumental; but it is deficient in life, and from the time of Justinian onward, it tended more and more to create immutable types and formulæ. These unfortunate tendencies are especially conspicuous towards the period of the artistic revival under the Palæologi (fourteenth century), a period which nevertheless produced the beautiful mosaics of Kahrié-Djami at Constantinople,

FIG. 156.—THE HOLY WOMEN AT THE TOMB.

Byzantine Bas-relief in Silver-gilt.

(The Louvre.) (Schlumberger, *Épopée Byzantine*, Paris.)

101

FIG. 157.

THE EMPEROR ROMANUS IV. AND
THE EMPRESS EUDOXIA CROWNED
BY CHRIST.

Byzantine Ivory in the Cabinet des
Médailles, Paris. (Schlumberger,
Épopée Byzantine, Paris.)

It is, indeed, misleading to speak of the utter decadence of Byzantine art after the eleventh century. Even after the fall of Constantinople, at the beginning of the sixteenth century the paintings in the Monastery of Mount Athos, attributed to the monk Panselinos, the "Raphael of Athos," mark a very original development of the same tradition, with its mixture of lofty qualities and incurable vices. At the close of the sixteenth century, the vices prevailed; Byzantine art, petrified into rigid formulæ, became an industry with a fixed tariff, and fell into a slumber from which it has not yet awakened, though it has never ceased to reign wherever the Greek schism has triumphed.

When, in the seventh century, the Arabs invaded Syria and Egypt, they found the higher tradition of Byzantine architecture still flourishing there, side by side with a debased style of painting and sculpture (Coptic art[1]). Inspired by these traditions, they modified them to suit their own requirements, and developed an original art, of which the mosques of Cairo (Fig. 158), and of Spain, give a very favourable impression. The mosque of Amrou at Cairo dates from 643 A.D.; the Alhambra, or "Red Palace," of Granada (Fig. 159), a marvel of Moorish architecture, from about 1300. Arab art, faithful to the prescriptions of the Koran, refrained in general, if not absolutely, from the representation of the human figure. But this very limitation necessitated a rich variety in the treatment of plant forms and geometric motives. Hence those admirable

FIG. 158.—MOSQUE OF KAIT BEY AT CAIRO.

(Photo. by Bonfils.)

[1] The Copts are the Christian natives of Egypt as distinguished from the Moslem invaders.

102

arabesques, the term retained by a complicated system of ornamentation, in which the Arabs of our own day still excel. Another original feature of Arab architecture is the stalactite vault, an aggregation of plaster prisms, producing a very picturesque effect (Fig. 159); the origin of these should probably be sought in the carvings of little wooden shrines.

Persian art, which had participated in the formation of Byzantine art, was in its turn affected by the latter, and exercised its own influence on Arab, Turkish, and Hindoo art. On the other hand, the north of Europe, especially Russia, converted to Christianity by the Byzantines about the year 1000, received and held fast the Byzantine tradition. The great churches of Kiev, Moscow, and St. Petersburg are directly derived from St. Sophia. Southern Italy, long in the hands of

FIG. 159.—COURT OF LIONS IN THE ALHAMBRA, GRANADA.

the Byzantines, retained the impression left by them so faithfully that it took no part in the work of the Italian Renaissance. Even Western Europe did not altogether escape it, for Byzantium, with her wealth, her far-reaching commerce, her monuments sparkling with gold and jewels, was the admiration and envy of Occidentals until the dawn of the Renaissance in Italy. St. Mark's at Venice (Fig. 160) is a Byzantine church, built about the year 1100, on the model of the Church of the Holy Apostles at Constantinople,[1] which also inspired the architect of the Cathedral of St.

FIG. 160.—CHURCH OF ST. MARK AT VENICE.
(Photo. by Alinari.)

Front at Périgueux. The ivories, enamels, and embroideries of the Byzantines spread throughout Europe and were imitated in every

[1] This church no longer exists.

103

country. It is not surprising that the art of mediæval Europe should show so many analogies with that of Byzantium; rather is it surprising that it should have retained such a large measure of independence. This is not only an occasion for wonder, but for rejoicing. For the Byzantine influence was baleful, bringing the seeds of decay and death with it; the superficial pomp and splendour of Byzantine works barely conceal their emptiness, their lack of thought and inspiration. According to the myth accepted by Vasari, it was by Byzantine artists that the elements of drawing were brought to Florence in the thirteenth century. It is true that there were always Byzantine artists and Byzantine works of art in Italy; far too many, indeed! But the great achievement of Duccio, and, above all, of Giotto, was that they broke vigorously with this moribund tradition to find a new artistic formula in the observation of life.

BIBLIOGRAPHY OF CHAPTER XI.

H. Cabrol, *Dictionnaire d'Archéologie chrétienne*, vol. i., Paris, 1903; A. Michel (and others), *Histoire de l'Art*, vol. i., Paris, 1905; X. Kraus, *Geschichte der christlichen Kunst*, vol. i., Freiburg, 1896; A. Pératé, *L'Archéologie chrétienne*, Paris, 1894; M. Laurent, *L'Art chrétien primitif*, 2 vols., Brussels, 1911; H. Marucchi, *Eléments d'Archéologie chrétienne*, 3 vols., Rome, 1899, 1905; J. Wilpert, *Die Malereien der Katakomben*, Freiburg, 1903 (267 plates); L. Bréhier, *La Querelle des Images*, Paris, 1904; *L'Art chrétien*, Paris, 1917; A. Venturi, *Storia dell' Arte italiana*, vol. i., Milan, 1901; Jos. Strzygowski, *Orient oder Rom*, Leipzig, 1901; *Byzantinische Denkmäler* vol. iii., Leipzig, 1903; *Kleinasien* (Christian Asia Minor), Leipzig, 1903 (cf. Ch. Diehl, *Journal des Savants*, 1904, p. 239); E. Dobbert, *Zur Geschichte der altchristl. und frühbyzant. Kunst* (*Repertorium*, 1898, p. 1, 95); H. Holtzinger, *Die altchristl. und byzantinische Baukunst*, 2d ed., Stuttgart, 1899; A. Choisy, *Histoire de l'Architecture*, vol. ii., Paris, 1899; L. Lindenschmit, *Handbuch der deutschen Altertumskunde*, Brunswick, 1880–1889 (The Barbaric Art of the West); J. Hampel, *Alterth. des Mittelalters in Ungarn*, 3 vols., Brunswick, 1905; C. Barrière-Flavy, *Les Arts industriels de la Gaule du V⁰ au VII⁰ siècle*, 3 vols., Toulouse, 1901; Cl. Boulanger, *Le Mobilier funéraire gallo-romain et franc*, Paris, 1905; A. Marignan, *Un Historien de l'Art français, Louis Courajod; Les Temps francs*, Paris, 1889 (cf. *Repertorium*, 1902, p. 101); L. Bréhier, *Les Colonies d'Orientaux en Occident au Commencement du Moyen Age* (*Byzantinische Zeitschrift*, 1903, p. 1).

M. de Vogüé and Duthoit, *L'Architecture civile et religieuse en Syrie*, 3 vols., Paris, 1866, 1877; H. C. Butler, *Expedition to Syria, Architecture*, New York, 1903 (600 illustrations); O. Dalton, *Catalogue of Early Christian Antiquities in the British Museum*, London, 1901; Ph. Lauer, *Le trésor du Sancta Sanctorum* (*Monuments Piot*, vol. xv.); H. Graeven, *Frühchristl. und mittelälterliche Elfenbeinwerke*, Rome, 1898 et seq.; A. M. Cust, *The Ivory Workers of the Middle Ages*, London, 1903; A. Haseloff, *Codex Purpureus Rossanensis*, Leipzig, 1899; H. Omont, *Peintures d'un Manuscrit grec de l'Evangile* (*Mon. Piot*, vol. vii., p. 175); Herm. Vopel, *Die altchristl. Goldgläser*, Freiburg, 1899; Jul. Kurth, *Die Wandmosaiken von Ravenna*, Leipzig, 1902 (cf. *Repertorium*, 1903. p. 339); Ch. Diehl, *Ravenne*, Paris, 1903; P. Leitshuh, *Geschichte der Karolingischen Malerei*, Berlin, 1894; G. Swarzenski, *Karoling. Malerei und Plastik* (*Jahrbücher* of the Berlin Museums, 1902); K. Künstle, *Die Kunst des Klosters Reichenau*, Fribourg, 1906; E. Babelon, *Histoire de la Gravure sur gemmes en France*, Paris, 1902; J. Labarte, *Recherches sur la Peinture en émail*, Paris, 1856.

Ch. Diehl, *Manuel d'art byzantin*, Paris, 1910; O. M. Dalton, *Byzantine Art and Archeology*, Oxford, 1911; J. P. Richter, *Quellen der byzantinischen Kunstgeschichte*, Vienna, 1896; D. Ainalow, *Origines hellénistiques de l'Art byzantin* (in Russian), St. Petersburg, 1900 (cf. *Repertorium*, 1902, p. 35); Ch. Diehl, *Justinien et la Civilisation byzantine au VI⁰ siècle*, Paris, 1901; *Etudes byzantines*, Paris, 1905; G. Millet, *L'Ecole grecque dans l'Architecture byzantine*, Paris, 1917; *L'Iconographie de l'Evangile*, Paris, 1916; Ch. Diehl, *L'Art byzantin dans l'Italie méridionale*, Paris, 1896 (cf. *Repertorium*, 1896, p. 49); E. Bertaux, *L'Art dans l'Italie méridionale*, vol. i., Paris, 1903; Ch. Diehl, Le Tourneau, H. Saladin, *Monuments chrétiens de Salonique*, Paris, 1918; J. Ebersolt and J. Thiers, *Les Eglises de Constantinople*, Paris, 1917; R. W. Schultz and S. H. Barnsley, *The Monastery of St. Luke of Stiris in Phocis*, London, 1901; G. Millet, *Le Monastère de Daphni*, Paris, 1899; A. Ballu, *Le Monastère byzantin de Tébessa*, Paris, 1898; L. de Beylié, *L'Habitation byzantine*, Paris, 1902.

J. Tikkanen, *Die Byzantinischen Psalterillustrationen*, Helsingfors, 1895; Ch. Diehl, *Mosalques byzantines du Monastère de Saint-Luc* (*Gazette des Beaux-Arts*, 1897, i., p. 37; (cf. *Mon. Piot*, vol. iv. p.

CHRISTIAN ART IN THE EAST AND IN THE WEST

231); E. Bertaux, *Les Mosalques de Daphni* (*Gazette des Beaux-Arts*, 1901, i., p. 39); C. Bayet, *Recherches pour servir à l'Histoire de la Sculpture chrétienne en Orient*, Paris, 1879.

E. Saladin and G. Migeon, *Manuel d'Art musulman*, 2 vols., Paris, 1907; R. Kœchlin, *L'Art musulman* (*Revue de l'Art*, 1903; i., p. 409); J. Karabacek, *Das angebliche Bilderverbot des Islam*, Vienna, 1876; A. Gayet, *L'Art Copte*, Paris, 1901; *La Sculpture Copte* (*Gazette des Beaux-Arts*, 1892, i., p. 422); A. Riegl, *Koptische Kunst* (*Byzantinische Zeitschrift*, 1893, p. 114); G. Le Bon, *La Civilisation des Arabes*, Paris, 1893; A. Gayet, *L'Art arabe*, Paris, 1893 (cf. *Repertorium*, 1896, p. 358); Herz Bey, *Le Musée national du Caire* (*Gazette des Beaux-Arts*, 1902, i., p. 45); G. Migeon, *Les Cuivres arabes* (*ibid.*, 1899, ii., p. 462); Owen Jones, *The Alhambra*, 2 vols., London, 1842; C. Nizet, *La Mosque de Cordoue*, Paris, 1905; C. Blochet, *Les Miniatures des manuscrits musulmans* (*Gazette*, 1897, i., p. 281; cf. *Burlington Magazine*, 1903, ii., p. 276); A. Gayet, *L'Art persan*, Paris, 1895; Fr. Sarre, *Denkmäler persischer Baukunst*, Berlin, 1901 (Islamite epoch); H. Wallis, *La Céramique persane au XIIIe siècle* (*Gazette des Beaux-Arts*, 1892, ii., p. 69); C. Blochet, *Peinture en Perse* (*Revue Archéol.*, 1905, ii., p. 121); Claude Anet, *Persian Miniatures* (*Burlington Magazine*, Oct., Nov., 1912); A. van de Put, *Hispano-Mauresque Ware of the XVth Century*, London, 1904 (cf. *Gazette des Beaux-Arts*, 1905, i., p. 351); Jul. Lessing, *Orientalische Teppiche*, Berlin, 1891; A. Riegl, *Altorientalische Teppiche*, Vienna, 1891 (cf. *Gazette des Beaux-Arts*, 1895, i., p. 168; 1896, i., p. 271); W. Bode, *Westasiatische Knüpfteppiche* (*Jahrbücher* of the Berlin Museums, vol. xiii., 1892, p. 26); S. Humphries, *Oriental Carpets*, London, 1909; G. Le Bon, *Les Civilisations de l'Inde*, Paris, 1887; *Les Monuments de l'Inde*, Paris, 1893; M. Maindron, *L'Art indien*, Paris, no date; *Arts décoratifs de l'Inde* (*Gazette des Beaux-Arts*, 1898, ii., p. 511); J. F. Fergusson, *History of Indian Architecture*, London, 1876; E. B. Havell, *Indian Sculpture and Painting*, London, 1908 (see above, p. 30).

The best general survey of the art of the non-Christian countries of the East and of Arab art (India, Egypt, and Spain) is that in K. Woermann's *Geschichte der Kunst*, vol. i., Leipzig, 1900, pp. 479–606.

XII

ROMANESQUE AND GOTHIC ARCHITECTURE

The term Romance or Romanesque.—Inaccuracy of the term Gothic.—Its First Use by Raphael. —A Comparison of Romanesque and Gothic Architecture.—The Celtic Influence on the Art of Northern Europe.—Græco-Syrian Elements.—Influence of the Byzantine Cities, Constantinople and Ravenna.—Phases of the Transition from Romanesque to Gothic.— Characteristics of Romanesque Architecture.—Of Gothic.—The Invention of the Pointed Arch.—The Age of Cathedral-building.—The Three Periods of Gothic.—Town-halls, Dwellings, and Fortresses.—The Architecture of the Future Foreshadowed by Gothic.

ARCISSE DE CAUMONT, who died in 1873, was the first writer to apply the term *Romance* or *Romanesque* to the art which

FIG. 161.—TYPES OF VAULTS.

1. Barrel vault.   2. Extrados of a groined vault.
3. Intrados of a Roman groined vault.   4. Intrados of a groined vault with salient ribs.

(Reusens, *Archéologie Chrétienne.*)

obtained in the West of Europe after Charlemagne. This term was very happily chosen. On the one hand, it recalls the affinities of this art with that of Rome, and on the other, its intermediate position as between a national style and one of foreign origin. The Romance tongue and Romanesque art were parallel and contemporary phenomena, although the Roman element, fortified by Christianity, is much more apparent in the latter than in the former.

The expression *Gothic Art* is, on the contrary, inaccurate, for the art which succeeded to Romanesque art was neither created nor propagated by the Goths. The term is said to have been first used by Raphael, in a report he addressed to Leo X., dealing with the works projected in Rome, *Gothic* being used at that period as a synonym of *barbarous*, as opposed to Roman. The use of the expression still survives in the term "Goth," denoting an uncouth and mannerless person. The use of the epithet *Gothic* was popularised by the historian of Italian art, Vasari (1574), and still persists. The substitution of the term *French Art* for that of *Gothic* persists. The substitution of the term *French Art* for that of *Gothic Art* has been suggested; but the expression is equivocal, unless we add: of *the last third of the Middle Ages*, which makes the expression clumsy and diffuse. It will be better, therefore, to keep to the consecrated phrase.

If we examine a Romanesque church and a Gothic church, we easily recognise the essential differences of the two styles. The first is still somewhat heavy and depressed, in spite of the towers that raise and dominate it; the impressions most strongly conveyed by the second are those of height and lightness. In the former, the solid surfaces are in excess of the apertures, and the converse

FIG. 162.—ROMANESQUE CHURCH AT ANGOULÊME.
(*Monuments Historiques.*)

may be said of the latter, which is made up of windows, rose-windows, pinnacles, and lace-like traceries of stone. The decoration of the former is conventional, fantastic, or geometrical; that of the latter is based directly upon Nature; round-headed arches and horizontal lines characterise the former; in the latter the most striking features are its vertical lines and its pointed arches. To sum up, a Romanesque church suggests the idea of serene majesty and conscious strength; and a Gothic church, the lifting-up of the soul to God.

FIG. 163.—BAMBERG CATHEDRAL, BAVARIA.

(Lübke, *Architektur*, vol. i., Seemann, Leipzig.)

The Celts, like the Germans and Scandinavians, raised no stone buildings; but they had a decorative art quite distinct from the Græco-Roman style, which is manifested notably in their personal ornaments. This art was not crushed by Roman domination and influence; it revived with great intensity in the fourth century, when the barbaric world resumed its attacks upon Rome. This is an element that should not be overlooked in studying the art of the Middle Ages; it may be characterised as *Northern*, bearing in mind that the barbaric tribes were in constant communication with Central Asia and Persia, by way of the Russian steppes, a fact which goes far towards explaining the presence of Oriental elements in the Northern style.

FIG. 164.—BAPTISTERY, CATHEDRAL, AND LEANING TOWER OF PISA.

A second element, the influence of which was felt at an early period, was the Græco - Syrian. Marseilles was a Greek town; ancient relations, never interrupted, connected the south of Gaul with the Asiatic coast. As early as the fifth century, the western region of Asia, where, as we have seen, the Byzantine style developed, exercised its influence upon Gaul, which was frequented by Asiatic merchants and workmen.

Italy herself, from the fourth century onward, received the Byzantine imprint more and more profoundly; for Constantinople began, almost from its first foundation, to play the part formerly filled by Alexandria. Sheltered from the invasions that devastated Rome and Italy, it became the centre of civilisation and art; Ravenna, the imperial residence in the fifth and sixth centuries, was a Byzantine town. Thus, the influence exercised by Italy over Gaul during the first centuries of the Middle Ages was rather Byzantine than Italian.

This mixture of Northern, Asiatic, Syrian, and Byzantine elements is apparent, though difficult to analyse, in the evolution which gave birth successively to Romanesque and Gothic art. It should be noted that down to the eleventh century, the Northern element was perpetually reinforced by the afflux of new invaders, Saxon and Norman; from the eleventh

FIG. 165. — FLYING BUT-TRESSES OF STE. GUDULE. BRUSSELS.

(Reusens, *Archéologie Chrétienne*.)

century onward, the Syrian and Byzantine elements were in their turn accentuated by the results of the Crusades, which brought the Western nations into permanent contact, in place of intermittent relation, with Byzantines, Syrians, and Arabs. The Græco-Roman element became fainter and fainter, till it almost disappeared in Gothic architecture. Indeed, the principle of architectural art in the Middle Ages was not so much the development as the gradual elimination of Græco-Roman principles, under the dual influence of Asiatic and Byzantine art on the one hand, and of the barbaric temperament on the other.

FIG. 166.—NOTRE DAME, PARIS, WEST FRONT.

Romanesque architecture marks the first stage in this progression, Gothic architecture the second. The result was gradually achieved by transitions it is possible to demonstrate; and thus, without denying the intervention of foreign elements in the development of Western art, we can trace the evolution of architecture as if it had been perfectly spontaneous. The tendency induced by adventitious elements did not arrest evolution, but it explains its course. Let us briefly point out the principal phases of this transformation.

FIG. 167.—CHEVET OF NOTRE DAME, PARIS.

Tracing the evolution of the Romanesque church back to its source, we shall find that, like the Gothic church, it owed its origin to the Roman basilica of the fourth century. But it was found necessary to cover this basilica to fit it for public worship, and the time came when architects rejected the timber roof, as over-liable to destruction by fire, and also roofs constructed of large horizontal stones, as involving immense labour and difficulty

FIG. 168.—CHARTRES
CATHEDRAL.
(*Monuments Historiques*.)

in transport and manipulation. They accordingly adopted the vault, which enabled them to use large quantities of small stones.

The section of a vault may be semi-cylindrical; or it may be a pointed arch, that is to say, an angle formed by the intersection of two arches. In the same way, the lintel surmounting a door or window may be replaced by a round-headed arch or a pointed arch. The round-headed arch may be called the vital principle of Romanesque architecture, the pointed arch that of Gothic architecture.

These two types differ not merely in form, but in construction. There are two kinds of vaults: the barrel vault, a hollow demi-cylinder with or without arcs-doubleaux; and the groined vault, the exterior, or extrados, of which shows four groins, and is formed by the intersection at right angles of two demi-cylinders. An essential variation of the groined vault as known to the Romans is the groined vault with projecting ribs. Whereas the Romanesque vault is a homogeneous dome, owing its solidity to its points of support, the groined vault with projecting ribs owes its solidity to the network of arches, or elastic ossature, which holds it up as if in equilibrium.

The groined vault with projecting ribs was first used in Italy after the eighth century, by the Lombard architects, whose art, though it developed under Byzantine influences, was not merely an imitation of Byzantine art.

The Roman basilica, roofed and enclosed, had become the Christian church. The same model did duty in the West for four centuries. After the death of Charlemagne, civil war, internal anarchy, and the Norman incursions checked the advance of civilisation; it was as if a

FIG. 169.—REIMS CATHEDRAL.
(Photo. by Courleux.)

"thick darkness" had descended upon Western Europe. When this was dissipated, a period of great activity set in, described by the chronicler, Raoul Glaber (who died in 1050), in a famous passage: "It was as if the world, shaking off its old tatters, desired to re-clothe itself in the white robes of the Church." The same writer tells us that some time after the year 1000 "all religious buildings, cathedrals, country churches, village chapels, were transformed by the faithful into something better." This "something better" refers to stone vaults, to Romanesque architecture, in fact.

FIG. 170.—AMIENS CATHEDRAL.
(Photo. by Neurdein.)

One of the most learned historians of architecture, M. Choisy, attributes the introduction of the vault in Western churches to Byzantine and Syrian influences. The growth of the trade between Venice and Byzantium on the one hand, and Venice and the West on the other, the frequent pilgrimages made by Occidentals to Palestine, and finally the commerce of Asia with the ports of the Rhine and the Loire, may be put forward to support this theory. But it is possible that the sight of the Roman arcades which still existed may have helped, or even sufficed, to suggest to Western architects the substitution of the round-headed arch for the horizontal entablature.

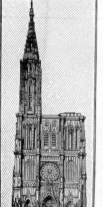

FIG. 171.—STRASBURG CATHEDRAL.

The Romanesque church differs in many particulars from the basilica. It was built in the form of a Latin cross, that is to say, the long nave was intersected at a point two-thirds of its length by a perpendicular transept; the roof was vaulted, the windows generally round-headed; finally, it had as a rule one or more towers, forming a corporate part of the building. These modifications, and several others, were not at once adopted; we can trace their evolution down to the middle of the twelfth century, and even later. But the general conception was the same: a central

FIG. 172.—COLOGNE CATHEDRAL.

nave, lighted laterally, ending in an apse, and side aisles, generally two in number.

To support the weight of their vaults, the Romanesque architects were obliged to increase the thickness of their walls and pillars. Thick, solid walls admit of few apertures; the lighting of Romanesque churches is consequently insufficient. The same exigencies of stability led the Romanesque architects to increase the width and diminish the height of their buildings; hence a certain heaviness is inseparable from this kind of construction.

The oldest and finest of the Romanesque churches in France are found south of the Loire. This architectural style was fostered mainly by the monks of Cluny, whose vast Abbey church, destroyed under Napoleon I., was imitated everywhere, even in the Holy Land. Numerous local schools sprang up, in Burgundy, Auvergne, Périgord, &c. That on the banks of the Rhine, which was influenced by Lombard architecture, was perhaps the most recent, but the great churches built at Spires, Mayence, Worms, and Bamberg are among the masterpieces of religious architecture. In Italy, the principal monument of Romanesque art is the Cathedral of Pisa (1063-1118). A good example still exists in Paris, though it has been much altered and restored, the ancient Church of St. Germain-des-Prés. [In England, the rude architecture of the Saxons, of which only negligible fragments survive, gave place to the Romanesque imported by the Norman conquerors. The earliest English examples (parts of Canterbury, Winchester, and Rochester Cathedrals) are therefore closely akin to French Norman buildings. But the independent genius of the English soon made itself felt in this as in other domains. By the be-

FIG. 173.—SAINTE CHAPELLE, PARIS.
(Photo. by Levy.)

ROMANESQUE AND GOTHIC ARCHITECTURE

Ornaments (England and France), London, 1831; L. de Fourcaud, *L'Art gothique* (*Gazette des Beaux-Arts*, 1891, ii., p. 89); Clara Perkins, *French Cathedrals and Châteaux*, 2 vols., Boston, 1903.

Eug. Lefèvre-Pontalis, *L'Architecture religieuse dans l'ancien diocèse de Soissons*, Paris, 1897; *L'Architecture gothique dans la Champagne méridionale*, Paris, 1904; C. Enlart, *Origines françaises de l'Architecture gothique en Italie*, Paris, 1895 (cf. *Revue archéologique*, 1893, ii., p. 284); *Origines de l'Architecture gothique en Espagne et en Portugal* (*Bulletin du Comité* 1894, p. 168); E. Bertaux, *Castel del Monte et les Architectes français de Frédéric II* (*Comptes rendus de l'Académie des Inscriptions*, 1897, p. 432); Francis Vond, *Gothic Architecture in England*, London, 1905 (cf. Lasteyrie, *Journal des Savants*, 1908, p. 57); E. Corroyer, *L'Architecture gothique*, Paris, 1891, English trans., London, 1893; Edw. S. Prior, *A History of Gothic Art in England*, London, 1900; P. A. Ditchfield, *The Cathedrals of Great Britain*, London, 1912, 4th ed.; *Westminster Abbey*, London, 1909; P. Biver, *Westminster*, Paris, 1913; C. Enlart, *L'Art gothique et la Renaissance en Chypre*, 2 vols., Paris, 1899; Fergusson, *Handbook of Architecture*, London, 1859, and *History of Architecture*, 2 vols., London, 1865, 1874; G. Gilbert Scott, *Lectures on the Rise and Development of Mediæval Architecture*, 2 vols., London, 1879.

G. Durand, *Monographie de la Cathédrale d'Amiens*, 2 vols., Amiens, 1901, 1903; J. Denais, *Monographie de la Cathédrale d'Angers*, Paris, 1899; Abbé Bulteau, *Monographie de la Cathédrale de Chartres*, 2nd ed., Chartres, 1902 (cf. *Bull. monumental*, 1903, p. 581); R. Merlet, *La Cathédrale de Chartres*, Paris, 1908; P. Vitry and G. Brière, *Saint Denis*, Paris, 1908; *Notre Dame de Paris*, Paris, 1909; Eug. Lefèvre-Pontalis, *Histoire de la Cathédrale de Noyon*, Paris, 1900; *Le Château de Coucy*, Paris, 1909; L. Bréhier, *La Cathédrale de Reims*, Paris, 1916; E. Male, *L'Art allemand et L'Art français du Moyen Age*, Paris, 1917; L. Demaison, *La Cathédrale de Reims* (*Bulletin monumental*, 1902, p. 3); Bégule and Guigne, *La Cathédrale de Lyon*, Lyons, 1880; E. Lambin, *L'Eglise de Saint-Leu d'Esserent* (*Gazette des Beaux-Arts*, 1901, i., p. 305); H. Stein, *Pierre de Montereau, architecte de Saint Denis* (*Mém. de la Soc. des antiq.*, 1900, vol. lxi., p. 79); *Le Palais de Justice et la Sainte Chapelle*, Paris, 1912; G. Delahache, *La Cathédrale de Strasbourg*, Paris, 1910; P. Gout, *Le Mont Saint-Michel*, Paris, 1910; C. Romussi, *Le Dome de Milan*, Milan, 1911; A. de Geymüller, *La Cathédrale de Milan* (*Gazette des Beaux-Arts*, 1890, i., p. 152).

For the supposed "terrors of the year 1000," see the trenchant article by Dom Plaine, in the *Revue des Questions historiques*, 1873, p. 145.

XIII

ROMANESQUE AND GOTHIC SCULPTURE

The Church the Patroness of Art in the Middle Ages.—The Origin of Painted Glass.—Illuminated Manuscripts.—Decorative Sculpture in Romanesque and Gothic Churches.—Conventional Character of Romanesque Ornament.—Realistic Character of Gothic.—The "Vintage Capital" at Reims.—The Educational Intention of the Gothic Cathedral.—Vincent de Beauvais' Miroir du Monde.—The Supposed Ascetic Character of Gothic Art Denied.—The Anti-Clerical Tendencies of the Gothic Imagiers a Romantic Fiction.—Portrait Statues on Tombs.—Statuettes in Wood and Ivory.—The Serenity of Gothic Art.—The Rise of the Burgundian School.

THE Church was not only rich and powerful in the Middle Ages; it dominated and directed all the manifestations of human activity. There was practically no art but the art it encouraged, the art it needed to construct and adorn its buildings, carve its ivories and reliquaries, and paint its glass and its missals. Foremost among the arts it fostered was architecture, which never played so important a part in any other society. Even now, when we enter a Romanesque or Gothic church, we are impressed by the might of that vast force of which it is the manifestation, a force which shaped the destinies of Europe for a thousand years.

FIG. 181.—INTERLACED ORNAMENT.
From the Irish manuscript known as the Book of Durrow (seventh century) (Trinity College, Dublin).
(Photo. by Lawrence.)

Wall painting, the special art of primitive Christianity, was relatively neglected both in the Romanesque and Gothic periods. This was primarily a result of construction. The Romanesque churches were dark, and the Gothic churches had very few flat surfaces suitable for decoration. On the other hand, these latter had lofty windows, which had to be filled in and beautified with coloured glass. The art of glass painting is inseparable from Gothic art, and it was during the apogee of this art, in the thirteenth century, that the glass painters lavished their masterpieces on the churches of St. Denis, Chartres, Poitiers, and Sens. The brilliant and somewhat crude colour proper to coloured glass exercised an undeniable influence on the painting of the fifteenth century. Some time had to elapse before the eye could accustom itself to tones more fused and discreet.

While glass painting was in its glory, the illumination of manuscripts was also practised. But it was not until the middle of the fourteenth century that this art achieved any pre-eminent results. Down to this time, illuminators and calligraphers worked from coloured designs which they transmitted to one another. Originality was shown chiefly in the initials and the borders, which were sometimes treated with amazing richness of invention (Figs. 181, 182).

FIG. 182.—ILLUMINATED INITIAL WITH INTERLACED ORNAMENT.

From the Irish manuscript known as the Book of Kells (eighth century) (Trinity College, Dublin).
(Photo. by Lawrence.)

The decoration of Romanesque churches was often carried out by the monks who built them; that of Gothic churches was essentially the work of lay sculptors, *imagiers*, and stone-carvers, who formed themselves into guilds. In both epochs the favourite form of decoration was the bas-relief. The Romanesque sculptors ornamented the tympana of porches with large religious compositions; they also carved " histories," and figures of men and of animals on the capitals of columns and on friezes. The Gothic sculptors, more especially in France, introduced reliefs and statues in all parts of the vast buildings, in the porches, the galleries, and the choir-stalls. It has been calculated that Chartres Cathedral contains no less than

FIG. 183.—THE LAST JUDGMENT.
Tympanum in Porch of Autun Cathedral.
(Photo. by Giraudon.)

10,000 figures—statues and reliefs, persons and animals painted on glass.

Although the transition between Romanesque and Gothic sculpture was not abrupt, and there are monuments in which the characteristics of the two are associated, it may be said that, taken as a whole or at the apogee of each, the contrast between them is very striking.

FIG. 184.—CHRIST WITH THE EVANGELISTS AND THE ELDERS OF THE APOCALYPSE.
Tympanum in Porch of Abbey Church at Moissac. (Photo. by Giraudon.)

Romanesque sculpture is the product of very diverse influences, which vary in intensity according to the country; foremost among them was the persistent influence of Roman art—especially in Italy and the south of France—and to this were added Byzantine, Arab, and Persian elements, transmitted by war or commerce, and the influence of the art of northern countries, with its taste for complicated forms and interlacements. One influence is lacking in this composite art, that of Nature, studied at first hand. The Romanesque sculptors, having eyes, saw not. Their art is sometimes majestic, powerful, and decorative; but it is always abstract, conventional, and indifferent to reality.

One of the most characteristic examples that can be quoted is the tympanum of the Cathedral of Autun, representing the Last Judgment (Fig. 183). This vast composition, dating from about 1130, is not lacking in grandeur; it even reveals a remarkable taste for vivacity

FIG. 185.—"THE VINTAGE CAPITAL."
(Reims Cathedral.) (Photo. by Thuillot.)

of movement. But the drawing is grotesque, the bodies ludicrously elongated, the draperies stiff and meagre. The tympanum of the Church of Moissac (Tarn et Garonne), later by some twenty years than that of Autun, is hardly less barbarous (Fig. 184). But here again, while the drawing is very defective, we note a mobility and variety of attitude which show that the vitality of native tendencies had not succumbed to Byzantine hieraticism.

In contrast to this Romanesque art, as yet in bondage to convention, ignorant or disdainful of Nature, the mature Gothic art of the thirteenth century appeared as a brilliant revival of realism. The great sculptors who adorned the cathedrals of Paris, Amiens, Reims, and Chartres with their works, were realists in the highest sense of the word. They sought in Nature, not only their knowledge of human forms, and of the draperies that cover them, but also that of the principles of decoration. Save in the gargoyles of cathedrals and in certain minor sculptures, we no longer find in the thirteenth century those unreal figures of animals, nor those ornaments, complicated as nightmares,

FIG. 186.—THE MEETING BETWEEN
ABRAHAM AND MELCHISEDECH.
(Reims Cathedral.)
(Photo. by Giraudon.)

FIG. 187.—GROUP FROM THE
VISITATION.
(Reims Cathedral.)
(Photo. by Giraudon.)

which load the capitals of Romanesque churches; the flora of the country, studied with loving attention, is the sole, or almost the sole, source from which decorators take their motives. It is in this charming profusion of flowers and foliage that the genius of Gothic architecture is most freely displayed. One of the most admirable of its creations is the famous *Vintage Capital* (Fig. 185) in Notre Dame at Reims, carved about the year 1250. Since the first century of the Roman Empire (see p. 91) Art had never imitated Nature so perfectly, nor has it ever since done so with a like grace and sentiment.

The Gothic cathedral is a perfect encyclopædia of human knowledge. It contains scenes from the Scriptures and the legends of the saints; motives from the animal and vegetable kingdom; representations of the seasons, of agricultural labour, of the arts and sciences and crafts, and finally moral allegories, as, for instance, ingenious personifications of the virtues and the vices. In the thirteenth century a learned Dominican, Vincent of Beauvais, was employed by St. Louis to write a great work which was to be an epitome of all the knowledge of his times. This compilation, called *The Mirror of the World*, is divided into four parts: the *Mirror of Nature*, the *Mirror of Science*, the *Moral Mirror*, and the *Historical Mirror*. A contemporary archæologist, M. E. Male, has shown that the works of art of our great cathedrals are a translation into

FIG. 188.—A PROPHET.
(Reims Cathedral.)
(Photo. by Giraudon.)

stone of the *Mirror* of Vincent of Beauvais, setting aside the episodes from Greek and Roman history, which would have been out of place. It was not that the *imagiers* had read Vincent's work; but that, like him, they sought to epitomise all the knowledge of their contemporaries. The first aim of their art is not to please, but to teach; they offer an encyclopædia for the use of those who cannot read, translated by sculptor or glass-painter into a clear and precise language, under the lofty direction of the Church, which left nothing to caprice. It was present always and everywhere, advising and superintending the artist, leaving him to his own devices only when

he modelled the fantastic animals of the gargoyles, or borrowed decorative motives from the vegetable kingdom.

There are certain prejudices against this admirable, though incomplete art, which it is difficult to destroy. It is often said, for instance, that all Gothic figures are stiff and emaciated. To convince ourselves of the contrary we need only study the marvellous sculpture of the meeting between Abraham and Melchisedech, in Reims Cathedral (Fig. 186); or again, the Visitation,[1] the seated Prophet, and the standing Angel, in the same cathedral, or the exquisite Magdalen of Bordeaux Cathedral (Figs. 187—190). What can we see in

[1] The author of this amazing group must certainly have seen and studied antique statues. But which and where were these?

these that is stiff, sickly, and puny? The art that has most affinity with perfect Gothic is neither Romanesque nor Byzantine, but the Greek art of from 500 to 450 B.C. By a strange coincidence, the Gothic artists even reproduce the somewhat stereotyped smile of their forerunners.

It has also been said that Gothic art bears the impress of ardent piety and emotional mysticism, that it dwells on the sufferings of Jesus, of the Virgin, and of the martyrs with harrowing persistency. Those who believe this have never studied Gothic art. It is so far from the truth that, as a fact, the Gothic art of the best period, the thirteenth century, never represented any sufferings save those of the damned. The Virgins are smiling and gracious, never grief-stricken. There is not a single Gothic rendering of the Virgin weeping at the foot of the Cross. The words and music of the *Stabat Mater*, which are sometimes instanced as the highest expression of the religion of the Middle Ages, date from the end of the thirteenth century at the very earliest, and did not become popular till the fifteenth century. Jesus himself is not represented as suffering, but with a serene and majestic expression. The famous statue known as the *Beau Dieu d'Amiens* may be instanced as typical.

FIG. 189.—AN ANGEL.
(Reims Cathedral.)
(Photo. by Giraudon.)

I may remark, in this connection, that Gothic art treated but few Scripture episodes, choosing those which conveyed some doctrine and tended to edification, that is to say, to the glorification of the faith. Such was the meeting of Abraham and Melchisedech, because Melchisedech, like Jesus, was both priest and king, and because in offering bread and wine to Abraham, he prefigured the institution of the Eucharist. On the other hand, as M. Male has pointed out, mediæval artists seem to have been insensible to the more human, tender, and picturesque elements of the Old and New Testaments. The artists themselves were not theologians, but they were directed by theologians. Now the theology of this period, as represented by the *Summa* of St. Thomas Aquinas, was by no means sentimental. It was a haughty and positive science, much addicted to the chopping of logic, which aspired to secure man's salvation by appealing to his reason, and not by touching his

FIG. 190.—ST. MARY MAGDALEN.
(Bordeaux Cathedral.)
(Photo. by Giraudon.)

heart. It is strange that the same mistake should have been made in estimating Dante, the great poet of the thirteenth century. Because we find in his works a Beatrice and a Francesca da Rimini, he is credited with modern ideas, a sentimental melancholy, when he was above all things a theologian, a logician, and a politician. The sickly, tearful, plaintive Middle Age is an absurd invention of the Romantic school of the nineteenth century.

No less false is the idea popularised by Victor Hugo, that the *imagiers* had escaped from the influence of the Church, that they were independent and seditious spirits, and that liberty of architecture was the mediæval equivalent for modern liberty of the press. It was highly dangerous to appear independent or seditious in the Middle Ages, especially when the authority of the Church was involved. Such spirits ran the risk of the stake or imprisonment for life. From 1234 to 1239, in the reign of St. Louis, about the time of the completion of the Sainte-Chapelle, Robert, Inquisitor of France, caused 222 persons suspected of holding "opinions" to be burnt alive in Flanders, Picardy, and Champagne. The *imagiers*, as I have already said, were only allowed a free hand in the execution of minor decorations; in all the sacred or profane subjects they treated, the "clerks," in other words, the Church, guided their hands. Much

FIG. 191.—STATUE ON TOMB OF HAYMON,
COUNT OF CORBEIL. (C. 1320.)
Church of St. Spire, Corbeil, Seine et Oise.

has been made of certain caricatures of monks which figure in the reliefs of some cathedrals; but these do not appear at all till the end of the fourteenth century, and besides, they are much less malicious than they are said to be. The theory of the anti-clerical *imagier* is piquant, no doubt; but it is pure romance.

Gothic sculpture was not confined to the decoration of cathedrals; it produced, especially from the fourteenth century onwards, a number of memorial statues for tombs, which gradually became portraits. It was portraiture—of which we find isolated examples as early as the thirteenth century—which led Gothic art

FIG. 192.—STATUE ON TOMB OF ROBERT D'ARTOIS, BY PÉPIN DE HUY. (C. 1320.)

Church of St. Denis, near Paris.

from realism to naturalism, to the rendering of individual expression. In this it was assisted by the practice of moulding from nature. Its first essays were the *gisants* and *gisantes, i.e.,* recumbent male and female figures, representing deceased persons lying in calm, serene attitudes; in the sixteenth century this type was replaced by that of the defunct kneeling, with hands folded in prayer, which was borrowed from the votive figures of *donors,* and lasted almost to our own times. The fine recumbent statues of Haymon, Count of Corbeil, and of Robert d'Artois (Figs. 191, 192) are preserved at Corbeil and at St. Denis; those of Philip VI. and Charles V., the works of André Beauneveu, a sculptor of Hainault, who worked in France, are in the Louvre.

FIG. 193.—VIRGIN AND CHILD.

Ivory Statuette. French. (The Louvre.)

(Photo. by Giraudon.)

The chief masterpieces of Gothic sculpture other than church decorations are statuettes and bas-reliefs in wood and ivory, which were often painted and gilded, of which the most beautiful specimens known are in France (Figs. 193, 194). Ivory was a material much prized, more especially by the craftsmen of the fourteenth century; but the curved form of the elephant's tusk often forced the artist to make the standing figures he carved in it protrude in the middle, as if the weight of the torso were thrown backwards on the hips.

I have spoken several times of the *serenity* of Gothic art; this is a word I have scarcely had occasion to use since I spoke of Greek art. Indeed, the more one considers the matter, the more clearly

127

APOLLO

one perceives that Greek and Gothic art are sisters, long hostile, but at last reconciled. The superiority of Greek art is undeniable, and this superiority arises, above all, from the important fact that Gothic art is essentially the art of draped figures. The prejudice of the age in which it flourished, and the nature of the religious monuments it

FIG. 194.—VIRGIN AND CHILD.
Ivory Statuette, French.
(Martin-Le Roy Collection, Paris.)

adorned, forbade the representation of the nude almost absolutely. Even when it was thought permissible to represent it, the result is timid and mediocre; Gothic art produced no satisfactory figure of the Infant Jesus, of Adam or of Eve. It must further be remembered that the evolution of Greek art continued for some thousand years, whereas Gothic art, from the beginning of the fourteenth century, began to show signs of exhaustion, and became mannered and complex. A kind of revival took place, it is true, in the middle of the fourteenth century but mainly in memorial sculpture. A new spirit, breathing from beyond the Alps, brought the lessons of the Italian *Trecento*. The acting of religious plays or *mysteries* went far towards substituting naturalism for symbolism and introduced new *motifs*. These elements were combined and developed in Paris, around the Court of Charles V., and reached their highest fruition in the Flemish School of Burgundy, during the last quarter of the fourteenth century. Yet there is no solution of continuity in the history of sculpture; the genius of the thirteenth-century *imagiers* merely became more expressive and more varied; it continued its course in the great Franco-Flemish School, and exercised a fruitful influence upon the painting of the day.

BIBLIOGRAPHY OF CHAPTER XIII.

Viollet-le-Duc's *Dictionaries*, works by A. Michel, Gonse, Bertaux, given on p. 118.—W. Lübke, *Geschichte der Plastik*, vols. i. and ii., 3rd ed., Leipzig, 1884; L. Gonse, *La Sculpture française depuis le XIVe siècle*, Paris, 1895; L. Courajod and F. Marcou, *Le Musée de Sculpture comparée du Trocadéro*, Paris, 1892; L. Courajod, *Leçons professées à l'Ecole du Louvre*, vol. ii., Paris, 1901; R. Allen, *Celtic Art*.

ROMANESQUE AND GOTHIC SCULPTURE

London, 1904; E. Male, *L'Art religieux du XIIIe siècle en France*, 2nd ed., Paris, 1902 (cf. Bertaux, *Revue des Deux-Mondes*, May 1, 1899); *L'Art religieux de la fin du Moyen Age*, Paris, 1908; E. Lambin, *La Flore sculpturale du Moyen Age* (*Gazette des Beaux-Arts*, 1899, i., p. 291).

M. Vöge, *Die Anfänge des monumentalen, tiles im Mittelalter*, Strasburg, 1894 (supposed priority of the Provençal school to that of the Île de France); *Der provenzalische Einfluss in Italien* (*Repertorium*, 1902, p. 409); R. de Lasteyrie, *Etudes sur la Sculpture française au Moyen Age* (*Monuments Piot*, vol. viii., 1902); porch of Chartres and discussion of Vöge's thesis; L. Pillon, *La Sculpture française du XIIIe siècle*, Paris, 1912; G. Fleury, *Portails imagés du XIIIe siècle*, Mamers, 1904.

R. Köchlin, *La Sculpture belge et les Influences françaises aux XIIIe et XIVe Siècles* (*Gazette des Beaux-Arts*, 1902, ii., p. 519); K. Franck, *Der Meister der Ecclesia und Synagoge am Strasburger Münster*, Düsseldorf, 1903 (influence of Chartres upon Strasburg); Ad. Goldschmidt, *Studien zur Geschichte der Sächsischen Skulptur*, Berlin, 1902; A. Weese, *Die Bamberger Domskulpturen*, Strasburg, 1898; M. Vöge, same subject (*Repertorium*, 1901, p. 255); Max Zimmermann, *Oberitalienische Plastik im Mittelalter*, Leipzig, 1897; A. Venturi, *Storia dell' arte italiana*, vols. i.–iii., Milan, 1901, 1902, 1903; H. v. der Gabelentz, *Mittelalterliche Plastik in Venedig*, Leipzig, 1903.

H. Otte, *Handbuch der kirchlichen Kunstarchäologie des deutschen Mittelalters*, 5th ed., Leipzig, 1883–1885; E. Molinier, *Les Ivoires*, Paris, n. d.; *La Descente de la Croix, groupe en ivoire du XIIIe siècle au Louvre* (*Monuments Piot*, vol. iii., p. 121); Berlin Museum, *Die Elfenbeindilder*, Berlin, 1903; O. Merson, *Les Vitraux*, Paris, 1895; H. Oldtmann, *Geschichte der Glasmalerei*, Cologne, 1898; Lecoy de la Marche, *Les Manuscrits et la Miniature*, Paris, n. d.; A. Labitte, *Les Manuscrits*, Paris, 1893; A. Haseloff, *Les Psautiers de Saint Louis* (*Mém. de la Soc. des Antiquaires*, 1900, vol. lviii., p. 18).

XIV

THE ARCHITECTURE OF THE RENAISSANCE AND MODERN ARCHITECTURE

*Gothic Architecture Alien to the Italian Genius.—Renaissance Architecture in Italy.—
"Renaissance Art" a Misleading Term.—The Florentine Palaces Types of Renaissance
Architecture.—The Differences between Gothic and Renaissance Churches.—The Duomo of
Florence.—The Riccardi and Strozzi Palaces.—St. Peter's, Rome.—The Disastrous In-
fluence of Michelangelo on his Imitators.—The Baroque Style.—The Palazzo Pesaro or
Bevilacqua, Venice.—Renaissance Architecture never fully accepted by the Northern
Nations.—French Castles and Mansions of the Renaissance Period.—The Louvre.—Château
of St. Germain.—Heidelberg.—Renaissance Buildings in Paris and London.—The Rococo
Style.—The Empire Style.—French Architecture of the Second Empire.—Renaissance
Architecture in Germany.—Modern Gothic in England.—The "New Art," or Anglo-
Belgian Movement.*

GOTHIC architecture, essentially a northern, Franco-Germanic manifestation, struck no very deep roots in Italy. It seems strange at

FIG. 195.—RICCARDI (MEDICI) PALACE,
FLORENCE.

first sight that Græco-Roman architecture should have found no imitators till so late. If the statues
and paintings of ancient Rome had
disappeared, or were buried under
ruins, the soil of the peninsula was
covered with Roman monuments,
to which no single Italian builder
for ten centuries had dreamt of
turning for inspiration. Indeed, far
from this, architects often demolished
them to make use of the dressed
stones. But the time came when
Humanism, by which we mean a
taste for the literature and history of
the ancients, drew the attention of
artists to the character of their
monuments. It was then that the
architecture of the Renaissance
arose; it must be looked upon as a consequence of the Humanist
movement, together with which it spread into the West of
Europe.

The term "Renaissance" is by no means a happy one, for it

130

implies two mistaken ideas: that art was dead, and that it rose again in its old form. As a fact, art was not dead, for dead things are not capable of evolution; and at the beginning of the revival, classic art found disciples, but not copyists. The men of the Renaissance themselves may have cherished the delusion that they were repeating the lessons of Rome, but in reality they were merely innovators, who had profited by these. The new art, which borrowed the forms and the setting of antiquity, was animated by a very different spirit, a spirit modified by ten centuries of Christianity. Humanity no more repeats its past than a river flows back to its source; what we take sometimes for resurrections are syntheses.

FIG. 196.—COURT OF THE PALAZZO DELLA CANCELLERIA, ROME.

The first period of Renaissance architecture in Italy, which extended through almost all of the fifteenth century, may be characterized as the attempted fusion of the forms of the Middle Ages and those of antiquity. Novelty is less apparent at first in the conception of buildings than in their decorations, in which Græco-Roman motives play a part. There are ornaments intended to embellish or to vary the surfaces which do not affect the structural framework of the monuments. Other needs —those of the civilisation of that period in Italy—soon tend to have a profound effect upon their character. For the first time since the fall of the Empire, civil architecture becomes more important than religious architecture. This was a consequence of the progress of the secular spirit. The type of the new art is the Florentine palace, a massive

FIG. 197.—"GROTESQUE" DECORATION BY PERUGINO.
In the Cambio at Perugia.

131

structure built round a quadrangular court with a columned portico (Figs. 195, 196). The exterior still preserves the character of the mediæval fortresses, in which solid surfaces occupy far more space than apertures, for the palace must be able to defend itself from

FIG. 198.—FRAGMENT OF SCULPTURED FRIEZE.
Ducal Palace, Urbino.

the street. It is in the interior, with its arcades, its rows of columns, the decoration of its pilasters and vaults that the imitation of antique models manifests itself (Figs. 197, 198).

Some of this decoration, no longer realistic but fantastic, was inspired by that of the Roman tombs lately excavated and known as *grottoes*; hence the term *grotesque*, which, in its original sense, implies no sort of censure or ridicule.

The Renaissance church differs from the Gothic church, mainly in that it is generally crowned by a cupola square on plan; clustered columns are replaced by pillars, the vault on intersecting arches by a barrel vault or a horizontal coffered ceiling; on the exterior we find columns, pediments, and niches, all the various elements of Roman art.

The Florentine Brunellesco (1377-1466) was the initiator of the first Renaissance. From 1420 to 1434 he raised the dome of the Cathedral of Florence (Fig. 199) to a height of about 300 feet. This Romanesque building was begun in 1294 by Arnolfo di Cambio, and continued after 1357 by Francesco Talenti on a modified plan. It was also Talenti who, in 1358,

FIG. 199.—THE DUOMO AND CAMPANILE, FLORENCE.

finished the beautiful Gothic campanile, begun under Giotto's direction, and from his plan (1334-1336). About the year 1445, Brunellesco began the Pitti Palace at Florence. It is a building characterised by a severe beauty, due mainly to the clarity of the design and the perfection of the proportions[1] (Fig. 200).

Classic influences are more apparent in the Riccardi Palace, the work of Michelozzo about 1440 (Fig. 195), and in the Strozzi Palace, Florence, built about 1489 by Benedetto da Majano and Cronaca. This is surmounted by an attic or cornice inspired by the best Roman models and justly celebrated. As in the Pitti Palace, the facing stones are rough hewn; this manner of dressing them, known as *rustica,* which is adopted in many Florentine

FIG. 200.—VIEW OF THE PITTI PALACE, FLORENCE.

buildings, emphasises the projections of the stones, and induces a rich play of light and shade on the façade. The Renaissance architecture later penetrated to Venice and there took on an aspect much less severe than at Florence. The great number of windows, the luxury of exterior decoration bear testimony to the survival of the Gothic style and to the influence of the Orient. The Venetian palaces have a gay and welcoming appearance which distinguishes them from all other Italian buildings (Fig. 201).

The marvellous façade of the Certosa at Pavia (Fig. 206) was built in 1491, two years later than the Strozzi Palace. Here decoration abounds, infinitely rich and varied; if it borrows elements from antique art, it lavishes them with truly Gothic exuberance. The architectural lines disappear under the profusion of statues and reliefs. This peculiarity makes it a type of the transition from the ogival churches to those in which the Roman constructive elements predominate.

FIG. 201.—VENDRAMINI PALACE, VENICE.
Built by P. Lombardo, 1481.

The centre of true Renaissance architecture, characterised by the constructive, non-decorative use of columns and pilasters, was not Florence but Rome, where the monuments of antiquity

[1] The greater part of the Pitti Palace was built by Ammanati about 1568.

furnished models. It began with Bramante of Urbino (1444-1514), the director of the first works undertaken at St. Peter's (Fig. 207). His

FIG. 202.—COURT OF THE PALAZZO MARINO, MILAN.

influence was principally exercised to restrain parasitical decoration and emphasise the structure of a building; this formula has become the law of modern architecture. Perhaps the most gifted of his successors was Andrea Palladio, who worked at Vicenza and at Venice (1518-1580). A characteristic work by him is the Church of the Redentore in that city. As an example of a palace built in this second phase of the Renaissance, we may cite the beautiful Library of St. Mark at Venice (Fig. 208), the work of Jacopo Tatti, called Sansovino (1486-1570), with its Doric ground floor, its Ionic first floor, its graceful frieze and balustrade enriched with statues.

The third period was entirely dominated by the influence of Michelangelo (1475-1564), especially from about the year 1550 onwards. This redoubtable genius imposed picturesque elements and individual fancies upon architecture. He continued, but did not finish, the enormous Church of St. Peter, the plans of which had already been modified by several architects, Raphael among the number. After the death of Michelangelo, the huge cupola, some 430 feet high, was finished from his designs; but the façade was spoilt in the seventeenth century by Maderna, and more especially by Bernini, the author of two lateral towers by no means pleasing

FIG. 203.—PROCURATIE NUOVE, VENICE.

in their effect. To Bernini, nevertheless, we owe the double colonnade, which gives the whole piazza the appearance of a vast vestibule before the church (Fig. 209). The interior, completed in the seventeenth century, is grandiose and splendid to a degree, in spite of the occasional over-exuberance of the decoration (Fig. 210); the exterior can only be appreciated from a distance, and has an illusory effect upon the visitor when viewed from the piazza. It is the largest church ever built, covering a superficies of over 225,000 square feet, while Milan Cathedral and St. Paul's in London occupy only some 118,300, St. Sophia some 107,000, and Cologne Cathedral some 86,000. But true greatness is a result rather of proportion than

FIG. 204.—SANTA MARIA DELLA SALUTE, VENICE.

dimension, and St. Peter's, the work of various architects and of two centuries, is not a well-proportioned building.

The example of Michelangelo inspired a taste for the colossal and a straining after effect, to the detriment of simplicity and good taste. His disciples have left many powerful and original works, which are marred by too great an exuberance of fancy. This tendency developed, at the close of the sixteenth century into the style known as Baroque, from the name given by the Portuguese to ir-

FIG. 205.—PALAZZO CARIGNANO, TURIN.

regularly shaped pearls (*barocco*). It is a kind of degenerescent Renaissance art, allied by its defects to the Flamboyant Gothic of the fifteenth century, its most pronounced characteristic being the preference of the curved to the straight line. In the interior of the churches of this period the so-called Jesuit style held sway; it aimed at dazzling the eye by wealth and variety of motive, without regard to the true function of ornament, which is to emphasise form. This was the period

135

of decoration treated as an end in itself, introduced everywhere and in the most contradictory fashion, resulting in feverish visions of

FIG. 206.—FAÇADE OF THE CERTOSA, PAVIA.

tortured lines and unexpected reliefs. The genius of the Renaissance succumbed at last in this decorative orgy, though down to the end of the eighteenth century it never ceased to produce buildings remarkable for their boldness or their elegance. As an example of the latter, we may mention the Palazzo Pesaro, or Bevilacqua, at Venice, where, in spite of the profusion of useless ornament, the eye is charmed by the nobility of the proportions and the playful fancy of the decorations (about 1650).

Just as Gothic architecture took but a feeble hold of Italy, so that of the Renaissance was not readily accepted by the northern nations. In France, as in Germany, it was introduced by princes and nobles; it was used for country houses and palaces long before it was adopted for churches. When at length it gained ground in these countries, the Italian Renaissance took on an individual character, a savour of the soil; the French and German architects emulated the Italians; they did not imitate them.

Many French buildings of the first half of the sixteenth century, formerly attributed to Italian artists, are, as documents in the archives have shown, the work of French architects. Among these was Pierre Chambiges, who built a part of the palace of Fontainebleau, and the *châteaux* of St. Germain and Chantilly, and also took part in the construction of the Hôtel de Ville of Paris, begun by Domenico da Cortona, called Il Boccador, in 1533.

The oldest monuments of the French Renaissance are the country mansions built in the valley of the Loire. They retain the high sloping roof, the towers, turrets, and spiral staircases of

FIG. 207.—BRAMANTE'S DESIGN FOR ST. PETER'S, ROME.

the Middle Ages; it is only in the decoration, especially that of the pilasters, that Italian influences are revealed.

In Germany, the resistance offered by national art was even more determined. Towns like Nuremberg, Hildesheim, and Augsburg preserved until the nineteenth century the high gabled houses which perpetuate the tradition of the Middle Ages, side by side with their Italianised churches and palaces (Fig. 211).

We need go no further than Paris to study the beautiful gate of the Château de Gaillon (1502–1510), built by the Cardinal d'Amboise, and now erected in the courtyard of the École des Beaux-Arts. A bolder example of the style is Chenonceaux, on the Cher (1512–1523), a well-preserved building, in which Gothic forms are everywhere perceptible, under the veil of Renaissance decoration (Fig. 212). The masterpiece of this style is Chambord, the work of Pierre Trinqueau (c. 1523), with its forest of chimneys and gables, a fairy apparition rising in the midst of a desolate sandy plain (Fig. 213).

FIG. 208.—LIBRARY OF ST. MARK'S, VENICE.

But if we examine it closely, we are struck by the incongruities of construction: a Gothic roof, a Renaissance main building, and massive Romanesque towers. The older parts of the Castle of Blois (especially on the north) abound in charming Renaissance details, still allied to Gothic elements (Fig. 214). Fontainebleau is more severe in style, even a trifle wearisome; the most severe of all Francis I.'s châteaux is that of St. Germain, where the austerity of the façade and the flat roof recall the Florentine palaces of the early Renaissance (Fig. 215).

The hybrid union of Gothic and Renaissance is found in several of the churches of this period, as, for instance, in St. Etienne-du-Mont (1517-1541-

FIG. 209.—VIEW OF ST. PETER'S, ROME.
With Bernini's Colonnade.

137

1610) and St. Eustache (1532) in Paris. Towards 1540 a purifica-
tion of style took place. Pierre Lescot, who worked at the Louvre

from the year 1546; Jean Bull-
ant (1515-1578), who built
Ecouen and began the Tui-
leries, completed by Philibert
Delorme, were thoroughly
saturated with the spirit of
the Italian Renaissance, but
they also developed a decorative and picturesque talent
which presaged the French
art of the seventeenth century.

Even in this rapid sketch
I cannot refrain from a passing reference to the Castle of
Heidelberg (1545-1607), the
masterpiece of the German Renaissance, a work which, while Italian
in decoration, remains profoundly Gothic in sentiment (Figs. 216, 217).

FIG. 210.—INTERIOR OF ST. PETER'S, ROME.
(Photo. by Alinari.)

An interesting phenomenon in the history of architecture is the
period of simplicity it entered upon in France between 1580 and
1650. The combination of stone and
brick gave an air of gaiety to the façades
of buildings, while at the same time the
suppression of mouldings and superfluous ornament diminished the cost
of labour. This style, applied to the
houses of the Place des Vosges, Paris,
and to the nucleus of the Castle of
Versailles, under Louis XIII., owed its
acceptance to economical exigencies,
when France was still suffering from the
miseries wrought by the religious wars;
but in its clarity and quiet dignity it
realised the classic ideal of Malherbe,
the literary reformer of the age.

The masterpiece of French Renaissance architecture, and perhaps of
all modern architecture, is the Louvre.
Of the many who have seen it, but few

FIG. 211.—HOUSE AT HILDESHEIM,
HANOVER.

know it, for its different portions date from various periods, and it
requires careful scrutiny to grasp the distinctive characteristics.

The Louvre is bounded on the north by the Rue de Rivoli, on the east by the Rue du Louvre, on the south by the quay, on the west by the Rue des Tuileries. We will begin with the northwest. From the Pavillon de Marsan, built under Louis XIV., to the angle of the courtyard of the Louvre, the whole was built by Napoleon I., Louis XVIII.,

FIG. 212.—CHATEAU OF CHENONCEAUX.

and Napoleon III., whose architects were Percier, Fontaine, Visconti, and Lefuel. The buildings that enclose the courtyard of the Louvre date from the reign of Louis XIV. (1660-1670), with the exception of the southwest angle, begun under Henry II., which is by Pierre Lescot (1546-1578), and the rest of the west side, including the Pavillon de Sully, or de l'Horloge, built in the reign of Louis XIII. On the quay, as

FIG. 213.—CHÂTEAU OF CHAMBORD.

far as the gateway of the Carrousel, the buildings date from the time of Catherine de' Medici (1566-1578). The rest of the Louvre on the riverside was constructed by Ducerceau under Henry IV., but was restored by Lefuel under Napoleon III. (1863-1868).

The part of the Louvre courtyard which we owe to Lescot (southwest) struck the note that was taken up by his successors, and it is not too much to say that this courtyard affords the most admirable view of a palace in existence (Fig. 218). On the outside, facing the Rue du Louvre, Louis XIV. commissioned Claude Perrault to build a long monotonous façade with

FIG. 214.—STAIRCASE IN THE CASTLE OF BLOIS.

139

double columns (Fig. 219), which gives the measure of the distance between the art of the French Renaissance and that of the age of Louis XIV.

FIG. 215.—SAINT GERMAIN-EN-LAYE.
(Restoration.)

Even the exquisite grace of a Lescot seemed frivolous to that age; its artists no longer sought inspiration in the Italy of the fifteenth century, but found their models in imperial Rome. The style then adopted is known as the *academic* style, because it was enforced mainly by the Academies of Sculpture, Painting, and Architecture, founded by Mazarin (1648) and by Colbert (1671). Perrault's colonnade and the façade of the Palace of Versailles, completed by Jules Hardouin Mansard (1646-1708), are memorable examples of this sad, solemn, and lofty style, in which

FIG. 216.—CASTLE OF HEIDELBERG.
Part built by the Elector-Palatine
Otto Henry (1556–1559).

FIG. 217.—CASTLE OF HEIDELBERG.
Part built by the Elector-Palatine
Frederick IV. (1601–1607).

symmetry is the supreme law and every picturesque and unexpected element is banished. Mansard's best work is the dome of the Invalides (1675-1706), which rises to a height of about 340 feet, the silhouette of which, at once elegant and majestic (Fig. 220), is much

finer than that of the Panthéon, by Soufflot (1757-1784). The imposing façade of St. Sulpice (1733) is the work of an Italian architect, Servandoni (Fig. 221). The two Garde-Meubles, on the Place de la Concorde, akin to Perrault's colonnade, but greatly superior

FIG. 218.—COURTYARD OF THE LOUVRE, WEST FRONT.

to it, are due to Gabriel, the best architect of the time of Louis XV. These fine buildings have one very unsuitable feature, the flat Italian roofs, so ill-adapted to the climate of Paris. As it is absolutely necessary to warm them, the roofs have been crowned by a forest of chimney-pots, which produce a somewhat grotesque effect.

Gothic architecture endured longer in England than elsewhere, and took a new lease of life under the name of Tudor Style (1485-1558). [To this transitional style belong the Royal Chapels, St. George's at Windsor and Henry VII.'s Chapel, Westminster Abbey (Fig. 222), with their unique system of fan-vaulting. Hamp-

FIG. 219.—COLONNADE OF THE LOUVRE.

ton Court Palace is a charming example of the Tudor Style as applied to domestic architecture (Fig. 234).] Renaissance architecture only

FIG. 220.—THE DOME OF THE INVALIDES, PARIS.

flourished in the time of the Stuarts [Charles I.], when it was represented principally by Inigo Jones (1572-1662), the author of the beautiful Banqueting Hall of Whitehall, London (Fig. 223), and by Christopher Wren (1632-1723), the architect of the vast church of St. Paul's, a building inspired by St. Peter's at Rome, though not copied from it (Fig. 224).

The delightful art of the eighteenth century showed its influence on architecture only in little sylvan buildings and in interiors. The origin of the style known as Rococo is probably to be found in the ornamentation of woodwork, which passed from furniture to rooms. Pilasters, colonnades, and flat mouldings disappear, and are replaced by garlands, festoons, shells, a profusion of sinuous lines entwining and interlacing; every detail of ornament aims at coming as a surprise to the spectator. With all this we find an exquisite sense of proportion and marvellous dexterity of execution (Fig. 225).

FIG. 221.—ST. SULPICE, PARIS.

At the outset of Louis XVI.'s reign a reaction, which had been in process of preparation from about the year 1760, declared itself; this was the revival of the Academic Style, improperly called the Empire Style, because it reached its apogee under Napoleon I. Here, again, it was not the Italy of the Renaissance which gave the example; the antique was the avowed source of inspiration, and architects even ventured to set up in Paris copies of Roman

FIG. 222.—HENRY VII.'S CHAPEL, WESTMINSTER ABBEY.
(Photo. by Spooner.)

monuments, such as the Madeleine (begun in 1764), the triumphal arches of the Carrousel and of the Étoile (Fig. 226), and the Vendôme column. One general even proposed, about the year 1798, to bring the Trajan column to Paris.

These were errors of taste that had never been committed during the Renaissance. The qualities of the Empire style are purely executive; invention and sentiment have no part in them. Under the Restoration and the July Monarchy these qualities were lost, and no compensating originality replaced them. Happily, this disastrous mania for the imitation of the antique was

FIG. 223.—BANQUETING HALL, WHITEHALL, LONDON.
(Photo. by Spooner.)

tempered in certain artists— notably Duban, the author of the École des Beaux-Arts, completed about 1860—by a delicate feeling for detail derived from the direct study of Greek monuments, and by a return to the severe elegance of great Florentines such as Brunellesco and Bramante (Fig. 227).

At the same time, Viollet-le-Duc, a learned writer of the highest order, who was also a distinguished architect, boldly enounced the programme of a new architecture, emancipated from the exclusive cult of past styles, and seeking its way in the rational satisfaction of modern wants. He foretold the advent of construction in iron, and its promotion from the domain of industry to that of art. Labrouste, in the Bibliothèque Ste. Geneviève, and the Reading Room of the Bibliothèque Nationale (1859), and Duc, in the Salle des Pas

FIG. 224.—ST. PAUL'S CATHEDRAL, LONDON.

Perdus of the Palais de Justice, admirable constructions well suited to their respective uses, seem to have been inspired by these ideas, which did not reach full fruition till much later.

143

FIG. 225.—DECORATIVE PANEL IN THE CHÂTEAU OF VERSAILLES.

The close of the Second Empire witnessed a revival of Italian architecture, especially the Venetian architecture of the sixteenth and seventeenth centuries, to which are due Ballu's Church of La Trinité and Garnier's Grand Opera House (Fig. 228). This tendency still persists, modified by a rather more severe taste. The last important buildings erected in Paris, the Grand Palais and the Petit Palais (Fig. 229), are Renaissance buildings, the decorative elements in which are borrowed from antiquity, but which are no mere copies of Greek or Roman monuments. On the other hand, works of metallic architecture, which have multiplied rapidly since 1878, mark a more or less deliberate reaction against the traditional art of the schools. Engineering feats, like the Tour Eiffel and the Palais des Machines, with their soaring vertical lines, the marked predominance of empty spaces over solid surfaces, and the lightness of their frankly displayed framework, are much more closely akin to the conceptions of Gothic architecture, a renaissance of which, in different materials, and governed by a secular spirit, is quite among the possibilities of the future.

The examples I have given here are mainly French. I have chosen these as conveniently typical, and not because other countries have not also produced notable monuments, as the vast Escorial palace, the first monument of Renaissance architecture in Spain. In the case of these, I can only indicate the filiation of styles. The German Renaissance,

FIG. 226.—ARC DE TRIOMPHE DE L'ÉTOILE, PARIS.

144

interrupted by the Thirty Years' War, was followed by the imitation of French and Italian styles, by the Academic, the Baroque, and the Rococo styles.

The finest example of the Baroque style in Germany is the Pavilion of the Zwinger (bastion) at Dresden (Fig. 230), the work of Pöppelmann (1715). The builder of the Royal Palace of Berlin, Andreas Schlüter (d.1714),

FIG. 227.—COURTYARD OF THE ÉCOLE DES BEAUX-ARTS, PARIS.

author of the fine bronze statue of the Great Elector in the same city, revealed superior gifts in unfavourable surroundings. In the nineteenth century with Schinkel and Klenze the neo-Greek style, cold like all imitations, wearisome like all anachronisms, dominates at Berlin and Munich. Meanwhile, at Dresden and at Vienna, a new evolution in the direction of the Italian Renaissance took place about 1850. It is to this movement that Vienna owes her fine modern buildings, notably the two Imperial Museums by Semper and Hasenauer (Fig. 231).

FIG. 228.—FAÇADE OF THE OPERA HOUSE, PARIS.

[In England, the national variant of the Renaissance style was carried on in the eighteenth century by the followers of Wren, Vanbrugh, Colin Campbell, Kent, Lord Burlington, Gibbs, and the Brothers Adam. *Pari passu* with the architecture of these men advanced a charming style of furniture and decoration, of which Sheraton, Chippendale, and Hepplewhite were the chief exponents. On their works the style so greatly in vogue at the present day is based. The neo-Greek style, suggested by the publications of Stuart, Revett, and others, followed closely upon this renaissance; the Baroque and Rococo styles were hardly known in England.] Then, as if by way of return to the national style, there was a recrudescence of perpendicular Gothic, the most important example of which is the Houses of Parliament (Fig. 232), built by Barry

FIG. 229.—THE PETIT PALAIS, PARIS.

on the banks of the Thames (1840-1860). Finally Belgium raised in the nineteenth century the most huge accumulation of freestone in Europe, the Palais de Justice at Brussels (Fig. 233), in style a conglomeration of Assyrian and Renaissance influences, the effect of

FIG. 230—PAVILION OF THE ZWINGER, DRESDEN.
(Lübke, *Architektur*, Seemann, Leipzig.)

FIG. 231.—NEW IMPERIAL MUSEUM, VIENNA.
(*L'Art en Tableaux*, Seemann, Leipzig.)

which is by no means proportionate to the vast expense and labour involved.

RENAISSANCE AND MODERN ARCHITECTURE

Nevertheless, in England and Belgium there has sprung up within the last few years a new style, which seems destined to put an end to the imitation of antique and Renaissance models in our day, even more effectually than the introduction of iron buildings. It was in England, under the influence of the æsthetic writer Ruskin, William Morris, and other artists, seconded by the painters Burne-Jones and Walter Crane, that

FIG. 232.—HOUSES OF PARLIAMENT, LONDON.

FIG. 233.—PALAIS DE JUSTICE, BRUSSELS.

the movement originated which transformed the interiors of houses, substituting for trite and conventional models, in furniture, hangings, and applied ornaments, expressive forms, or at least forms which are intended to be expressive. Then two Belgian architects, Hankar and Horta, ventured, towards the year 1893, to apply equally bold principles to external decoration, waging war upon imitation and breaking with all tradition. An Austrian, Otto

FIG. 234.—WEST SIDE OF THE GREAT QUADRANGLE, HAMPTON COURT PALACE.
(Photo. by Spooner.)

147

APOLLO

Wagner, became acquainted with this Belgian movement, and initiated a new school of construction at Vienna, to which the term "Secessionist" was applied, a name which sufficiently indicates its independent and even rebellious character. From Vienna, the "heresy" spread to Berlin, Darmstadt, and even Paris, but so far the new style has had no opportunity of manifesting itself there in a public building. To define this new Anglo-Austro-Belgian style would be almost impossible, for it has no credo, and seeks its way in very diverse directions. But its existence is a well-established fact, which proclaims itself in the disposition and arrangement of private buildings. In its determination to belong to its own times, to reject anachronisms, it is related, in spite of individual aberrations, to the great programme of good sense and good taste laid down about 1860 by Viollet-le-Duc.

BIBLIOGRAPHY OF CHAPTER XIV.

W. Lübke, *Geschichte der Architektur*, 6th ed., 2 vols., Leipzig, 1886; E. Müntz, *Histoire de l'Art pendant la Renaissance*, 3 vols., Paris, 1889–1891; E. Hänel, *Spätgothik und Renaissance*, Stuttgart, 1899; J. Durm, *Die Baukunst der Renaissance in Italien*, Stuttgart, 1903; A. G. Meyer, *Oberitalienische Frührenaissance*, Berlin, 1896; L. Palustre, *La Renaissance en France* (*Le Nord*, 2 vols., Bretagne, 1 vol.), Paris, 1879–1888; *L'Archit. de la Renaissance*, Paris, no date; W. H. Ward, *Architecture of the Renaissance in France*, London, 1911; W. Lübke, *Geschichte der Renaissance in Frankreich* (*Architektur*), Stuttgart 1883; H. von Geymüller *Die Baukunst der Renaissance in Frankreich*, Stuttgart, 1901; M. Vachon, *L'Hôtel de Ville de Paris*, (*Bulletin Monumental*, 1903, p. 438); G. von Bezold, *Die Baukunst der Renaissance in Deutschland, Holland, Belgien und Dänemark*, Stuttgart, 1899; M. Reymond, *Les Débuts de l'Architecture de la Renaissance* (*Gazette*, 1900, i., p. 89); H. Moore, *Renaissance Architecture*, London, 1905; A. Doren, *Zum Bau der Florentiner Domkuppel* (*Repertorium*, 1898, p. 249); J. Wood Brown, *The Builders of Florence*, London, 1908; C. von Fabriczy. *Fil. Brunelleschi*, Stuttgart, 1892; M. Reymond, *Brunelleschi*, Paris, 1912; L. Scott, *Brunellesco*, London, 1902; Luca Beltrami, *Storia Docum. della Certosa di Pavia*, Milan, 1896; A. G. Meyer, *Die Certosa bei Pavia*, Berlin, 1900; Aug. Schmarsow, *Barok und Rokoko*, Leipzig, 1896; Gust. Eve, *Die Schmuckformen der Monumentalbauten, VI. Spätrenaissance und Barockperiode*, Berlin, 1896; L. Milman, *Christopher Wren*, London, 1908; C. Gurlitt and M. Junghändel, *Die Baukunst der Spanier*, Dresden, 1899; A. F. Calvert, *Moorish Remains in Spain*, London, 1906; A. Haupt, *Die Baukunst der Renaissance in Portugal*, 2 vols., Frankfort, 1894; C. Justi, *Philipp II. als Kunstfreund* (*Zeitschrift für bildende Kunst*, 1881, p. 342, on the Escorial); M. Rosenberg, *Quellen zur Geschichte des Heidelberger Schlosses*, Heidelberg, 1882; A. Haupt, *Peter Flettner, der erste Meister des Otto-Heinrichbaus zu Heidelberg*, Leipzig, 1904 (cf. *Repertorium*, 1905, p. 63).

H. Clouzot, *Philibert de Lorme*, Paris, 1910; H. Guerlin, *Chambord*, Paris, 1912; C. Lemmonier, *Philibert de Lorme* (*Revue de l'Art*, 1898, i., p. 123); Cᵗᵉ de Clarac, *Le Louvre et les Tuileries* (vol. i. of the text of the *Musée de Sculpture*), Paris, 1841; A. Babeau, *Le Louvre*, Paris, 1895; L. Vitet, *Le Nouveau Louvre* (*Revue des Deux Mondes*, July 1, 1866); E. Bonnefon, *Claude Perrault* (*Gazette*, 1901, ii., p. 209); P. de Nolhac, *Histoire du Château de Versailles*, Paris, 1899; *La Création de Versailles* (*Revue de l'Art*, 1898, i., p. 399); *Le Versailles de Mansart* (*Gazette*, 1902, i., p. 209); L. Courajod, *Leçons professées au Ecole du Louvre*, vol. iii., Paris, 1903 (*Origines de l'Art moderne, rococo, baroque, style jésuite, académisme*); Lady E. Dilke, *French Architects and Sculptors of the XVIIIth Century*, London, 1900; F. de Fels, *Gabriel*, Paris, 1912; F. Mazerolle, *J. D. Antoine, architecte de la Monnaie* (*Réunion des Sociétés savants des Beaux-Arts*, 1897, p. 1038); R. Milès, *Les Maisons de plaisance du XVIIIᵉ siècle*, Paris, 1900; C. Sédille, *Charles Garnier* (*Gazette*, 1898, ii., p. 341); O. Reichelt, *Das Zwingergebäude in Dresden* (*Deutsche Bauzeitung*, 1898, p. 410); H. Ziller, *Schinkel*, Bielefeld, 1896; L. Gonse, *Les Nouveaux Palais des Musées à Vienne* (*Gazette*, 1891, i., p. 353); C. Sédille, *L'Architecture moderne en Angleterre* (*Gazette*, 1886, i., p. 89); H. Fiérens-Gevaert, *Nouveaux Essais sur l'Art contemporain*, Paris, 1903 (on the new Austro-Belgian school, and kindred tendencies); D. Joseph, *Geschichte der Baukunst des XIX Jahvh.*, 2 vols., Leipzig, 1910; A. de Bandot, *L'Architecture et le ciment armé*, Paris, 1905.

XV

THE RENAISSANCE AT SIENA AND FLORENCE

The Renaissance in Italy no mere Revival of Classicism.—The First Renaissance the Logical Development of Gothic Art.—The Apulian School of Sculptors.—Niccolà Pisano.—The Legend of Cimabue and Giotto a Myth.—Duccio of Siena and his School.—Giotto and his Frescoes at Assisi and Florence.—The Giotteschi.—Fra Angelico and Benozzo Gozzoli.—Masaccio, Paolo Uccello, Andrea del Castagno.—Verrocchio, Sculptor and Painter.—Botticelli.—Ghirlandajo.—Filippino Lippi.—Piero di Cosimo and Lorenzo di Credi.—Piero dei Franceschi and Luca Signorelli.—The Character of Florentine Painting.—Florentine Sculpture.—Donatello, Verrocchio, Desiderio da Settignano.—Jacopo della Quercia.—Luca della Robbia.—Andrea Sansovino.—Fifteenth Century Florence compared with the Athens of Pericles.—The Living, or Tactile Quality of the Highest Art.

THE plastic and pictorial art of the Renaissance is not to be defined as an imitation of classic models. In Italy, as in the north and east of France, there was an initial Renaissance in the fourteenth century, which owed little, if anything, to antiquity. It was the logical development of the great Gothic style, passing gradually to naturalism, from the art of the *imagiers* under St. Louis, to that of the por-

FIG. 235.—THE CRUCIFIXION.
NICCOLÀ PISANO.
(Pulpit in the Baptistery at Pisa.)

traitists of the time of Charles V. Gothic naturalism found its way into Italy, and awoke Italian realism, which had been slumbering for ten centuries (*cf.* p. 91). But whereas in France and Flanders, naturalism was unbridled and soon degenerated into triviality, in Italy, thanks to the dawn of Humanism and the study of antique examples, it was chastened and disciplined, and learned to desire beauty even

FIG. 236.—THE NATIVITY.
NICCOLÀ PISANO.
(Pulpit in the Baptistery at Pisa.)

before expression. Thus the part played by antiquity was that of a teacher, not of a mother; it regulated, but it did not create, the Renaissance.

FIG. 237.—CHRIST BEFORE PILATE. DUCCIO.
(Siena Cathedral.)
(Photo. by Lombardi.)

One art does not act upon another by mere propinquity. Before any such action takes place, the second must have reached a point in its natural evolution at which it is peculiarly sensitive to the first. From the fifth to the fifteenth century it never occurred to the Italians to imitate their antique buildings; they used them merely as quarries. A barbaric Rome rose side by side with imperial Rome. About the year 1240, a school of sculptors and engravers, who took as their models the busts and coins of the Roman Empire, rose in Apulia, under the fostering guidance of the Emperor Frederick II. This school lasted barely forty years. Niccolà of Apulia, an artist who had worked for Frederick, and who was afterwards more famous as Niccolà Pisano, came to Pisa, and there, in 1260, carved the pulpit of the Baptistery, a work which, while Gothic in form, is decorated with bas-reliefs so skilfully imitated from those on Roman sarcophagi that they might easily be mistaken for antiques (Figs. 235 and 236). He shows himself no less facile an imitator in decorating a pulpit of the Siena Cathedral (1268). This astounding resurrection of the antique ideal is an isolated phenomenon, and bore no fruit. Niccolà's own son, Giovanni Pisano, was a pure realist of the Gothic school, who probably drew his inspiration from French and Rhenish sources. Before Italy became susceptible to the

FIG. 238.—HEROD'S FEAST.
GIOTTO.
(Church of S. Croce, Florence.)

teachings of her Roman past, she had to pass through a Gothic period, of which the first Renaissance, made memorable by Giotto and Duccio, marks, not the close, but the apogee. Indeed, the Gothic spirit, modified by the influences of Flanders and the valley of the Rhine, did not die out in Italy till the sixteenth century. It was only then that Græco-Roman æsthetics definitely prevailed, and inaugurated the propagandist movement which has assured its domination down to our own times.[1]

In the middle of the sixteenth century it was generally believed in Florence that certain Byzantine painters, who had been summoned to the town about the year 1260,

FIG. 239.—THE ANNUNCIATION.
FRA ANGELICO.
(Church of Cortona.)

awakened the latent talent of Cimabue, and that this artist was the first Italian painter, just as Adam was the first man. The legend went on to tell how Cimabue, in his turn, discovered the genius of the shepherd, Giotto, by seeing him draw the outline of a sheep on the rock with a sharp stone. These tales are mere fables. Cimabue was a worker in mosaic; no authenticated pictures by him are known to us. Siena, the rival city of Florence, produced the first Italian painter of genius, Duccio, who had evidently seen and studied the Byzantine paintings and enamels (1255-1319). Duccio combined with a sense of grandiose composition a broad, if as yet not very delicate, feeling for line (Fig. 237). He was the

FIG. 240.—THE CORONATION OF THE VIRGIN.
FRA ANGELICO.
(The Louvre.)

[1] These ideas, which I have summed up in a few lines, were formulated by Léon de Laborde in 1849, and further developed by Courajod in 1890.

first to translate into true pictures, that is to say, expressive group-
ings of figures, the painted chronicles of the Middle Ages, which pious
souls had spelt out for centuries as a kind of Bible for the unlettered.

FIG. 241.—THE ADORATION OF THE MAGI.
BENOZZO GOZZOLI.
(Palazzo Riccardi, Florence.)

Duccio was the progenitor
of a numerous family of painters at Siena, among them Simone Martini, called Memmi,
the Lorenzetti, and Taddeo
Bartolo, who, though they did
not equal the Florentines in
power, surpassed them perhaps
in passion, poetry, and tenderness. A little Sienese picture
of the highest quality is a
feast for the eyes; but works
of the first rank are rare in
this school, which produced
too quickly and too abun-
dantly. The weakness of the Sienese school was, that it aimed
rather at expression and emotion than at perfection of form, that
it "marked time," so to speak, and was incapable of following
the Florentines on the salutary path of naturalism while preserv-
ing its distinctive charm. By the middle of the fifteenth century, the vitality of the Sienese school was exhausted. Thence-

FIG. 242.—THE MEDICI WATCHING THE BUILDING
OF THE TOWER OF BABEL.
BENOZZO GOZZOLI.
(Fresco in the Campo Santo, Pisa.)

forth, Florence, who had learnt
from her in the beginning, sent
artists to her.

The first of the great Florentine painters was Giotto,
who died in 1336. His real
master seems to have been the
Roman mosaicist, Pietro Cavallini, admirable frescoes by
whom have recently been discovered in Rome (S. Cecilia in
Trastevere). To understand
Giotto it is necessary to study
his frescoes; but the excellent
picture by him in the Louvre,
St. Francis receiving the Stigmata, gives some idea of his powers.
Giotto's drawing is not always correct, his draperies are sometimes
heavy and his heads vulgar; but with what clarity and poetry

he expresses what he has to say!
Giotto's frescoes at Assisi, illustrating the life of St. Francis, and those at Padua and in the Church of Santa Croce at Florence (Fig. 238) are among the most charming achievements of painting, although not one of the figures they contain is above criticism.

Giotto was inspired by the Gothic masters, notably by Giovanni Pisano (d. 1329), but, above all, by Nature. His disciples were nearly all merely *Giottesques*, who escaped from the salutary contact with realities. Their very prolific school extended throughout Italy. It produced many ingenious and inventive illustrators, such as the unknown painters of the great frescoes in the Campo Santo of Pisa; but, preoccupied above all with narrative, they made no

FIG. 243.—SS. PETER AND JOHN GIVING ALMS.
MASACCIO.
(Church of the Carmine, Florence.)

progress towards greater purity and precision of form. Giottism produced but one great artist, the monk Fra Angelico, of Fiesole (1387-1455), and even he was influenced by Masaccio,

FIG. 245.—THE LAST SUPPER.
ANDREA DEL CASTAGNO.
(Sant' Apollonia, Florence.)

an uncompromising realist. Fra Angelico was the painter *par excellence* of Christianity as preached by St. Francis of Assisi. The joys of belief, the happiness of suffering for the

FIG. 244.—PORTRAIT OF PIPPO SPANO.
ANDREA DEL CASTAGNO.
(Sant' Apollonia, Florence.)

153

APOLLO

FIG. 246.—MADONNA WITH TWO SAINTS.
VERROCCHIO AND LORENZO DI CREDI.
(Pistoia Cathedral.) (Photo. by Alinari.)

faith, the beatitude of the elect, have never been more eloquently expressed than by him. He was also, though this has been often overlooked, a learned painter, whose knowledge of the human form was far greater than that of Giotto; but his mystic lyre had but few chords. There is a certain insipidity in his genius, the reflection of a somewhat puerile soul, whose outlook was bounded by the walls of a cloister. His suave virgins and angels delight us at first, and finally pall on us; we long for a few wolves in this impeccable sheepfold (Figs. 239-240). Fra Angelico's best pupil, Benozzo Gozzoli (1420-1498) reveals himself as the most exquisite and naïve storyteller

FIG. 247.—FRAGMENT OF THE CORONA-
TION OF THE VIRGIN.
FILIPPO LIPPI.
(Florence.)
(Photo. by Anderson.)

FIG. 248.—VIRGIN AND CHILD WITH TWO
ANGELS.
VERROCCHIO.
(National Gallery, London.)
(Photo. by Hanfstaengl.)

154

of the Renaissance in his frescoes in the Palazzo Riccardi at Florence; his visions of the world are the golden dreams of a child (Figs. 241, 242). But the world is not peopled by children, nor can it live by golden dreams alone.

Giottism would have dragged down Florentine art to the puerility of pietistic illustration, if the naturalism so brilliantly vindicated by Donatello in sculpture had not also found a great pictorial interpreter in Masaccio (1401-428). The Brancacci Chapel, in the Church of the Carmine at Florence, decorated by Masaccio with frescoes, was a source of virile inspiration to all the Florentine artists of the fifteenth century (Fig. 243). His contemporaries, Paolo Uccello, the first painter of battles and of perspective, and Andrea del' Castagno, a master of almost brutal vigour, completed the work begun by him and disgusted the Florentines with insipidity (Figs. 244, 245). Fra Filippo Lippi, another monk, but a monk who had not altogether broken with the world (1406-1469), was, as it were, the synthesis of Fra Angelico and Masaccio; strength—still somewhat rugged in its vigour — is happily married to tenderness in his best works, examples of which are to be seen both in the National Gallery of London and the Louvre (Fig. 247). Verrocchio (1435-1488), who is best known as a sculptor, proves himself a master of

FIG. 250.—ALLEGORY OF SPRING.
BOTTICELLI.
(Academy, Florence.)

line in his rare pictures (Figs. 246, 248); he was, moreover, the first of the Florentines to understand landscape, and the part played

FIG. 251.—MADONNA AND ANGELS
BOTTICELLI.
Ambrosiana, Milan. (Photo. by Alinari.)

therein not only by forms, but by light and air. We must not, however, forget that twenty years before the birth of Verrocchio, the Van Eycks had painted exquisite landscapes in Flanders. Italian art, as Courajod has well said, was the favoured child, but not the eldest one of the Renaissance.

Botticelli (1444-1510), a somewhat younger master than Verrocchio, was the pupil of Fra Filippo, but, like Verrocchio, he was much influenced by the realist, Antonio Pollaiuolo (Fig. 249), a pupil of Donatello and of Uccello. He was one of the most original of painters, a creative genius, but fantastic, restless, and vehement, an artist who, in his passion for expressive line, often overshot the mark, and became violent rather than suggestive. The very mixed pleasure caused by his works is a kind of nervous vibration or hyperæsthesia. We have heard of the " superman," a creation of the disordered brain of Nietzsche; Botticelli may be styled the "super-painter." Without being a colourist, without even desiring to be one, he succeeds in emphasising the continuous and contagious *tremolo* of his line by colour. When he is at his best, as in the *Spring*, at Florence, he gives us the most perfect expression of Humanism, the very quintessence of Florentine distinction. (Figs. 250, 251.)

FIG. 252.—THE VISITATION.
D. GHIRLANDAJO.
(The Louvre.)

Botticelli has found his most fervent adorers among the neurasthenic spirits of the close of the nineteenth century. They fall into ecstatic swoons (for this is the fashion in which such persons proclaim admiration), as they contemplate, not only his defects, but those of his coarsest imitators. To recognise the real strength and the subtle vitality of his art, the equipment of a connoisseur is necessary.

Two painters of the most amazing facility, ingenious, graceful, and pellucid, admirably summed up the amiable qualities of the High Renaissance in Italy. The older of these, Domenico Ghirlandajo (1449-1494) is a somewhat suaver Verrocchio, whose large religious compositions are enlivened by gay and transparent colour (Figs. 252-254). One of his

FIG. 253.—ADORATION OF THE MAGI.
D. GHIRLANDAJO.
(Church of the Innocents, Florence.)
(Photo. by Alinari.)

masterpieces, the *Visitation*, is in the Louvre. The younger artist, Filippino Lippi, is not represented there, but may be studied in two fine examples in the National Gallery. The son of Fra Filippo Lippi and the pupil of Botticelli, he was to his master

FIG. 254.—THE BIRTH OF JOHN THE BAPTIST.
D. GHIRLANDAJO.
(Church of Santa Maria Novella, Florence.)

what Ghirlandajo was to Verrocchio. A very gifted, though uninventive artist, he has given several exquisite works to painting, the best of which is the *Virgin appearing to St. Bernard*, in the Badia at Florence (Figs. 255-257). To the same group of artists belongs Piero di Cosimo, the creator of charming idylls, an exquisite portrait-painter, and Lorenzo di Credi, the unequal fellow-student of Leonardo, whose large picture, painted in collaboration with his master, Verrocchio, adorns the Cathedral of Pistoia (Fig. 246).

The two giants of the Florentine Renaissance, Leonardo da Vinci and Michelangelo, must be reserved for special consideration. But there are two masters, of S o u t h e r n Tuscany and the Romagna respectively, whom we must mention here: Piero dei Franceschi and his pupil, Luca Signorelli.

Piero (1416-1462), master of the graceful Melozzo, cold

FIG. 255.—THE ADORATION OF THE MAGI.
FILIPPINO LIPPI.
(Uffizi, Florence.)

and impersonal, occupies a place apart in Italian art; there is something spectral and disquieting, together with a touch of melancholy disdain, in his pale straight figures (Fig. 258). Signorelli (1441-1523) is the Dante of fifteenth century painting; he, too, is sad, and almost fierce in his energy, even in the rendering of his admirable Virgins with their powerful chins. There is tenderness under this mask of strength, but it conceals itself. His *End of the World* (Fig. 262), in the Cathedral of Orvieto, presages Michelangelo's *Last Judgment* in the Sistine Chapel. His *Education of Pan*, in the Berlin Museum, is a masterpiece of severe and sculpturesque design (Fig. 260).

Thus we see that Florentine painting moves between two extremes, mystic suavity and melancholy power. It is a perfect reflection of an agi-

FIG. 256.—THE VIRGIN APPEARING TO ST. BERNARD.
FILIPPINO LIPPI.
(Church of the Badia, Florence.)
(Woermann, *Geschichte der Malerei*, Seemann, Leipzig.)

THE RENAISSANCE AT SIENA AND FLORENCE

tated society, fevered by luxury and enjoyment, and afire with civil discords, a society in which the fanatical Christianity of a Savonarola jostled the almost pagan Humanism of the Medicean Court. Classic art gave it lessons in design, and furnished it with examples of the correct interpretation of forms, but left it entirely untouched by its spirit. All the roots of the Florentine soul were deep-set in the Middle Ages; it was neither Greek nor Roman, because it was still profoundly religious, alternately illumined

FIG. 257.—THE VIRGIN ADORING THE INFANT CHRIST.
SCHOOL OF FILIPPINO LIPPI.
(Pitti Palace, Florence.)   (Photo. by Alinari.)

and obscured by the radiant or terrible visions of another world.

Florentine sculpture began with Lorenzo Ghiberti (1378–1465), who modelled the marvellous series of scriptural bas-reliefs which decorate the two great bronze doors of the Baptistery at Florence,

FIG. 258.—THE DREAM OF CONSTANTINE.
PIERO DEI FRANCESCHI.
(Church of S. Francesco, Arezzo.)

between 1405 and 1452. Of the second, Michelangelo said that it was worthy to figure on the gates of Paradise (Fig. 263). These bas-reliefs are treated pictorially, with plans in perspective, and the more distant figures in lower relief than the rest. Like Masaccio's frescoes, they were a source of inspiration to the whole Florentine School.

At the same period, the great Donatello (1386–1466) set the example of a vivid naturalism in his statues of saints, his portraits, and his bas-reliefs, as well as that of an exquisite grace in the representation of childhood (Figs. 264–267). Donatello's naturalism is seen in the manner in which he

159

gave life in bronze or marble to models conforming to the Florentine ideal, slender, muscular, energetic, and expressive from head to foot. This ideal is almost the antithesis of that of classical antiquity, but it is identical with that of modern art, emancipated from academic bondage. Rodin and Constantin Meunier are the heirs of Donatello, who is himself much more akin to the Gothic masters than to the Greeks.

One of Donatello's pupils, Verrocchio (1435–1485), was both painter and sculptor. The master of Leonardo da Vinci, of Lorenzo di Credi, and many others, he created the most beautiful equestrian figure of the Renaissance, the statue of the *condottiere* Colleone, at Venice (1479) (Fig. 268). I do not except even Donatello's *Gattemalata* at Padua.

Another pupil of Donatello's, Desiderio da Settignano (Fig. 269), who died young, in 1464, was the leader of a fascinating group of workers in marble, suaver and more idealistic than Donatello, who has left us heads of the Virgin, and portraits of women and children, marked by a sweetness

FIG. 260.—THE EDUCATION OF PAN.
LUCA SIGNORELLI.
(Museum, Berlin.)   (Photo. by Hanfstaengl.)

160

veiled with sadness, and touched by a sentiment quite unknown to antique art. To this group belong Mino da Fiesole (d. 1484), Antonio Rossellino (d. 1478), and Benedetto da Majano (d. 1497). They were chiefly employed on portraits, votive bas-reliefs, altars, and tombs in churches (Figs. 270–272).

Jacopo della Quercia of Siena, contemporary with Donatello, was Michelangelo's exemplar. A powerful and original sculptor, he was certainly influenced

FIG. 261.—MARY SALOME.
LUCA SIGNORELLI.
(Fragment of a Crucifixion at Borgo San Sepolcro.) (Photo. by Alinari.)

by Flemish and Burgundian realism. The delightful artist, Luca della Robbia, whose glazed polychrome bas-reliefs afforded one of the sources of Raphael's inspiration, worked at Florence itself; other members of his family, Giovanni and Andrea, carried on the manufacture of these glazed terra-cottas till about the year 1530. Jacopo Tatti, called Sansovino (1486–1570), the pupil of Andrea Sansovino (Fig. 277) gave noble expression to the

FIG. 262.—THE DAMNED.
SIGNORELLI.
Fragment of Fresco at Orvieto.
(Photo. by Anderson.)

FIG. 263.—THE STORY OF ISAAC AND JACOB.
GHIBERTI.
(Second Gate of the Baptistery, Florence.)

FIG. 264.—DAVID.
DONATELLO.
(Florence.)

FIG. 265.—ST. JOHN.
DONATELLO.
(Duomo, Florence.)

plastic genius of the Renaissance, because, like Raphael in painting, he was able to reconcile the classic and the Christian spirit (Fig. 276).

Nearly all the great works of the Florentine sculptors have remained in their native land, whereas those of the painters have migrated to the museums of other countries in large numbers. Hence it is that the former are less widely known, though they are no less worthy of fame. Even had the painting of the fifteenth century disappeared like Greek painting, the whole genius of the Renaissance would still survive in the works of the great Florentine sculptors.

But what a difference there is between Florence, the Athens of the fifteenth century, and the Athens of Pericles! At Florence, there is no serenity, nothing which attests a happy equilibrium between the faculties of the mind and the feelings; now we have an agitated, poignant, almost painful realism, now a languorous grace, melancholy even in the rendering of joy. For between Athens and Florence stood Christianity, a purely spiritual religion, which deifies suffering and anathematises the flesh. After the dry, dogmatic phase which ended in the thirteenth century, Christianity became,

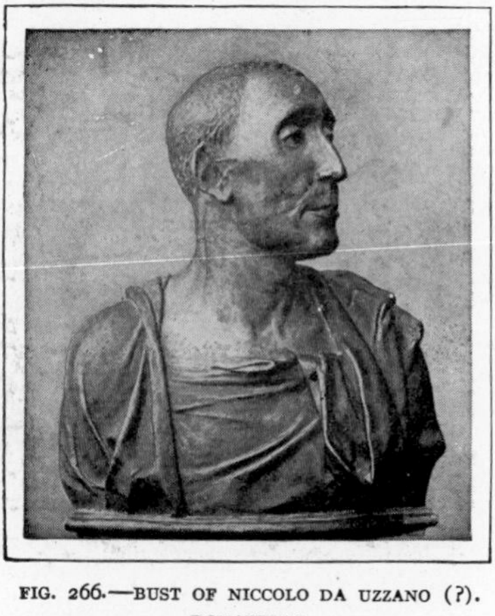

FIG. 266.—BUST OF NICCOLO DA UZZANO (?).
DONATELLO.
(Museum, Florence.)

FIG. 267.—ANGEL WITH
TAMBOURINE.
DONATELLO.
(Berlin Museum.)   (Photo., Seemann.)

FIG. 268.—EQUESTRIAN STATUE OF
COLLEONE.
VERROCCHIO.
(Venice.)

FIG. 269.—MADONNA AND CHILD.
DESIDERIO DA SETTIGNANO.
(Florence.)

FIG. 270.—MADONNA WITH SAINTS.
MINO DA FIESOLE.
(Cathedral, Fiesole.)

FIG. 271.—THE NATIVITY.
A. ROSSELLINO.
(Church of Monte Oliveto, Naples.)
(Photo. by Alinari.)

FIG. 272.—THE ANNUNCIATION.
BENEDETTO DA MAJANO.
(Church of Monte Oliveto, Naples.)
(Photo. by Alinari.)

thanks mainly to St. Francis of Assisi (d. 1226), a religion of mystic tenderness and fervid asceticism. In an estimate of the art of the High Renaissance, it is impossible to overstate the importance of the moral revolution accomplished by the disciples of St. Francis.

FIG. 273.—ADAM AND EVE.
JACOPO DELLA QUERCIA.
(Church of San Petronio, Bologna.)

The dominant quality of Florentine sculpture, a quality to be recognised also, though less definitely, in the painting, is the delicate firmness of the lines, a something we might call their *quality*. Why is it that the copy of a masterpiece is rarely itself a masterpiece? It is because the personal sentiment of a great artist manifests itself not only in the invention and disposition of the figures, but in the infinitely subtle shades of form which escape the attention of a copyist. A very just distinction has been drawn between *living* lines and surfaces, and *dead* lines and surfaces. Only the first have what a contemporary critic, Mr. Berenson, calls *tactile* values, that is to say, the almost imperceptible quiver of life, the effect of which on the eye is analogous to that of living flesh against the finger-tips. An artist of genius has the faculty of infusing life into each sinuosity of contour, each square inch of surface. In a work of art the presence of dead lines and surfaces, that is to say, of flat or rounded surfaces, insignificant and void of expression, suffices to show that it is either

FIG. 274.—THE MADONNA WITH TWO SAINTS.
LUCA DELLA ROBBIA.
(Cathedral, Prato.)

a copy, or the work of a mediocre artist. In this connection there is nothing more instructive than such a comparison as may be made in the Louvre between one of Michelangelo's *Slaves*, in which every inch of the marble seems to vibrate, and a statue of Canova's

FIG. 275.—THE VISITATION.
ANDREA DELLA ROBBIA.
(Church of San Giovanni, Pistoja.)

FIG. 276.—BACCHUS.
JACOPO SANSOVINO.
(Museum, Florence.)

APOLLO

FIG. 277.—TOMB OF CARDINALS
SFORZA AND DELLA ROVERE.
ANDREA SANSOVINO
(Church of S. Maria del Popolo, Rome.)

or Pradier's, where the grace of the general effect, that is to say, of the silhouette, does not atone for the coldness of the modelling, the facile and flaccid execution.

The ancients were well aware that this faint quiver of life is the supreme quality of a masterpiece: *spirantia mollius aera*, said Virgil.

BIBLIOGRAPHY OF CHAPTER XV.

Work by X. Kraus, A. Venturi, Michel, given p. 104. —L. Courajod, *Leçons professées à l'Ecole du Louvre*, vol. ii., Paris, 1901 (the origin of the Renaissance; cf. *Gazette du Beaux-Arts*, 1888, i., p. 21); E. Müntz, *Histoire de l'Art pendant la Renaissance en Italie*, 3 vols., Paris, 1889–1395; J. Burckhardt, *Der Cicerone*, 8th ed. by Bode, 3 vols., Leipzig, 1901; *Die Cultur der Renaissance in Italien*, 8th ed. by Geiger, 2 vols., Leipzig, 1901; L. Pastor, *Geschichte der Päpste*, 4th ed., vol. i–iii., Freiburg, 1900 (period of the Renaissance); E. Müntz, *Les Précurseurs de la Renaissance*, Paris, 1882 (an Italian edition, with considerable additions, Florence, 1902); H. Wölfflin, *Die klassische Kunst, Einführung in die italienische Renaissance*, Munich, 1901 (evolutionist point of view), English edition, *The Art of the Italian Renaissance*, London, 1903.

J. Crowe and G. Cavalcaselle, *A New History of Painting in Italy*, 3 vols., 1864–66 (a new Italian edition in 5 vols., 1889–1892; two new English editions have appeared, London, 1903, 1912); Woermann and Woltmann, *Geschichte der Malerei*, 3 vols., Leipzig, 1879–1888; English transl. ed. by S. Colvin, London, 1880; J. Lermolieff (pseudonym of Morelli), *Kunstkritische Studien über italienische Malerei*, 3 vols., Leipzig, 1890–1893 (English and Italian editions); B. Berenson, *The Study and Criticism of Italian Art*, vol. ii., London, 1902 (with an exposition of the Morellian method[1]); G. Lafenestre, *La Peinture italienne jusqu' à la fin du XVᵉ siècle*, Paris, 1900; H. Thode, *Franz von Assisi und die Anfänge der Kunst in Italien*, Berlin, 1903; L. Gillet, *Histoire artistique des Ordres Mendiants*, Paris, 1912.

W. Lübke, *Geschichte der Plastik*, 3rd ed., 2 vols., Leipzig, 1880; Ch. Perkins, *Italian Sculptors*; W. Bode, *Die italienische Plastik*, 3rd ed., Berlin, 1902; L. F. Freeman, *Italian Sculptors of the Renaissance*, London, 1902; W. S. Waters, *Italian Sculptors*, London, 1912; Venturi, *op. cit.*, Milan, 1905.

A. Brach, *Niccolà una Giovanni Pisano*, Strasburg, 1903; Apulian origin of Niccolà Pisano: Polaczek, *Repertorium für Kunstwissenschaft*, 1903, p. 361 (against); E. Bertaux, *L'Art dans l'Italie mérid.*, Paris, 1903, vol. i., p. 787 (for); cf. Male, *Gazette des Beaux-Arts*, 1905, i., p. 117.

L. Douglas, *A History of Siena*, London, 1902; W. Rothes, *Die Blütezeit der Sienesischen Malerei*, Strasburg, 1904; W. Heywood and Lucy Olcott, *A Guide to Siena (History and Art)*, Siena, 1903; S. Borghesi and L. Banchi, *Nuovi documenti per la storia dell' arte senese*, Siena, 1898; F. Wickhoff, *Ueber die Zeit des Guido von Siena (Mittheil. des Instit. für oester. Geschichtsforschung*, 1889, vol. x., 2; refutation of the legend of Cimabue); A. Aubert, *Die Cimabufrage*, London, 1907 (cf. article *Cimabue* in Thieme's *Künstlerlexicon*); A. Pératé, *Duccio (Gazette des Beaux-Arts*, 1893, i., p. 89); E. H. Weigelt, *Duccio*, Leipzig, 1911; B. Berenson, *A Sienese Painter of the Franciscan Legend, Sassetta (Burlington Magazine*, 1903, iii., p. 3; cf. L. Douglas, *ibid.*, 1903, ii., p. 265); E. Bertaux, *Sancta Maria di Donna Regina e l'arte senese à Napoli nel secolo XIV.*, Naples, 1899 (cf. *Repertorium*, 1899, p. 401); A. Gosche, *Simone Martini*, Leipzig, 1899; B. Supino, *Arte Pisana*, Florence, 1903.

R. Davidsohn, *Geschichte von Florenz*, vol. i., Berlin, 1896 (cf. *Repertorium*, 1897, p. 215); E. Müntz, *Florence et la Toscane*, Paris, 1896.

Berenson, *The Drawings of the Florentine Painters*, 2 vols., London, 1903 (enormous folios, exceedingly costly and difficult to handle); *The Florentine Painters of the Renaissance*, 2nd ed., London, 1900, G. Lafenestre and E. Richtenberger, *Florence*, Paris, 1895 (Painting); M. Zimmermann, *Giotto und die Kunst Italiens in Mittelalter*, 2 vols., Leipzig, 1899–1900; H. Thode, *Giotto*, Bielefeld, 1900; John Ruskin, *Giotto and his Works in Padua*, London, 1900; M. Perkins, *Giotto*, London, 1902; J.-B. Supino, *Il Campo Santo di Pisa*, Florence, 1896 (cf. *Repertorium*, 1897, p. 67); O. Siren, *Don Lorenzo Monaco*,

[1] This method consists in deciding upon the authorship of works of art by studying minute details of execution. Cf. *Revue critique*, 1895, i., p. 271.

THE RENAISSANCE AT SIENA AND FLORENCE

Strasburg, 1905; *Giottino,* Leipzig, 1908; L. Douglas, *Fra Angelico,* 2nd ed., London, 1902; L. Pichon, *Fra Angelico,* Paris, 1911; U. Mengin, *Benozzo Gozzoli,* Paris, 1909; Aug. Schmarsow, *Masaccio-Studien,* Cassel, 1895–1900 (on the Brancacci Chapel and the authorship of its frescoes), cf. *Gazette des Beaux-Arts,* 1902, i., p. 89); W. Weisbach, *Francesco Pesellino,* Berlin, 1901 (cf. *Gazette des Beaux-Arts,* 1907, i., p. 341); C. Loeser, *Paolo Uccello* (*Repertorium,* 1898, p. 83); Wolfram Waldschmidt, *Andrea del Castagno,* Berlin, 1900; M. Cruttwell, *A. Pollaiuolo,* London, 1907; H. Ulmann, *Bilder und Zeichnungen der Brüder Pollajuoli* (*Jahrbücher* of the Berlin Museums, 1894, p. 230); M. Cruttwell, *Verrocchio,* London, 1904; M. Reymond, *Verrocchio,* Paris, no date; H. Ulmann, *Sandro Botticelli,* Munich, 1893; E. Steinmann, *Botticelli,* Bielefeld, 1867 (Eng. transl., London, 1901); H. Horne, *Botticelli,* London, 1908; Ch. Diehl, *Botticelli,* Paris, 1912; Oppé, *Botticelli,* Paris, 1912; E. Jacobsen, *Allegoria della Primavera di Botticelli* (*Archivio storico dell' Arte,* 1897, p. 321); H. Mackowsky, *Jacopo del Sellaio* (*Jahrbücher* of the Berlin Museums, 1899); E. Steinmann, *Ghirlandajo,* Bielefeld, 1897; G. Davies, *D. Ghirlandajo,* London, 1908; E. Strutt, *Fra Filippo Lippi,* London, 1902; J.-B. Supino, *Les deux Lippi,* French transl. by Crozals, Florence, 1904; W. G. Waters, *Piero della Francesca,* London, 1901; B. Berenson, *Alessio Baldovinetti et Piero della Francesca* (*Gazette des Beaux-Arts,* 1898, ii., p. 39); F. Wilting, *Piero dei Franceschi,* Strasburg, 1898; Maud Cruttwell, *Signorelli,* London, 1902; Mancini, *Signorelli,* Florence, 1903; F. Knapp, *Piero di Cosimo,* Halle, 1899; H. Haberfeld, *Piero di Cosimo,* Breslau, 1901; E. Steinmann, *Die Sixtinische Kapelle,* vol. i., Munich, 1901 (period of Sixtus IV.); W. Kallab, *Die Toskanische Landschaftsmalerei* (*Jahrbücher* of the Vienna Museums, 1900); J. Guthmann, *Die Lanschaftsmalerei der toskanischen und umbrischen Kunst,* Leipzig, 1902; F. Rosen, *Die Natur in der Kunst,* Leipzig, 1903.

M. Reymond, *La Sculpture florentine,* Florence, 1898; W. Bode, *Florentinische Bildhauer der Renaissance,* Berlin, 1902; M. Reymond, *Lorenzo Ghiberti* (*Gazette des Beaux-Arts,* 1896, ii., p. 125); A. G. Meyer, *Donatello,* Bielefeld, 1902; Frida Schottmüller, *Donatello,* Munich, 1905 (cf. *Repert.,* 1905, p. 384); E. Müntz, *Andrea Verrocchio et le Tombeau de Francesca Tornabuoni* (*Gazette des Beaux-Arts,* 1891, ii., p. 27); F. Wolff, *Michelozzo di Bartolomeo,* Strasburg, 1900; M. Cruttwell, *Luca and Andrea della Robbia,* London, 1902; A. Marquand, *The Della Robbias,* 4 vols., Princeton (1914–1922); cf. Mary Logan (*Gazette des Beaux-Arts,* 1905, i., p. 256); S. Weber, *Die Entwickelung des Putto in der Plastik der Frührenaissance,* Heidelberg, 1898.

F. Lippmann, *Der Kupferstich,* 3rd ed., Berlin, 1905; A. M. Hind, *History of Engraving,* London, 1908; Kristeller, *Kupferstich und Holzschnitt,* 2nd ed., Berlin, 1911; L. Rosenthal, *La Gravure,* Paris, 1910; H. Delaborde, *La Gravure,* Paris, no date; Armand, *Les Médailleurs italiens des XVᵉ et XVIᵉ siècles,* 2nd ed., 3 vols., Paris, 1883–1887; A. Heiss, *Les Médailleurs de la Renaissance,* 7 vols., Paris, 1881–1887; C. von Fabriczy, *Medaillen der ital. Renaissance,* Leipzig, 1903 (cf. Bode, *Zeitschrift für bildende Kunst,* 1903, ii., p. 36); G. Hill, *Portrait Medals of Italian Artists,* London, 1912; E. Molinier, *Les Plaquettes,* Paris, 1886; J. Maindron, *Les Collections d'armes du Louvre et du Musée d'Artillerie* (*Gazette des Beaux-Arts,* 1891, ii., p. 466; 1893, ii., p. 265); *Les Armes,* Paris, no date.

A. de Champeaux, *Le Meuble,* vol. i., Paris, 1888; E. Molinier, *Les Meubles du Moyen Age et de la Renaissance,* Paris, 1896; *Les Ivoires,* Paris, 1896; *L'Emaillerie,* Paris, 1901; A. Maskell, *Ivories,* London, 1905; J.-W. Bradley, *A Dictionary of Miniaturists, Illuminators,* etc., London, 1888; F.-H. Jackson, *Intarsia and Marquetry,* London, 1908; Drury Fortnum, *Maiolica,* London, 1896; O. von Falke, *Majolika,* Berlin, 1896; W. Bode, *Altflorentinische Majoliken* (*Jahrbücher* of the Berlin Museums, 1898, p. 206); H. Wallis, *Early Italian Majolica,* London, 1901 (cf. *Gazette des Beaux-Arts,* 1902, i., p. 352); A. Darcel, *La Céramique italienne* (*ibid.,* 1892, i., p. 136); E. Molinier, *La Céramique italienne au XVᵉ siècle,* Paris, 1888; R. Davillier, *Les Origines de la Porcelaine en Europe,* Paris, 1882; G. Vogt, *La Porcelaine,* Paris, no date; R. L. Hobson, *Porcelain,* London, 1906; Th. Deck, *La Faïence,* Paris, no date; H. Cunynghame *European Enamels,* New York, 1907; E. Müntz, *La Tapisserie,* 3rd ed., Paris, 1888; W. G. Thomson, *A History of Tapestry,* London, 1907; G. Migeon, *Les Tissus,* Paris, 1909; Isab. Errera, *Collection d'anciennes Etoffes,* 2nd ed., Brussels, 1907; H. Moore, *The Lace Book,* New York, 1904; Handbooks of the Victoria and Albert Museum, South Kensington, London.

XVI

VENETIAN PAINTING

The Origin of the Venetian School.—The Vivarini.—The Bellini.—The Influence of Padua upon Venice.—Mantegna.—Antonello da Messina.—Internal Prosperity and Social Brilliance of Venice.—Sante Conversazioni.—The Joyousness of Venetian Art.—Crivelli.—Carpaccio.—Cima.—Giorgione.—Titian.—Palma.—Lorenzo Lotto.—Sebastiano del Piombo.—Tintoretto.—Paolo Veronese.—Tiepolo.—The Enduring Influence of the Venetian School.

ALTHOUGH in the fifteenth and sixteenth centuries, Venice produced such excellent sculptors as the Lombardi, it is always of her painters that we think when the Venetian school is in question; I therefore propose to deal only with painting.

FIG 278.—VIRGIN AND CHILD WITH INFANT ANGELS.

ALVISE VIVARINI.

(Church of the Redentore, Venice.)

The Venetian school, as it existed in the second half of the fifteenth century, sprang from two earlier schools. The first of these centred in the Island of Murano, where a Byzantine style, tempered by Sienese influences, long prevailed. Towards the middle of the fifteenth century, the most prominent masters of this school belonged to the Vivarini family; the most distinguished of the Vivarini, Alvise, born in 1450, seems to have been the master of Lorenzo Lotto (Fig. 278).

The second of the primitive Venetian schools was founded by Jacopo Bellini, the father of the two great painters, Gentile and Giovanni. Jacopo was the pupil of the Umbrian painter, Gentile da Fabriano; but he seems to have been more affected by the school of Padua, which was the true mother of the great Venetian School.

Padua, which was politically dependent on Venice, had, from the year 1222 onwards, owned a flourishing university, which was in close touch with France and the Valley of the Rhine; it soon became the intellectual centre of all northern Italy. At a very early date, Florentine artists began to arrive at Padua, notably Giotto and Donatello, who spent ten years there (1443-1453). The Paduan school is a combination of Florentine elegance, and of a style founded on that of Græco-Roman bas-reliefs. Nowhere is the influence of antique sculpture on a basis of ancient Gothic severity more marked. Mantegna, the pupil of Squarcione (1431-1506), was a mighty genius who is well represented in the National Gallery and in the Louvre, though his more important works are his frescoes at Padua and Mantua. His sculp-

FIG. 279.—THE MARTYRDOM OF ST. JAMES. MANTEGNA.
(Fresco in the Eremitani, Padua.)

turesque and abstract style, in which classic and Gothic reminiscences play an equal part, has a severity marked by a sort of haughty correctness; it should be studied not only in his pictures, but in his admirable engravings and in his drawings (Figs. 279-281). His ruggedness is healthy and virile, as far removed from Giottism as from the emasculated classicism of the academic school. Mantegna's influence upon the Venetian school of Bellini, and even on the rival school of Murano, was immense. It is not too

FIG. 280.—BARBARA OF BRANDENBURG, MARCHESA DI GONZAGA AND HER COURT.
MANTEGNA.
(Fresco in the Palace at Mantua.)

much to say that the highest qualities of the great Venetian art of the fifteenth century were derived from him.

FIG. 281.—THE TRIUMPH OF CÆSAR.
MANTEGNA.
(Fragment of the Cartoon at Hampton Court.)

A third element on which much stress is to be laid is the part played by Antonello da Messina, a painter who, though by birth a Sicilian, worked at Venice. Born in 1444, he went, it is said, to study in Flanders, and there learned the process of painting in oil from one of the successors of Van Eyck, perhaps Petrus Cristus. (It is, however, quite possible that the Venetians, who were constantly in communication with Flanders, knew the process before his time.) Antonello is the author of the beautiful portrait in the Louvre known as the *Condottiere;* he painted several others almost equally fine, that, for instance, in the Casa Trivulzio, at Milan (Fig. 282), and certain little pictures,

marvellously dexterous in execution, among them the *Crucifixion* in the Antwerp Gallery, and the St. Jerome in the London National Gallery, which also owns the reputed *Portrait of Himself*, and his earliest signed work, the *Salvator Mundi*. It will be well to explain here that at this period oil-colours were only used to give superficial lustre to very carefully executed painting in tempera (pigment mixed with white of egg), which formed the basis of the picture. The first artist who used oil as his sole medium was the Spaniard, Velasquez.

Venice was better governed than the other towns of Italy. Her trade with the East had

FIG. 282.—PORTRAIT OF A MAN.
ANTONELLO DA MESSINA.
(Trivulzio Collection, Milan.)
(Photo. by Anderson.)

made her rich and prosperous; civil war was unknown to her. Religion was respected within her territory, but was less tyrannical than elsewhere; even in the thirteenth century Venice held her own against the Inquisition, and reserved the right of punishing heretics for her own magistrates, to the exclusion of monks sent from Rome. Social life had developed brilliantly; the Venetians loved pleasure, fine clothes, courtly assemblies, and stately pageants, in which all the representative bodies took part. These tendencies are reflected in Venetian painting; it is gay, luminous,

FIG. 283.—"CONCERT CHAMPÊTRE."
GIORGIONE.
(The Louvre.)

full of the joy of life; it loves to render magnificent processions—as in Gentile Bellini's famous picture at Venice—or social gatherings, sacred and profane. The sacred groups are the *Holy Conversations*, a kind of composition peculiar to Venetian painting, in which male and female saints and Scriptural characters are gathered together without any apparent reason, for the mere pleasure of meeting. The secular assemblies are of the type of Giorgione's exquisite *Concert Champêtre* in the Louvre (Fig. 283), a group of nude women and musicians in a rich landscape. Such gatherings certainly never took place in Venice; but the painters of *Conversazioni* were not concerned with actualities; they wished to paint beautiful bodies and gorgeous costumes, to suggest the idea of free

FIG. 284.—PIETÀ.
GIOVANNI BELLINI.
(Brera, Milan.)

and joyous life against a luminous background of landscape, and in this they succeeded.

From the close of the fifteenth century the Madonnas and Saints

FIG. 285.—VIRGIN AND CHILD.
GIOVANNI BELLINI.
(Academy, Venice.) (Photo. by Naya.)

of the Venetian painters were no longer ascetic and morose persons, but beautiful young women and handsome young men, with blooming complexions and sunny hair, who loved to deck themselves with gorgeous stuffs, and held life to be well worth living.

This smiling optimism is the essential characteristic of Venetian painting, and is expressed chiefly in the radiant splendour of its colour. It is inadmissible to explain this by the climate, for the skies of Naples are much more brilliant than those of Venice, and Neapolitan colour is grey and black. It was a result of moral and physical health at Venice, as in the Flanders of Rubens. At Florence, even in the works of delicate and skilful colourists, the colour is more or less an accessory of the drawing; at Venice, from the time of Giorgione onwards, it was painting itself, and this seems sometimes less intent upon the objects it represents than upon the atmosphere in which they are bathed, the light that penetrates and envelops them. The Venetians were not only colourists, but luminists. Giovanni Bellini, who lived eighty-six years (1430-1516), passed through such a variety of stages that he was a school of painting in himself, rather than a single painter. His first works are subtle and somewhat dry, akin to those of Mantegna, with a certain hardness and eccentricity in the drawing. The compositions of his maturity are masterpieces in which scarcely any quality is lacking, not even a reflec-

FIG. 286.—VIRGIN AND CHILD.
GIOVANNI BELLINI.
(National Gallery, London.)

172

FIG. 287.—THE VIRGIN AND CHILD WITH SAINTS
GIOVANNI BELLINI AND BASAITI.
(Benson Collection, London.)
(Photo. by Rischgitz.)

FIG. 288.—VIRGIN AND CHILD.
CRIVELLI.
(Benson Collection, London.)
(Photo. by Braun, Clément and Co.

FIG. 289.—VIRGIN AND CHILD WITH
TWO SAINTS.
CIMA DA CONEGLIANO.
(Museum, Vienna.)

FIG. 290.—HISTORY OF ST. URSULA.
CARPACCIO.
(Academy, Venice.)

tion of the colour cf his pupil, Giorgione, who died six years before him. In his laborious life this great artist traversed all the road that led from Mantegna to Titian. One single gift was denied him: the power, or the desire, to represent movement (Figs. 284-287).

Crivelli, on the other hand, who was formed at Murano but influenced by the school of Padua (1430-1494), never ceased to be a primitive. In his fragile Virgins, with their slight grimace, their slim, nervous figures, their quivering contours and dazzling draperies, the rich lustre of Japanese lacquer is united to the subtle elegance of Gothic art (Fig. 288).

Carpaccio (1460-1522) and Cima da Conegliano (1460-1517) are the most lovable personalities among this group of men of genius. In his series illustrating the Legend of St. Ursula in the Venice Academy (Fig. 290), Carpaccio is a story-teller both amused and amus-

FIG. 291.—THE ENTOMBMENT.
TITIAN.
(The Louvre.)

ing, less smiling than Benozzo Gozzoli, but more thoughtful and suggestive. Cima is the delightful painter of Virgins who are still serious, but conscious of their own beauty, whose softly rounded forms are in strong contrast to the ascetic, bony frames of the Florentines (Fig. 289).

Giorgione, in the course of his brief life (1478-1510), united the gaiety of Carpaccio to the poetry and delicacy of his master, Bellini; but he surpassed all his contempora-

FIG. 292.—AN INVITATION TO LOVE.
(SACRED AND PROFANE LOVE.)
TITIAN.
(Borghese Gallery, Rome.)

ries by the extraordinary magic of his brush (Figs. 283, 294). His *Conversazioni*, his mythological and allegorical pictures, and

FIG. 293.—PORTRAIT OF
FRANCIS I.
TITIAN.
(The Louvre.)

his portraits had an immense success, attested by numerous copies and still more numerous imitations; the Venetian Renaissance acclaimed its most perfect expression in this painter of light and of glowing flesh.

FIG. 294.—THE VIRGIN AND CHILD
WITH SS. GEORGE AND LIBERALE.
GIORGIONE.
(Church of Castelfranco.)
(Gazette des Beaux-Arts.)

Titian did not, as was formerly believed, live to be ninety-nine, but died at the ripe old age of eighty-eight. Born about 1488, and collaborating, while still a youth, with Giorgione, he finished one of his master's most beautiful works, the *Reclining Venus*, at Dresden, and inherited his splendour of colour, while surpassing him in fertility of invention.

Titian never ceased to advance in his art, even in his extreme old age. His first pictures, without being dry, are still somewhat timid in touch; as an old man, he painted with unprecedented fire and boldness, preparing the way for Velasquez and the French painters of our own day. He essayed every class of subject, including great episodes of pagan mythology, in which his passionate love of life, of movement, and

FIG. 295.—THE THREE SISTERS.
PALMA.
(Dresden Gallery.)

of beautiful nature are more perfectly expressed than elsewhere. Even his sacred pictures often share the radiant gaiety of his

FIG. 296.—THE ANNUNCIATION.
LORENZO LOTTO.
(Church of S. Maria, Recanati.)
(Photo. by Anderson, Rome.)

FIG. 297.—PORTRAIT OF LAURA DI POLA
LORENZO LOTTO.
(Brera, Milan.)
(Photo. by Brogi.)

FIG. 298.—THE RESURRECTION OF
LAZARUS.
SEBASTIANO DEL PIOMBO.
(National Gallery, London.)
(Woermann, *Geschichte der Malerei.*
Seemann, Leipzig.)

FIG. 299.—PORTRAIT OF A ROMAN LADY,
WITH THE ATTRIBUTES OF
ST. DOROTHEA.
SEBASTIANO DEL PIOMBO.
(Museum, Berlin.)

Bacchanals. As to his portraits, such as the *Man with the Glove* and *Francis I,* in the Louvre, and the seated *Charles V.,* at Munich, they are pages of profound psychology as well as rich æsthetic feasts (Figs. 291-293, 300, 301).

Palma Vecchio (1480–1528), a painter somewhat older than Titian, who died long before the latter, was, like him, a successor of Giorgione, though of a temperament calmer and less original (Fig. 282). His *Adoration of the Shepherds,* in the Louvre, is one of the most charming idylls of Venetian painting; lacking the genius of Titian, it has all the seduction of his brush.

A very different master was Lorenzo Lotto (1480–1556), the most individual of the great Venetians, who felt the influence of Giorgione less than any of his contemporaries. In his art there is a touch of melancholy, and a sympathetic suavity which strikes a strangely modern note in his best pictures and is even echoed in his admirable portraits (Figs. 296, 297). This gentle sadness of Lotto's must have been the outcome of personal temperament; if it were to be accounted for by the political events of his maturity—the abasement of Venice, the beginning of the Counter-Reformation — we should find traces of the same sentiment in other painters of his day. A fact

FIG. 300.—THE MADONNA OF THE PESARO FAMILY.

TITIAN.

(Church of the Frari, Venice.)

that remains inexplicable is the resemblance between certain works by Lotto and those of Correggio, an artist with whom it is highly improbable that he ever came in contact, and who worked at Parma, a city Lotto is not likely to have visited.

The youngest of the great painters of this generation, Sebastiano del Piombo (1485–1547), was a highly gifted artist, who began by successfully imitating Giorgione; but going to Rome, he came under the influence first of Raphael, and afterwards of Michelangelo, to

FIG. 301.—THE ASSUMPTION OF THE VIRGIN.

TITIAN.

(Academy, Venice.)
(Photo. by Alinari.)

such an extent that he lost his individuality. He remained a Venetian, however, in the fine intensity of his colour. In his best works, such as the *Resurrection of Lazarus*, in the National Gallery, he approaches Titian and Michelangelo; in his portraits he is closely akin to Raphael, for whom he is often mistaken (Figs. 298, 299).

But the true Michelangelo of Venice was Tintoretto (1518–1594), who, together with Paolo Veronese (1528–1588), dominates the second epoch of the Renaissance in Venice with his feverish and somewhat trivial activity. Michelangelo's frescoes in the Sistine Chapel have inspired hundreds of artists; but how few had the temperament of their exemplar! Tintoretto was one of these few; he was not an imitator of the great Florentine, but a younger brother, born under serener skies. Amazing in his fecundity, eager for difficulties to overcome, fiery and unequal, Tintoretto sought and found in violent contrasts of light and shade grandiose effects unknown to his predecessors. As a draughtsman he is often brutal and incorrect, but never commonplace; as a painter he took up the tradition of the aged Titian, who, weary of the russet and golden tones so lavishly used in the Venetian Renaissance, had created a new palette for himself, in which silvery greys and blues predominated over more brilliant colours (Figs. 302, 303). Nearly all Tintoretto's large pictures have blackened; but

FIG. 302.—THE PRESENTATION OF THE VIRGIN IN THE TEMPLE.

TINTORETTO.

(Church of S. Maria dell' Orto, Venice.)
(Photo. by Naya.)

we may form some idea of his gifts as a colourist from his small sketches and his portraits.

Paolo Caliari, called Veronese, sprang from a family of painters at Verona, in spite of which he has expressed the luxurious life of Venice, in the second half of the sixteenth century, without a touch of provincialism in his accent. Something of the pomp and solemnity of Spain, whose ascendency weighed heavily upon Italy in his time, mingles in his fine compositions with his essentially Venetian love for clear light and splendid costumes (Figs. 304, 305). He also shows a marked preference for silvery tones; it may truly be said that in Venetian painting the silver age succeeded the golden age.

FIG. 303.—THE ORIGIN OF THE MILKY WAY.
TINTORETTO.
(National Gallery, London.)

The fact that there were two Renaissances at Venice, in spite of the political and commercial decay of the city after the League of Cambrai (1512), shows how favourable her soil had proved to the development of Renaissance tendencies. Venice was, further, fortunate enough to escape the academic eclecticism which, after the fruition of the Roman School under Raphael, destroyed the great schools of painting in Italy.

FIG. 304.—THE RAPE OF EUROPA.
PAUL VERONESE.
(Doges' Palace, Venice.)

Even in the middle of the eighteenth century Venice possessed one great Renaissance artist, Tiepolo (1696–1770). She was still the loveliest and the gayest city in the world, the trysting-place of pleasure and elegance; as of old, the scene of magnificent processions and imposing ceremonies.

Life there was easy and comparatively free, in a marvellous setting, enveloped in a transparent atmosphere, which first Canaletto, and then Guardi, the painters *par excellence* of the lagoons, rendered with such infinite truth and charm. Tiepolo gave final expression to these splendours. His genius is akin to that of Tintoretto, but he has more moderation, more elegance; he was the painter of a polished aristocracy, conscious of its superiority to the crowd, whose religion, modified by Spain, the Counter - Reformation, and the Jesuits, was a subtle mingling of devotion and worldliness (Figs. 306, 307). Tiepolo, it has been truly said, was the last of the old painters and

FIG. 305.—INDUSTRY.
PAUL VERONESE.
(Doges' Palace, Venice.)

FIG. 306.—ST. JOSEPH AND
THE INFANT JESUS.
TIEPOLO.
(Academy, Venice.)
(Photo. by Alinari.)

FIG. 307.—THE ADORATION OF THE
MAGI.
TIEPOLO.
(Munich.)
(Photo. by Hanfstaengl.)

the first of the moderns; nearly all the great decorators of the nineteenth century were inspired by him.

VENETIAN PAINTING

The influence of the Venetian School was immense. In Italy it gave birth to various local schools, Verona, Vicenza, and Brescia, the last-named memorable as having produced the great Moretto (1498–1555), who forestalled Tintoretto and Veronese in the use of silvery tones (Fig. 308). Tintoretto, and Bassano (1510–1592), one of the creators of modern landscape, were the first exemplars of Velasquez. Titian inspired Rubens and Reynolds; Tiepolo was imitated by the Spaniard, Goya, to whom we may, in a measure, ascribe the origin of French painting in the second half of the nineteenth century. In these, her offspring, it may be said that the Venetian School still exists, differing essentially in this respect from that of Florence, which has known but one ephemeral and artificial resurrection in the group of English Pre-Raphaelites. We have seen, in our survey of architecture, that the palaces of Venice continued to serve as models, whereas the severe art of Bramante merely inspired isolated imitations. The Renaissance triumphed at Venice, and was widely propagated by her. But something was lacking to her that was the glory of Florence: gravity of life and depth of thought.

FIG. 308.—ST. JUSTINA.

MORETTO.

(Museum, Vienna.)

BIBLIOGRAPHY OF CHAPTER XVI

B. Berenson, *The Venetian Painters*, 3rd ed., London, 1897; Lafenestre and Richtenberger, *Venise*, Paris, 1897 (Painting); P. Paoletti, *L'Architecture et la Sculpture de la Renaissance à Venise*, Venice, 1899; P. Paoletti and G. Ludwig, *Neue archiv. Beiträge zur Gesch. der venez. Malerei* (*Repertorium*, 1899, p. 427; 1900, p. 274); L. Venturi, *Pittura Veneziana*, Venice, 1907; E. M. Philipps, *The Venetian School*, London, 1912; T. Borenius, *Painters of Vicenza*, London, 1909; Romain Rolland, *La Décadence de la Peinture italienne* (*Revue de Paris*, 1896, i., p. 168; excellent notes on Mantegna, Titian, Paul Veronese, etc.).

P. Schubring, *Altichiero und seine Schule*, Leipzig, 1898; J. Ffoulkes, *Vincenzo Foppa* (*Burlington Magazine*, 1903, i., p. 103).

P. Kristeller, *Andrea Mantegna*, Berlin, 1902 (English ed., 1901); Maud Cruttwell, *Mantegna*, London, 1902; Blum, *Mantegna*, Paris, 1912; F. Knapp, *Mantegna*, Stuttgart, 1910 (photographs of all works).

P. Molmenti and G. Ludwig, *Carpaccio*, Milan, 1905 (cf. Mary Logan, *Burlington Magazine*, 1903, ii., p. 317); L. Venturi, article *Antonello da Messina* in Thieme's *Künstlerlexicon*, 1907.

G. Gronau, *Die Bellini*, Bielefeld, 1909; Cammaerts, *Les Bellini*, Paris, 1912.

R. Fry, *Giovanni Bellini*, London, 1899; R. Burckhardt, *Cima da Conegliano*, Leipzig, 1905; J. Rushforth, *Carlo Crivelli*, London, 1900; H. Cook, *Giorgione*, London, 1900; L. Venturi, *Giorgione*, Milan,

1913; Crowe and Cavalcaselle, *Titian*, 2 vols., London, 1877; G. Gronau, *Titian*, London, 1904; L. Hourticq, *La jeunesse de Titien*, Paris, 1920; M. Hamel, *Titien*, Paris, 1903; O. Fischel, *Tizian*, Stuttgart, 1904 (photographs of all his pictures); G. Gronau, *Tizian's himmlische und irdische Liebe* (*Repertorium*, 1903, p. 177; an explanation of the picture known as *Sacred and Profane Love*; for other explanations cf. *Revue Archéologique*, 1905, ii., p. 393; that we have adopted under Fig. 292 is due to Riese). On the date of Titian's birth: H. Cook, *Repertorium*, 1902, p. 98, and *Nineteenth Century*, 1902.

B. Berenson, *Lorenzo Lotto*, 3rd ed., London, 1905; P. d'Achiardi, *Seb. del Piombo*, Rome, 1908; H. Thode, *Tintoretto*, Bielefeld, 1901; Soulier, *Le Tintoret*, Paris, 1911; P. Caliari, *Paolo Veronese*, Rome, 1908; B. S. Holborn, *Tintoretto*, London, 1903; F. H. Meissner, *Paolo Veronese*, Bielefeld, 1896; L. Zottmann, *Die Bassani*, Strasburg, 1908; Simonson, *Guardi*, London, 1904; P. Molmenti, *Tiepolo*, Milan; 1909 (French translation); H. de Chennevières, *Les Tiepolo*, Paris, 1898; F. H. Meissner, *Tiepolo*, Bielefeld, 1896; H. Modern, *G. B. Tiepolo*, Vienna, 1902.

FIG. 309.—THE LAST SUPPER.
LEONARDO DA VINCI.
(Refectory of Santa Maria delle Grazie, Milan.)
(From Raphael Morghen's engraving.)

XVII

LEONARDO DA VINCI AND RAPHAEL
THE MILANESE SCHOOL, THE UMBRIAN SCHOOL, AND THE ROMAN SCHOOL

Leonardo's Genius a Synthesis of the Renaissance.—His Birth.—His Works for Lodovico Sforza.—His Manuscripts: Scientific Writings.—Leonardo as a Sculptor.—Leonardo's Pictures.—Raphael's Birth and Parentage.—Timoteo Viti his first Master.—The Knight's Dream.—Raphael Perugino's Assistant.—The Sposalizio.—Raphael at Florence.—The Madonnas of the Florentine Period.—Raphael at Rome.—Giulio Romano his Assistant.—The Vatican Frescoes.—Madonnas and Portraits of the Roman Period.—An Appreciation of Raphael's Genius.

ALL the intellectual curiosity of the Renaissance, its dreams of glory and of infinite progress, its enthusiasm for science and for beauty, were combined with many other attributes of genius in Leonardo. Born at Vinci, between Pisa and Florence, in 1452, he died at Amboise in 1519, having spent his youth in Florence, his maturity in Milan, and the last three years of his life in France, where he seems to have become too feeble to work. Few artists have been more industrious, but few have produced less; in science as in art, he was tormented by a passion for innovation, a desire to strike out new paths. In some respects he recalls those alchemists of the Middle Ages, who squandered the most brilliant gifts in the pursuit of a chimerical ideal.

When, in 1483, Leonardo offered his services to Lodovico il Moro, Duke of Milan, in a letter that has been preserved, he

FIG. 310.—THE VIRGIN OF THE ROCKS.
LEONARDO DA VINCI.
(The Louvre.)

recommended himself as an inventor of engines of war, a builder of movable bridges and chariots, an engineer skilled in the science of artillery and sieges. At the end of his letter he adds: "*Item,* I will execute sculpture in marble, bronze, or terra-cotta; also in painting I can do as much as any other, be he who he may." It was evidently as an engineer and inventor that he esteemed himself most highly.

His manuscripts, the majority of which are preserved in the library of the Institut de France, bear witness to his passionate interest in science, and more particularly in mechanics. He believed he had made a practical design for a flying machine. The value of Leonardo's scientific work has been successively exaggerated and depreciated. His manuscripts contain many notes and extracts which merely reproduce the ideas of others, but, on the other hand, he certainly foreshadowed many important discoveries, and, more especially in geology, he had formed opinions far in advance of his times.

In his capacity as a sculptor, Leonardo worked for seventeen years at an equestrian statue of Francesco Sforza, the father of Lodovico il Moro. The plaster model of the horse, without the rider, was shown in 1493, and destroyed in 1501 by the archers of Louis XII. It is not even certain that any copies have been preserved. No trace remains of his other works in sculpture, which were not numerous. The beautiful profile head of Scipio in a helmet, bequeathed to the Louvre by M. Rattier, has been attributed to him.

FIG. 311—THE VIRGIN AND CHILD WITH ST. ANNE.
LEONARDO DA VINCI.
(The Louvre.) (Photo. by Neurdein.)

FIG. 312.—MONNA LISA GIOCONDA.
LEONARDO DA VINCI.
(The Louvre.)

FIG. 313.—VIRGIN AND CHILD.
BELTRAFFIO.
(Poldi Pezzoli Collection, Milan.)

FIG. 314.—VIRGIN AND CHILD.
BELTRAFFIO.
(National Gallery.)
(Photo. by Hanfstaengl.)

FIG. 315.—VIRGIN AND CHILD.
(Vierge au Coussin Vert.)
ANDREA SOLARIO.
(The Louvre.)

FIG. 316.—CARTOON FOR A HOLY FAMILY.
LEONARDO DA VINCI.
(Royal Academy, London.)

The extant paintings by Leonardo comprise four masterpieces of the highest rank, three of which are in the Louvre: *The Last Supper*, painted in oil on the wall of the refectory at Santa Maria delle Grazie at Milan (1497), a work that is now a wreck, but of which some twenty good copies exist; the *Virgin among the Rocks*,[1] painted about 1483; the *Virgin with St. Anne*, painted about 1502, and, finally, the famous portrait of Monna Lisa Gioconda, executed from 1502 to 1506 (Figs. 309-312).

Leonardo's pictures at Florence and in the Vatican, *The Adoration of the Magi* and the *St. Jerome*, are unfinished. Others ascribed to him in Paris and elsewhere have been very much repainted, or are the works of pupils. Among these disputable works there are, however, two of great beauty, the so-called *Portrait of Lucrezia Crivelli* and the *John the Baptist*, the latter marred by a certain affectation. Both are in the Louvre. Even the three great pictures I have grouped with the *Last Supper* are almost in a state of ruin. Modern restorers are not responsible for this. Leonardo did nothing with simplicity. His oil-painting was a complicated *cuisine* predestined to scale and blacken. Nevertheless, the *Virgin among the Rocks* and the *Gioconda* suffice to give the measure of his genius.

Leonardo, unlike his master

FIG. 317.—THE ADORATION OF THE MAGI.
LEONARDO DA VINCI.
(Fragment of a Drawing in the Louvre.)

[1] A replica, probably painted in Leonardo's studio, is in the National Gallery

Verrocchio, his contemporary Botticelli, and the great Florentines of the fifteenth century in general, sought to express the fluidity of atmosphere, and discarded the dry, angular manner of the Primitives. But this did not lead him into inaccuracy or flaccidity. With him, rigour of drawing and impeccable refinement of line were completed by the art of veiling them under the fusion of modelling and chiaroscuro, the manner called by the Italians *lo sfumato*. Precision of outline is, indeed, but a first stage, leading to a precision subtler and more difficult of attainment, that of planes. By the middle of the sixteenth century, the *Gioconda* was accepted in Italy as the inimitable masterpiece of the art of portraiture, the greatest effort of the painter setting himself to compete with Nature. It was

FIG. 318.—THE VIRGIN WITH THE SCALES. CESARE DA SESTO. (?)
(The Louvre.)

said that Leonardo worked at it for four years, and that to call up the sweet and smiling expression on his sitter's face, he caused her to be entertained with music and other diversions. It was not until modern times that a mysterious and romantic character was attributed to Monna Lisa, a sphinx-like gaze, a scornful irony, and a hundred other things undreamt of by Leonardo.

Leonardo's type of the Madonna,—whence he took that he has impressed on the Gioconda, for the portraits of an artist of genius always show the influence of his ideal—is akin to the favourite type of his master Verrocchio. Leonardo embellished and spiritualised it, eliminated its harshness and dryness, and endowed it with that smile which had already taken

FIG. 319.—THE MARRIAGE OF THE VIRGIN.
LUINI.
(Fresco in the Church of Saronno.)

on a touch of affectation in the *St. Anne*, and was destined to become still more exaggerated and insipid in the hands of his imitators.

FIG. 320.—THE NATIVITY.
LUINI.
(Fresco in the Church of Saronno.)
(Photo. by Anderson.)

The *Last Supper* at Milan shows with what deep attention to the underlying thought Leonardo grouped his figures. The subject had been very often treated before, but he laid down a quasi-definitive formula for it. Jesus has just said: "One of you shall betray Me," and He bows His head, as if to the blast of emotion He has evoked. It is not only a great work of art, but a page of the profoundest psychology, a study of character and feeling, translated at once by the expressions of the faces, the gestures, and the attitudes.

In addition to these beautiful but half-ruined works, we have happily a good many of Leonardo's drawings, which are to be reckoned among the undisputed masterpieces of the Renaissance,

FIG. 321.—ST. VICTOR.
SODOMA.
(Palazzo Pubblico, Siena.)

FIG. 322.—THE VISION OF ST. CATHERINE
SODOMA.
(Church of San Domenico, Siena.)

LEONARDO DA VINCI AND RAPHAEL

and would suffice of themselves to make the glory of a great artist. Two of these drawings may be mentioned as incomparable: the cartoon of the *Virgin with St. Anne* (Fig. 316), in the Royal Academy of London, and the *Adoration of the Magi* (Fig. 317), in the Louvre.

At Milan a local school existed, derived from that of Padua, and founded about 1450 by Vincenzo Foppa. At the time of Leonardo's arrival (1483) it boasted an exquisite master, at once Mantegnesque and Umbrian, Ambrogio Borgognone (Fig. 324). Leonardo himself formed several pupils, or inspired several artists of talent, Beltraffio, Solario, Cesare da Sesto, Gaudenzio Ferrari (Figs. 313–315, 318), but

FIG. 323.—VIRGIN AND CHILD WITH SAINTS.
SODOMA.
(Museum, Turin.)
(Photo. by Anderson.)

also a large proportion of clumsy and mediocre imitators. The most popular of these disciples was and is Luini, who may be said to have translated the ideal of Leonardo into simple terms, a process

FIG. 324.—VIRGIN AND CHILD.
A. BORGOGNONE.
(National Gallery, London.)
(Photo. by Hanfstaengl.)

FIG. 325.—THE VIRGIN AND CHILD WITH SAINTS
AND ANGELS.
PERUGINO.
(The Louvre.)   (Photo. by Neurdein.)

189

FIG. 326.—THE ENTOMBMENT.
PERUGINO.
(Pitti Palace, Florence.)

FIG. 327.—THE VIRGIN IN GLORY.
PERUGINO.
(Museum, Bologna.) (Photo by Alinari.)

FIG. 328.—MARY MAGDALENE.
TIMOTEO VITI.
(Museum, Bologna.)

FIG. 329.—VIRGIN AND CHILD WITH DONOR.
PINTORICCHIO.
(Cathedral of San Severino.) (Photo. by Alinari.)

he carried out not altogether without vulgarity, for his elegance is superficial, his drawing uncertain, and his power of invention limited.

His most characteristic trait is a certain honeyed softness that delights the multitude; but he rose to great heights in his frescoes in the Church of Saronno, where he appears as the Filippino Lippi of the Milanese School (Figs. 319, 320). Leonardo's influence is also very apparent in the work of the Vercellese Sodoma, who worked at Siena (d. 1549), an artist who, though unequal and mannered, is sometimes very happily inspired (Figs. 321-323). Finally, Leonardo is the artist whom the Flemings

FIG 330.—THE RETURN OF ULYSSES.
PINTORICCHIO.
(National Gallery, London.)

of the first half of the sixteenth century imitated more than any other Italian; many of the reputed Leonardos of our museums are nothing but Flemish pasticci.

The life of Raphael Santi (or Sanzio) is a complete contrast to

FIG. 331.—VIRGIN AND CHILD.
COSIMO TURA.
(Accademia Carrara, Bergamo.)

FIG. 332.—VIRGIN AND CHILD WITH SAINTS.
ERCOLE ROBERTI.
(Brera, Milan.)

FIG. 333.—SS. PETER AND JOHN.
FRANCESCO DEL COSSA.
(Brera, Milan.)

that of Leonardo. If the latter, in the course of his long life, produced so little, Raphael, who died at the age of 37, left an immense artistic legacy behind him, which has come down to us almost in its entirety.

To understand this passionately acclaimed artist, we must first get a clear idea of the origin of his talent; for no painter was more open to influences, or even more prone to imitate. The truth about the formation of Raphael's genius was discovered by Morelli about 1880; it is the more necessary to insist upon it, because it has not yet become an accepted fact in the teaching of art history.

We will first take a rapid survey of Raphael's more remote precursors. The Umbrian School, the offspring of the Sienese School, revealed itself towards the close of the fourteenth century in Gentile da Fabriano's (1360–1428) *Adoration of the Magi*, in all the freshness of its youthful visions, its gay tints, and amusing narrative. At Venice, Gentile collaborated with his friend, the Veronese Pisanello, the engraver of admirable medals, a draughtsman of genius, and, further, the first Italian who observed animals, and rendered their attitudes and action faithfully. When Roger Van der Weyden visited Italy about 1450, he expressed his admiration for the works of

FIG. 334.—VIRGIN AND CHILD WITH SAINTS
LORENZO COSTA.
(Church of S. Giovanni in Monte, Bologna.

FIG. 335.—THE ADORATION OF THE INFANT
JESUS.
FRANCIA.
(Museum, Bologna.)

FIG. 336.—THE ENTOMBMENT.
FRANCIA.
(Museum, Turin.)
(Photo. by Anderson.)

Pisanello and Gentile; the great artist from the North recognised
in them talents akin to his own. It is indeed probable that both
Pisanello and Gentile, but
more especially the former,
were familiar with the masterpieces of the Flemish School,
and were influenced by them.
Verona was in constant communication with the Court of
Burgundy, and as early as
the year 1400 Philip the
Bold bought Italian medals.
The precursors of the Van
Eycks, and doubtless Hubert
Van Eyck himself, learned
much from Italy, though it is
not easy to say on which side
of the Alps the loans were
most numerous and most important.

FIG. 337.—THE KNIGHT'S DREAM.
RAPHAEL.
(National Gallery.) (Photo. by Hanfstaengl.)

In the second half of the fifteenth century the Umbrian towns,
notably Perugia, developed a school of painting very unlike that of

FIG. 338.—THE MARRIAGE OF THE
VIRGIN (*Sposalizio*).
RAPHAEL.
(Brera, Milan.)

FIG. 339.—THE MADONNA "DEL GRAN
DUCA."
RAPHAEL.
(Pitti Palace. Florence.)

Florence. Taking up, as it were, the tradition of the Sienese, they

FIG. 340.—THE MADONNA DELLA CASA
TEMPI.
RAPHAEL.
(Pinacothek, Munich.)
(Photo. by Hanfstaengl.)

opposed a soft and dulcet suavity
to the austere elegance of the
Florentines. They are fascinating
masters, full of freshness and poetry,
but with something childish and
limited in their art. If the Florentines are over intellectual, they
are often puerile. The two great
Umbrian masters were Vannucci,
called Perugino, born in 1446, and
Betti, called Pintoricchio, born in
1454. Perugino had an instinct
for large, airy compositions, and
golden, transparent colour, an exquisite sense of reverie and ecstasy
(Figs. 325–327). Such qualities
may be admired to the full in the
beautiful triptych of the National
Gallery and the delicate *tondo* in
the Louvre. But he could not represent movement, and when he

194

attempts to set his figures in motion, they skip rather than walk. Pintoricchio, for a time the foreman of Perugino's studio, had certain gifts which were denied his master (Figs. 329, 330); but he drew worse, and thought even less; his large compositions, such as the series in the Libreria at Siena and the frescoes of the Borgia Rooms in the Vatican, are decorative and seductive, though not powerfully conceived. But he is a very interesting figure in the history of art, for it was he who created, or at least developed, the exquisite type of the Umbrian Madonna, transmitting the ideal to Raphael.

A malady of taste common among novices in connoisseurship

FIG. 341.—"LA BELLE JARDINIÈRE."
RAPHAEL.
(The Louvre.)

FIG. 342.—THE "MADONNA DEL PRATO."
RAPHAEL.
(Museum, Vienna.)

FIG. 343.—THE "MADONNA DI FOLIGNO."
RAPHAEL.
(Museum of the Vatican.)

FIG. 344.—THE MADONNA DI SAN SISTO.
(Virgin and Child with St. Barbara and
Pope Sixtus II.)
RAPHAEL.
(Dresden Gallery.)

FIG. 345.—THE MADONNA WITH THE
FISH.
RAPHAEL AND GIULIO ROMANO.
(Prado Museum, Madrid.)
(Photo. by Manzi, Joyant & Co.)

leads them to prefer Perugino and Pintoricchio to Raphael, and
even to all other Italian painters. The remedy is a simple one: go
to Perugia. The patient will return disillusioned and cured.

We have seen that the Venetian School had thrown out innumerable offshoots in the
north of Italy. One of its
colonies, Bologna, produced a
distinguished master, Francia
(b. 1450), who came very near
to being a genius. In style he
was halfway between Giovanni
Bellini and Raphael. His
pupil and foreman, about 1490,
was one Timoteo Viti (Fig.
328).

FIG. 346.—LA DISPUTA, OR TRIUMPH OF THE
CHURCH.
RAPHAEL.
(Fresco in the Vatican.)

Born at Urbino in 1483,
Raphael was eleven years old
when he lost his father, Giovanni Santi, a mediocre painter
to whom he owed nothing, not
even the first principles of his art. Soon after this (1495), Timoteo
Viti quitted Francia's studio to set up for himself at Urbino. He

196

was Raphael's first master, and grounded him in the manner of Francia. It was from him that Raphael acquired a certain predilection for round and opulent forms, which is in itself the negation of the ascetic ideal. About 1499, at the age of sixteen, Raphael painted the charming little picture in the National Gallery, the *Vision of a Knight* (Fig. 337). Nothing in this work recalls Perugino, as whose pupil and successor Raphael has so long passed.

FIG. 347.—THE SCHOOL OF ATHENS.
RAPHAEL.
(Fresco in the Vatican.)

The following year (1500), Raphael entered Perugino's workshop at Perugia, not as his pupil but as assistant. The master, then overwhelmed with work, was at Florence; Pintoricchio was the foreman of the studio. Raphael, whose nature was peculiarly impressionable, drew his inspiration for some four years from Pintoricchio and Perugino; there are pictures by him painted at this period the cartoons and studies for which are by one or the other of his Umbrian masters. Thus his first sympathetic manner was evolved by a blending of the styles of Francia and Perugino. He is, however, more akin to the former than to the latter in the masterpiece of his youth, the *Sposalizio*, or *Marriage of the Virgin*, at Milan (1504) (Fig. 338). It was long supposed that this picture was almost an exact copy of a large composition attributed to Perugino in the Museum of Caen. But Mr. Berenson found the Caen *Sposalizio* to be no Perugino at all, but a feeble Umbian imitation, probably by Lo Spagna, of Raphael's *Sposalizio*.

FIG. 348.—POPE LEO I. CHECKING THE ADVANCE OF ATTILA.
RAPHAEL.
(Fresco in the Vatican.)

From 1504 to 1508 Raphael was at Florence, already famous, and advancing from one success to another. This was the period of the beautiful Madonnas, for which the civilised world has eagerly competed for some four centuries, the Munich *Madonna*, the so-called *Madonna del Gran Duca* in the Pitti Palace, the *Belle Jardiniere* of the Louvre, the *Madonna del Prato* at Vienna (Figs. 339-342). At Florence, Raphael began to imitate Leonardo da Vinci, Michelangelo, and Fra Bartolommeo, a languid draughtsman, but a remarkable composer and colourist. One reason of the unparalleled popularity of Raphael was that faculty for adaptation and intelligent imitation which made his art the synthesis and quintessence of all that was most fascinating in Italian genius.

FIG. 349.—HELIODORUS DRIVEN FROM THE TEMPLE.
RAPHAEL.
(Fresco in the Vatican.)

Summoned to Rome in 1508, Raphael became successively the favourite painter of Julius II. (d. 1513) and of Leo X. Honours were showered upon him, and he was overwhelmed with commissions. He had not only a numerous school, but a veritable court. From this time forward, it was his almost invariable practice to furnish only the cartoons for pictures, leaving the execution of them to his pupils, and retouching them before sending them home to his clients. The most active and gifted of his pupils, Giulio Romano, painted carnations with a peculiar brick-red tone, which appears as the assistant's signature in many pictures of Raphael's Roman period. This tone was admired and imitated by the fervent Raphaelites of the nineteenth century, though it is now universally held to be very unpleasant.

FIG. 350.—THE LOGGIE OF THE VATICAN.
(Decorated under the direction of Raphael.)

The great task confided to Raphael in Rome was the decoration of certain rooms in the Vatican (*le Stanze*) and of a long covered gallery round the Courtyard of San Damasio (*le Loggie*). The *Stanze* contain vast historical, allegorical, and religious compositions, such as the *Dispute of the Sacrament* (more exactly described as *The Triumph of the Church*), *The School of Athens, Parnassus, Heliodorus driven from the Temple, Pope Leo Checking the Advance of Attila, L'Incendio del Borgo* (Figs. 346-349). The *Loggie* are decorated with a series of frescoes commonly known as *Raphael's Bible*, representing scenes in sacred history, and a profusion of ingenious ornaments imitated from ancient

FIG. 351.—PORTRAIT OF JULIUS II.
(FRAGMENT.)
RAPHAEL.
(Pitti Palace, Florence.)
(Photo. by Anderson.)

Roman paintings (Fig. 350). In spite of these labours, which might have filled a whole lifetime, Raphael found time to paint admir-

FIG. 352.—PORTRAIT OF BALTHAZAR CASTIGLIONE.
RAPHAEL.
(The Louvre.) (Photo by Neurdein.)

able portraits (Figs. 351, 352), and, aided by his pupils, to complete large pictures such as the *Madonna di San Sisto* at Dresden, the *Madonna di Foligno* in the Vatican, and the *Holy Family of Francis I.* in the Louvre. He began, but left unfinished, one of his most grandiose works, the *Transfiguration*, which was completed after his death by Giulio Romano (Fig. 353). In addition to all this, Raphael had been appointed architect of St. Peter's after the death of Bramante, and inspector of the antiquities and monuments of Rome. If we further accept the statement that he led a life of pleasure, and was

199

FIG. 353.—THE TRANSFIGURATION.
RAPHAEL AND GIULIO ROMANO.
(Museum of the Vatican.)

the assiduous worshipper of a lady of whom he has left a fine portrait, the *Donna Velata* in the Pitti Palace, we can only wonder that for twelve years of untiring productiveness he was able to withstand so many causes of nervous fatigue, especially as he seems from his portraits to have been by nature frail and delicate, almost effeminate. An anthropologist, examining a cast of his skull, supposed it to be that of a woman. His art, with its predominance of sweetness over strength, and its susceptibility to novel influences, has indeed a certain feminine and receptive character. The darling of the Papacy and of the Church, the object of a worship from which there was hardly any dissent down to the middle of the nineteenth century, Raphael is now beginning to expiate his glory, and his imprudence in relying too much on the help of his assistants. As is always the case in such matters, the reaction has gone too far. Raphael, in the *Stanze* and the *Loggie,* shows himself the greatest illustrator that ever lived; pagan and Christian antiquity alike furnished him with immortal images which realised the ideal of the Renaissance and have been graven in the minds of men for four centuries. His type of the Virgin, half Christian, half pagan, neither too ethereal nor too sensual, has won all hearts, and still retains its sovereignty. It seems as if the momentary fusion of two hostile worlds, Paganism and Christianity, had been brought about by the genius of Ra-

FIG. 354.—THE ENTOMBMENT.
RAPHAEL.
(Borghese Gallery, Rome.)

phael; if others were the flowers of the Renaissance, he was its perfect fruit.

To admite the faults of a genius is not to discredit him. Raphael, the marvellous creator of images, was a mediocre colourist (save in a few portraits such as the *Balthazar Castiglione* in the Louvre); and, though Ingres would never have allowed this, his drawing was often commonplace and nerveless. There is no picture by him in which an impartial critic may not find loose, inaccurate, and inexpressive contours. The work in which he attempted to compete with Michelangelo, the *Entombment*, in the Borghese Gallery in Rome, has all the frigidity of a seventeenth century "academy." Not without reason has the decadence of art been dated from the apogee of Raphael's glory.

The worship of Raphael, "the divine painter," has had its day. His works must now be analysed and judged one by one, not as those of a god in the form of a painter, but as the creations of an artist of great genius, fallible like the rest of mankind, and deified by irresponsible enthusiasm. All that is truly great in his art can but gain by being studied critically, not in the spirit of depreciation, but, on the other hand, without a blind determination to admire at any price.

BIBLIOGRAPHY OF CHAPTER XVII

Works and articles already quoted (pp. 166, 181) by Burckhardt, Morelli (essential for Raphael), Romain-Rolland, Venturi, Wölfflin, and Woltmann.

J. P. Richter, *Literary Works of Leonardo da Vinci*, 2 vols., London, 1888; Léonard, *Traité de la peinture*, French translation by Péladan, Paris, 1910; E. Müntz, *Léonard de Vinci*, Paris, 1898; English edition, London, 1898; B. Berenson, *The North Italian Painters*, London, 1907 (School of Leonardo); G. Gronau, *Leonardo da Vinci*, London, 1903; Seidlitz, *Leonardo*, 2 vols., Berlin, 1909; H. Cook, *Le Carton de Léonard à la Royal Academy* (*Gazette des Beaux-Arts*, 1897, ii., p. 371); G. Carotti, *Le Opere di Leonardo*, Bramante e Raffaello, Milan, 1905; (cf. P. Gautlriez, *Ouvrages récents sur Léonard*, in *Gazette des Beaux-Arts*, 1907, i., p. 505); S. Reinach, *Art Journal*, 1912, pp. 6–25 (*Virgin of the Rocks, Gioconda*, etc.); F. Malaguzzi-Valeri, *Pittori lombardi dal quattrocento*, Milan, 1902; P. Toesca, *Pittura e miniatura lombarda*, Milan, 1911; S. Weber, *Piemont, Malerschule*, Strasburg, 1912; Eth. Halsey, *Gaudenzio Ferrari*, London, 1903; M. Reymond, *Cesare da Sesto* (*Gazette des Beaux-Arts*, 1892, i., p. 314); G. Williamson, *Bernardino Luini*, London, 1899; Beltrami, *Luini*, Milan, 1911; F. Malaguzzi-Valeri, *La Corte di Lodovico il Moro*, Milan, 1913–1917; R. H. Cust, *Bazzi* (*Sodoma*), London, 1906; H. Hauvette, *Sodoma*, Paris, 1912.

B. Berenson, *The Central Italian Painters*, London, 1898 (Raphael); A. Venturi, *Gentile da Fabriano e Pisanello*, Florence, 1896; L. Courajod, *Leçons*, vol. ii., Paris, 1900 (*Pisanello et les écoles du Nord*); E. Müntz, *Pisanello* (*Revue de l'Art*, 1897, i., p. 67); A. Gruyer, *Vittore Pisano* (*Gazette des Beaux-Arts*, 1893, ii., p. 353); G. Hill, *Pisanello*, London, 1905 (cf. *Burlington Magazine*, September, 1910); J. Williamson, *Francia*, London, 1901; S. Weber, *Fiorenzo di Lorenzo*, Strasburg, 1904; Mrs. Graham, *Fiorenzo di Lorenzo*, Rome, 1904; O. Okkanen, *Melozzo*, Helsingfors, 1911; Abbé Broussolle, *La Jeunesse de Pérugin et les Origines de l'Ecole ombrienne*, Paris, 1901; E. Steinmann, *Pinturicchio*, Bielefeld, 1898; C. Ricci, *Pintoricchio*, London, 1902; A. Schmarsow, *Raphael und Pinturicchio in Siena*, Berlin, 1903; F. Ehrle and E. Stevenson, *Gli affreschi del Pinturicchio nell' Appartamento Borgia*, Rome, 1897 (cf. *Repertorium*, 1897, p. 318); A. Schmarsow, *Giovanni Santi*, Berlin, 1887.

A. Rosenberg and Gronau, *Raffael*, Stuttgart, 4th ed., 1909 (reproductions of all his pictures); A. Springer, *Raffael und Michelangelo*, 2nd ed., Leipzig, 1895; E. Müntz, *Raphael*, new ed., Paris, 1900; English edition, London, 1882; Julia Cartwright, *Raphael*, London, 1895[1]; H. Knackfuss, *Raphael*, 4th ed.,

---

[1] Of all the illustrated books on Raphael this is, in my opinion, the best one to read.

APOLLO

Bielefeld, 1896; Crowe and Cavalcaselle, *Rafaello*, new ed., Florence, 1901; Alex. Amersdoffer, *Kritische Studien über das venezianische Skizzenbuch* (wrongly attributed to Raphael), Berlin, 1902 (cf. *Repertorium*, 1902, p. 130); B. Berenson, *Le Sposalizio du Musée de Caen* (*Gazette des Beaux-Arts*, 1896, ii. p. 273); *The Study and Criticism of Italian Art*, vol. ii., London, 1902; G. Gronau, *Aus Raphaels florentiner Tagen*, Berlin, 1903; H. Dollmayr, *Raffaels Werkstätte* (*Jahrbuch* of the Vienna Museums, 1895; cf. *Repertorium*, 1896, p. 368); *Giulio Romano und das klassische Altertum*, Vienna, 1902; Lafenestre and Richtenberger, *Rome*, vol. i., Paris, 1903 (detailed study of the frescoes of Raphael in the Vatican); J. Klaczko, *Rome and the Renaissance, the Pontificate of Julius II.*, London, 1903 (English illustrated translation; Melozzo da Forli, Michelangelo).

On the feminine character of Raphael's skull, see *Bonner Jahrbücher*, vol. lxxiii., p. 182.

XVIII

MICHELANGELO AND CORREGGIO

The Development of the Florentine School after Leonardo.—Fra Bartolommeo, Andrea del Sarto, and Michelangelo.—Pontormo and Bronzino.—The Extinction of the Florentine School hastened by Michelangelo.—The Titanic Nature of Michelangelo's Genius.—His Early Masterpieces of Sculpture.—The Ceiling of the Sistine Chapel.—The Unfinished Tomb of Julius II.—The Medici Chapel, Florence.—The Fresco of The Last Judgment, in the Sistine Chapel.—Pictures by Michelangelo.—Sebastiano del Piombo, Daniele da Volterra, Benvenuto Cellini, Giovanni da Bologna.—Correggio.—His Decoration of the Cupola of Parma Cathedral.—His Type of the Virgin.—His Art the Expression of the Counter-Reformation.

THE genius of Leonardo summed up and dominated the second period of the Florentine Renaissance, inaugurated by Masaccio's frescoes in the Carmine. But Leonardo's pupils and imitators were all Milanese. At Florence the development of the school proceeded on independent lines. In the sixteenth century it could boast three other great names, Fra Bartolommeo, Andrea del Sarto, and Michelangelo.

After Botticelli, Ghirlandajo, and Filippino Lippi, painting had to make a certain progress in its special domain, that of colour. The somewhat crude methods of the illuminators were to be superseded by the use of warm, brilliant tones, brought into harmony by chiaroscuro, and that of delicate tints, on a golden or silvery base, in which Venice and Brescia excelled. Leonardo had set the example in the employment of

FIG. 355.—MADONNA WITH SAINTS AND ANGELS.

FRA BARTOLOMMEO.
(Cathedral, Lucca.)

chiaroscuro, though he aimed at fusion rather than at brilliance of colour. The first Florentine who competed with the Venetians in this domain, though he did not equal them, was Baccio della Porta, the friend of Savonarola, who became a Dominican monk

FIG. 356. —THE VIRGIN APPEARING TO ST. BERNARD.
FRA BARTOLOMMEO.
(Academy, Florence.)

under the style of Fra Bartolommeo, after Savonarola had expiated his reforming zeal at the stake in 1498.

Fra Bartolommeo (1475-1517) had another merit, the instinct for rhythmic composition, scientifically balanced and pyramidally arranged. By virtue of this quality and of his gifts as a colourist he exercised a very happy influence on the youthful Raphael from the year 1504 onwards. He would have been a master of the first rank if he had been able to create types; unfortunately, the faces of his personages are inexpressive, and lack both originality and charm (Figs. 355, 356).

His pupil, Andrea del Sarto (1486-1531), was a yet more skilful colourist, the Florentine who approached most nearly to Giorgione. He was influenced by Leonardo, from whom he borrowed his *sfumato*, and later by Michelangelo, often an unhealthy source of inspiration, who gave him a taste for heavy draperies. Andrea, although a commonplace thinker, was a great painter. Like Fra Bartolommeo, he composed skilfully, and he excelled his compatriot in giving movement to his figures, bathing them in a soft and luminous atmosphere, and suggesting ten-

FIG. 357.—THE BIRTH OF THE VIRGIN.
ANDREA DEL SARTO.
(S. Annunziata, Florence.)

derness without affectation. He had, further, the rare gift of narrative, and his great mural paintings at Florence, such as the

Birth of the Virgin in the Convent of the Annunziata, add to their other fine qualities that of being delightful illustrations. His fresco of the *Last Supper*, at San Salvi, near Florence, is admirable, even if we come to it after seeing Leonardo's great work (Figs. 357-360). These frescoes of Andrea's, which must be studied in Tuscany, are of the greatest importance historically, for if we compare

FIG. 358.—THE LAST SUPPER.
ANDREA DEL SARTO.
(S. Salvi, near Florence.)

them with similar works of the fifteenth century—Andrea del Castagno's *Last Supper*, for instance—we realise what progress had been made by art towards the goal of complete emancipation. Not only has all Gothic rigidity disappeared, but sentiment has under-

FIG. 350.—CHARITY.
ANDREA DEL SARTO.
(The Louvre.) (Photo. by Neurdein.)

FIG. 300.—THE MADONNA DELLE ARPIE.
ANDREA DEL SARTO.
(Pitti Palace, Florence.)

gone a complete change; harshness has given place to sweetness, asceticism to a playful and smiling humour. Finally, Andrea was

FIG. 361.—PORTRAIT OF THE DUCHESS
ELEONORA OF TOLEDO AND HER SON
FERDINAND.
BRONZINO.
(Uffizi, Florence.)

FIG. 362.—PIETÀ
MICHELANGELO.
(St. Peter's, Rome.)
(Photo. by Anderson.)

one of the rare artists who created a novel and enduring type of Virgin, with large, liquid, dark eyes, an exquisite mingling of pride and simplicity. One of the most beautiful examples of the type is the *Madonna delle Arpie* at Florence (1517), where the Virgin is enthroned on a pedestal decorated with figures of harpies (Fig. 360).

The Florentine School produced a few more good artists, such as Pontormo (1494-1557), and Bronzino (1502-1572), who painted excellent portraits (Fig. 361) and mannered religious compositions. Broadly speaking, however, it ceased to exist before the end of the sixteenth century. This sudden extinction was not due to political revolutions, but to the crushing superiority of Michelangelo. Though a Florentine, he worked in Rome,

FIG. 363.—HEAD OF THE DAVID.
MICHELANGELO.
(Academy, Florence.)

made it the centre of Italian art, and, in his life-time, founded a school which his violent personality governed like a new ideal. Venice alone, where Titian outlived Michelangelo, preserved a local tradition; everywhere else, Michelangelo held undisputed sway. Florentine art, uprooted and Romanised, died like a luxuriant plant that has flowered too freely, and grown too tall.

Michelangelo was born near Florence in 1475, the same year as Fra Bartolommeo. He died in 1564, forty-four years after Raphael, and eighteen years after Raphael's most active disciple, Giulio Romano.

Poet, architect, sculptor, and painter, Michelangelo Buonarroti felt himself, and claimed to be, exclusively a sculptor. At Rome, after 1508, when he was painting the ceiling of the Sistine Chapel,

FIG. 364.—FRAGMENT OF CEILING IN THE SISTINE CHAPEL, ROME.
MICHELANGELO.

he signed his letters ostentatiously: Michelangelo, Sculptor. And, indeed, the genius he applied to painting was a purely sculptural and plastic one. To chiaroscuro, landscape, and local colour he was indifferent. One thing absorbed all his interest, man; not man in the variety and mutability of actual life, but man as he conceived him, a sombre giant with eloquent gestures, brusque and vehement attitudes, and a formidable tension of the muscles, which touches the limits of possibility, even when it does not overstep them. Michelangelo plays with the

FIG. 365.—MOSES.
MICHELANGELO.
(Church of S. Pietro in Vincoli, Rome.)

207

FIG. 366.—JEREMIAH.
MICHELANGELO.
(Sistine Chapel, Rome.)

human body as on an instrument, from which he continuously draws the most piercing, strident, and sonorous sounds. On that summit which others only reach occasionally, as if by accident, he maintained himself habitually without apparent fatigue; the exceptional became his normal standard. Those who imitated him without possessing his temperament fell into mannerism, that is to say, the affectation of an emotion they did not feel. This was why the stormy Titanism of Michelangelo was more pernicious to art than the dawning Academicism of Raphael.

Michelangelo lived to be eighty-nine; he did not begin his artistic career with the Titanic fervour of his later life. The pupil of Ghirlandajo and of a sculptor formed in the school of Donatello, he was strongly influenced by the vigorous works of Jacopo della Quercia (Fig. 273), and also, in his Florentine period, by the antique marbles of the Medici collections. The story of his *Cupid*, the statue he buried to make it pass for a Roman antique, is well known; the work was acclaimed with all the more fervour because its admirers thought it was fifteen centuries old. But Michelangelo's genius had nothing in common with antique art save the predilection for general types. Serenity was unknown to him, and all tradition was intolerable to him. This is apparent even in his early masterpieces (Figs. 362, 363): the *Pietà*, in St. Peter's, Rome (1498), the *Virgin and Child*, at Bruges (1501), and the *David*, at Florence (1504). The David, a masterpiece of anatomy, seems to some critics to offend against taste, but the two Madonnas are admirable, and reveal a great genius already mature. Michelangelo boldly placed the naked body of

FIG. 367.—FETTERED SLAVE.
MICHELANGELO.
(The Louvre.)

MICHELANGELO AND CORREGGIO

Jesus on the knees of a draped Madonna, winning a very striking effect from this contrast. The Virgin suffers in silence; she is too proud and too majestic for tears. The conception of the Bruges group is no less bold. The Child is not on his mother's lap. This was the traditional attitude, and Michelangelo accordingly rejected it. He stands between her knees, a sturdy, thoughtful boy. She, too, is robust and thoughtful, displaying neither emotion nor tenderness, but vibrating with restrained vitality. The fingers of her right hand, which hold a book, seem to quiver. All the genius of Michelangelo is already present in these works, for those who look at them with knowledge and sympathy.

FIG. 368.—LORENZO DE MEDICI.
(Il Pensieroso.)
(Medici Chapel, Florence.)

Pope Julius II., the most energetic of the successors of St. Peter, was worthy to understand and admire such a man. In 1508 he commissioned him to decorate the ceiling of the Sistine Chapel in the Vatican. The vast work, carried out by Michelangelo in four years, is unrivalled and even unapproached in the history of painting. These scenes from the Old Testament, these Prophets, Sibyls, and seated Slaves, resemble nothing the world had ever seen (Figs. 364–366). These colossal, statuesque figures, resplendent with muscular strength and athletic effort, in attitudes disconcertingly bold and novel, are the representatives of a race at once human and superhuman, in which Michelangelo realised his vision of wild energy and grandeur.

Entrusted with the execution of the tombs of Julius II., and of the Medici at Florence, Michelangelo carried the truculent visions of the Sistine Chapel into his chosen domain of sculpture. The tomb of Julius was never finished; the *Moses* sculptured for it, and now in the

FIG. 369.—DAWN.
MICHELANGELO.
(Medici Chapel, Florence.)

Church of San Pietro in Vincoli in Rome, is an extraordinary creation, full of "repressed movement" [1] and vibrating with wrath and passion, the sublimity of which affects one like some great natural spectacle (Fig. 365). Two of the Slaves designed for the tomb are among the most precious possessions of the Louvre; they are standing figures, but bent, twisted, and oblique, marking the extreme of reaction against primitive

FIG. 370.—ANGELS BEARING THE CROSS.
MICHELANGELO.
(Fragment from the Fresco of the *Last Judgment*.)
(Sistine Chapel, Rome.)

art, in which the law of frontality prevailed (Fig. 367). The Medici Chapel at Florence was also left unfinished. Michelangelo completed only the two niches, where the seated statues of Giuliano and Lorenzo de' Medici (Fig. 368) dominate two groups of figures reclining on the sarcophagi, *Evening* and *Dawn*, *Day* and *Night*. The seated princes are not portraits, but personifications of melancholy power; they are like two Prophets descended from the Sistine ceiling, and like them are robust, sombre, and contemplative (Fig. 366). A still higher degree of strength, a strength which finds expression in impatient contortions, characterises the four reclining figures, whose audacious attitudes and violent play of muscle evoke both admiration and stupefaction (Fig. 369).

FIG. 371.—HOLY FAMILY.
MICHELANGELO.
(Uffizi, Florence.)

[1] A very apt term used by H. Wölfflin, *The Art of the Italian Renaissance*, Heinemann, London.

MICHELANGELO AND CORREGGIO

On his return to Rome, Michelangelo, at the request of Pope Paul III., began, in 1535, to paint the *Last Judgment* on the end wall of the Sistine Chapel (Fig. 370). This colossal fresco, on which he worked for seven years, is a mistake as a whole, but it is the most complete expression of his genius. In it he exhausted all the possibilities of movement and of line, creating a sinister world of exasperated giants, some victorious, others vanquished, all naked and muscular as athletes. Christian sentiment is conspicuously absent from this conception, which is like the nightmare of some fevered Titan. What trace of Christianity is to be seen in the avenging Christ with his herculean frame, and the terrified Virgin who cowers beside her Son? The sublimity of the *Last Judgment* verges on insanity; neither Æschylus, nor Dante, nor Victor Hugo ever carried the audacity of substituting personal vision for a given argument to such lengths as this.

FIG. 372.—GROUP KNOWN AS " THE CLIMBERS."
(From Marc Antonio Raimondi's Engraving of a Fragment of the Cartoon by Michelangelo, *The Pisan War*.)

There are very few pictures by Michelangelo (Fig. 371), and the most famous of his cartoons, executed for the city of Florence in 1505, has perished. Fortunately, Marc Antonio, the engraver, the friend of Raphael, engraved a fragment of it, representing Florentine soldiers surprised by the Pisans while bathing (Fig. 372). Antique art has given us nothing superior to these naked bodies in their athletic vigour, and the elegance that sets off their strength. If this engraving were all we had by which to judge Michelangelo,

FIG. 373.—THE DESCENT FROM THE CROSS.
DANIELE DA VOLTERRA.
(Church of S. Trinità dei Monti, Rome.)
(Photo. by Anderson, Rome.)

we should recognise the giant in it, as we know the lion by his paw.

The Venetian, Sebastiano del Piombo, owed the epic grandeur of his *Resurrection of Lazarus* in the National Gallery to Michelangelo's collaboration (Fig. 298). One of Michelangelo's pupils, Daniele da Volterra, imitating his master, achieved the sublime in the great *Crucifixion* of the Church of the Trinità, at Rome (Fig. 373). A sculptor of the same school, Benvenuto Cellini (1500–1572), who was also a goldsmith and chaser of metal, and an

FIG. 374.—PERSEUS.

BENVENUTO CELLINI.

(Loggia dei Lanzi, Florence.)

FIG. 375.—MERCURY TAKING FLIGHT.

GIOVANNI DA BOLOGNA.

(Bargello, Florence.)

adventurer and charlatan to boot, rose to great heights in his *Victorious Perseus* (Fig. 374) at Florence, inspired both by Donatello and Michelangelo. Giovanni da Bologna (Boulogne in France and not Bologna), a French sculptor, settled in Italy, was the author of an admirable *Mercury taking Flight*, in which both Michelangelo and the classic sculptors are imitated (Fig. 375). But with very few exceptions, the crowd that made up the other disciples of the master did nothing but imitate his gestures, dislocate colossal figures for no apparent reason, and, " running amok " in colo blood, overstep the narrow boundary that separates the sublime from the ridiculous.

Younger by some twenty years than Michelangelo, whom he nevertheless predeceased by thirty years, a Parmesan painter, Antonio Allegri, called Correggio, exercised almost as great an influence over the Italian art of the sixteenth and seventeenth centuries. He seems to have been formed in the School of Ferrara, and to have been the pupil of the

FIG. 376.—FRAGMENT OF THE VIRGIN AND CHILD WITH ST. JEROME.
CORREGGIO.
(Parma Gallery.)

painter, Bianchi, of whom there is a beautiful example in the Louvre. He was of a gentle, sensuous temperament, equally attracted by the romantic myths of paganism and the pious legends of Christianity.

FIG. 377.—VIRGIN AND CHILD WITH ST. GEORGE.
CORREGGIO.
(Dresden Gallery.)

He treated both in the same spirit, and with the same delight in flickering and caressing light, mellow, vaporous forms, and the languorous softness of chiaroscuro. Leonardo inspired him first, then Michelangelo. From the latter he took his taste for aërial movement, for figures hovering in mid-air, soaring overhead, riding on clouds, dumbfounding the spectator by foreshortenings that seem incredible and are perfectly true to nature. These audacities of draughtsmanship were a strange innovation in religious painting, but one to which Italian taste speedily reconciled itself. To this sentimental Michelangelo, who was a painter to his finger-tips, and had none of the sculptor's severity, we owe one of the great achievements of art, the decorations of the dome of Parma Cathedral, where the Virgin ascends in the midst of saints borne up heavenwards like herself;

a tumult of legs and fluttering draperies dominated by ecstatic heads in perspective.

Of the pictures which shed lustre on his brief career, the most characteristic are those at Parma and Dresden (Figs. 376, 377), in which there is a good deal of Francia and of Michelangelo, but above all, of Correggio, that is to say, of a soul enthralled by beauty, light, and joy, and carrying its worship for loveliness to the very verge of effeminacy. His two pictures in the Louvre, one essentially profane, the *Jupiter and Antiope*, the other full of tender sentiment, if not of religious feeling, the *Marriage of St. Catherine* (Fig. 378), give an almost perfect idea of his genius; [the same may be said of the two analogous works in the National Gallery, the *Mercury instructing Cupid*, and the delightful little *Madonna della Cesta*.] He created a type of Virgin of exquisite but superficial charm, the influence of which was the more far-reaching in that, on the morrow of the Reformation, it harmonised with the new departure of Catholicism.

FIG. 378.—THE MYSTIC MARRIAGE OF
ST. CATHERINE.

CORREGGIO.

(The Louvre.)

The Catholic Renaissance, provoked by the schism of Luther towards 1540, had nothing in common with the triumphant and dogmatic religion of the Middle Ages. The task in hand was not to govern minds, but to win hearts. The shrewd and energetic Popes who saved Catholicism from ruin, and helped it to regain the ground lost during the first years of the Reformation, had as their auxiliaries the Jesuits, who made religion easy, and the artists, who made it attractive. In contrast to austere Protestantism, the enemy of art, to whom mystic fervours were suspect, and who sought to restrict the way of salvation, the Counter-Reformation decked the old Roman creed with all the seduction of beauty accessible to the multitude, with all the blandishments of devotion and ecstasy. The art which it protected and which grew up under its influence, notably in Italy and Spain, is typified in church architecture by the Jesuit style, and in painting by the

MICHELANGELO AND CORREGGIO

somewhat sensual mysticism, the first examples of which were furnished by Correggio. There is nothing here which resembles the great Christian art of the Middle Ages, not even that of the fifteenth century, which, while it borrowed forms from paganism, remained austere and Christian in thought. To this very day, popular religious illustrations, multiplied *ad infinitum* by chromolithography, must be finally referred to the master who painted the *Antiope*, to the decorator of the cupola of Parma Cathedral.

BIBLIOGRAPHY OF CHAPTER XVIII

Works already quoted by Berenson (more especially *The Drawings of Florentine Painters*), by Burckhardt, by Müntz, and by Woermann.—C. Cornelius, *Jacopo della Quercia*, Halle, 1896 (cf. *Gazette des Beaux-Arts*, 1897, ii., p. 172); A. Michel, *Madone et Enfant de Jacopo della Quercia au Louvre* (*Monuments Piot*, vol. iii., p. 261); H. Grimm, *Leben Michel-Angelo's*, 10th ed., 2 vols., Stuttgart, 1901; (for more recent works, see *Repertorium*, 1910, p. 166); J. A. Symonds, *The Life of Michel-Angelo*, 3rd ed., 2 vols., London, 1899; H. Wölfflin, *Die Jugendwerke des Michelangelo*, Leipzig, 1891; *Die Klassische Kunst*, Munich, 1899, p. 42, English trans., London, 1903; C. Justi, *Michelangelo*, Leipzig, 1900; F. Knapp, *Michelangelo*, Stuttgart, 1906 (photographs of all his works); C. Ricci, *Michel-Ange*, transl. Crozals, Florence, 1902; Ch. Holroyd, *Michel Angelo*, London, 1903; Romain Rolland, *Michel-Ange*, Paris, 1905; H. Thode, *Michel Angelo und das Ende der Renaissance*, vols. i. and ii., Berlin, 1903–1904; K. Lange, *Der schlafende Amor des Michelangelo*, Leipzig, 1898; H. Focillon, *Benvenuto Cellini*, Paris, no date; J. B. Supino, *Benvenuto Cellini*, Florence, 1901; A. Desjardins, *Jean Bologne*, Paris, 1901; P. de Bouchaud, *Jean Bologne* Paris, 1906; H. Guinness, *Andrea del Sarto*, London, 1901; Schulze, *A. Bronzino*, Strasburg, 1911.

Burlington Club, School of Ferrara-Bologna, London, 1894 (very important for Correggio, but not in circulation); H. Cook, *Francesco Bianchi-Ferrari* (*Gazette des Beaux-Arts*, 1901, i., p. 376; cf. for the School of Ferrara, Venturi, *Jahrbücher* of the Berlin Museums, 1887, p. 71; 1888, p. 3); H. Thode, *Correggio*, Bielefeld, 1898; C. Ricci, *Correggio*, London, 1897; B. Berenson, *Study and Criticism of Italian Art*, London, 1901 (p. 20, Correggio); T. S. Moore, *Correggio*, London, 1906; J. Strzygowski, *Das Werden des Barock bei Raphael und Correggio*, Strasburg, 1898.

XIX

THE RENAISSANCE IN FRANCE AND IN FLANDERS

The Union of Flanders and Burgundy.—The Valois Dukes of Burgundy and their Patronage of Artists.—The Rise of the School of Burgundy at Dijon.—The Early French Renaissance Checked by National Calamity.—Flanders in Advance of Italy at the Beginning of the 15th Century.—Early Flemish Artists.—Claux Sluter and his Works at Dijon.—The Brothers Limbourg.—The Book of Hours at Chantilly.—The Painter Malouel.—The Affinity between the Flemish and Italian Primitives.—The Reciprocal Influence of the Two Schools.—The Supposed Invention of the Oil Medium by Van Eyck.—The Brothers Hubert and Jan van Eyck.—The Polyptych of the " Adoration of the Lamb."—The Masterpieces of Jan van Eyck.—His followers: Albert van Ouwater, Thierry Bouts, Roger van der Weyden.—The Flemish School at its Apogee.—Jacques Daret, Simon Marmion.—Hugo van der Goes, and the Portinari Altar-piece.—Memling, Gerard David, Quentin Matsys.—The Italianised Flemings: Mabuse, B. van Orley.—The Realists: Jerome Bosch, Breughel the Elder.—The Realistic Tendencies of Flemish Art.—The Franco-Flemish School at Paris, Avignon, and the Court of King René.—Froment, Jean Fouquet.—The Clouets.—The School of Fontaine-bleau.—Michel Colombe, Germain Pilon, and Barthélemy Prieur.—Jean Goujon.—The Rise of the Dutch School.—The Leyden Painters: Engelbrechtsen and Lucas van Leyden.

IN 1361, Jean le Bon, King of France (1350-1364), inherited the Duchy of Burgundy on the death of the last native Duke, Philippe

de Rouvre. He gave this fair domain to his fourth son, Philippe le Hardi, who married Marguerite, heiress of the Counts of Flanders, and thus Burgundy and Flanders were united in 1384.

This union lasted throughout the reigns of the princes of the House of Valois, who were all zealous protectors of art and artists, Jean Sans Peur (1404-1419), Philippe le Bon (1419-1467), Charles le Téméraire (1467-1477). Very close relations were established between Burgundy, Flanders, France, and Italy; many Flemish artists came to work at Dijon, and there founded the School of Burgundy, which is but a branch of the Flemish School, itself a graft on the French Gothic trunk.

The eldest son of Jean le Bon, who reigned in France under the name of Charles V. (1364-1380), was a great lover of books and

THE RENAISSANCE IN FRANCE AND FLANDERS

works of art. His court painter was Jean Bandol of Bruges, the author of the cartoons for the tapestries in Angers Cathedral. Another son of Jean le Bon, Jean, Duc de Berry, who died in 1416, surrounded himself with a brilliant court at Bourges, and collected a magnificent library of manuscripts illuminated by Flemish artists, a good number of whom worked in Paris.

This city was the great artistic and intellectual centre of Europe at the end of the fourteenth century. Flemish art, a little heavy in Flanders and Burgundy, had in Paris taken on a character of urbanity and refinement which manifested itself in the miniatures of manuscripts.

FIG. 380.—THE WELL OF MOSES.
CLAUX SLUTER.
(Chartreuse of Champmol, near Dijon.)

A brilliant French Renaissance was about to unfold there, when the Civil War (1410), the disaster of Agincourt (1415), and the Treaty of Troyes (1420), plunged France into misery. Art took flight towards the Duchy of Burgundy, and it was there, and not in Paris, that the Franco-Flemish Renaissance culminated.

FIG. 381.—THE DUC DE BERRY AT TABLE.
PAUL DE LIMBOURG.
(Miniature from the Book of Hours, at Chantilly.)
(*Chantilly*, Plon, Nourrit and Co., Paris.)

Gothic art had developed in Flanders together with the wealth of the country, which, from the beginning of the fourteenth century, excited the wonder and the envy of all Europe. About 1390, Melchior Broederlam, of Ypres, painter to Philippe le Hardi, painted the shutters of a carved reredos preserved at Dijon. At the same time, a sculptor of genius, Claux Sluter, arrived from Flanders in Burgundy. He left there some master-

217

FIG. 382.—TOMB OF PHILIPPE POT, SENESCHAL
OF BURGUNDY.
(The Louvre.)

pieces of expressive realism, notably the porch of the Carthusian Monastery of Champmol, near Dijon (Fig. 379), and (in the same place) the famous *Well of Moses*, the hexagonal base of a Calvary, each compartment of which is ornamented with statues of prophets (Fig. 380). The group of the Virgin and Child, the smiling and somewhat silly figure of Duc Philippe and that of Marguerite of Flanders, are admirable details which worthily sustain the great tradition of the *imagiers*. The Moses is a mighty figure, at once scriptural and realistic. All this was finished before 1395; now Ghiberti's beautiful gates for the Baptistery at Florence are later by thirty years, and Masaccio was not born till 1401. It is, therefore, evident that, at the beginning of the fifteenth century, Flanders was greatly in advance of Italy.

And this was not only true as regards sculpture. Before 1416, the date of the Duc de Berry's death, Paul de Limbourg and his brothers illuminated the exquisite Book of Hours which is the glory of the Musée Condé at Chantilly (Fig. 381). This was no isolated masterpiece. There is in the Louvre a *Trinity* by the Guelderlander Malouel, probably the uncle of the Limbourgs, who was working in Paris about 1400. In this many of the finest qualities of the Book of Hours are foreshadowed. We must therefore look

FIG. 383.—CHOIR OF
ANGELS.
HUBERT AND JAN VAN
EYCK.
(Museum, Berlin.)

FIG. 384.—VIRGIN READING.
HUBERT VAN EYCK.
(Fragment of the Polyptych,
*The Adoration of the
Lamb.*)
(Church of St. Bavon,
Ghent.)

upon it as a product of the Parisian Renaissance, born from the contact of artists of Flemish birth with the taste and refinement that distinguished the court of the Valois.

At this period (1400-1410), Franco-Flemish art had spread throughout France, and invaded the valley of the Rhine. Social and commercial intercourse soon carried it beyond the Alps; we may note that the Duke of Orleans, assassinated in 1407, had married a Visconti, Valentina of Milan. About the year 1400, Philippe le Hardi was buying Italian medals and ivories; an Italian, Pietro of Verona, was his librarian. On the other hand, Flemish art was finding its way

FIG. 385.—THE JUST JUDGES AND THE KNIGHTS OF CHRIST.

HUBERT AND JAN VAN EYCK.

(Shutters of the Polyptych, *The Adoration of the Lamb.*)

(Museum, Berlin.)

into Italy, and this migratory movement continued throughout the fifteenth century. The artistic affinities of the Limbourgs, the Van Eycks, Gentile da Fabriano, and Pisanello are obvious. Now it is

more than probable that rich and prosperous Flanders did not borrow everything from Italy. It may even be that the realistic influence of Flemish art had its share in Masaccio's reaction against Giottism. These are points a good deal discussed just now, which will no doubt be presently solved.

Although the sculptors of the Flemish Renaissance left us many important works which upheld the tradition of Claux Sluter—it will be enough to give as examples the tombs

FIG. 386.—THE VIRGIN AND CHILD WITH A CARTHUSIAN DONOR.

HUBERT OR JAN VAN EYCK.

(G. de Rothschild Collection, Paris.)

(Photo. by Lévy and Son.)

of the Dukes of Burgundy at Dijon and at Bruges, and that of Philippe Pot in the Louvre (Fig. 382)—I shall confine myself here

FIG. 387.—JAN ARNOLFINI AND HIS WIFE.
JAN VAN EYCK.
(National Gallery, London.)

FIG. 388.—THE RAISING OF LAZARUS.
A. VAN OUWATER
(Museum, Berlin.)   (Photo. by Hanfstaengl.)

to painting, the art in which its genius was most brilliantly manifested.

The Italians of the middle of the fifteenth century were well aware that the Flemish painters had no compeers; they collected their works eagerly, and sent them many pupils.[1] Common opinion even attributed the invention of oil-painting to the Van Eycks, though the method had been known since the twelfth century, and the Flemings had merely perfected drying mediums, and given a new splendour and intensity to colour. Superior as the Italians were to the Flemings in the decorative style, they admitted their inferiority in the rendering of life. Later on opinion became less equitable, and even somewhat oblivious. It was only in the

FIG. 389.—ST. FRANCIS RECEIVING THE STIGMATA.
(Museum, Turin.)   (Photo. by Anderson.)

[1] In 1460, Bianca Maria Sforza, Duchess of Milan, sent the youthful painter Zanetto Bugatto to Brussels, to study in Roger van der Weyden's *atelier*. In 1463, Zanetto returned and the Duchess wrote to Roger to thank him. (Malaguzzi Valeri, *Pittori, Lombardi*, Milan, 1902.)

THE RENAISSANCE IN FRANCE AND FLANDERS

nineteenth century that full justice began to be rendered to those admirable artists, the Van Eycks, Roger van der Weyden, Hugo van der Goes, Thierry Bouts, Memling, Gerard David, Albert van Ouwater, and Quentin Matsys.

The great altar-piece of *The Adoration of the Lamb* at Ghent was all, and even more, to Flemish painting, that Masaccio's frescoes were to the Italian School. This work, now divided between the towns of Ghent, Brussels, and Berlin, was begun about the year 1420 by Hubert van Eyck, and finished in 1432 by his brother Jan. It is not easy to assign to each brother his part in the work; but I am inclined to think that Jan's share was confined to the two magnificent portraits of the donors. The angels playing musical instruments, the processions of the

FIG. 390.—THE MEETING OF ABRAHAM AND MELCHISEDECH.

THIERRY BOUTS.

(Pinacothek, Munich.) (Woermann, *Geschichte der Malerei*. Seemann, Leipzig.)

Soldiers of Christ and of the Just Judges, the figures of Adam and Eve, the great central panel, which is all that remains at Ghent,

FIG. 391.—THE DESCENT FROM THE CROSS.
R. VAN DER WEYDEN.
(Museum, Madrid.) (Photo. by Lacoste.)

moved Fromentin to say that in this work art had achieved perfection in a first effort (Figs. 383-385). But the miniatures in the Chantilly Book of Hours, which were unknown to Fromentin, attest that the Van Eycks had their peers. It is quite evident that they were not the disciples of the brothers Limbourg; the two families were contemporary manifestations of two kindred styles, the one (that of the Van Eycks), purely Flemish, the other modified by Italian influences, and refined by a Parisian environment.

221

Jan van Eyck (1385-1441) was employed by Philippe le Bon on various diplomatic missions. He visited Portugal, Spain, and the Hague. There is nothing to show that he was ever in Italy. From 1432 to 1440 he painted a whole series of signed and dated pictures, among them such incomparable portraits as those of his wife, of Canon Van de Paele at Bruges, and of the Arnolfini couple in the National Gallery (Fig. 387). The great picture at Bruges, in which Van de Paele appears as donor, enables us to appreciate both the greatness of Jan's genius and its limitations. He has no religious sentiment, no fervour; the Virgin is ugly, the Infant Jesus sickly; the St. George is a peasant in armour. But Jan van Eyck is the greatest portraitist of all time. Never did keener eye scrutinise the living form, never did more skilful hand fix its image on the panel.

FIG. 392.—THE JUDGMENT OF THE EMPEROR OTHO.
THIERRY BOUTS.
(Museum, Brussels.)
(Photo. by Hanfstaengl.)

There is also a little series of unsigned pictures, nearly all masterpieces, which are ascribed sometimes to Jan, sometimes to Hubert. Two of the most perfect of them are in Paris; one, in the Louvre, represents Rolin, Chancellor of Philippe le Bon, kneeling before the Virgin and Child, against a marvellous landscape background; the other, in M. Gustave de Rothschild's collection, shows the Vicar of the Carthusian monastery of St. Anne at Bruges, Hermann Steenken, before the Virgin, St. Anne, and St. Barbara, with the same landscape as the first. A third panel from the same *atelier*, representing St. Francis, is at Turin.

FIG. 303.—VIRGIN AND CHILD.
JACQUES DARET
(called the Master of Flémalle).
(Museum, Frankfort.)
(Photo. by Bruckman.)

FIG. 394.—THE BISHOP GUILLAUME FILLATRE
PRESENTS THE VOLUME TO PHILIPPE LE BON.

SIMON MARMION. (?)

(Frontispiece of a Manuscript in the Library
at St. Petersburg.)

FIG. 395.—ARRIVAL OF ST. URSULA AT
COLOGNE.

H. MEMLING.

(Shrine of St. Ursula.)

(Hospital of Bruges.)

During their long sojourn at the Hague, the two Van Eycks must have formed a certain number of pupils; the best known of these is Albert van Ouwater, the author of a masterpiece, *The Resurrection of Lazarus*, in the Berlin Museum (Fig. 388), which his pupil, Gerard of Haarlem (Geertgen), successfully imitated in a picture acquired by the Louvre in 1902. With these Dutchmen we must class a Haarlemer, who was perhaps a fellow-pupil of Ouwater's, Thierry Bouts (1410-1475), and who worked at Louvain about 1459. He was an artist whose vigour of temperament verged on brutality, whose realism led him into deliberate ugliness, and his desire for brilliance into crudity of colour. His best

FIG. 396.—THE NATIVITY.

HUGO VAN DER GOES.

(Academy, Florence.) (Photo. by Alinari.)

works, such as the *Judgment of Otho* at Brussels, are extraordinary in their intensity of tone and expression, but better in drawing

FIG. 397.—PORTRAIT OF MARTIN VAN NEWENHOVEN.

H. MEMLING.

(Hospital of St. John, Bruges.)

and painting than in composition (Figs. 390, 392).

Between 1435 and 1464, a painter of Tournai, Roger de la Pasture (in Flemish, Van der Weyden), worked at Brussels. He was the pupil of Robert Campin (1375-1444), to whom some have wished to attribute the magnificent paintings in the Mérode collection at Brussels, at Aix, and elsewhere. Until 1909, he was called the master of Mérode or of Flémalle (from the name of the Walloon abbey from which the Frankfort pictures

FIG. 399.—THE BANKER AND HIS WIFE.

QUENTIN MATSYS

(The Louvre.)

came) and wrongly believed to be the pupil of Rogier or identified with another of Campin's pupils, Jacques Daret. Campin and Van der Weyden strove for pathos. They had the religious and dramatic sentiment; unlike Van Eyck, they knew how to express the strong emotions of the soul. Van der Weyden's *Descent from the Cross* in the Escorial (Fig. 391) and his great pictures at Beaune, at Munich, and at Berlin will always be counted among the great masterpieces of art.

FIG. 398.—THE VIRGIN SURROUNDED BY SAINTS.

GERARD DAVID.

(Museum, Rouen)   (Photo. by Petiton.)

Between 1450 and 1490, the Dutch or Flemish school produced a long series of prodigies who are still in doubtful chronological order and whose works are uncertainly attributed. Marmion of Amiens—unless, indeed, it was Jean Hennecart—painted, about 1455 the admirable *Life of St. Bertin* (in the Berlin Museum and illuminated with exquisite miniatures a manuscript presented to Philippe le Bon (Fig. 394). About 1470, the Zeelander, Hugo van der Goes,

painted for Tommaso Portinari, the agent of the Medici at Bruges, a colossal *Nativity* (Fig. 396), which Portinari presented to the hospital at Florence, and from which the Italian painters Lorenzo di Credi, Ghirlandajo, etc., hastened to copy details. Finally, from 1468 to 1489, Memling produced his exquisite series of portraits and large religious compositions (Figs. 395, 397). Is there a more fascinating achievement in all the domain of painting than the *Shrine of St. Ursula* at Bruges? If we except those of Van Eyck, what portraits are superior to Memling's? He was, indeed,

FIG. 400.—THE VIRGIN AND ST ANNE.
QUENTIN MATSYS.
(Museum, Brussels.)   (Photo. by Hanfstaengl.)

the Raphael of Flemish art, the man in whom all the gentler gifts of his school were combined to the exclusion of all that was harsh and brutal. Inferior to Van der Weyden in his mastery of expressive line, and to Jan van Eyck in solid and plastic realism, the heir of the miniaturists rather than of the painters, he is the most attractive, if not the most original, of all these gifted masters.

Memling had a successor at Bruges, Gerard David, who flourished from 1488 to 1509. His masterpiece, a Virgin surrounded by Saints, is at Rouen (Fig. 398); we note therein, together with a return to the types of Van Eyck, indications of the increase of Italian influence. These are also apparent in the works of the Antwerp

FIG. 401.—THE JUGGLER.
JEROME BOSCH.
(Municipal Museum, St. Germain-en-Laye.)
(Photo. by Lévy and Son.)

FIG. 402.—VIRGIN AND CHILD.
JAN GOSSAERT, CALLED MABUSE.
(Museum, Berlin.)
(Photo. by Hanfstaengl.)

FIG. 403.—THE BURNING BUSH.
NICHOLAS FROMENT OF AVIGNON.
(Cathedral of Aix.)
(Photo by Neurdein.)

master, Quentin Matsys (1466-1530); but Van der Weyden's tradition is maintained in his *Descent from the Cross* at Antwerp, his *St. Anne* at Brussels (Fig. 400), and his head of the praying Virgin in the National Gallery. There is an idealistic element in Matsys' art, though he appears as a realist, and even a satirist upon occasions (Fig. 399), but he did not deliberately imitate the Italians.

Unfortunately, the Flemings were stirred to emulation by the glory of Leonardo da Vinci, Raphael, and Michelangelo. Certain very gifted painters, such as Jan Gossaert of Maubeuge (called Mabuse) and Barendt van Orley, went to Italy and brought back a style which harmonised ill with that they had received from native masters (Fig. 402.)

It is unnecessary to linger over

FIG. 404.—THE ADORATION OF THE MAGI.
J. FOUQUET.
(Miniature in the Musée Condé, Chantilly.)
(Photo by Braun, Clement et Cie.)

226

these hybrid, though often fascinating, works, in which Italian idealism, the imitation of the antique, and Flemish realism are associated but not assimilated. These Italianised painters reigned supreme throughout the second half of the sixteenth century, and had at at least this merit, that they prepared the way for Rubens. Side by side with them, as if in reaction, other Flemings were following a very different path, delighting in jests and satires, painting and working for people. These racy

FIG. 405.—TRIPTYCH PRESENTED BY PIERRE II. DE BOURBON AND ANNE DE BEAUJEU TO THE CATHEDRAL OF MOULINS.
(By a French Master, perhaps Jean Perréal.)
(Photo. by Neurdein.)

and spirited realists, Jerome Bosch (Fig. 401) and the elder Breughel, prepared the way for the Dutch Little Masters of the seventeenth century, who were to raise genre-painting to the level of great art.

This tendency to give poetry to realities, rather than to realise a conventional ideal, is prominent throughout the whole course of Flemish art. Painters were obliged to paint sacred pictures, Virgins, angels and martyrs, because their clients asked for these; but how clearly they show that all of them, even Memling himself, would gladly have painted anything else! The things that interest them, that they study and render most lovingly, are figures of donors, rich stuffs, distant glimpses of landscape. They are never so great as when they escape from the bondage of the given theme. There is one exception to this rule—Roger van der Weyden. But we know he had made a pilgrimage to Rome, and that he lived for a time at Ferrara. He was the sole mystic among the numerous Flemish painters of religious subjects.

FIG. 406.—PORTRAIT OF HENRY II.
F. CLOUET.
(The Louvre.)

The French branch of Flemish art in the fifteenth century followed a similar course, save that the realistic tendency here was early tempered by the essentially French taste

227

FIG. 407.—DIANA AND HER NYMPHS.
SCHOOL OF FONTAINEBLEAU.
(Museum, Rouen.)
(Photo by Petiton.)

for sobriety and elegance[1]. At the close of the fourteenth century, Paris was an artistic centre of the first rank. About 1410, the misfortunes that befell the monarchy scattered the artists of the capital to Burgundy, Touraine, and Provence. The establishment of the Papal court at Avignon in 1309 had created a centre of Italian art in the city, round which a local school soon grew up; the masterpiece of this school is the large *Pietà* of the hospital of Villeneuve (1470), now in the Louvre. Froment of Avignon, the

FIG. 408.—A CARDINAL
VIRTUE[2].
MICHEL COLOMBE.
(Figure from the Tomb of
François II. of Bretagne.)
(Nantes Cathedral.)

painter of the *Burning Bush* (Fig. 403) in the Cathedral of Aix, worked at the court of René of Anjou (1417-1480), who established himself in Provence after losing Naples and Sicily. During the reigns of Charles VII. and Louis XI. a very great artist flourished in France, Jean Fouquet (1415-1485), who was in Italy about 1445, and later at Tours. There are powerful portraits by him at Paris and at Berlin, and at Chantilly an admirable series of forty miniatures, painted about 1455 for the Book of Hours of

FIG. 409.—THE THREE
GRACES.
GERMAIN PILON.
(The Louvre)

Etienne Chevalier (Fig. 404). The decorative elements of these little pictures are Italian to some extent, but the sentiment is purely

[1] What Courajod calls "the relaxation of the French style."
[2] Temperance, with her attributes, a yoke and a clock.

French, and suggests a gentler Van Eyck. The colour is delicate, but lacking in brilliance, and occasionally in harmony. The school of the Bourbonnais, of which we are only just beginning to learn something, was formed under the influences of those of Touraine and Provence. A large picture in the Cathedral of Moulins, perhaps by Jean Perréal, painter to Charles VIII., shows strong Italian influences, together with a native taste for a somewhat mannered grace and pale, delicately shaded colours (Fig. 405). A yet finer work by this master is the *Nativity* in the Bishop's palace at Autun, the background of which reveals the influence of Van der Goes (cf. Fig. 396).

FIG. 410 —RELIEFS ON THE FON-
TAINE DES INNOCENTS, PARIS
JEAN GOUJON.
(Photo by Giraudon.)

A family of painters of Dutch origin, the Clouets, produced a large number of portraits from the time of François I. to that of Henry III., both in oils and crayons, in which lightness of touch, learned precision of line, and contempt for unnecessary detail presage the qualities of the classic spirit as manifested in France in the seventeenth century (Fig. 406). These fine portraits, so non-insistent, so reticent, and yet so delicately psychological, seem "made out of nothing," like Racine's tragedies. The Italians summoned to France in 1531-1532, Rosso and Primaticcio, busied themselves mainly in propagating the defects of the School of Michelangelo, but their imitators, who formed the so-called School of Fontainebleau, remained French rather than Italian. This is evident in the pictures of the school, which is well represented at the Louvre and at Rouen (Fig. 407). Their authors speak Italian, but with a strong French accent.

FIG. 411.—DIANA AND STAG.
ATTRIBUTED TO JEAN GOUJON.
(The Louvre.)

In sculpture, Italianism first invaded decoration, then bas-relief and statuary; but, here again, down to the end of the sixteenth century, the French element predominated, in the works of Michel Colombe (d. 1512), Germain Pilon, and Barthélemy Prieur, the contemporaries of Catherine de' Medici and Henri IV. (Figs. 408, 409). The most Italian and also, perhaps, the most gifted of the artists of this period was Jean Goujon, whose nymphs on the Fontaine des Innocents in Paris (1550) and the portal of the Louvre which bears his name are among the most delightful works of the Franco-Italian Renaissance (Fig. 410). These are decorative sculptures; but the portraits of the period, especially those of dead persons kneeling, are inspired rather by the French *imagiers* than by Italian models. French art was never completely Italianised, even under Louis XIV.; the history of national resistance to foreign taste may be followed throughout the seventeenth century and paves the way for the truly French school of the eighteenth.

FIG. 412.—THE TEMPTATION OF ST. ANTHONY.
(Engraving.)
LUCAS VAN LEYDEN
(Woermann, *History of Painting*, Seemann, Leipzig.)

At the beginning of the sixteenth century, a very individual school of Dutch painting arose. The centre of this school was Leyden, where Engelbrechtsen (d. 1533), the master of Lucas van Leyden (1494-1533), worked. Few pictures by Lucas have survived; the most important is the *Last Judgment* in the Leyden Museum. But he left nearly two hundred engravings, which will bear comparison with those of Dürer himself (Fig. 412). His taste for rustic and comic scenes, the boldness and facility of his burin, herald the development of familiar art in Holland.

Lucas, who died at the age of 39, was an artist of great capacity, Jacob Cornelisz of Amsterdam and Jan van Scorel of Utrecht were also gifted painters, less susceptible than their Flemish contemporaries to those transalpine influences which have nearly always proved pernicious to men of northern race. Holland, by espousing the cause of the Reformation, and breaking with Rome, preserved her

THE RENAISSANCE IN FRANCE AND FLANDERS

artistic originality to some extent, before she won her independence. This was done at the expense of cruel sacrifices; but she reaped the reward of her courage, in the seventeenth century, when she gave the world one of the heroes of art, Rembrandt, a genius at once Dutch and universal.

BIBLIOGRAPHY OF CHAPTER XIX.

A. Michel, *op. cit.*, p. 166; L. Courajod, *Leçons professées à l'Ecole du Louvre*, vol. ii., Paris, 1901; (Origins of the Renaissance, Burgundian art, the influence of Northern art on Italy); L. Courajod and F. Marcou, *Le Musée de Sculpture comparée du Trocadéro*, Paris, 1892; L. Gonse, *La Sculpture française depuis le XIVe siècle*, Paris, 1895; Hourtique, *Histoire de l'art en France*, Paris, 1911; *Vitry et Brière, Documents de Sculpture française, Renaissance*, Paris, 1911.

Sir Martin Conway, *The Van Eycks and Their Followers*, London, 1921; A. Michiels, *Histoire de la Peinture flamande*, 10 vols., Paris, 1865–1874; *L'Art flamand dans l'Est et le Midi de la France*, Paris, 1877; A. von Wurzbach, *Niederländisches Künstlerlexicon*, Vienna, 1906–1908; Fierens-Gevaert, *Les primitifs flamands*, 4 vols., Brussels, 1908–1912; C. Dehaisnes, *L'Art chrétien en Flandre*, Douai, 1860; *Histoire de l'Art dans la Flandre avant le XVe siècle*, 2 vols., Lille, 1886; A. Darcel, *L'Art dans les Flandres avant le XVe siècle* (Gaz. des Beaux-Arts, 1887, i., p. 153); E. Müntz, *Les influences classiques et le Renouvellement de l'Art dans les Flandres au XVe siècle* (*ibid.*, 1898, i., pp. 289, 472); M. Friedländer, *Meisterwerke der niederländischen Malerei*, Munich, 1903; J.Weale, *The Early Painters of the Netherlands* (Burlington Magazine, 1903, i., p. 41); F. Gevaert, *La Renaissance septentrionale*, Brussels, 1905; H. Hymans, *L'Exposition des Primitifs flamands à Bruges*, Paris, 1902; R. Fry, *The Exhibition of Early Flemish Art at Bruges* (The Athenaeum, September 13 and 20, 1902; cf. *Rev. archéol.*, 1903, i., p. 76); G. Hulin, *Catalogue critique de l'Exposition de Bruges*, Bruges, 1902 (cf. *Revue archéol*, 1903, i., p. 110; 1903, ii., p. 319); E. Male, *L'Art religieux de la fin du Moyen Age* (influence of the *Mystères*).

P. Durrieu, *L'Exposition des Primitifs français* (*Revue de l'Art*, 1904, i., p. 82); Bouchot, same subject, Paris, 1905 (with 100 illus.); R. Fry, same subject (Burlington Magazine, 1904, i., p. 279); Bouchot, Delisle, etc., *Exposition des Primitifs français au Louvre*, Paris, 1904; R. de Lasteyrie, *Les Miniatures d'André Beauneveu et de Jacquemart de Hesdin*, (Mon. Piot, vol. iii., p. 71); Delisle, *Les Heures du Duc de Berry* (Gaz. des B.-Arts, 1884, i., p. 401); A. de Champeaux and P. Gauchery, *Les Arts à la Cour du Duc de Berry*, Paris, 1894 (cf. B. Prost, Gaz. des Beaux-Arts, 1895, ii., p. 254, and for the works of this school. H. Bouchot and S. Reinach, *ibid.*, 1904, i., pp. 1 and 55); P. Durrieu, *Les très riches Heures du Duc de Berry*, Paris, 1904; *Les belles Heures d'Ailly* (Gazette des Beaux-Arts, 1906, i., p. 265); A. de Champeaux, *Le Duc de Berry et l'Art italien* (Gaz. des Beaux-Arts, 1888, ii., p. 409) (cf. Burlington Magazine, xviii, p. 144, and Monuments Piot, xviii., p. 183); *L'Ancienne Ecole de peinture de la Bourgogne* (*ibid.*, 1898, i., p. 36); A. Perrault-Dabot, *L'Art en Bourgogne*, Paris, 1894 (cf. Leprieur, *Repertorium*, 1895, p. 383); A. Kleinclausz, *Claus Sluter* (Gaz. des Beaux-Arts, 1903, i., p. 121, and Paris, 1905); *L'Art funéraire de la Bourgogne*, (*ibid.*, 1901, ii., p. 441; 1905, ii., p. 26).

J. Helbig, *La Sculpture au pays de Liège*, Liège, 1890; *La Peinture au pays de Liège*, Liège, 1903; F. G. Cremer, *Studien zur Geschichte der Oelfarbentechnik*, Düsseldorf, 1895; P. Durrieu, *Les Débuts des Van Eyck* (Gazette des Beaux-Arts, 1903, i., p. 1; The Book of Hours at Turin); L. Kämmerer, *Hubert und Jan Van Eyck*, Bielefeld, 1898; W. H. Weale, *The Van Eycks*, London, 1912; M. Dvorak, *Das Rätsel der Kunst der Van Eyck*, Vienna, 1904; W. Bode, *Le Retable de l'Agneau* (Gazette des Beaux-Arts, 1897, i., p. 211; cf. J. Six, *ibid.*, 1904, i., p. 177).

P. Lafond, *Rogier*, Brussels, 1912; L. Maeterlinck, *Rogier sculpteur* (Gazette des Beaux-Arts, 1901, ii., p., 265); M. Friedländer, *Bildniss des Meisters von Flemalle* (Jahrbücher of the Berlin Museums, 1902, p. 17); H. von Tschudi, *Der Meister von Flemalle* (*ibid.*, 1898, p. 8); G. Hulin *Darêt et Campia* (Burlington Magazine, July, 1909, p. 202); A. Wauters, *Hugo van der Goes*, Brussels, 1872 (cf. Gaz. des Beaux-Arts, 1910, ii., p. 104, on the picture discovered at Monfort, Spain); W. Bode, *Die Anbetung der Hirten von H. van der Goes* (Juhrbücher of the Berlin Museums, 1903, p. 99); C. Dehaisnes, *Recherches sur le retable de Saint-Bertin et sur Simon Marmion*, Lille, 1892 (cf. on Hennecart, Durrieu, Revue arch., 1909, ii., p. 287); A. Golfin, *Thierry Bouts*, Brussels, 1908; L. Kämmerer, *Memling*, Bielefeld, 1889; W. H. Weale, *Hans Memling*, London, 1901 (same subject in French, Bruges, 1903); K. Voll, *Memling*, Stuttgart, 1909 (photographs of all the works); G. Servières, *Le Polyptyque de Memling à Lubeck* (Gazette des Beaux-Arts, 1902, i., p. 119); E. von Bodenhausen, *G. David*, Munich, 1905; L. Balet, *Geertgen*, La Haye, 1912; C. Benoit, *La Résurrection de Lazare par Gérard de Harlem* (Monum. Piot, vol. xi., p. 73); J. de Busschère, *Z. Metsys*, Brussels, 1908; C. Benoit, *Jean Mostaert* (*ibid.*, 1899, i., p. 265); S. Pierron, *Les Mostaert*, Brussels, 1912; M. Gossart, *Jean Gossart de Maubeuge*, Lille, 1903; J. Bosch, Lille, 1907; A. Wauters, *Bernard van Orley*, Paris, 1893; H. Dollmayer, *Hieronymus Bosch* (Jahrbücher of the Vienna Museums, 1898, p. 284); L. Maeterlinck, *Une Œuvre inconnue de Jérome Bosch* (Gazette des Beaux-Arts, 1900, i., p. 68); H. Hymans, *Breughel le Vieux* (*ibid.*, 1890, i., p. 361); Basteleur and De Loo, *P. Breughel*, Brussels, 1906.

G. F. Warner, *Illuminated Manuscripts in the British Museum*, London, 1899 and after (facsimiles

---

[1] I have taken various items in Chapter XIX from these articles.

in colour); R. Beer, *Die Miniaturenausstellung in Wien* (*Kunst und Kunsthandwerk*, Vienna, 1902, p. 285); H. Martin, *Les Miniaturistes français*, Paris, 1906; J. A. Herbert, *Illuminated Manuscripts*, London, 1911; S. Reinach, *Un Manuscrit de Philippe-le-Bon à Saint-Pétersbourg* (*Gazette des Beaux-Arts*, 1903, i., p. 265; cf. *Monuments Piot*, vol. xi.); P. Durrieu, *Histoire du bon roi Alexandre* (*Revue de l'Art*, 1903, i., p. 49; miniatures by Ph. de Mazerolles); Aug. Schestag, *Die Chronik von Jerusalem* (*Jahrbücher* of the Vienna Museums, 1899, p. 195; manuscript illuminated for Philippe le Bon): J. Destrée, *Les Heures de N.-D. dites de Hennessy*, Brussels, 1896; P. Durrieu, *A. Bening et les Peintres du bréviaire Grimani* (*Gazette des Beaux-Arts*, 1891, i., p. 353); G. Pawlowski, *Le Livre d'Heures d'Alexandre Borgia* (*ibid.*, 1891, i., p. 511); Kämmerer, *Ahnenreihen aus dem Stammbaum des portugiesischen Königshauses* (Flemish miniatures in the British Museum), Stuttgart, 1903 (cf. Weale, *Burlington Magazine*, 1903, ii., p. 321); A. Lindner, *Der Breslauer Froissart*, Berlin, 1912.

H. Curmer, *Les Evangiles*, Paris, 1864 (chromos after miniatures of the 15th century); *Œuvres de Jean Fouquet*, Paris 1865 (chromos); H. Bouchot, *Jean Fouquet* (*Gazette des Beaux-Arts*, 1890, ii., p. 273); P. Leprieur, *Jean Fouquet* (*Revue de l'Art*, 1897, i., p. 25); G. Lafenestre, *Jean Fouquet* (*Revue des Deux-Mondes*, Jan. 15, 1902); M. Friedländer, *Die Votiftafel des Etienne Chevalier von Fouquet* (*Jahrbücher* of the Berlin Museums, 1897, p. 206); F. Gruyer, *Etienne Chevalier et Saint Etienne par Fouquet* (*Gazette des Beaux-Arts*, 1896, i., p. 89); *Les Quarante Fouquet* [Chantilly], Paris, 1900; E. Michel, *Les Miniatures de Fouquet à Chantilly* (*Gazette des Beaux-Arts*, 1897, i., p. 214); P. Durrieu, *Miniatures inédites de Fouquet* (Memo. of the Soc. des Antiquaires, 1903, vol. lxi., p. 105); P. Durrieu and J. J. Marquet de Vasselot, *Les Manuscrits à miniatures des Héroïdes d'Ovide* (*L'Artiste*, May, June, 1894; sequel to the school of Fouquet at Tours); Dorez, *Les Manuscrits de Holkham Hall*, Paris, 1908.

L. de Laborde, *La Renaissance à la Cour de France*, 2 vols., Paris, 1850, 1855; E. Müntz, *La Renaissance en Italie et en France à l'époque de Charles VIII*, Paris, 1885; H. Lemonnier, *Les Guerres d'Italie* (vol. v. of the *Histoire de France*, edited by Lavisse), Paris, 1902; L. Dimier, *French Painting in the XVIth Century*, London, 1904; P. Mantz, *La Peinture française du IXe au XVIe siècle*, Paris, 1898; C. Benoit, *La Peinture française à la fin du XVe siècle* (*Gazette des Beaux-Arts*, 1901, ii., pp. 89, 318; 1902, i., p. 65); G. Lafenestre, *La Peinture française du XVe siècle* (*ibid.*, 1900, ii., p. 377, and 1904, i., p. 353); P. Gélis-Didot, *La Peinture décorative en France, du XIe au XVIe siècle*, 2 vols., Paris, 1891; H. Laffillée, *La Peinture murale en France avant la Renaissance*, Paris, 1904; M. Poète, *Les Primitifs parisiens*, Paris, 1904; J. Déchelette and E. Brassart, *Les Peintures murales du moyen âge et de la Rencissance en Forez*, Montbrison, 1900; L. de Farcy, *Histoire et Description des Tapisseries de l'Eglise cathédrale d'Angers*, 1896 (extr. from the *Revue de l'Anjou*).

G. Lafenestre, *Nicolas Froment* (*Revue de l'Art*, 1897, ii., p. 305); L. Dehaisnes, *La Vie et l'Œuvre de Jean Bellegambe*, Lille, 1890 (cf. *Gazette des Beaux-Arts*, 1890, i., p. 514); R. Maulde de la Clavière, *Jean Perréal dit Jean de Paris peintre de Charles VIII*, Paris, 1896; E. Male, *Jean Bourdichon* (*Gazette des Beaux-Arts*, 1904, i., p. 185, and 1904, ii., p. 441); H. J. Hermann, *Ein unbekanntes Gebetbuch von Jean Bourdichon* (*Beiträge zur Kunstgeschichte Wickhoff gewidmet*, Vienna, 1903, p. 46).

H. Havard, *La Peinture hollandaise*, Paris, 1882; F. Dülberg, *Die Leydener Malerschule*, Berlin, 1399 (cf. *Repertorium*, 1899, p. 328); Th. Volbehr, *Lucas v. Leyden*, Hamburg, 1888.

F. Dimier, *La Primatice*, Paris, 1902; E. Müntz, *L'Ecole de Fontainebleau et le Primatice* (*Gazette des Beaux-Arts*, 1902, ii., p. 152); H. Bouchot, *Le Portrait en France au XVIe siècle* (*Gazette des Beaux-Arts*, 1887, ii., p. 108); *Les Clouet et Corneille de Lyon*, Paris, 1892; F. Wickhoff, *Die Bilder weiblicher, Halbfiguren* (*Jahrbücher* of the Vienna Museums, 1901; cf. *Chronique des Arts*, 1902, p. 240); Moreau-Nélaton, *Les Clouet*, Paris, 1908; S. Reinach, *Gaz. des Beaux-Arts*, August–October, 1920.

St. Lami, *Dictionnaire des Sculpteurs de l'Ecole française jusqu'à Louis XIV*, Paris, 1898; M. de Vasselot, *Antoine le Moiturier* (*Monuments Piot*, vol. iii., p. 247); R. Koechlin and M. de Vasselot, *La Sculpture à Troyes et dans la Champagne méridionale au XVIe siècle*, Paris, 1901 (cf. *Gazette des Beaux-Arts*, 1901, i., p. 260); E. Thiollier, *Sculptures foréziennes de la Renaissance* (*ibid.*, i., p. 496); P. Vitry, *Michel Colombe*, Paris, 1902 (cf. Lefèvre-Pontalis, *Bull. Monumental*, 1902, p. 111); Deuis, *Ligier Richier*, Paris, 1912; L. Palustre, *Germain Pilon* (*Gazette des Beaux-Arts*, 1894, i., p. 1); P. Vitry, *Jean Goujon* Paris, 1908; H. Jouin, *J. Goujon*, Paris, 1906.

L. Bourdery and E. Lachenaud, *Léonard Limosin*, Paris, 1897; Edm. Bonnaffé, *Les Faïences de Saint-Porchaire* (*Gazette des Beaux-Arts*, 1895, i., p. 277; P. Burty, *Bernard de Palissy*, Paris, 1886; C. Dupuy, *Bernard de Palissy*, Poitiers, 1902; H. Havard, *Histoire de l'Orfèvrerie française*, Paris, 1890; E. Molinier, *L'Orfèvrerie religieuse du Ve à la fin du XVe siècle*, Paris, no date; N. Dawson, *Goldsmiths and Silversmiths*, London, 1907; J. Guiffrey, *La Tapisserie, son histoire depuis le moyen âge jusqu'à nos jours*, Tours, 1836; *Les Tapisseries du XII–XIII Siècle*, Paris, 1912; E. Garnier, *Histoire de la Verrerie, et de l'Emaillerie*, Tours, 1886.

FIG. 413.—THE ADORATION OF THE MAGI.
STEPHAN LOCHNER.
(Cologne Cathedral.)

XX

THE RENAISSANCE IN GERMANY

The National Character of German Art.—The School of Prague.—Master Wilhelm of Cologne. —Stephan Lochner.—His Adoration of the Magi.—The School of Cologne.—The Master of the Altar of St. Bartholomew, and other anonymous Masters of the School.—The Lack of Refinement in German Art.—German Wood-carving and its Influence on Painting.—The Suabian School.—Martin Schongauer.—The School of Augsburg.—The School of Nuremberg.—Albert Dürer and his Pupils.—Holbein.—Lucas Cranach.—The School of Alsace.— Mathias Grünewald.—Hans Baldung Grien.—Joos von Cleve.—Barthel Bruyn.—The Extinction of National Art in Germany.

ITALIAN art dreamed of beauty and realised its dream. Flemish art was in love with truth, and "held the mirror up to nature." German art rarely achieved either truth or beauty. But it succeeded in rendering, with a fidelity that was often brutal, the character of the German people immediately before and after the Reformation.

The first School of German painting of which we have any knowledge flourished at Prague about the year 1360 under the Emperor Charles IV., who summoned the Modenese painter, Tommaso, from Italy to Bohemia. Somewhat later, in 1380, we hear of one Master Wilhelm, of Cologne, who is much lauded by the chroniclers of the time. Wilhelm was succeeded by Stephan Lochner, from the neighbourhood of Constance. About the year 1435, during the lifetime of Van Eyck, he completed the most important work produced by the German School in the Middle Ages, the famous *Adoration of the Magi* in Cologne Cathedral (Fig. 413). Lochner has been called the German Fra Angelico; his art is devout, radiant, and sentimental; his characters are rosy,

FIG. 414.—SS. COLOMBA AND ANDREW.
(School of Cologne. The Master of the Altar of St. Bartholomew.)
(Museum, Mainz.)

FIG. 415.—THE ANGELIC SALUTATION.
VEIT STOSS.
(Church of St. Lawrence, Nuremberg.)

chubby children, who are always good and go to church regularly. The Van Eycks were already famous in 1435, but the Cologne picture shows no trace of their influence. Lochner's art was derived from illuminated manuscripts, probably the work of the Flemish miniaturists who flourished at the end of the fourteenth century in Flanders, Burgundy, and Paris.

A novel tendency towards realism made its appearance towards 1460 in the numerous pictures of the Cologne masters. A pupil of Bouts founded a school there which became very flourishing. Henceforth, though it remained very German in its defects, the School of Cologne, which existed till the middle of the sixteenth century, was merely a Rhenish off-shoot of Flemish art. The two masters most imitated at Cologne were Bouts and Van der Weyden. The great, and as yet unknown, master who painted the Colognese *Descent from the Cross* in the Louvre was inspired by the latter and by Schongauer (p. 237); he is distinguished as the *Master of the Altar of St. Bartholomew*, from one of his works at Munich (Fig. 414). As a general rule, indeed, the artists of this prolific

FIG. 416.—THE TOMB OF ST. SEBALD.
PETER VISCHER.
(Church of St. Sebald, Nuremberg.)

THE RENAISSANCE IN GERMANY

school are anonymous, and are known as the *Master of the Lyversberg Passion* (from the name of the owner of the series), the *Master of the Life of the Virgin*, the *Master of the Holy Family* (*Heilige Sippe*), &c.

It was not only at Cologne that painters sought inspiration from the Flemings, but throughout Germany. But the political and social conditions of the country were not yet propitious to the fruition of a delicate art. There were no rich patrons, as in Italy and Flanders; the nation was backward, manners were rough. A great number of petty princes, civil and ecclesiastical, ordered pictures and expected to be served without delay; the artists, aided by their pupils, produced too much, and worked too rapidly. They imitated the brilliant colour of the Flemings, but without achieving their delicacy of touch. The colour of the German painters is harsh and often

FIG. 417.—THE VIRGIN IN THE ROSE-GARDEN. MARTIN SCHONGAUER. (Cathedral, Colmar.)

FIG. 418.—PORTRAIT OF THE ARTIST. ALBERT DÜRER. (Pinacothek, Munich.) (Photo. by Hanfstaengl.)

FIG. 419.—PORTRAIT OF OSWOLT KRELL. ALBERT DÜRER. (Pinacothek, Munich.)

heavy. They long continued to use gold backgrounds instead of landscapes as a setting for their figures, the former being more

235

FIG. 420.—PORTRAIT OF JEROME
HOLZSCHUHER.
ALBERT DÜRER.
(Museum, Berlin.)
(Photo. by Hanfstaengl.)

dazzling to the ignorant and easier of execution; aërial perspective was therefore developed very tardily. But the quality most conspicuously lacking in the Germans of the fifteenth and even of the sixteenth century was taste, the talent for selection. Their compositions are crowded with figures; these figures are often grotesque and grimacing; in place of strength and beauty, we find sometimes a sickly insipidity, sometimes a painful tension of style, sometimes an almost ridiculous mannerism of attitude and gesture. It is the art of devout peasants, at once coarse and sentimental, which attracts at first by its artlessness and vigour, and finally wearies by a vulgarity, now clamorous, now insignificant. Compared with Italian or Flemish pictures of the same period, a German picture appears as the work of a rustic beside that of a polished man of letters.

But the rustic is a good fellow, who has done his best; one of the virtues of this inferior art is its honesty.

The German art *par excellence* was wood-carving. Among its most gifted craftsmen were the Suabian, J. Syrlin of Ulm (d. 1491), and the Galician Veit Stoss (d. 1533, Fig. 415). At Nuremberg, where Stoss worked for many years, flourished the stone-carver, Adam Krafft (d. 1508). These masters carried on, with great skill and admirable vigour, the tradition of the realistic *imagiers* of the fourteenth century. They influenced the painters of their time, instead of being influenced by them. It was

FIG. 421.—THE FOUR PREACHERS.
ALBERT DÜRER.
(Pinacothek, Munich.)

they who were responsible for the long-continued prevalence in German art of broken draperies with deep and unnecessarily numerous folds, an angular style, and a taste for crowded compositions. But the types of old men created by Krafft, and of women created by Stoss, are among the most expressive in the whole range of sculpture, and their dense compositions are instinct with a fervid piety which makes those of the Italians seem almost frivolous and worldly.

FIG. 422.—THE ADORATION OF THE MAGI.
ALBERT DÜRER.
(Uffizi, Florence.)

The School of Nuremberg also produced sculptors of bronze, the Vischers, the best of whom, Peter Vischer, who died in 1529, translated the types and conceptions of the wood and stone carvers into metal (Fig. 416).

FIG. 423.—THE HOLY FAMILY RESTING ON THE FLIGHT INTO EGYPT.
ALBERT DÜRER.
Gazette des Beaux-Arts.

The school next in order of development after that of Cologne was the School of Suabia, the great master of which was Martin Schongauer of Colmar (1450-1491). Martin was a disciple of Roger van der Weyden, but he has a shade of sentimentality that is purely German. Like many of the German painters who had to provide pictures for the poor as well as for the rich, he engraved on wood and on copper; his engravings, characterised by much vigour and feeling in the line, are superior to his pictures, the best of which is the *Virgin in the Rose-garden* at Colmar (Fig. 417). Zeitblom of Ulm (d. 1517), a deeply religious painter, fascinating in spite of his incorrectness, had much in common with Schongauer.

The School of Augsburg developed side by side with those of

Colmar and Ulm. Its best painter was Burgkmair, a pupil of Schongauer, who went to Venice in 1508, and finally settled at Augsburg, where most of his works are preserved. Another Augsburg master, whose spirited and robust art is sometimes of a rather vulgar type, was Holbein the elder, father of the great Holbein. In his last pictures, he seems to be forsaking the Gothic style, and preparing the way for that emancipation of art which was to be consummated by his famous son.

Nuremberg, with its rich commercial class, was the Florence of Germany about the year 1500, but it was a coarser Florence, intent on expression rather than on beauty. It produced many masterpieces of

wood-carving. The head of its school of painting was Michel Wohlgemut (b. in 1434), a prolific but mediocre artist, whose chief title to fame is that he was the master of Dürer.

During the first half of the sixteenth century, Germany could boast two painters of genius, and one very richly gifted artist: Albert Dürer, Hans Holbein, and Lucas Cranach.

Dürer (1471-1528) was a thinker as well as an artist, and in this connection claims a place in the history of art side by side with Leonardo da Vinci and Michelangelo (Fig. 418). The Italians said he would have been the greatest of their artists had

THE RENAISSANCE IN GERMANY

he been born in Rome or Florence. A native of Nuremberg, he first learned the craft of a goldsmith, his father's calling, and in 1486 entered Wohlgemut's workshop. In 1490 he went to Colmar and Basle, and to Venice, where he came under the influence of Mantegna and Bellini. In 1497 he set up a studio in Nuremberg, and adopted his famous monogram, a D under an A. Even at this period, he painted admirable portraits, such as that of Oswolt Krell, at Munich (Fig. 419). In 1505 he went back to Venice, only returning to Nuremberg in 1507. It was after this that his period of great and feverish activity began, not only in the field of art, but also in that of the intellect and of literature, for Nuremberg had become a centre of Humanism, and Dürer was the friend and painter of the Humanists. In 1521, he visited the Netherlands, and was received with great honour.

FIG. 426.—THE VIRGIN WITH THE FAMILY OF THE BURGOMASTER MEYER.

(Castle, Darmstadt.)

It was after his return from this last visit that he painted his masterpieces, the portrait of Holzschuher at Berlin (Fig. 420) and the *Four Preachers* (Fig. 421) at Munich, works that were undoubtedly inspired by the Van Eycks. The latter, the most imposing picture of the German School, "a creation of superhuman types, a supreme effort towards simplicity and grandeur," attests the master's sympathy with the Reformation, which appealed to the Evangelists in order to bring Christianity back to the ancient paths.

FIG. 427.—PORTRAIT OF ERASMUS. HOLBEIN.

(The Louvre.)

Ecclesiastical architecture in Germany was ill adapted to mural painting. Dürer never painted on a wall. Some forty easel pictures and portraits by him exist; his most beautiful picture is the

239

Adoration of the Magi, at Florence (Fig. 422), a vigorous, profoundly thoughtful work, thoroughly German in its contempt for

FIG. 428.—CHARITY.

LUCAS CRANACH.

(Errera Collection, Brussels.)

FIG. 429.—PORTRAIT OF AN OLD MAN.

LUCAS CRANACH.

(Museum, Brussels.)

(Photo. by Hanfstaengl.)

elegance. When Dürer attempted to imitate the antique after the manner of the Italian masters, the result was almost grotesque, as in his *Lucretia*, at Munich. The Germans in general were even less skilful than the Flemings in the treatment of the nude. Sometimes they fell into a coarse realism; sometimes they disfigured borrowed types by the stiffness and dryness of their execution. But where Dürer was superior to the Italians, and equal to the greatest geniuses of all time, was in engraving. Compositions such as his *Repose in Egypt* (Fig. 423), *St. Jerome in his Cell*, *Melancholy*, and *Death and the Knight*, show

FIG. 430.—HERCULES AND OMPHALE.

LUCAS CRANACH.

(Museum, Brunswick.)

(Photo. by Bruckmann.)

a profundity of thought, a reticent poetry, and at the same time a knowledge of form only equalled in the works of Leonardo and

Michelangelo. At a period when Classicism reigned supreme, Goethe justly wrote: "When we know Dürer thoroughly, we recognise that in truth, nobility, and even grace, his only equals are the greatest of the Italians."

Among the pupils of Dürer who worked at Nuremberg and Ratisbon, two were artists of remarkable talent: Hans von Culmbach (Fig. 424) and Albrecht Altdorfer (Fig. 425).

Holbein (1497-1543), the second great master of the German Renaissance, was the son of the Augsburg painter I have already mentioned. Like Dürer, he travelled, going still further afield. In 1515 he was at Basle,

FIG. 431.—PORTRAIT OF A MAN.
CHR. AMBERGER.
(Museum, Brunswick.)
(Photo. by Bruckmann.)

and afterwards in England at the Court of Henry VIII., painting the king and his family, his ministers, several members of the English aristocracy, and the famous portrait-group of the two French envoys, known as *The Ambassadors*, in the National Gallery. Holbein has no affinities with Dürer. He is the only great German artist who shows a strong tendency to idealism. There is no trace of Gothicism in his manner, no touch of devotion and asceticism. The results of his German education are tempered by an elegance and reticence which make him the most French, rather than the most Italian of the Germans. Of his larger pictures, one is a masterpiece. This is the *Virgin and Child* (Fig. 426) at Darmstadt, of which there is a Dutch copy at Dresden, suaver but less expressive. In this work a result quite novel in Germany was achieved:

FIG. 432.—THE JUDGMENT OF PARIS.
LUCAS CRANACH.
(Museum, Carlsruhe.)
(Photo. by Bruckmann.)

character is reconciled to beauty. The important wall-paintings executed by Holbein at Basle are known to us only by sketches or fragmentary copies. Holbein's great title to glory is to be found in his series of engravings and his portraits. The Louvre possesses what is perhaps the finest of his portraits, that of Erasmus (Fig. 427), in which he equals Dürer in precision while surpassing him in freedom of touch. All deserve mention; but we must be content to name those of Amerbach, and of the painter's wife and children, in the Basle Museum, of the merchant, George Gisze, at Berlin [of Archbishop Warham at Lambeth Palace, of Sir Thomas More in Mr. E. Huth's collection, and the Sieur de Morette at Dresden]. His engravings have not the intellectual depth of Dürer's, but they charm by their wit and fertility of invention.

FIG. 433.—THE NATIVITY.
BALDUNG GRIEN.
(Museum, Frankfort.)
(Photo. by Bruckmann.)

Holbein's influence was far-reaching, extending into Holland and France. One of his imitators at Augsburg, Amberger, was a vigorous and penetrating portrait-painter (Fig. 431).

Lucas Cranach (1472-1553), the founder of the Saxon School, was a very different personality. Although he was the intimate friend of the Elector of Saxony, and familiar with Luther and Melanchton, whose portraits he painted, he is neither thoughtful nor subtle. The basis of his art is German rusticity, a rusticity with a veneer of literature and mythology, and a superficial elegance, such as might be acquired by a parvenu sprung from the peasan-

FIG. 434.—THE DEATH OF THE VIRGIN.
JOOS VON CLEVE.
(Pinacothek, Munich.)
(Photo. by Bruckmann.)

try. His science, which manifests itself in his fine portraits, seems rather thin in quality, especially as he produced very rapidly, and also signed many pictures painted by his pupils with his monogram, the dragon. His feminine type is a very peculiar one, with an enormous forehead and narrow oblique eyes. Unlike Dürer and Holbein, he was fond of treating the nude, not only Adam and Eve, whom all the German masters painted, but the goddesses of fable (Fig. 432). These nudities of Cranach's, often, as in his *Venus* in the Louvre, crowned with a large red velvet hat, are supremely comical. His painting, like his drawing, has a certain wooden quality in its dry uniformity; he is all the more a German, in that he suggests his national art, that of wood-carving. Sometimes, especially in his angels, he recalls Perugino, some of whose pictures he must certainly have seen. Cranach is the most diverting of painters, not only because he is eager to amuse, but because his artlessness and his false ideal of elegance often provoke a smile at his expense (Fig. 430). But he painted certain realistic portraits which are among the best works of the school (Fig. 429). As an engraver, he is inferior to Dürer and Holbein, but more popular and good-humoured. His son, Lucas the Younger, continued his art (I had almost said his trade), and flooded all Germany with facile pictures.

FIG. 435.—THE MAN WITH THE PINK.
BARTHEL BRUYN.
(Museum, Frankfort.)
(Photo. by Bruckmann.)

The school of Alsace produced an eminent artist in the sixteenth century, Mathias Grünewald, the forerunner, in his Carlsruhe *Crucifixion*, of the modern realists, and the first German who used colour, not in the manner of an illuminator, but as a painter. Hans Baldung Grien, who worked at Strasburg, and was influenced by Dürer, was a nervous draughtsman and a good colourist (Fig. 433). The school of Cologne fell more and more under the sway of the Netherlands and of Italy. A very prolific painter, thoroughly imbued with Italianism, who was known as the *Master of the Death of the Virgin* down to 1898, and has lately been identified as one Joos von Cleve, was born at Antwerp, and died in 1540 (Fig. 434).

APOLLO

This remarkable artist, who probably worked at Cologne, was the master of the last notable painter of that town, the portraitist Barthel Bruyn (Fig. 435). But from the second half of the sixteenth century German art may be considered dead, stifled on the one hand by imitators of the Italians, who produced only mediocre works without any character, and on the other by the religious wars, which devastated Germany and threw civilisation back by a full century. When the storm abated, the country was impoverished, and national tradition was interrupted. French and Italian art reigned alone; these were succeeded by Academicism, Neo-Hellenism, Raphaelism, and Impressionism. At present, though she boasts several great artists, Germany has no national school, and the worship she professes for her ancient masters has all the intensity of regret, nay, of remorse.

BIBLIOGRAPHY OF CHAPTER XX.

Works quoted on pp. 118 and 166 by Woermann and Michel.—Dohme, Bode, Janitschek, Lippmann and Lessing, *Geschichte der deutschen Kunst*, 5 vols., Berlin, 1885–1890; H. Janitschek, *Geschichte der deutschen Malerei*, Berlin, 1890; L. Reau, *Les primitifs allemands*, Paris, 1910; G. Ebe, *Der deutsche Cicerone*, Leipzig, 1901; W. Lübke and M. Semrau, *Die Kunst der Renaissance*, Stuttgart, 1903; A. Lehmann, *Das Bildniss bei den altdeutschen Meistern bis auf Dürer*, Leipzig, 1901.

J. von Schlosser, *Tommaso von Modena* (*Jahrbücher* of the Vienna Museums, 1898, p. 240); A. Marguillier, *Michel Pacher* (*Gazette des Beaux-Arts*, 1894, i., p. 327); L. Scheibler and C. Aldenhoven, *Geschichte der Kölner Malerschule*, Lubeck, 1897–1902 (with a portfolio of 131 photographs); E. Delpy, *Die Legende von der heiligen Ursula in der Kölner Malerschule*, Cologne, 1901.

P. Clemen, *Die rheinische und die westfälische Kunst*, Leipzig, 1903 (sculpture); *Meisterwerke westdeutscher Malerei*, Munich, 1905; F. Wanderer, *Adam Krafft und seine Schule*, Nuremberg, 1896 (with plates) B. Daun, *Adam Krafft*, Berlin, 1897; *Veit Stoss*, Leipzig, 1906 (cf. Michaelson, *Repertorium*, 1899, p. 395); G. Seeger, *Peter Vischer der Aeltere*, Leipzig, 1898; L. Reau, *P. Vischer*, Paris, 1909; E. Tönnies, *Tilmann Riemenschneider*, Strasburg, 1900; G. Hager, *Die Kunstentwicklung Altbayerns* (*Kongress kathol. Gelehrten*, Munich, 1901, p. 143); E. Müntz, *Syrlin* (*Gaz. des B.-Arts*, 1899, ii., p. 369).

F. von Reber, *Schwäbische Tafelmalerei im XIVten und XVten Jahrhundert* (*Sitzungsberichte der bayerischen Akademie*, 1894, iii., p. 343); M. Bach, *Schongauerstudien* (*Repertorium*, 1895, p. 253); *Bulletin de la Société Schongauer*; G. von Terey, *Hans Baldung Grien*, Strasburg, 1898; F. von Reber, *Hans Multscher von Ulm*, Munich, 1898.

M. Thausing, *Dürer*, 2 vols., Stuttgart, 1884; Ch. Ephrussi, *Albert Dürer et ses dessins*, Paris, 1882; F. Lippmann, *Zeichnungen von Albert Dürer*, 4 vols., Berlin, 1883–1896; H. Knackfuss, *Dürer*, 6th ed., Bielefeld, 1899; H. Woelfflin, *Die Kunst A. Dürer's*, Munich, 1905; M. Hamel, *Dürer*, Paris, 1904; *Derniers Travaux sur Dürer* (*Gazette des Beaux-Arts*, 1903, i., p. 59); L. Justi, *Dürers künstlerisches Schaffen* (*Repertorium*, 1903, p. 447); R. Thode, *Die Malerschule von Nürnberg*, Frankfort, 1891.

A. Woltmann, *H. Holbein und seine Zeit*, 2nd ed., Leipzig, 1874; P. Mantz, *H. Holbein*, Paris, 1879; H. Knackfuss, *Holbein der Jüngere*, 2nd ed., Bielefeld, 1896; H. Stein, *Bibliographie de Holbein*, Paris, 1897; G. S. Davies, *Hans Holbein*, London, 1903; Ganz, *H. Holbein*, Stuttgart, 1912 (photographs of all works); A. Goette, *Holbeins Totentanz und seine Vorbilder*, Strasburg, 1897; L. Dimier, *Les Danses des Morts dans l'Art chrétien*, Paris, 1903; E. Haasler, *Cristoff Amberger*, Königsberg, 1894.

E. Flechsig, *Cranachstudien*, Leipzig, 1900 (with a portfolio of 129 plates); M. Friedländer, *Die frühesten Werke Cranachs* (*Jahrbücher* of the Berlin Museums, 1902, p. 228); F. Lippmann, *Lucas Kranach Nachbildung seiner Holzschnitte und Stiche*, Berlin, 1896; Seidlitz, *L'Exposition de l'oeuvre de Cranach à Dresde* (*Gazette des Beaux-Arts*, 1899, ii., p. 191); H. Michaelson, *Lucas Cranach*, Leipzig, 1902; E. S. Heyck, *Cranach*, Bielefeld, 1908; Campbell Dodgson, *Bibliographie de Cranach*, Paris, 1900; Sturge Moore, *Altdorfer*, London, 1900; J. K. Huysmans, *Les Grünewald de Colmar*, Paris, 1905; F. Bock, *Grünewald*, Munich, 1909; E. Firmenich-Richartz, *B. Bruyn*, Leipzig, 1891.

XXI

THE ITALIAN DECADENCE AND THE SPANISH SCHOOL

The Phenomenon of Artistic Decadence.—The Decline of Art in Italy and its Causes.— The Jesuit Style.—Originality Checked by Excessive Admiration of the Great Renaissance Artists.—The Influence of the Decadent Italian Schools on France and Spain.—The Mannerists.—The Carracci.—The Frescoes in the Farnese Palace.—Albano, Domenichino, Guido, Guercino.—Guido's Religious Types.—Caravaggio and his School.—Pietro da Cortona and Luca Giordano.—The Neapolitan School.—Salvator Rosa and Bernini.— Sassoferrato.—The Allori.—Carlo Dolci.—Ribera and his Influence on the Spanish School. —Morales.—The School of Seville.—Herrera and Zurbaran.—Montañez and Alonzo Cano.—Velasquez.—His Technical Supremacy.—His Relations with the Spanish Court.— The Historical Significance of his Works.—The Impersonal Character of his Art.— Murillo.—His Qualities as a Colourist.—His Interpretation of Spanish Religious Sentiment. —Goya.—The Unimpaired Vigour of Modern Art in Spain.

THE word decadence, when applied to art, must not be taken in too strict a sense. Art never declines so far as to return to its point of departure; thus the Bolognese are in no way akin to the Giottesques, but are more remote from them than from the Florentines of the golden age. As a fact, evolution is always going on, even when artists believe that they are slavishly imitating their predecessors. But it sometimes happens

FIG. 436.—NEPTUNE AND AMPHITRITE.
ANNIBALE CARRACCI
(Farnese Palace, Rome.)
Woermann, *Geschichte der Malerei.* (Seemann, Leipzig.)

that the works of art of a country or of a period are more fitted to awaken curiosity than to excite admiration. This is true of those produced by the Italians from the death of Michelangelo to our own times, though we must make a reservation in the case of Venice. The other exceptions, some of which we will point out, have not sufficed to prevent us from talking of the decadence or decline of Italian art; but there has been neither retrogression nor stagnation.

Various causes have been assigned for this depressing phenomenon. Some urge the loss of Italian liberty, crushed successively under the heel of Spain and of Austria; others the Counter-Reformation (1545), which brought about the predominance of a religion whose chief preoccupation was to touch and to dazzle. It is certain that Italian art of the seventeenth century aims at effect, that it dwells unduly on

245

ecstasy and rapture, sentimental effusions, the physical tortures of the martyrs. It introduced a variety of new motives, such as that of

FIG. 437.—THE LAST COMMUNION OF
ST. JEROME.
DOMENICHINO.
(Museum of the Vatican.)
(Photo. by Anderson.)

FIG. 438.—ECCE HOMO.
GUIDO RENI.
(Gallery, Bologna.)
(Photo. by Brogi.)

Christ and the Virgin as half-length figures, with eyes cast mournfully heavenwards, an ex-voto of a vague and sickly piety quite unknown to the fifteenth century. In place of the Venuses of Titian and Giorgione, or even the Graces and Galateas of Raphael, art repeated to satiety the type of the repentant Magdalen, of which Morelli said that it was "the Venetian Venus translated into the Jesuit style." It shows an unpleasant mingling of sensuality and devotion.

FIG. 439.—AURORA.
GUIDO RENI.
(Rospigliosi Palace, Rome.)

Assuredly what is known, in architecture especially, as the Jesuit style had a disastrous influence in the domains of painting and sculpture. But why did this style, which was that of Rubens, produce masterpieces in Flanders and not in Italy? Here another cause of decay intervenes, the legitimate but stupefying admiration evoked by the great masters of the Renaissance. It was held that they had said everything to perfection; artists studied the masterpieces of the past rather than Nature, and in this study acquired a somewhat mechanical facility, which they abused. It is, of course, true that artists in all ages have been inspired by their masters; but these masters have been for the most part living. At the close of the sixteenth and throughout the seventeenth century, they took, sometimes as their only masters, dead men, Raphael, Michelangelo, Titian, Correggio, or more remote dead artists, the authors of antique statues and bas-reliefs. At Rome, in the fifteenth century, these works were comparatively rare; in the sixteenth century, thanks to the excavations that were carried on on every side, they multiplied rapidly, and the first museums were established at Rome and Florence. Italian art was the victim of

FIG 440.—MARY MAGDALENE.
GUERCINO.
(Spoleto.)   (Photo. by Alinari.)

many simultaneous tyrannies, that of the foreigner, that of the Counter-Reformation, that of the great men of the Renaissance, that of classic art. And yet, as we shall see, this art was vital and innovating. In Spain and in France, it threw out vigorous off-shoots, which have not yet ceased to bear fruit. A walk through the Musée du Luxembourg in Paris suffices to show that the Romans of the Empire and the Bolognese of the seventeenth century had a larger following in France than the Greeks of Phidias and the Florentines of Botticelli.

After the death of Michelangelo in 1564, a first period of unbridled imitation set in, that of the Mannerists, which lasted to the end of the century. An Antwerp painter, Denis Calvaert, founded a school at Bologna (about 1575), which thenceforth became what Florence and Rome had been, the most active centre of Italian art. It was there that

FIG. 441.—THE ENTOMBMENT.
CARAVAGGIO.
(Museum of the Vatican)
Woermann, *Geschichte der Malerei.*
(Seemann, Leipzig.)

247

FIG. 442.—THE DEATH OF THE VIRGIN.
CARAVAGGIO.
(The Louvre.) (Photo. by Neurdein.)

Lodovico Carracci, born at Bologna in 1515, opened jointly with his cousins, Agostino and Annibale, an Academy known as that of the Incamminati, which became the rival of Calvaert's school, and the seminary of art in the seventeenth century. Carracci taught eclecticism, instead of the imitation of Michelangelo; his theory was that from each school and each painter the artist should take what was best, so as to rise above the masters by combining their qualities. The practice of the Carracci was superior to their doctrine. The frescoes Annibale spent eight years in painting in the Farnese Palace in Rome show fine qualities of grace and invention (Fig. 436). The dominant influences in this school were those of Raphael and Michelangelo in drawing and composition, of Titian and Correggio in colour. These exemplars are not so diverse but that they might be imitated simultaneously.

The school of the Carracci produced certain painters who were formerly very famous, and are now somewhat unduly depreciated, Albano (1578-1660), who was called the Anacreon of Painting, Domenichino (1581-1641), who was compared to Raphael, Guido Reni (1575-1642), a clever and prolific decorator. These artists, to whom we must add Guercino (1591-1666), who, like them, was influenced by the Carracci, are the principal representatives of the Bolognese School. Their pictures are to be found in every town in Italy, and in every museum in Europe (Figs. 437-440).

Domenichino's masterpiece, *St. Je-*

FIG. 443.—APOLLO AND DAPHNE.
BERNINI.
(Borghese Gallery, Rome.)
(Photo. by Anderson.)

FIG. 444.—THE ECSTATIC VISION OF
ST. THERESA.
BERNINI.
(Church of Sta. Maria della Vittoria,
Rome.) (Photo. by Anderson, Rome.)

FIG. 445.—JUDITH WITH THE HEAD OF
HOLOFERNES.
CRISTOFORO ALLORI.
(Pitti Palace, Florence.) (Woermann, *Ge-
schichte der Malerei.* Seemann, Leipzig.)

rome's Last Communion, in the Vatican, gives a good general idea
of the Bolognese style (Fig. 437). It is an academic and eclectic
work, betraying the imitation of Raphael and Michelangelo, and show-

FIG. 446.—THE MADONNA OF THE
ROSARY.
SASSOFERRATO.
(Church of Sta. Sabina, Rome.)
(Photo. by Anderson.)

FIG. 447.—ST. CECILIA
CARLO DOLCI.
(Museum, Dresden.)
(Woermann, *Geschichte der Malerei.*
Seemann, Leipzig.)

FIG. 448.—THE ADORATION OF THE
SHEPHERDS.
RIBERA.
(The Louvre.)   (Photo. by Neurdein)

ing neither originality of conception nor depth of thought; nevertheless, it reveals a high degree of knowledge, and a sense of composition unknown to most of Raphael's predecessors. Guido Reni's famous painting, again, *Aurora,* in the Rospigliosi Palace at Rome (1609), though a little strident in its high-toned colour, and over-facile in drawing, is one of the great achievements of decorative painting (Fig. 439). Guido Reni further created types of Christ, the Virgin, and the Magdalen, which may not be free from the reproach of a certain sentimental vulgarity, yet whose prodigious popularity attests that they realised the religious ideal of the day, a merit that claims some recognition (Fig. 438).

The Academicism of the Eclectics was not long in provoking a reaction. Caravaggio, a plasterer, without any artistic education, but naturally gifted (1569-1609), preached a return to nature, not smiling and serene, but brutal and ugly. Painting in a dark studio, lighted by a trap-door in the roof, he obtained striking effects of colour and relief which were new to the Italians. If the illumination of his pictures is artificial, his types are those of the street, and even of the prison. Caravaggio was the first Italian who deliberately renounced idealism (Figs. 441, 442). In this respect he was the Manet of his day; but as he belonged essentially to that day, he had more in common with the Carracci than he supposed. His masterpiece, the *Death of the Virgin,* in the Louvre (Fig. 442), inspires a certain respect; only a true pioneer could have had the courage to hurl such a gage of naturalism in

FIG. 449.—VIRGIN AND CHILD.
MORALES.
(Pablo Bosch Collection, Madrid.)

the faces of Raphael's votaries. Besides his religious subjects, Caravaggio painted with evident gusto violent episodes of real life, murders, quarrels, tavern scenes, adventures of gipsies and vagabonds.

The Carraccists inveighed against Caravaggio, but nearly all of them succumbed to his influence. Guercino became his disciple, and Guido Reni imitated him so far as to abandon his light, crude colour, and paint figures that seem to be hiding in a cellar. Even now, the disciples of Caravaggio are more numerous than those of Raphael; and it was the reaction against this tenacious tradition in the second half of the nineteenth century that created the practice of painting in a strong light, in the manner described by the barbarous term *pleinairisme* ("open-airism").

FIG. 450.—A DOMINICAN MONK PRAYING.

ZURBARAN.

(National Gallery, London.)

Yet another decorator of astonishing spirit and vigour was Pietro da Cortona (1596-1669), who had a gifted but over-facile pupil in Rome, Luca Giordano, called *Fa presto* (does quickly), the author of numerous works preserved at Naples and at Madrid. The school of the *Cortonists* covered the churches and palaces of Italy with clamorous, rapidly executed compositions, the *brio* of which, to use the Italian term, does not compensate for their vulgarity and incorrectness.

FIG. 451 —THE CRUCIFIXION.

VELASQUEZ.

(Museum, Madrid.)
(Photo. by Lacoste.)

After Bologna, Naples and Genoa witnessed the rise of schools which played an important part in the second half of the seventeenth century. Naples was the field of the greatest landscape and battle painter of Italy, Salvator Rosa (1615-1673), whose violent, sombre style is akin to that of Caravaggio. Naples also produced the most distinguished Italian sculptor of the seventeenth century, Bernini (1598-

251

FIG. 452.—THE INFANT, BALTAZAR CARLOS.
VELASQUEZ.
(Museum, Madrid.)

1680), who was invited to Paris by Louis XIV., and who, thanks to the protection of successive Popes, exercised a sort of artistic dictatorship in Rome (Figs. 443, 444). His contemporaries acclaimed him as a second Michelangelo. He was, in reality, the Rubens of sculpture, the representative *par excellence* of the Jesuit style. But his abuse of pathetic gestures, fervid expressions, fluttering draperies, and superfluous ornament should not blind us to the fact that his works are those of a marvellously gifted artist, thoroughly familiar with all the resources of his art, and with all the intellectual vices of his time, and making use of the one to flatter the other.

In the seventeenth century the Roman School dragged on an inglorious existence. Its best artist, Sassoferrato (1605-1685), imitated Raphael's Florentine manner with some success, and painted sentimental canvases in a silvery tone which has a certain charm. His masterpiece, the *Madonna of the Rosary* (Fig. 446), recently stolen from the Church of Sta. Sabina in Rome, was recovered by the Italian police and restored to its place. Even a *masterpiece* by Sassoferrato did not find an immediate purchaser!

At Florence, the two Allori, Alessandro and Cristoforo, showed genuine artistic qualities. Cristoforo's *Judith* (about 1600) is a fine academic work, which Musset eulogised as one of the supreme pictures in Italy (Fig. 445). But even in this we note, instead of the austere grace of the earlier

FIG. 453.—THE MAIDS OF HONOUR.
VELASQUEZ.
(Museum, Madrid.)

252

masters, a deplorable taste for a liquid fusion of surface, for languid syrupy colour. The most popular representative of this style was Carlo Dolci (1616-1686), whose works are often to be met with in English and German collections; the Louvre, fortunately, has no example of him. His most characteristic productions are half-length figures, blue, waxen, and streaky, which mark the transition from the amenities of Correggio to our most nauseous religious prints (Fig. 447).

FIG. 454.—THE FORGE OF VULCAN.
VELASQUEZ.
(Museum, Madrid.) (Woermann, *Geschichte der Malerei.* Seemann, Leipzig.)

An artist of Valencia, Ribera (1588-1652), arrived in Italy when still a youth. He was fascinated by the style of Caravaggio, then went to Parma to copy Correggio's works, and returned to found a school at Naples. Philip IV. of Spain took him under his protection. He carried the style of Caravaggio into Spain, where it found congenial territory, and exercised an influence that has never died out. Ribera was a true artist and a true Spaniard. "In his choice of subjects and still more in their interpretation, he always shows an intense realism, which in the execution, and in the expression of form, sometimes betrays a sort of instinctive ferocity. He took pleasure in the rendering of tortures and martyrdoms. Beggars and old men with deep wrinkles are his favourite models."[1]

FIG. 455.—VIRGIN AND CHILD.
MURILLO.
(Pitti Palace, Florence.)

Ribera's violent illumination was derived from Caravaggio; but his types are nobler and his drawing better than those of the Neapolitan. He sometimes approaches Correggio, as in the beautiful *Adoration of the Magi* in the Louvre (Fig. 448). It is mainly owing to Ribera that Caravaggio's manner has persisted in modern

Bonnat, *Gazette des Beaux-Arts,* 1898, i., p. 180.

FIG. 456.—ST. ELIZABETH OF HUNGARY.
MURILLO.
(Museum, Madrid.)

art. A skilful imitator thereof in our own times was the French painter, Théodule Ribot.

Toledo was the adopted home of a mystical and fantastic Cretan, Theotocopuli, called El Greco (1550-1614), a pupil of Titian at Venice, the gifted and often extravagant imitator of Tintoretto. Velasquez had in his studio four of Greco's paintings which he called "the Bible of painting." His extreme spiritualisation of form partakes of contempt for form. He is the most daring and even in his aberrations the most admired precursor of Impressionism.

The natural tendencies of Spanish art were monkish and ascetic. In the middle of the sixteenth century a belated mystic of considerable talent, Morales, called the Divine, was still painting emaciated Virgins and Christs inspired by Roger van der Weyden (Fig. 449). But at the same time the influences of the Italian Renaissance took root in Seville, the school of which city became the centre of Spanish art. There again eclectic classicism provoked a reaction. About 1620, the elder Herrera set the example of a brutal and impetuous naturalism, aptly interpreted by an amazing breadth of touch. (It is said that he painted with reeds instead of brushes.) The most gifted of his successors, Zurbaran, born in 1598, has been called the Caravaggio of Spain. He was primarily a painter of religious scenes, of ecstatic visionary monks. The *Kneeling Dominican,* in the National Gallery of London, is a picture which compels a painful admiration, and lingers hauntingly in the memory (Fig. 450).

A contemporary of Zubaran's at

FIG. 457.—THE IMMACULATE
CONCEPTION.
MURILLO.
(Museum, Madrid.)
(Photo. by Lacoste.)

Seville, Montañez, was the head of the school of Spanish sculpture. At once ascetic and brutally realistic, he produced a series of terrifying works, quivering with a mournful and intense vitality, the eloquence of which appeals rather to the senses than to the mind. His best pupil, Alonzo Cano (1601-1667), painter and sculptor, rebelled against the excesses of naturalism, and turned again to Italian idealism without ceasing to be touching and expressive.

Younger by a year than Zurbaran, and brought up like him at Seville, Velasquez, brimming over with health and strength, escaped from the influence of Caravaggio and the paralysing grip of Spanish mysticism (1599-1660). His career, like that of Raphael, was a long series of triumphs. He knew neither the difficulties of a beginning, nor the melancholy of a neglected old age. Velasquez studied the admirable series of pictures by Titian which the Emperor Charles V. had collected at Madrid; he also spent two years in Italy. But the Venetians merely revealed to him his own profoundly personal genius. As regards technique, he was perhaps the greatest painter the world has ever seen. Let us hear how some distinguished modern masters, his most fervent worshippers, speak of his art: "She [*i.e.*, Art,]" said Whistler, "dipped the Spaniard's brush in light and air," and Bonnat tells us of his "clear colouring, limpid as water-color, brilliant as a precious stone," of "his grey, golden, and silvery tones," of "the happy union and exquisite tenderness of the most delicate tints in his works. His method is surprisingly simple. He paints his composition directly on the

FIG. 458.—BOYS EATING MELONS.
MURILLO.
(Pinacothek, Munich.)

FIG. 459.—LAS MAJAS ON THE BALCONY.
GOYA.
(Museum, Madrid.)
(Photo. by Lacoste.)

255

canvas. The simplified shadows are merely rubbed in, all the high lights are laid on in a rich impasto; and the result, with its broad, delicate, and justly executed tonalities, is so perfect in value that the illusion is complete." Yet withal, he does not, like Rembrandt, create an artificial atmosphere for his personages. "The air he breathes is our own, the sky above him is that under which we live. Before his creations we receive the same impression as that made upon us by living beings." "Before a work of Velasquez," wrote Henri Regnault, "I feel as if I were looking at reality through an open window." Velasquez' portraits are miracles of truth, of power, of implacable psychological analysis; in his large pictures, he combines with his high qualities as a painter clarity of composition and a grandiose simplicity. "He envelops his models in ambient air, and places them so exactly on the planes they ought to occupy that we feel as if we were walking round them."

FIG 460.—LA MAJA CLOTHED.
GOYA.
(Museum, Madrid.)

Velasquez painted not only individuals but a whole society, a whole epoch. The Spanish court and aristocracy live again on his canvases in all their pride, their melancholy, the sinister indications of their physical degeneracy. What lessons in history we may read in his sickly Philip IV., in his prematurely serious royal children, with their unhealthy faces and rigid attitudes! On the other hand, when he painted his mythological or genre pictures, Velasquez took his models from the robust Madrilene populace, which attracted Murillo also, when he wearied of Virgins and saints. Velasquez, the painter of an anæmic court, turned from it occasionally to the people, where he found not only physical health but a joy of life which echoed his own.

If this great observer, this prodigious craftsman, felt a heart beating strongly in his breast, if he knew sympathies and antipathies, love and hate, he has not confided them to us. He is a haughty and indifferent genius, whose soul never appears in his pictures; he is content to live and to make others live. The warmest of painters was, at least apparently, as cold as a photographer's lens (Figs. 451-454).

Very different was the gentle Murillo (1617-1682), also a native of Seville, who studied Rubens and Van Dyck at Madrid, and created a style of his own, sometimes devout and sentimental, as in his numerous pictures of the Virgin, sometimes realistic, but tempered by a certain pity and tenderness, as in his charming boys and girls of the people. Murillo is weak and wanting in distinction as a draughtsman. His much admired Virgins are fundamentally com-

monplace; but he was a master of vaporous colour, sometimes silvery, sometimes golden, always suave and caressing. This colour is not merely spread
upon his figures, but around them; it
is like a nimbus from which they
emerge, embellished by its glamour.
Murillo was the most eloquent interpreter of that tender and sensuous
piety which, in his country of strange
contrasts, flourishes together with a
taste for bloody spectacles and the disdainful indifference of the hidalgo
(Figs. 455-458).

FIG. 461.—PORTRAIT OF DONA ISABEL
Y CORCEL.
GOYA.
(National Gallery, London.)

Spanish art never lost sight of these
traditions. Goya (1746-1828) appeared as a second Velasquez at a
time when scarcely anyone in Europe
knew how to paint. The French colourists of the nineteenth century felt
his influence as they did that of the English successors of Titian and Rubens. If he carried his taste for realism to the verge of vul-garity, it was tempered, both in his pictures and engravings, by a strong dramatic instinct, and the mordant vigour of the satirist (Figs. 459-461). No painter has spared less the vices and defor-mities of his time. Spain suffered very little from the disease of Aca-demicism, which ravaged Italy, France, and Germany. The love for true painting was never extinguished there. Those of our con-temporaries who have lived in Spain, Regnault, Bonnat, and Carolus Duran, have come back colourists. "I was brought up in the wor-ship of Velasquez," wrote Bonnat in 1898. And in recent exhibitions we have seen pictures signed with Spanish names—such as Zuloaga and Bilbao—that no Italian, no German, and no Englishman could have painted. They bear eloquent testimony to the vitality of a school which prides itself on its descent from the great Velasquez, a school which perhaps reserves for the Europe of the twentieth cen-tury the apparition of some new genius of the first rank.

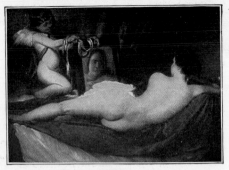

VENUS.

VELASQUEZ.

(National Gallery.)

BIBLIOGRAPHY OF CHAPTER XXI.

C. Ricci, *L'art de l'Italie du Nord*, Paris (1911), p. 329; work by Woltmann quoted on p. 166.—G, Ebe, *Die Spät-Renaissance Kunstgeschichte der europäischen Länder von der Mitte des XVIten bis zum Ende des XVIIIten Jahrhunderts*, 2 vols., Berlin, 1886; G. Gurlitt. *Geschichte des Barockstiles*, 3 vols., Stuttgart, 1887–1889; A. Riegl, *Entstehung der Barockkunst*, Vienna, 1912; Ch. Scherer, *Studien Zur Elfenbeinplastik der Barockzeit*, Strasburg, 1898; J. Strzygowski, *Das Werden des Barock bei Raphael und Correggio*, Strasburg, 1898; L. Serra, Il *Dominichino*, Rome, 1909; L. Ozgala, *Salvator Rosa*, Strasburg, 1909; M. von Boehn, *Guido Reni*, Bielefeld, 1910; W. Rolfs, *Geschichte der Malerei Neapels*, Leipzig, 1910; M. Reymond, *L'école bolonaise* (*Rev. des deux Mondes*, January 1, 1910); M. Reymond, *Le Bernin*, Paris, 1910.

S. Fraschetti, *Il Bernini*, Milan, 1900: *La Sainte-Cécile de Maderna* (*Gazette des Beaux-Arts*, 1892, i., p. 37); E. Steinmann, *Sassoferrato's Madonna del Rosario* (*Kunstchronik*, 1901–1902, p. 27).

C. Justi, *Miscellaneen* (Spanish and Portuguese Art), 2 vols., Berlin, 1909; P. Lefort, *La Peinture espagnole*, Paris, 1894; S. Saupere y Miquel, *Los Cuatrocentistas catalanes*, 2 vols., Barcelona, 1906 (cf. *Burlington Magazine*, November, 1906, p. 99); *L'Ecole espagnole au Prado* (*Gazette des Beaux-Arts*, 1894, ii., p. 405); Manuel Cossio, *El Greco*, Madrid, 1908; C. G. Hartley, *A Record of Spanish Painting*, London, 1904; Roblot-Delondre, *Portraits d'infantes XVIe siècle*, Brussels, 1913; A. L. Mayer, *Ribiera*, Leipzig, 1908; *Sevillaner Malerschule*, Leipzig, 1911; N. Sentenach, *Painters of Sevilla*, London, 1911; Manuel Cassio, *El Greco*, Madrid, 1908; Meier-Graefe, *Spanische Reise*, Berlin, 1910 (Velasquez sacrificed to Greco); Barres and Lafond, *Le Greco*, Paris, 1911; A. F. Calvert, *El Greco*, London, 1909; P. Lefort, *Zurbaran* (*Gazette des Beaux-Arts*, 1892, i., p. 365); Sir Walter Armstrong, *Velasquez* (Portfolio Monographs), London, 1897; A. de Beruete, *Velasquez*, Paris, 1898: *The School of Madrid* (*Velasquez School*), London, 1909; L. Bonnat, *Velasquez* (*Gazette des Beaux-Arts*, 1898, i., p. 177); H. Knackfuss, *Velasquez*, Bielefeld, 1896; C. Justi, *Diego Velasquez*, Bonn, 1889 (English translation, London, 1890); R. Stevenson, *Velasquez*, 2nd ed., London, 1899; E. Faure, *Velasquez*, Paris, 1903; W. Gensel, *Velasquez*, Stuttgart, 1905 (photographs of all his pictures); A. Bréal, *Velasquez*, London, 1905; P. Leprieur, *La Vénus au Miroir*, acquired by the London Gallery in 1905 (*Gazette des Beaux-Arts*, i., p. 452); C. Justi, *Murillo*, Leipzig, 1892; A. L. Mayer, *Murillo*, Stuttgart, 1913 (photographs of all works); P. Lefort, *Murillo et ses Elèves*, Paris, 1892; H. Knackfuss, *Murillo*, 2nd ed., Bielefeld, 1896; Ch. Ynarte, *Goya*, Paris, 1867; P. Lafond, *Goya*, Evreux, 1902 (cf. *Revue de l'Art*, 1899, i., p. 133); V. von Loga, *Francisco de Goya*, Berlin, 1903; A. F. Calvert, *Goya*, London, 1909; P. Lafond, *Ignacio Zuloaga* (*Revue de l'Art*, 1903, ii., p. 163); G. de Frenzi, *Zuloaga*, Rome, 1912; C. S. Ricketts, *The Prado*, London, 1904.

P. Lafond, *La Sculpture espagnole*, Paris, 1908; B. Händcke, *Studien zur Geschichte der spanischen Plastik* (*Montanez, Alonzo Cano, Pedro de Mena, Zarcillo*), Strasburg, 1900; M. Dieulafoy, *La Statuaire polychrome en Espagne* (Mon. Piot. vol. x., p. 171), Paris, 1908; *Le Siècle d'Or*, Paris, in progress (1906); on the Renaissance in Portugal: Bertaux, in Michel, *Histoire de l'Art*, iv., p. 869; J. de Figueiredo, *Nuno Goncales*, Lisbon, 1910.

XXII

ART IN THE NETHERLANDS IN THE SEVENTEENTH CENTURY

The Revolt of the Netherlands.—The Separation of Dutch and Flemish Schools.—The Character of Dutch Art Determined by Social Conditions.—The Non-literary Quality of Dutch Art.—Frans Hals.—Adriaen Brouwer and Adriaen van Ostade.—The Ruisdaels. —Rembrandt.—His Life and Work.—The Originality of his Art.—His Etchings.—Masters of the Second Rank.—The Decline of Dutch Art under Italian Influences.—Flemish Art.— Rubens.—The Fecundity of his Genius.—Jordaens.—Van Dyck.—David Teniers.

IN 1556, the Netherlands, which had formed a part of the Empire of Charles V., passed to the Kingdom of Spain. For some thirty years past the Reformation had made steady progress in the Low Countries, in spite of persecutions and tortures. In 1564 the up-heaval began, which brought about the Union of Utrecht after terrible carnage; the Dutch Provinces formed the Republic of the Seven United Provinces. In 1648 the Peace of Westphalia recog-nised the independence of Holland, which was then allied to France. In the seventeenth century, in spite of the unjust and cruel war waged against her by Louis XIV., she was the richest and most civilised country of Europe, the heir of the glory and prosperity of Venice.

FIG. 462.—THE ARTIST AND HIS WIFE.
FRANS HALS.
(Museum, Amsterdam.)

Thus, from the end of the sixteenth century onwards, there is a very clear distinction between Belgium, which had remained Spanish and Catholic, and Holland, which was free and Protestant. The lower Meuse separated two different civilisations. This is a fact of which the historian must take account in a comparative study of Dutch and Flemish art.

The Holland of the seventeenth century, wealthy and industrious,

259

was a domain very propitious to the development of art, and especially of painting. But this could not be applied to the decoration of churches, which was disapproved by Protestantism. There was consequently no monumental art, and therefore very little Academicism. The private houses, narrow, high, and dark, required small pictures; for the town-halls and the halls of the various corporations, groups of portraits, representing sheriffs, archers, surgeons, directors of charitable institutions, were in request, to satisfy the desire of this rich commercial community to commemorate the services rendered by them. This explains the double preference shown in Dutch art for little pictures, interiors, and landscapes, dealing but rarely with religious or historic themes, and for portraits, either of individuals, or groups of persons.

FIG. 463.—THE MARSH.
J. VAN RUISDAEL.
(The Hermitage, St. Petersburg.) Woermann,
Geschichte der Malerei. (Seemann, Leipzig.)

The Dutch loved nature and painting with a sort of artistic sensuality. They did not, like the Italians, look to them for the expression of subtle ideas. Their art is realistic, and, in general, non-intellectual—art for art's sake. The result was firstly, an extraordinary development of technical skill, which made it possible to render the most fugitive gradations of Dutch sunlight, filtering through the damp atmosphere in a pale golden rain; and secondly, a comparative indifference to the meaning of the subject treated.

FIG. 464.—THE MILL.
J. VAN RUISDAEL.
(Van der Hoop Museum, Amsterdam.)

The little masters restrict themselves to a certain number of general themes; the doctor and his patient, the pangs of love, the message, the concert, the inn; the landscape painters represent the forest, the cascade, the sea, or the seashore, a bit of a town, a quay. They are no story-tellers in quest of piquant or edifying anecdotes; they give us nothing akin to Fragonard's *Swing*, or Greuze's *Father's Curse*. All the wit of this painting lies in the execution, in the actual handling of the colours. Unlike the French masters of the eighteenth and nineteenth centuries, the Dutch put no literature into their painting.

FIG. 465.—THE ANATOMY LESSON. REMBRANDT. (Museum, The Hague.)

One point that seems difficult to explain is that this nation, which had bought liberty at the price of such heroic sacrifices, which, in the course of the seventeenth century, distinguished itself by brilliant victories on land and sea, should have almost entirely neglected historical painting. When we compare Meissonier to the Dutch masters, we forget that the French painter, though he may have been somewhat Dutch in technique, was by no means Dutch in sentiment. He was, above all things, a historical painter. But perhaps the Dutch had no appreciation of a style of painting in which art is less important than narrative; and perhaps they held that war, even when glorious and justifiable, causes so much misery that pictures dealing with its incidents must be repellent.

At the end of the sixteenth and the beginning of the seventeenth centuries, Holland came under the influence of Italian art, firstly, that of Raphael,

FIG. 466.—THE PRESENTATION IN THE TEMPLE. REMBRANDT. (Museum, The Hague.)

FIG. 467.—PORTRAIT OF THE ARTIST.
REMBRANDT.
(Etching.)

then that of Caravaggio. Thenceforward, it may be said that Italianism remained in a latent state in Holland. But realism asserted itself triumphantly at Haarlem, in the person of Frans Hals (d. 1666), the greatest portrait painter of Holland, after Rembrandt (Fig. 462). Hals' last works reveal a most penetrating observation, and a frankness of touch comparable to that of Velasquez. But in every other respect, he is the antithesis of the austere Spaniard. Hals is the laureate of laughter; he has observed and recorded laughter in all its phases; a monograph on the smile and the laugh might be fully illustrated from the works of Hals alone!

This robust master formed numerous pupils, among others two painters of rustic subjects, who combine admirable technique with a lively and brilliant imagination, sometimes rather too coarse for modern taste, Adriaen Brouwer (1606-1638), and Adriaen van Ostade (1610-1685). It is interesting to compare them with the more refined painters of the following generation, Terborch, Metzu, and the delightful master of bright and cosy middle-class interiors, Pieter de Hoogh. With these, subject and action are reduced to a minimum; Brouwer and Ostade have much more *verve* and invention. Ostade's masterpiece is perhaps the little *Schoolmaster* in the Louvre. It hung for many years beside Correggio's *Antiope* in the Salon

FIG. 468.—THE ARTIST AND HIS WIFE.
REMBRANDT.
(Museum, Dresden.)

Carré and was well able to bear such a juxtaposition.

The School of Haarlem also produced some wonderful landscape painters. First Everdingen (1621-1675), who journeyed as far afield as Norway to study mountains and waterfalls; then the uncle and nephew, Solomon and Jacob van Ruisdael, the latter of whom (d. 1682) is the greatest landscape-painter of Holland. If we compare him with the landscape-painters of the nineteenth century, we cannot call him a realist, for he composes; he does not paint haphazard some slice of nature or some effect of light; but with the possible exception of Corot, no painter has put more of his own soul into Nature, none has

FIG. 469.—FRAGMENT OF MANOAH'S PRAYER.
REMBRANDT.
(Museum, Dresden.)

made it more moving and eloquent, none has more adequately felt and rendered the transparence of air and water. Ruisdael's masterpiece is *The Marsh,* at St. Petersburg; but his great pictures in the Louvre, at Dresden and in London are scarcely less admirable. Philips Wouwerman, a painter rather older than Ruisdael (1619-1668),

FIG. 470.—THE NIGHT-WATCH.
(March out of the Civic Guard.)
REMBRANDT.
(Museum, Amsterdam.)

263

is famous as a painter of horses and horsemen; his prolific talent would be more fully appreciated now if he had applied it to a wider range of subjects.

Amsterdam succeeded Haarlem as the centre of Dutch art when

FIG. 471.—THE SYNDICS.
REMBRANDT.
(Museum, Amsterdam.)

FIG. 472.—ST. MATTHEW.
REMBRANDT.
(The Louvre.)

Rembrandt settled there in 1631. Born at Leyden in 1606, he passed through the studio of an obscure painter, one Lastman, who had studied in Italy and had felt the influence of Caravaggio; some

FIG. 473.—PORTRAIT OF REMBRANDT
WITH HAGGARD EYES.
REMBRANDT.
(Etching.)

FIG. 474.—REMBRANDT'S MOTHER.
REMBRANDT.
(Etching.)

of his pictures offer contrasts of light and shade which seem to foreshadow the great works of his pupil. A most industrious worker (600 of his pictures and 300 of his engravings are extant), Rembrandt lived, happy and envied, till 1650; at this period, his extravagant habits, or rather his inveterate passion for collecting, landed him in bankruptcy and ruin (1656). The close of his life was overshadowed by sorrow and misfortune, in spite of the devotion of a faithful servant, and of his son, Titus. But Rembrandt's biography is of little importance, taking into account the regular and logical development of his genius. Like Hals, he passed from a firm but somewhat frigid technique, to an amazing boldness of handling; he ended by painting with all the freedom of

FIG. 475.—THE BANQUET OF THE GUILD OF CROSSBOWMEN.

B. VAN DER HELST.

(Museum, Amsterdam.)

Velasquez, though with a very different system of illumination. This system is the essential characteristic of Rembrandt's manner. It does not lie, as with Caravaggio, in the brutal opposition of livid whites to opaque blacks, but rather in the blending by imperceptible

FIG. 476.—INTERIOR.

PIETER DE HOOGH.

(National Gallery, London.)

FIG. 477.—THE ARTIST IN HIS STUDIO.

JAN VERMEER (OF DELFT).

(Czernin Collection, Vienna.)

(Photo. by Stoedner, Berlin.)

gradations of the most brilliant light with the deepest shadow in the midst of an ever luminous atmosphere. Luminous atmosphere! I had almost said luminous shadow—this was Rembrandt's great achievement. Just as Michelangelo created a race of giants for his own use, and manipulated them as his genius dictated, so Rembrandt created a light all his own, which is possible without being real, and plunged all nature into this bath of gold.

FIG. 478.—THE MILL.
M. HOBBEMA.
(The Louvre.)

Everything in Rembrandt's sum of achievement—large compositions like the *Night Watch* (1642), which is, in reality, the march-out of a company of cross-bowmen in broad daylight; like the *Syndics*, also in the Amsterdam Ryksmuseum; like the *Manoah's Sacrifice* at Dresden, —compositions minute as to scale, but infinitely great in conception, like the *Philosophers* and the *Supper at Emmaus* in the Louvre; portraits of himself, of his wife, Saskia, of his servant; landscapes, still-life pieces, all partake of this same character, which becomes more and more pronounced as the master becomes freer, as he gives himself up more completely to his genius.

In the course of his prolific career (1609-1669), Rembrandt essayed nearly every subject which could invite an artist's brush. His universality is equalled only by the originality of his vision, thanks to which he gave new life to the most commonplace motives, and to themes which had been treated again and again by his predecessors.

It is true that he did not see Nature with the eyes of the Italians of the Renaissance; he preferred character

FIG. 479.—THE BULL.
PAUL POTTER.
(Museum, The Hague.)

to beauty, and sought to express the infinite by light rather than by line. But his glory need not fear comparison with any other. Familiarity with his genius brings ever-increasing appreciation of its greatness; and he who can delight in it has studied in a good school.

Like Dürer, Rembrandt appealed not only to the rich but to the poor; he reached the masses with his incomparable etchings, the charm of which lies not only in the colour—no other master ever made white paper radiate as he did—but in the inimitable expressive power of the line, where the slightest stroke, the lightest emphasis give utterance to a deep intention. Everyone knows the unfinished plate called *The Hundred Guilder Piece*, representing Christ healing

FIG. 480.—DUTCH LANDSCAPE WITH CATTLE.
A. CUYP.
(National Gallery, London.)

the sick; or at least everyone in London and in Paris should know it, for there are fine impressions of it in the Print Room of the British Museum, in the Cabinet des Estampes, and in the Dutuit Collection at the Petit Palais.

As a portrait-painter Rembrandt had a rival in Van der Helst of Haarlem, the author of the famous portrait-group of the Archers' Guild of Amsterdam (Fig. 475). Set side by side with Rembrandt, he seems somewhat cold: but how many painters can bear the ordeal of such proximity? There are perhaps two who do not suffer from it; one is Pieter de Hoogh, who worked at Amsterdam (1630-1677), and who, under Rembrandt's influence, learned to shed a light at once intense and diffused over his canvases. He is a painter of quiet interiors bathed in sunlight, with glimpses into an outer world in which a warm and velvety atmosphere seems to circulate (Fig. 476). The other is the

FIG. 481.—THE MUSICIAN.
TERBORCH.
(Museum, Berlin.)

267

FIG. 482.—THE CONSULTATION.
JAN STEEN.
(Museum, Amsterdam.)
(*Gazette des Beaux-Arts.*)

prodigious Vermeer of Delft (1632-1675), also influenced by Rembrandt, the author of some dozen luminous masterpieces which are among the most beautiful works in the world; the finest of them is in the Czernin collection at Vienna (Fig. 477).

It is always irksome to have to observe limits in the rapid review of a great school. But how doubly painful is the duty of brevity, when it compels us to pass over landscape-painters like Van Goyen, Aart van der Neer, and Hobbema (Fig. 478), the rival of Ruisdael; animal-painters like Paul Potter and Cuyp (Figs. 479, 480), the greatest of all masters in this genre; painters of gallant and domestic motives such as Terborch (Fig. 481), Metzu, and

FIG. 483.—THE DESCENT FROM THE CROSS
P. P. RUBENS.
(Cathedral, Antwerp.)

FIG. 484.—THE PAINTER AND HIS WIFE
AND CHILD.
RUBENS.
(Alphonse de Rothschild Collection, Paris.)

Steen (Fig. 488), who are great masters of their craft, and Gerard Dou and Mieris, who are delightful exponents of it. I have said nothing of the painters of church interiors, of flowers, fruit, still-life, and poultry-yards. The task of sketching the history of art in twenty-five rapid summaries has never seemed so difficult to me as now. I will only add that all these gifted men appeared and disappeared in a short space of time. In the eighteenth century there was not a single great name. Dutch painting became minute and china-like, in imitation of Gerard Dou and Mieris; Academicism and Italianism held sway; a long twilight succeeded to the most brilliant of days.

In Catholic Flanders, painting reckons fewer great names, but among them is one of the greatest of all time, that of Rubens.

The Italian style, that insidious enemy of Northern art, had taken possession of Flanders from the middle of the sixteenth century. Of the two masters of Rubens, one, Adam van Noort, is almost unknown; the other, Otto Venius, was a distinguished but frigid Italianiser. Born in 1577, Rubens studied at Antwerp, where he seems to have been more influenced by the works left by Quentin Metsys and his pupils than by his own masters[1]. In 1600, at the age of 23, his talent was already formed. He then trav-

FIG. 485.—THE CRUCIFIXION.
(Le Coup de Lance.)
RUBENS.
(Museum, Antwerp.)

elled to Italy, and remained there eight years, living chiefly in Venice, Mantua, Rome, and Genoa. In 1609 he settled at Antwerp, and set out on a triumphal career which was only interrupted by his sudden death in 1640. Like Jan van Eyck, Rubens was entrusted with diplomatic missions and lived on terms of intimacy with kings and princes. He was wealthy, greatly admired, the head of a numerous band of pupils who helped him in his overwhelming undertakings; in 1611

---

[1] It seems to me that we are too prone to lose sight of the affinity between the first paintings of Rubens and the last works attributed to Metsys, as, for example, the touching *Pietà* of Munich.

FIG. 486.—THE MIRACLE OF ST. IGNATIUS.

RUBENS.

(Museum, Vienna.)

he wrote to a friend that he had been obliged to refuse over a hundred pupils. Rubens had a special tariff for the pictures he painted and those of which he merely superintended the execution. But the canvases on which he represented himself with the two women he successively married, Isabella Brandt and Helena Fourment, or the beautiful children they bore him, are, like his sketches, entirely by his own hand, and suffice to prove that the fine works to which he owes his fame were to a great extent sketched out and finished by himself.

Rubens was a creator of unparalleled fecundity; a portrait-painter, landscape-painter, a painter of religious, historical, allegorical, and domestic subjects, of hunting-pieces, fêtes and tournaments. He had a passion for grandiose decoration; even his small pictures, which are comparatively rare, look like reductions of huge canvases. The modifications in his manner as he advanced in years are not very important. His handling, at first smooth and slightly thin, became bolder and more expeditious; but he never loaded his impasto, and always remained faithful to a very simple palette, from which he drew a thousand different effects with the skill of a magician. His style was from the beginning, and remained, that of an eloquent narrator, himself amused by his loquacity, playing with difficulties, never moved or troubled, even when he moves and troubles

FIG. 487.—THE RAPE OF THE DAUGHTERS OF LEUCIPPUS BY CASTOR AND POLLUX.

RUBENS.

(Pinacothek, Munich.)

others, never harassing himself with subtle research, loving beautiful forms and rich colours, delighting in clarity and strength rather than

FIG. 488.—THE CORONATION OF MARIE DE' MEDICI.
RUBENS.
(The Louvre.)

in depth and distinction. His numerous obligations to the antique, the Venetian masters, Michelangelo and Caravaggio, in no degree impaired his somewhat vulgar originality, the reflex of an essentially Flemish temperament, in which sensuality was always on the alert, even when he treated sacred subjects. The Venetians, alone among the Italians, were also more sensual than intellectual; but with them sensuality is beautified by a higher aspiration, rising from the individual to the type; whereas Rubens is a giant who seizes Nature with eager hands, kisses her with an eager mouth; he is not concerned to express the inexpressible, nor even the hidden delicacy of things. Compare the naked woman in Giorgione's *Concert* with any one of Rubens' redundant

FIG. 489.—A FAMILY BANQUET.
JORDAENS.
(Museum, Dresden.)
Woermann, *Geschichte der Malerei*. (Seemann, Leipzig.)

nudities, and you will be able to measure the interval that separates poetry from prose, the form dreamt of from the form actually seen, even in the higher regions of art.

The *Descent from the Cross* (Fig. 483), in Antwerp Cathedral, is generally, but by no means correctly, described as Rubens' master-piece. This picture was painted in 1611, directly after his return from Italy. It is a magnificent canvas, but one of the least Flemish and least characteristic of the master's works. Italian influences are apparent, not only in the composition, which is for the most part borrowed, but in the colour, which is still timid. On the other hand, the *Coup de Lance* (*Crucifixion*), in the Antwerp Museum (Fig. 485), dated 1620, belongs to the period of Rubens' splendid maturity, immediately before the extraordinarily rapid execution of the twenty-four great pictures of the Medici Gallery in the Louvre (1622-1625). The *Coup de Lance* reveals all the genius of Rubens, and all its limitations. In vain are the faces expressive, the composition learned, the colour glowing; this theatrical art is altogether earthy and material; it appeals to the sensibility of the herd, not to that of the elect. It is like the sermon of a grandiloquent preacher, whose style is florid and full of imagery. It was just such declamatory and emotional pictures as this that the Jesuits demanded; to dazzle, to seduce, to speak plainly, and strike hard—such was the programme of these protectors of the arts. To Rubens belongs the dubious honour of having carried it out better than any other artist. His picture lacks the pearly and mysterious note, an echo from the *Fioretti* of the saints of Assisi, which breathes from the Florentine pictures of the Golden Age.

FIG. 490.—LORD JAMES AND LORD BERNARD STUART.

VAN DYCK.

(Late in the Darnley Collection, Cobham Hall.)

FIG. 491.—PIETÀ.

VAN DYCK

(Museum, Antwerp.)

If, in this domain, Rubens is inferior to the Italians and even to the Spaniards, how greatly he surpasses them all in pictures where a robust gallantry, brilliance, sensuality even, are appropriate to the theme, as in his admirable *Rape of the Leucippidae,* at Munich, the dare-devil *Kermess,* in the Louvre, and a score of dashing Hunting Scenes. As a portrait-painter, especially as the limner of his own family, he is no less marvellous; and if Rembrandt and Titian surpass him in depth of expression, he has a power they lack of initiating the spectator into his joy of life, the optimism of his love and health. Then there are his landscapes, his animals, his garlands of flowers and angels! The commission appointed at Antwerp in 1879 to collect reproductions of all his works, reckoned up a total of 2,235

FIG. 492.—KERMESS.

D. TENIERS.

(Pinacothek, Munich.)
(Photo. by Hanfstaengl.)

in museums and private collections, all of which they had not exhausted. In all history there is no other such example of fecundity combined with such imaginative power and such prodigious creative faculty.

Rubens' fellow-student Jordaens, a brilliant but vulgar painter (1593-1678), sometimes caricatures Rubens, and at others appears

FIG. 493.—THE TEMPTATION OF ST. ANTHONY.

. TENIERS.

(The Louvre.)

as his compeer in boisterous good-humour (Fig. 489). Rubens' best pupil, Van Dyck, was of a very different stamp (1599-1641). If Jordaens is Rubens at the Kermess, Van Dyck is Rubens as ambassador. He spent the greater part of his life in Italy and in England, in a world of princes and great ladies, whose favourite painter he was, and who delighted in his elegance and his courtly manners. His aristocratic portraits (Fig. 490), which reflect his delicate nature, are psychological and historical documents of the highest value, as well as a feast for the eyes. As a painter of sacred subjects (Fig. 491), he is distinguished without being powerful; but his delightful colour, more subtle in its gradations than that of Rubens, atones for a touch

273

of effeminacy in his drawing and of conventionality in his pathos. It is difficult to understand how an artist so constantly taking part in the diversions of a Court, and who lived barely forty-four years, could have painted nearly 1,500 pictures, the majority of them portraits, and also have executed a very considerable number of engravings. It is true that he was largely aided by assistants—in most of his full-length portraits only the heads are entirely by his own hand but, nevertheless, his extraordinary industry is only surpassed by that of Rubens.

Genre-painting developed less brilliantly in Catholic Flanders than in Holland; but David Teniers of Antwerp (1610-1690), who was inspired by Rubens, is one of the greatest painters of peasants, of drolleries, and innocent deviltries. The wine-shop, the fair, the booth, have no secrets for him, and his touch is no less brilliant than his observation (Figs. 492, 493).

Twenty other names rise to my lips, names of genre-painters, landscape-painters, still-life painters; but what would it profit us to give them, *verba et voces*, without the few words of information that would fix their artistic rank? I prefer to be silent rather than merely to enumerate them. Purely verbal erudition is especially odious in the history of art, for this history deals with the filiation of styles, and it would destroy its very conception to lower it to mere recitation.

BIBLIOGRAPHY OF CHAPTER XXII.

E. Fromentin, *Les Maîtres d'autrefois*, Paris, 1876 (numerous editions and translations); W. Bode, *Dutch and Flemish Painting*, London, 1909; A. J. Wauters, *La Peinture flamande*, Paris, 1883; H. Havard, *La Peinture hollandaise*, Paris, 1881; W. Bode, *Studien zur Geschichte der holländischen Malerei*, Brunswick, 1883; *Rembrandt und Seine Zeitgenossen*, Leipzig, 1906; A Riegl, *Das Holländische Gruppenporträt* (*Jahrbücher* of the Vienna Museums, vol. xxiii., 1902, p. 71); L. Rosenthal, *La Gravure*, Paris, 1909; A. M. Hind, *History of Engraving*, London, 1908; H. Delaborde, *La Gravure*, Paris, no date; F. Lippmann, *Der Kupferstich*, Berlin, 1893.

G. Davies, *Frans Hals*, London, 1902; E. W. Moes, *Frans Hals*, Brussels, 1909; E. Michel, *Rembrandt*, Paris, 1893 (English trans., London, 1894); C. Neumann, *Rembrandt*, Stuttgart, 1903; A. Bréal, *Rembrandt*, London, 1902; Hope Rea, *Rembrandt*, London, 1903; A. Rosenberg, *Rembrandt*, Stuttgart, 3rd ed., 1909 (photographs of all the pictures); W. Bode, *Die Bildnisse der Saskia als Braut und junge Gattin* (*Jahrbücher* of the Berlin Museums, 1897, p. 82); *Rembrandt und seine Zeitgenossen*, Leipzig, 1906; H. W. Singer, *Rembrandt's Radirungen*, Stuttgart, 1906 (reproductions of engravings); W. Bode and Ch. Sedelmeyer, *Rembrandt, Catalogue illustré de son oeuvre*, 6 vols. fol., Paris, 1897, *et seq.* (2000 francs); F. Lippmann and C. Hofstede de Groot, *Zeichnungen von Rembrandt*, Berlin, 1901, and Harlem, 1906; W. von Seidlitz, *Kritisches Verzeichnis der Radierungen Rembrandts*, Leipzig, 1895.

A. Rosenberg, *Adrian und Isack van Ostade*, Bielefeld, 1900; W. Bürger, *Jan Vermeer* (*Gazette des Beaux-Arts*, 1866, i., p. 297); E. Plietzsch, *Vermeer*, Leipzig, 1912; E. Michel, *Gerard Ter Borch* (*ibid.*, 1886, ii., p. 388); W. Martin, *Jan Steen*, Amsterdam, 1909; F. Hellens, *Terborch*, Brussels, 1911; Martin David, *Gerard Dow*, London, 1902; E. Michel, *Les Cuyp* (*Gazette des Beaux-Arts*, 1892, i., p. 1); *Les Maîtres du Paysage*, Paris, 1906 (on *Everdingen*, see *Gazette des Beaux-Arts*, 1902, ii., p. 262); P. Mantz, *Van Goyen* (*Gazette des Beaux-Arts*, 1875-1878).

M. Rooses, *Rubens*, 5 vols. (432 pl.), Paris, 1886-1892; *Rubens, sa vie et ses oeuvres*, Anvers, 1901; E. Michel, *Rubens*, Paris, 1900 (English trans., London, 1899); E. Knackfuss, *Rubens*, Bielefeld, 1895; A. Rosenberg, *Rubens*, Stuttgart, 1905 (photographs of all the pictures); J. Guiffrey, *Antoine van Dyck*, Paris, 1882; L. Cust, *Anthony van Dyck*, London, 1900; H. Hymans, *Van Dyck* (*Gazette des Beaux-Arts*, 1899, ii., p. 226); E. Schaeffer, *Van Dyck*, Stuttgart, 1909 (photographs of all works); E. Knackfuss, *Van Dyck*, Bielefeld, 1896; F. Gevaert, *Jordaens*, Paris, 1905 (cf. *Gazette des Beaux-Arts*, 1905, ii., p. 247, and *Magazine of Fine Arts*, 1905, vol. i.).

FIG. 494.—FRAGMENT OF THE LAST JUDGMENT.
JEAN COUSIN.
(The Louvre.)

XXIII

THE ART OF THE SEVENTEENTH CENTURY IN FRANCE

The Imitation of Italian Art in France.—Jean Cousin.—Philippe de Champaigne.—Jacques Callot.—Simon Vouet.—The Frigidity of French Art in the XVIIth Century.—Le Brun, Nicolas Poussin.—Le Sueur.—Jouvenet.—Claude Lorrain.—Hyacinthe Rigaud.—Largillière.—Mignard.—Molière the Apologist of Academic Art.—The Sculptors of the Grand Siècle: Guillain, Girardon, the Coustous, and Coysevox.—Puget.—The Industrial Arts under Louis XIV.—The Foundation of the Gobelins.—Boulle and Caffieri.—The Decadence of French Art at the Close of Louis XIV.'s Reign.

AT the beginning of the seventeenth century, French art, both painting and sculpture, was given over to the imitation of the Italians. The favourite exemplars among these were themselves eclectics, and the works they inspired were generally inferior to their own. Jean Cousin, the author of the *Last Judgment* in the Louvre (Fig. 494), was a mediocre artist, an illustrator of books rather than a painter, who by no means deserves the title given him of "founder of the national school." With the exception of immigrant Flemings, like Philippe de Champaigne, a Brussels master, who is represented by several admirable portraits in the Louvre, there were few distinguished painters in France before the accession of Louis XIV. One, however, Jacques Callot of Nancy, claims an honourable place; he was a pitiless realist, who drew and engraved beggars and incidents of war (1593–1635) (Fig. 495). This popular vein, which was destined soon to be stifled by official art, was also worked by the three brothers Le Nain, who were all received as members of the Academy of Painting on the same day. They are akin to the Dutch in their choice of familiar and intimate subjects, but their painting is black and heavy; the influence of Caravaggio told unfavourably upon them (Fig. 496).

The most popular and prolific painter of the reign of Louis XIII. was Simon Vouet (1590–1649), an imitator of the Carracci, who lived in Rome fourteen years before he was appointed painter to the king. He was a conscientious artist, distinguished by that somewhat cold and solemn integrity that often gave a certain prestige to mediocrity in the art of the "great century."

The most famous members of the school were Le Brun, Le Sueur, and Mignard, who were more gifted than himself, but who drew their inspiration from his examples and his lessons.

FIG. 495.—THE CRIPPLE.
J. CALLOT.
(Engraving.)

Names famous in the annals of painting abound in the reign of Louis XIV.: Poussin, Le Sueur, Le Brun, Jouvenet, Claude Lorrain, Hyacinthe Rigaud, Largillière, Mignard, and many others. Yet when we pass from the great Italian gallery in the Louvre to that of the French painters of the seventeenth century, we cannot but feel chilled, and even to some extent, bored. But if we take two or three pictures, even at random, and study them closely, we discover certain fine qualities due to technical knowledge and conscientious work, together with an air of nobility by no means superficial. Even so, however, the impression of coldness persists. All these artists, indeed, lacked fire and

FIG. 496.—PEASANTS AT TABLE.
LE NAIN.
(The Louvre.)

passion; they were over-intellectual; they rationalised their conceptions over-much, and above all, they lacked freedom: some were held in thrall by classic and Italian models, others by French academicism, of which Le Brun was the high priest.

This Le Brun was a fine draughtsman in the grand style, a learned and inventive decorator, but a wearisome painter, and a servile and tyrannical courtier. Quinault wrote thus to him:

"Au siècle de Louis l'heureux sort te fit
   naître.
Il lui fallait un peintre, il te fallait un
   maître."

FIG. 497.—SHEPHERDS OF ARCADIA.
N. POUSSIN.
(The Louvre.)

No satire could be more mordant than this eulogy. Although Le Brun showed something akin to genius in his decorations of the Galerie d'Apollon in the Louvre[1] and indisputable talent in the design of his *Battles of Alexander*, which are spoilt by their ugly brownish colour, he was *par excellence* the type of the official painter, under a *régime* when it was the function of art to glorify absolute power, to subserve and contribute to its pomp. For even art in the seventeenth century was kept in tutelage. Mazarin and Colbert founded the Academies of Painting, Sculpture, and Architecture. Le Brun, who was Professor at the Academy of Painting from 1648, became permanent Chancellor in 1663, and was Director from 1663 till his death in 1690. His authority was well-nigh supreme. He cannot be accused of having favoured only the incapable,

FIG. 498.—THE FORD.
CLAUDE LORRAIN.
(The Louvre.)

but he certainly stifled or discouraged independence.

The greatest artist of the period, Nicolas Poussin (1594-1665), passed nearly his whole life in Italy. Summoned to Paris in 1641

[1] Let me remind the reader that the central painting of the ceiling is by Delacroix.

to direct certain official works, he was so disgusted by the intrigues of the Court that he made a pretext for returning to Italy. Poussin

FIG. 499.—THE LANDING OF CLEOPATRA.
CLAUDE LORRAIN.
(The Louvre.)

had admirable gifts, a delicate, *Racinian* sentiment, and a fine sense of grand historic landscape. But his pictures, though vigorously conceived and composed, are painted bas-reliefs. His figures, always correctly drawn, are curiously insignificant; there is nothing individual in their features, nothing vibrant in their flesh. Poussin painted many Bacchanals without a smile, without a touch of voluptuousness. His colour is at once dull and harsh, a kind of polychromy applied reluctantly, and as an afterthought. His landscape backgrounds alone are harmonious in their discreet tonality. A slave to the antique, he was also in bondage to allegory. One of his best works, the *Shepherds of Arcadia* (Fig. 497), is unintelligible without a commentary, and even now it is not quite certain what he meant by it. Nevertheless, Poussin's renderings of Scriptural subjects are among the finest illustrations that have been made of the Bible. In this domain he hardly falls short of Raphael.

Le Sueur (1616–1655) was a somewhat over-rated painter, whose work, preserved almost in its entirety in the Louvre, is interesting when carefully studied, but unattractive as a whole. In the twenty-two pictures dealing with the life of St. Bruno, there are many excellent compositions, and even some very fine figures. But the imitation of Raphael is as

FIG. 500.—PORTRAIT OF BOSSUET.
H. RIGAUD.
(The Louvre.)
(Photo. by Neurdein.)

obvious as is the lack of warmth and inspiration. His colour, less dull than that of Poussin, is harsher and cruder. Those who

call him the Racine of painting must have mis-read the
poet, or confounded him with
Campistron.

Jean Jouvenet (1644–1717)
the *protégé* of Le Brun, was,
like him, an imitator. His *Descent from the Cross* has been
given a place of honour in the
Salon Carré of the Louvre,
and holds it satisfactorily.
It is superior to kindred compositions by the Bolognese;
but it shows more rhetoric
than eloquence, more academic
knowledge than emotion.

FIG. 501.—PORTRAIT OF THE ARTIST WITH HIS
WIFE AND DAUGHTER.
N. DE LARGILLIÈRE.
(The Louvre.)
(Photo. by Neurdein.)

Claude Lorrain (1600–1682) lived in Italy like his friend Poussin,
and was the favourite of three successive Popes. He is the undisputed master of that false and conventional style which is called
Italian landscape, in which the great background of nature, skilfully
manipulated, serves as setting for a historical or mythological composition. Claude Lorrain's temples,
trees, and rocks have little reality, his
figures even less; but what redeems
his pictures, and ensures them legitimate
admiration, is the poetic sentiment of
space, sky, water, and light. This flood
of light, never darkened by a single
cloud, has a certain artificial and theatrical character, compared with the diffused
light of a Cuyp or a Vermeer; but
there is a kind of heroic beauty in
Claude's sunny landscapes (Figs. 498,
499). Turner, who bequeathed his
pictures to the National Gallery of
London, requested that two of them
should be placed there side by side with
two masterpieces by Claude. They still
hang together, and attest the influence
of the great luminist of the seventeenth
century upon his more richly gifted rival
of the nineteenth.

FIG. 502.—LOUIS XIII.
SIMON GUILLAIN.
(The Louvre.)

FIG. 503.—THE DUCHESS OF
BURGUNDY AS DIANA.

COYSEVOX.

(The Louvre.)

From the beginning of the reign of Louis XIV. to our own times, France has produced excellent portraits. Portraiture has become a national art, and strangers come from afar to sit to distinguished French portrait-painters. This is to be explained by the fact that the academic convention has less force in this than in any other genre. The artist, whether he will or no, is confronted with nature, in contact with her, and he must perforce open his eyes and look at her. In the reign of Louis XIV., however, life had become so artificial that even portraits take on an air of affectation and tension; we may instance Hyacinthe Rigaud's portraits of Louis XIV. and of Bossuet (Fig. 500), which are fine works, but fine in a cold and pompous style. The best of the portrait-painters of this period was Largillière; his masterpiece, a family group of himself, his wife and his daughter, is in the Salle Lacaze, in the Louvre (Fig. 501). It is a charming work, but one which makes us smile perhaps rather more broadly than the artist intended us to do; the dignified attitude of the parents is so prim, the young girl's grace so mincing! Mignard, the adversary of Le Brun, and his successor as Director of the Academy of Painting, is a seductive portraitist, though his handling is timid and pedantic. Poussin bestowed on his portraits the unpleasant epithets "froids et fardés." In his own day he was chiefly famous as a painter of large compositions, notably his frescoes in the cupola of the Val-de-Grâce Chapel, which were lengthily and emphatically eulogised by Molière. This mediocre epistle by the great poet is very instructive; it shows us what criticism demanded of art in the seventeenth century. According to Molière, it should be:—

FIG. 504.—MILO OF CROTONA

PUGET.

(The Louvre.)

"Assaisonné du sel de nos grâces antiques,
Et non du fade goût des ornements gothiques,
Ces monstres odieux des siècles ignorants,
Que de la barbarie ont produit des torrents
Quand leurs cours, inondant presque toute
la terre,
Fit à la politesse une mortelle guerre,
Et, de la grande Rome abattant les remparts,
Vint, avec son Empire, étouffer les Beaux-
Arts."

The duty of French artists was clearly to imitate the antique, to despise the national tradition, and to make full restitution of the rights of "politeness." This is pretty well; but let us hear the sequel:—

"Il nous dicte amplement les leçons de dessin,
Dans la manière grecque et dans le goût
romain,
Le grand choix du vrai beau, de la belle
nature,
Sur les restes exquis de l'antique sculpture."

FIG. 505.—HORSES OF MARLY.
G. COUSTOU.
(Champs-Elysées, Paris.)
(Photo. by Giraudon.)

Painting that imitates sculpture! This was, in fact, the pernicious ideal of Academicism. It is equally ready with its formula in the matter of colour:—

" Et quel est ce pouvoir qu'au bout des doigts tu portes,
Qui sait faire à nos yeux vivre des choses mortes,
Et d'un peu de mélange et de bruns et de clairs
Rendre esprit la couleur, et les pierres des chairs."

Molière seems to have a great opinion of these "browns"; he returns to the charge a little further on:—

"Le gracieux repos que, par des soins
communs
Les bruns donnent aux clairs, comme les
clairs aux bruns."

Antique art for drawing, browns and high tones for painting, such were the formulæ of great art. Not one word of nature as we see it, as it presents itself to us without any intermediary. And the supreme judge in art matters was,

FIG. 506.—THE RHONE.
COUSTOU.
(Hotel de Ville, Lyon.)

not the public, not any among the artists themselves, but Louis XIV., whose preferences were infallible:—

> "Mais ce qui plus que tout élève son mérite,
> C'est de l'auguste Roi l'éclatante visite,
> Ce monarque dont l'âme, aux grandes qualités,
> Joint un goût délicat des savantes beautés,
> Qui, séparant le bon d'avec son apparence,
> Décide sans erreur et loue avec prudence,
> Louis, le grand Louis, dont l'esprit souverain
> Ne dit rien au hasard et voit tout d'un œil sain,
> A versé de sa bouche, à ces grâces brillantes
> De deux précieux mots les douceurs chatouillantes,
> Et l'on sait qu'en deux mots ce Roi judicieux
> Fait des plus beaux travaux l'éloge glorieux."

Such words from the pen of a man of genius are even more distressing than ridiculous.

FIG. 507.—BOULLE CABINET.

(Palace of Versailles.)

In sculpture, as in painting, it was portraiture which most worthily sustained the national tradition; Simon Guillain's Louis XIII. (Fig. 502) and Girardon's Louis XIV., to mention but two out of a hundred, are full of life and spirit. Nevertheless, when Coysevox (1640-1720), his pupils, the Coustous (Figs. 503, 505, 506), and even the frigid Girardon, threw off the trammels of allegory, their knowledge of form and their innate nobility of taste showed themselves in works that command respect. We recognise this when we look at Coysevox's *Fames* at the entrance to the Tuileries, and at Guillaume Coustou's *Horses of Marly* at the entrance to the Champs-Elysées.

These sculptors were the favourites of the Court and of the town; the really great artist of the century was an independent and lonely figure, Pierre Puget (1622-1694). Like Poussin and Claude Lorrain, he lived principally in Italy and in the South of France, far from the desiccating tyranny of Le Brun. Puget's genius, a somewhat academic reflection of that of Michelangelo modified by the influence of Bernini, was not appreciated at its true worth, though Colbert, who was friendly to him, commissioned him to decorate the prows of the royal galleys. He was not employed on the sumptuous decorations of Versailles, where Girardon's empty talent triumphed. His works have a character of severe and haughty grandeur, the impress of a solitary life devoted to art, and of the noble pride which made him say at the age of sixty, after finishing his *Milo of Crotona* (Fig. 504): " I at home among great things, I soar when I am at work upon them, and the marble trembles before me, however big it may be."

Louis XIV. was not content with the institution of official painting and sculpture. He wished even the industrial arts to bear the *imprimatur* of his majesty, and in 1661 he founded the Gobelins manufactory, where not only carpets and hangings were made, but furniture, goldsmiths' wares, and candelabra. What is known in furniture as the Louis XIV. style is sometimes a compromise between the Flemish tradition and Italianism, sometimes a sort of severe Baroque, in which French taste proclaims itself, notably in the choice of materials and the fine quality of the execution. Boulle the furniture-maker won lasting fame with his cabinets incrusted with copper, brass, and tortoiseshell; they lack grace, but are impeccable in technique. The best worker in bronze and chaser of metals of the period was Caffieri, an Italian immigrant, the head of a family of clever artists.

The last twenty years of Louis XIV.'s reign were a lamentable decadence. But if the old king died all too slowly, France, in spite of the disasters he had let loose upon her, remained vital and laborious, though impoverished by the loss of thousands of skilled workmen that the revocation of the Edict of Nantes had driven out to Holland and to Prussia. In the dull silence imposed upon her by an effete despotism, she was preparing the brilliant Renaissance of the eighteenth century, which was to burst forth like a trumpet-blast of deliverance, on the very morrow of Le Roi Soleil's death.

BIBLIOGRAPHY OF CHAPTER XXIII.

L. Hourticq, *Histoire de l'Art en France*, Paris, 1911; L. Gonse, *La Sculpture française depuis le XIVe siècle*, Paris, 1894; Ch. Blanc, *L'Ecole française de peinture*, 3 vols., Paris, 1862; O. Merson, *La Peinture française au XVIIe et au XVIIIe siècle*, Paris, 1900; L. Gonse, *Les Chefs-d'oeuvre des Musées de France, la Peinture*, Paris, 1900; *La Sculpture*, Paris, 1904; St. Lami, *Dictionnaire des Sculpteurs . . . sous Louis XIV*, Paris, 1906; E. Bourgeois, *Le Grand Siècle*, Paris, 1896; E. Müntz, *L'Enseignement des Beaux-Arts en France, le Siècle de Louis XIV.* (*Gazette des Beaux-Arts*, 1895, ii., p. 367); L. Courajod, *Leçons professées à l'Ecole du Louvre*, vol. iii., Paris, 1903 (the origin of modern art, the resistance of the national style to academicism; H. Lemonnier, *L'Art au temps de Richelieu et de Mazarin*, Paris, 1893.

H. Bouchot, *J. Callot*, Paris, 1889; G. Grandin, *La Famille Lenain* (*Réunion des Sociétés des Beaux-Arts*, 1900, p. 475); A. Valabrègue, *Les Frères Lenain*, Paris, 1904; H. Jouin, *Ch. Le Brun et les Arts sous Louis XIV.*, Paris, 1890; O. Merson, *Charles Le Brun* (*Gazette des Beaux-Arts*, 1899. ii., p. 353); Ch. Le Brun à la Manufacture royale (*ibid.*, 1895, i., p. 89); P. Marcel, *Charles Le Brun*, Paris, 1909;

J. Guiffrey. *L'Exposition des Gobelins* (*ibid.*, 1902, ii., p. 265); H. Bouchitté, *Le Poussin*, Paris, 1858; Eliz. Denio, *Nicolas Poussin*, Leipzig, 1898 (English trans., London, 1899); P. Desjardins, *Poussin*, Paris, 1903; Mrs. Mark Pattison (Lady Dilke), *Claude Lorrain*, Paris, 1884; P. Mantz, *Largillière* (*Gazette des Beaux-Arts*, 1893, ii., p. 89); P. Lalande, *L'Art du portrait au XVIIe siècle* (*Grande Revue*, Nov. 15, 1904); E. Michel, *Etudes sur l'Histoire de l'Art*, Paris, 1896 (Flemish landscape, Claude Lorrain).

A. Lagrange, *P. Puget* (*Gazette des Beaux-Arts*, 1865–1867); P. Auquier, *Puget*, Paris, 1903; G. le Breton, *L'Hercule de Puget au Musée de Rouen* (*ibid.*, 1888, i., p. 224); Lady Dilke, *Les Coustou* (*ibid.*, 1901, i., p. 1).

A. de Champeaux, *Le Meuble*, 2 vols., Paris, 1885–1901; A. Molinier, *Le Mobilier au XVIIe et au XVIIIe siècle*, Paris, no date; *Le Mobilier français au Musée du Louvre*, Paris, 1903; *La Collection Wallace, Meubles et Objets d'art français*, Paris, 1903; *The Louis XIV. Style* (*Burlington Magazine*, 1903, i., p. 25); H. Havard, *Les Boulle*, Paris, 1893; J. Guiffrey, *Les Caffieri, Sculpteurs et Fondeurs-Ciseleurs*, Paris, 1877; Chr. Scherer, *Elfenbeinplastik seit der Renaissance*, Leipzig, 1903; E. Molinier, *Les Ivoires*, Paris, no date.

XXIV

FRENCH ART IN THE EIGHTEENTH CENTURY. THE RISE OF THE ENGLISH SCHOOL

FRANCE breathed freely once more on the death of Louis XIV. For fifteen years past she had been but half alive, holding her breath in an atmosphere of suffering, mediocrity, and sour prudery. Paris was transformed almost within twenty-four hours. The actors of the Italian theatre, expelled in 1697, returned to the capital; fêtes, balls, and pleasure-parties took place on every side. Society, with the Regent at its head, determined to be gay and natural once more. But, unable to shake off all its habits in a day, it halted mid-way, and, instead of returning to true nature, invented a nature of gallantry and masquerade. As inter- preters of its love of pleasure,

FIG. 508.—FÊTE CHAMPÊTRE.
WATTEAU.
(Royal Palace, Berlin.)
(Woermann, *Geschichte der Malerei.* (Seemann, Leipzig.)

its elegance, its easy morality, it found Watteau and his successors. These charming painters, winding like a garland throughout the eighteenth century, seem to many people to have summed up all its tastes. But this is a mistaken notion. The century that rapturously applauded Voltaire's dreary tragedies, that was roused to enthusiasm by the *Esprit des Lois* and *Emile*, was far from being a frivolous age.

although it was given to frivolity, as to other amenities of social life. It was still saturated with classicism, and it was inevitable that it should have been so, since education was based exclusively on a study of the Greeks and Romans. But side by side with this classical current, which was never interrupted, and overflowed towards the end of Louis XV.'s reign, there was another, that had its rise in a reaction of the French spirit against the tyrannical supremacy of the past. This current reflected a desire for emancipation, gaiety, and amiable epicurean-

FIG. 509.—OATH OF THE HORATII.
DAVID.
(The Louvre.)

ism, which is one of the charms of the eighteenth century. We are, it is true, accustomed to vilify it; we have all heard covert allusions to the corruption of the times, its license to which nothing was sacred, its scandalous impiety. This is because our educators were themselves formed during the political and religious reaction which occupied nearly the whole of the nineteenth century, and made a sort of bogey of its predecessor. This is not the place to attempt a refutation of this prejudice; suffice it to say that the eighteenth century, taken as a whole, marked a return to nature, to truth, to life. Pedants and hypocrites, the Trissotins and Tartuffes, the most dangerous enemies of the French genius, should stand alone in condemning it on these grounds.

FIG. 510.—AUTUMN.
LANCRET.
(Edmond de Rothschild Collection, Paris.)

In the seventeenth century the public was mainly the King, as we have seen from Molière's verses to Mignard (pp. 281, 282). In the eighteenth century it had not yet come to mean everybody, but it included a great number of courtiers, men of letters and of science, citizens, financiers, and—above all—pretty women. Art worked for them, to please them, to affirm their attraction and their power. We should seek in vain in the eighteenth century for a painter like Meissonier, whose brush almost ignored woman. At no period did she exercise a greater influence over the intelligence; and if the reaction of the nineteenth century dethroned her, it is not unlikely that she will have her revenge in our own day.

FIG. 511.—THE BATHERS.
BOUCHER.
(The Louvre.)
(Photo. by Neurdein.)

The advent of a new style in art did not lead to the abolition of Academies or of Academicism. The last disciples of Le Brun joined hands with Coypel, Van Loo, and Lagrenée, the representatives of that empty and theatrical art which preceded the

FIG. 512.—LE CHIFFRE D'AMOUR.
FRAGONARD.
(Wallace Collection, London.)
(Photo. by Mansell.)

FIG. 513.—STUDY.
FRAGONARD.
(The Louvre.)

more austere academicism of Vien and of David. There is little to say of these painters, save that they were affected, more perhaps

FIG. 514.—GRACE BEFORE MEAT.
CHARDIN.
(The Louvre.)

FIG. 515.—THE MORNING TOILETTE.
CHARDIN.
(Museum, Stockholm.)
Gazette des Beaux-Arts.

than they themselves were aware, by the delicate art that fluttered round them. Some of Coypel's Scriptural subjects, painted on a colossal scale, look like overgrown paintings for fans. The best representative of academicism before David was not a Frenchman, but an Italianised German, Raphael Mengs, who lived mainly in Italy (1728-1779). If this highly gifted artist produced no masterpieces, it was because, like the Carracci, he was led astray by the fatal seductions of eclecticism, which knows beauty only at second-hand.

The great master of the eighteenth century school, the school of gallant amenities, was Antoine Watteau of Valenciennes, who came to

FIG. 516.—THE VILLAGE BRIDE.
GREUZE.
(The Louvre.)

FIG. 517.—MADAME DE POMPADOUR.

QUENTIN LA TOUR.

(Pastel in the Museum, St. Quentin.)

FIG. 518.—MADEMOISELLE DE LAMBESC AND
THE COMTE DE BRIONNE.

NATTIER.

(The Louvre.)

FIG. 519.—MADAME DE CRUSSOL.

MADAME VIGÉE LE BRUN.

(Museum, Toulouse.)

Gazette des Beaux-Arts.

FIG. 520.—THE MILKMAID.

GREUZE.

(The Louvre.)

Gazette des Beaux-Arts.

Paris in 1702 and died there in 1721. He had seen some of Rubens' great canvases in his native town; in Paris he saw others, those of the Luxembourg series, now in the Louvre. He also made the acquaintance of a clever decorator, Gillot, who painted theatrical subjects. His *Fêtes galantes* and *Fêtes pastorales* owe something to Gillot and much to Rubens; but their poetry, their delicate sensibility, is all his own (Fig. 508). The nineteenth century long despised them, in the name of "high art." But are we to find fault with masterpieces such as the *Embarkation for Cythera* (1717) because they glorify the joy of life and the delight of sharing it with another? Is it not, indeed, the function of art, or at least a part of its function, to purify what is sensual by grace, to render beauty amiable and attractive, to gladden life and quicken its pulsations?

FIG. 521.—MADAME RÉCAMIER.
DAVID.
(The Louvre.)

Watteau is an exquisitely refined colourist, whose palette was as subtle as that of Van Dyck; his weakness was that the world appeared to him like a scene at the opera lighted by Bengal fire, that he felt neither passion nor emotion, and trifled with the surface of things. His imitators, Lancret and Pater, more sensual and less delicate than himself, were nevertheless true artists (Fig. 510). Can we say the same of Boucher, the most prolific of this generation of painters (1704-1770)? He was an ingenious decorator, a draughtsman who delighted in those undulating, sinuous lines which are, as it were, the graphic formula of the Rococo Style. But Boucher drew for effect, without having studied nature; he painted his pictures like screens with a monotonous prodigality of blue

FIG. 522.—MADAME SÉRIZIAT.
DAVID.
(The Louvre.) (*Gazette des Beaux-Arts.*)

FIG. 523.—STATUE OF PETER THE GREAT.

FALCONET.

(St. Petersburg.)

FIG. 524.—TOMB OF MARSHAL
DE SAXE.

PIGALLE.

(Strasburg Cathedral.)

and pink; his colour has a spurious gaiety, but is often crude, pallid, and tart (Fig. 511). The Painter of the Graces, as he was called, was, in truth, often superficial and vulgar, whose boldest inventions are not even sensual but rather insipid or sentimental. Fragonard (1732-1806) was greatly superior to him; he is even superior to Watteau in his sense of reality and his ingenious variety of motives (Figs. 512, 513). Poor Frago, so lively and so radiant, died forgotten and misunderstood under the Empire, after having witnessed the triumph of painters who reviled him as a corrupter of public morals and lacked both his imagination and his technical skill.

By the middle of the eighteenth century the wearisome frivolity of Boucher and his numerous imitators had provoked a double reaction

FIG. 525.—VOLTAIRE.

HOUDON

(Théâtre Français, Paris.)

FIG. 526.—DIANA.
HOUDON.
(The Louvre.)

—on the one hand, in favour of antique art; on the other, in favour of moral art. We will consider the former movement first.

It is often assumed that the classic reaction began with the great Revolution. This is an error: it was inaugurated in the reign of Louis XV. The first important discoveries among the ruins of Pompei and Herculaneum were made in 1755, and excited a lively curiosity as to antique art. A German scholar, Winckelmann (1717–1768), struck by the decay of art in Germany and Italy, exhorted artists to take their models from antiquity. His *History of Art among the Ancients* was translated into French in 1764, and had a great success in Paris. Meanwhile, from 1756 to 1785, the graceful and vigorous burin of the Italian engraver, Piranesi, multiplied reproductions of Roman monuments, sculptured vases, candelabra, and bas-reliefs. The influence of these was not confined to the decorative arts, though these were the first in which it was apparent.

At the time of Louis XVI.'s accession, in 1774, the taste of the

FIG. 527.—BACCHANALS.
CLODION.
(Edmond de Rothschild Collection, Paris.)

FIG. 528.—CUPID AND PSYCHE.
CANOVA.
(The Louvre.)

day had already turned to antiquity, the art and manners of which were all the more fervently admired because they were so sharply opposed to those of the moment. The new king—pious, a good husband, of a somewhat narrow understanding—established at least an outward show of decency at Court, which was in sharp contrast to the riotous license of the last years of Louis XV. All these elements went to make up the Empire style, which was considerably anterior to Napoleon, though it dominated without a rival at the period when the reinstatement of the principle of authority—in other words of despotism—brought back in its train the vagaries of the reign of Louis XIV., and upheld them for some fifteen years.

FIG. 529.—SIR PHILIP SIDNEY.
ISAAC OLIVER.
(Miniature at Windsor Castle.)

Vien and his pupil David were not, then, the authors of the revolution by which they profited; but it is only just to say that they ensured its triumph in painting, in which the taste for pink and blue gallantries obstinately survived after the death of Louis XV.

FIG. 530.—COMTESSE DE GRAMONT.
LELY.
(Hampton Court Palace.)

The reign of the Greeks and Romans began in 1784 with David's picture, the *Oath of the Horatii*, a fine bas-relief flatly coloured, which was received with a frenzy of admiration. The Revolution and the Empire made David what Le Brun had been under Louis XIV., the dictator of art: we shall see in our next chapter how this dictatorship came to an end.

In his famous essays on the Salons of 1765 to 1767, Diderot can hardly find terms of abuse sufficiently strong for Boucher and his disciples—with whose style he already contrasts "the grand taste of classic severity "—or panegyrics sufficiently fervid for Chardin and Greuze, in whom he hails the moral regenerators of art. According

FIG. 531.—THE MARRIAGE À LA MODE.
HOGARTH.
(National Gallery, London.)

to Diderot, it is not enough that art should be decent; he required that it should preach the domestic virtues, benevolence, sensibility. Siméon Chardin was an excellent painter, akin to the Dutch naturalists, though more refined than they, whose technical skill was justly appreciated by Diderot; his painting was anecdotic, familiar, and honest, but above all it was good of its kind (and " good painting is a mighty good thing," as he himself said), a return to Nature as we see her in the light of day, and not in the glare of the opera-house (Figs. 514, 515). Greuze, on his part, produced virtuous and sentimental pictures, which seem barely tolerable to-day. His *Paternal Curse,* a sermon in paint, is a very wearisome homily. But in the elements of his talent, as they appear in his charming heads of young girls, in his *Broken Pitcher,* in his *Milkmaid,* he shows himself an adherent of the amiable and graceful art of the eighteenth century (Fig. 520). He helped to crush Boucher, but was in his turn crushed by David, who drew no distinctions between sensual and sentimental art when neither was inspired by Greece and Rome. "We must go back to raw antiquity," he said savagely. A sculptor of the Revolutionary period, an acolyte of David's, demanded that all Flemish pictures

FIG. 532.—NELLY O'BRIEN.
SIR JOSHUA REYNOLDS.
(Wallace Collection, London.)

should be proscribed, on the ground that "they ridicule human nature," and that all non-patriotic subjects (by which we may understand subjects not inspired by the events of the Revolution or by Plutarch) should be forbidden to artists.

The only branch of art which continued to produce masterpieces in eighteenth-century France was portraiture. The pastellist La Tour has bequeathed to us a series of the most charming, the most *spirituel* faces, touched in with colours like the dust on the wings of butterflies (Fig. 517). Nattier, perhaps a little monotonous in his grace, has left us many delicious portraits of dainty, be-rouged womanhood (Fig. 518).

FIG. 533.—THE DUCHESS OF DEVONSHIRE
WITH HER BABY.
SIR JOSHUA REYNOLDS.
(Duke of Devonshire.)

Tocqué, a profounder and more learned artist, was the author of one of the finest portraits in the Louvre, that of Marie Leczynska, the neglected wife of Louis XV. Madame Vigée-Lebrun, who lived till 1842, but who belongs to the reign of Louis XVI. by her talent, painted sentimental, affected beauties with a certain emotional grace (Fig. 519). Finally, the classicists, with David at their head, produced admirable portraits; confronted with living nature, these learned men forgot Greece and Rome, to find inspiration at the fountain-head. The French school has no better title to fame than the group of portraits by David in the Louvre, that of Madame Récamier (Fig. 521), flanked by those of M. and Madame Sériziat (Fig. 522).

FIG. 534.—THE BLUE BOY.
GAINSBOROUGH.
(Grosvenor House, London.)

The two tendencies, frivolous and academic, appear in juxtaposition, nay, in intimate union, in the sculpture of the eighteenth century. The Louis XIV. style survives in the great allegorical

FIG. 535.—THE MORNING WALK.
GAINSBOROUGH.
(Lord Rothschild's Collection, Tring
Park.)

monuments and in mythological groups; the new art manifests itself in works of small dimensions and in portraits. The earliest among the good sculptors of the period, Lemoyne, was still imbued with the tradition of Coysevox and the Coustous; he was the master of Falconet, who executed the colossal *Peter the Great* at St. Petersburg (Fig. 523), an academic and declamatory work; in Paris, he produced his charming *Bather,* and the *Three Graces* of the famous Camondo clock. The second half of the eighteenth century witnessed the rise of two great sculptors, Pigalle and Houdon; the first was the author of the magnificent tomb of Marshal de Saxe in Strasburg Cathedral, and of a seated *Mercury,* a very happy imitation of the antique; the second, who may be ranked among the greatest interpreters of nature, was the sculptor of the incomparable *Voltaire* in the Théâtre Français, the *Dianas* of the Louvre and of St. Petersburg, and a long series of portraits sparkling with truth and intelligence (Figs. 525, 526). Among the boudoir sculptors, whose talents were unfettered by scruples, but who were seductive delineators of feminine grace, the most fascinating was Clodion, "leader of the chorus of frisky Bacchanals"[1] (Fig. 527). Like Fragonard, he outlived the era of light manners, and, when the Græco-Roman reaction had changed the tastes of his public, he was reduced to sculpturing Cato for a livelihood!

FIG. 536.—HON. MRS. GRAHAM.
GAINSBOROUGH.
(National Gallery, Edinburgh.)

[1] André Michel, *Notes sur l'Art moderne.* Paris, 1896. In this chapter and in the following I have borrowed several passages from that excellent little book; they are here printed in quotation marks.

Italy was the chief centre of the classic Renaissance. Canova (1757-1822) thought himself the rival of the Greeks, but was a very effeminate Praxiteles (Fig. 528); following in his wake, the German Danneker, the Englishman Flaxman, and the Dane Thorwaldsen usurped reputations which now cause us some surprise. About the year 1800, this school reigned supreme; it was the apotheosis of false elegance and insipidity. The distinguishing characteristic of these artists was that they had never felt the pulsation of living flesh. Their idealism led them to eliminate from art the main element of its superiority to literature: plastic expression and intensity.

FIG. 537.—MRS. MARK CURRIE.
ROMNEY.
(National Gallery, London.)

England, turned aside from art by Puritanism, long knew only imported painters, such as Holbein, Rubens, and Van Dyck. The beautiful works of a few gifted miniaturists, such as Hilliard, the Olivers, and Cooper, alone foreshadow the growth of a national taste (Fig. 529). [Under Charles I. this taste began to manifest itself in a reawakened interest in art and beauty, fostered by the cultured king and great nobles, such as Arundel, Pembroke, and Buckingham. A magnificent collection of pictures was gathered together by Charles, aided, in many instances, by the counsels of Rubens. It was sold under the Commonwealth, and its masterpieces are now among the gems of various foreign collections. The Louvre owns several of the most famous. Van Dyck, settling in England, may be said to have founded the national school. Among his imitators and successors were the Englishman William Dobson and

FIG. 538.—PORTRAIT OF A LADY.
HOPPNER.
(Fleischmann Collection, London.)

297

the Scotchman George Jamesone. Checked by the fanaticism of the Revolution, English art, reviving under Charles II., found its ex-

FIG. 539.—PORTRAIT OF A LADY.
RAEBURN.
(Schwabacher Collection, London.)

FIG. 540.—MRS. CUTHBERT.
LAWRENCE.
(Comte de Beistegui's Collection, Paris.)

ponent in another foreigner, the Westphalian Peter van der Faes, known as Sir Peter Lely, whose proficient technique and voluptuous manner embodied the very spirit of brilliant and cynical licence that marked the reaction against Puritanism. His famous series of Court Beauties is preserved at Hampton Court (Fig. 530). He was suc-

FIG. 541.—LANDSCAPE.
JOHN CROME.
(Mr. Fleischmann's Collection.)

ceeded by another German of inferior gifts, Godfrey Kneller, and by a number of French-men, Nicholas Largillière among the number, who worked chiefly as decorators and restorers. Sir James Thornhill, who imitated their manner, is now chiefly re-membered as the master of Hogarth, with whom the rep-resentative art of England began. Hogarth (1697-1764) was a moralist, not gently sentimental like Greuze, but harsh and satiric as Callot. He is best known by his famous series of painted narratives, *The Marriage à la Mode* (Fig. 531), *The Rake's Progress, The Election,* and others, but he was also a portrait-painter of great vigour and original-ity. His reputation suffers from the persistence with which writers have dwelt upon the subjects of his pictures, which are witty and entertain-ing, for he was also a master of technique—"the only *great*

FIG. 542.—SALISBURY CATHEDRAL. CONSTABLE.
(Victoria and Albert Museum, London.)

English painter," according to Whistler!] But it is important to note that his pictures set forth edifying histories and dwell upon de-tails, for this didactic tendency has persisted in English art. It has been justly said that Hogarth's anecdotic rebus prepared the way for Burne-Jones' psycho-logical rebus.[1]

Towards the middle of the eighteenth century a generation of remarkable portrait-painters grew up under the influence of Rubens and Van Dyck, Titian and Murillo, whose master-pieces were already numerous in English collections, and also under that of French art, which was never more popular than at this period. Joshua Reynolds (1723-1792), Gainsborough (1727-1788), Hoppner (1759-1810), Allan Ramsay (1713-1784), Romney (1734-1802), Raeburn (1756-1823), Opie (1761-1807), and Lawrence

FIG. 543.—THE CORNFIELD. CONSTABLE.
(National Gallery, London.)
(Photo. by Hanfstaengl.)

(1769-1830), unlike the French portraitists, were, above all, colour-ists, masters of tonalities at once intense and vaporous. Unlike the

[1] R. de la Sizeranne, *La Peinture anglaise contemporaine.* Paris, 1895.

APOLLO

great Venetians, they concerned themselves less with truth than with
grace. Their portraits immortalise a highly polished aristocracy,
like that which furnished sitters for Van Dyck, but healthier and
better equipped for action (Figs. 532-540). [Joshua Reynolds is
generally accepted as the greatest representative of this school, and
his wider sympathies and more intellectual vision may perhaps en-
title him to the first rank. But Gainsborough surpasses him in
purely artistic qualities, in the incomparable grace and spontaneity
of his art. As limners of character, of manly dignity, of womanly
beauty and distinction, of childish grace and innocence, these masters
need not fear comparison with the greatest of any school. Their
successors, though on a lower plane, worthily upheld their tradition, and in their finest achievements fall not very far short of
their masters. With Lawrence (1769-1830) and his brilliant superficial art, the glory of the English school of portraiture began to
pale. William Beechey was the last upholder of the great tradition,
which was finally overwhelmed by the puerilities of the early Vic-
torian period. Landscape flourished too.] Gainsborough, Crome,
and, above all, Constable (1776-1837) (Figs. 542, 543), took up the
tradition of Ruisdael, transformed it with their insular originality,
and inaugurated the modern school of realistic landscape. The best
French landscapes of the eighteenth century, if we except one or
two small canvases by Joseph Vernet, still looked to the Italian tradition for inspiration; the English were the first to cast off these
trammels and to venture upon "setting up an easel in the fields."
Thenceforth, England became an important factor in the artistic activity of the world; she continues to give more than she receives, and
both in portraiture and landscape remains English, essentially English, though French art reigns supreme almost everywhere else.

BIBLIOGRAPHY OF CHAPTER XXIV.

P. Lacroix, *Le Dix-huitième siècle*, Paris, 1875; E. and J. de Goncourt, *L'Art du XVIIIe siècle*, 3rd
ed., 2 vols., Paris, 1880-1883; Lady Dilke, *French Engravers and Draughtsmen of the XVIIIth Century*,
London, 1903; *French Architects and Sculptors; French Painters*, London, 1900; C. Justi, *Winckelmann
und seine Zeitgenossen*, 2nd ed., Leipzig, 1898; L. Hautecœur, *Rome, les origines de l'art Empire*, Paris,
1912; P. Seidel, *Die Kunstsammlung Friedrichs des Grossen auf der Weltausstellung*, Berlin, 1900 (French
trans., Paris, 1901).
P. Marcel, *La peinture française au début du XVIIIe siècle*, Paris, 1906; J. Foster, *French Art from
Watteau to Prudhon*; A. Valabrègue, *Claude Gillot* (*Gazette des Beaux-Arts*, 1899, i., p. 385); P. Mantz,
A. Watteau, Paris, 1892 (cf. *Gazette des Beaux-Arts*, 1889, i., p. 5); A. Rosenberg, *Watteau*, Bielefeld,
1896; E. Hannover, *Watteau*, Berlin, 1889; G. Séailles, *Watteau*, Paris 1901; L. de Fourcaud, *Watteau*
(*Revue de l'Art* 1901, i., p. 87); Th. de Wyzewa, *Watteau* (*Revue des Deux-Mondes*, Sept. 15, 1903);
H. Zimmermann, *Watteau*, Stuttgart, 1912 (photographs of all works).
P. Mantz, *Boucher, Lemoyne et Natoire*, Paris, 1880; A. Michel, *Boucher*, Paris, 1886; O. Fidière,
Alex. Roslin (*Gazette des Beaux-Arts*, 1898, i., p. 45); P. Mantz, *Nattier* (*Gazette des Beaux-Arts*, 1894,
i., p. 91); P. de Nolhac *Nattier* (*ibid.*, 1895, i., p. 457); P. Mantz, *Louis Tocqué* (*ibid.*, 1894, ii., p.
455); L. de Fourcaud, *Chardin*, Paris, 1900 (cf. *Revue de l'Art*, 1899, ii., p. 383); Lady Dilke, *Chardin*
(*Gazette des Beaux-Arts*, 1899, ii. p. 177); G. Schefer, *Siméon Chardin*, Paris, 1903; H. Furst, *Chardin*,
London, 1911; M. Tourneux, *Les Colson* (*Gazette des Beaux-Arts*, 1898, ii., p. 337); C. Gabillot, *Les*

Drouais (*Gazette des Beaux-Arts*, 1905, ii., p. 177); R. Portalis, *Fragonard*, Paris, 1899; E. de Goncourt, *La Tour* (*Gazette des Beaux-Arts*, 1867, i., p. 127); M. Tourneux, *La Tour* (*ibid.*, 1899, i., p. 485); J. Flammermont, *Les Portraits de Marie-Antoinette* (*ibid.*, 1897, ii., p. 283; 1898, i., p. 183); Dumont-Wilden, *Le portrait en France* Brussels 1910; H. Bouchot, *Boilly* (*Revue de l'Art*, 1899 i., p. 339); H. Harrisse, *L. Boilly*, Paris, 1898; P. Seidel, *A. Pesne*, (*Gazette des Beaux-Arts*, 1891, i., p. 318); H. Bouchot, *Mme. Vigée Le Brun* (*Revue de l'Art*, 1898, i., p. 51); Ch. Pichot, *M. Vigée Le Brun*, Paris, 1892; Aubert, *J.-M. Vien* (*Gazette des Beaux-Arts*, 1867, i., p. 180); C. Gabillot, *Hubert-Robert et son Temps*, Paris, 1895; Ch. Saunier, *Louis David*, Paris, 1904.

L. Gonse, *La Sculpture française*, Paris, 1895; Lady Dilke, *French Architects and Sculptors of the XVIIIth Century*, London, 1900; A. Roserot, *J.-B. Bouchardon*, Paris, 1910; Rochéblave, *Pigalle* (*Revue de l'Art*, 1902, ii., p. 267); H. Thirion, *Les Adam et les Clodion*, Paris, 1885; J. Guiffrey, *Clodion* (*Gazette des Beaux-Arts*, 1892, ii., p. 478); H. Stein, *Pajou*, Paris, 1912; A.-G. Meyer, *Canova*, Bielefeld, 1898; Molamani, *Canova*, Milan, 1911.

A. de Champeaux, *Le Meuble*, 2 vols., Paris, 1885–1901; Lady Dilke, *French Furniture and Decoration in the XVIIIth Century*, London, 1902; E. Molinier, *Le Mobilier aux XVIIe et XVIIIe siècles*, Paris, 1899; *Le Musée du mobilier français au Louvre* (*Gazette des Beaux-Arts*, 1901, i., p. 441); P. de Nolhac, *La Décoration de Versailles au XVIIIe siècle* (*Gazette des Beaux-Arts*, 1895, i., p. 265); 1898, i., p. 63); G. Schefer, *Le style Empire sous Louis XV*. (*Gazette des Beaux-Arts*, 1897, ii., p. 481); P. Lafond, *L'Art décoratif et le Mobilier sous la République et l'Empire*, Paris, 1900; Robiquet, *Gouthière*, Paris, 1912; R. Nevill, *French Prints*, London, 1908; H. Cordier, *La Chine en France au XVIIIe siècle*, Paris, 1910; W. Armstrong, *Histoire de l'art en Grande-Bretagne*, Paris, 1910.

H. Bouchot, *La Femme anglaise et ses Peintres*, Paris, 1903; G. C. Williamson, *The History of Portrait Miniatures*, 2 vols., London, 1905; A. Dobson and W. Armstrong, *William Hogarth*, London, 1892; B. Brown, *Hogarth*, London, 1905; W. Armstrong, *Sir Joshua Reynolds*, London, 1901; *Gainsborough*, London, 1900 (French transl.); *Turner*, 2 vols., London, 1902; A. Wherry, *Turner*, London, 1903; Lord R. S. Gower, *Thomas Lawrence*, London, 1900; Th. de Wyzewa, *Thomas Lawrence* (*Gazette des Beaux-Arts*, 1891, i., p. 118); H. Maxwell, *George Romney*, London, 1903; A. B. Chamberlain, *Romney*, London, 1910; Cl. Phillips, *John Opie* (*Gazette des Beaux-Arts*, 1892, i., p. 299); W. Roberts, *Beechey*, London, 1907; A. B. Chamberlain, *Constable*, London, 1903.

FIG. 544.—CHEST BY RIESENER.
(Musée Condé, Chantilly.)

XXV

ART IN THE NINETEENTH CENTURY

AT the beginning of the nineteenth century, Louis David (1748—
1825) held undisputed sway in the world of French art. With
true Jacobin intolerance, he had laid down as essential dogmas in art

FIG. 545.—SABINE WOMEN INTERVENING BETWEEN
ROMANS AND SABINES.
DAVID.
(The Louvre.)

the imitation of antique
statues and bas-reliefs,
a contempt for all genre
subjects, and for every-
thing in the nature of
sensual, and even of
gay and agreeable paint-
ing. But his practice
was better than his
precepts, as his admir-
able portraits (Figs. 522,
523) testify, and also
his grandiose *Corona-
tion of Napoleon I. in
Notre Dame* (Fig. 546),
a truly epic rendering
of a great historical
event, unrivalled in its

kind. In 1815, David, who had voted for the death of Louis XVI.,
was banished from France as a regicide. He died ten years later
in Belgium, where he painted several fine portraits, which show a
great increase in breadth of handling, and seem to reveal a tardy
modification of manner under the influence of Frans Hals.

David's contemporaries, though more or less subservient to his rule, were more independent than those of Le Brun. The least personal among them, Guérin, is also the one who is more nearly forgotten than the rest. The insipid Gérard is more akin to Canova than to his master: in his *Cupid and Psyche* he seems to prepare the way for the sickly painters of the Second Empire. Girodet sought inspiration from Macpherson's *Ossian*, which Napoleon I. thought equal to the poems of Homer; his painting, classic in form, thin and flaccid in execution, is already romantic in spirit.

FIG. 546.—CORONATION OF NAPOLEON IN NOTRE DAME.
DAVID.
(The Louvre.)

Gros, the author of the *Pestiférés de Jaffa* (*Plague-stricken at Jaffa*) (Fig. 548) and the *Napoleon at Eylau*, two fine works, inaugurated Romanticism by his taste for modern subjects and his indifference to the Græco-Roman tradition. David disapproved and advised him " to turn over the pages of Plutarch "; but Brutus, Cato and the Gracchi had had their day, in art as in literature.

The most original of the painters of the Empire period was Prudhon, one of the most fascinating of the great French masters (1758—1823). He had studied Correggio, and Leonardo, whom he called his " master and his hero," and whom he preferred to Raphael. He excelled in chiaroscuro, in rendering the play of light as it caresses white and velvety flesh. A harmonious and sometimes powerful colourist, a somewhat nerveless draughtsman, he remained severely classic in

FIG. 547.—ZEPHYR AND PSYCHE.
PRUDHON.
(The Louvre.)
(Photo. by Neurdein.)

his choice of types and subjects, the André Chénier, as it were, of painting (Figs. 547, 549). All the artists of this period, even Gérard, painted sincere and solid portraits; some of Prudhon's, notably those of Madame Copia and of Josephine, are masterpieces.

FIG. 548.—BONAPARTE AMONG THE PLAGUE-STRICKEN AT JAFFA.
GROS.
(The Louvre.)

From the year 1806 onwards, a pupil of David's, Ingres, executed a series of portraits in pencil which must always be reckoned among the marvels of art (Fig. 551). This artist, a man of iron temperament, who lived over eighty years, began almost as an independent; he was denounced as a Gothic master, an imitator of the Pre-Raphaelites. He became in time an uncompromising classicist, a subtle and nervous draughtsman, more keenly sensitive to tactile values than any artist of his age, but incapable of expressing passion, emotion, or thought. Not only was he a bad painter, but he despised painting, spoke of it as a negligible adjunct, and gave it as his opinion that what is well drawn is always painted well enough. Save in one or two little pictures and in some exquis-itely treated portraits—those, for instance, of Madame De-vauçay, Madame de Senonnes (Figs. 550, 552) — Ingres' painting was merely tinting on a grand scale. To quote Delacroix' epigram, he applied colour as one sticks comfits on a cake. Before his *Vierge à l'Hostie* Horace Vernet, himself a mediocre colourist, cried one day: "To think that he has been plastering us with these blues for the last twenty years!"

FIG. 549.—JUSTICE AND DIVINE VENGEANCE PURSUING CRIME.
PRUDHON.
(The Louvre.)

It is the colour, at once dull and violent, which makes his *Apotheosis of Homer* almost execrable, in spite of the fine qualities

FIG. 550.—PORTRAIT DE MDE. DE SENONNES.
INGRES.
(Museum, Nantes.)
(*Gazette des Beaux-Arts.*)

FIG. 551.—THE STAMATI FAMILY.
INGRES.
(Drawing.)
(Bonnat Collection, Bayonne.)

to be discovered in it on careful examination. To give some idea of Ingres' puerile intolerance, I may mention that he excluded Shakespeare and Goethe from the gathering of great men around the Father of Poetry, because he suspected them of Romanticism! His nude female figures, *The Spring*, *Andromeda*, and the *Odalisque*, are still justly admired; but they are more pleasing in black-and-white reproductions than in the originals. "Why does he not write in prose?" said Boileau of Chapelain. Ingres might have been asked very pertinently why he painted.

Géricault (1791—1824), whose life was very short, played an important part in the history of French art, taking up the tradition of Gros with greater boldness and power. His *Raft of the Medusa* (1819), like the *Pestiférés de Jaffa*, is more akin to Michelangelo than

FIG. 552.—PORTRAIT OF M. BERTIN.
INGRES.
(The Louvre.)

to the antique (Fig. 554). With this masterpiece "movement and pathos made a brilliant return to art." Géricault went to England

FIG. 553.—STRATONICE.
INGRES.
(Musée Condé, Chantilly.)

to exhibit his *Raft*, and brought back new ideas on the beauty of colour, as distinguished from the colouring of the Davidians. He resembles the English and Rubens in his admirable studies of horses, such as the *Derby* (Fig. 555) in the Louvre, the first example of the "flying gallop" in French art.[1] His *Wounded Cuirassier* and his *Chasseur Officer*, large epic figures, painted before his visit to England, are still very conventional in tone and design.

Géricault's heir was Delacroix (1799—1863), who was looked upon as the leader of the Romantic School. The word Romanticism is a somewhat vague term; the movement to which it is applied was, above all, a protest against the tyranny of Greece and Rome, a vindication of the art of the Middle Ages and of modern times as against the unjust contempt with which it was treated. Delacroix took the subject of his most famous pictures from Dante (Fig. 557), Shakespeare, Byron, the history of the Crusades, of the French Revolution, and of the Greek revolt against

FIG. 554.—THE RAFT OF THE MEDUSA.
TH. GÉRICAULT.
(The Louvre.)

the Turks. He painted as a pupil of Géricault, Rubens, and Paul Veronese, with a somewhat defective mastery of drawing, but with a feverish energy of life and expression, a deep and poetic

[1] This motive is, in point of fact, a conventional one, and is not to be found in any of the instantaneous photographs of equine movement (see p. 7). It was an invention of Mycenæan artists, and was adopted in Southern Russia, in Sassanian Persia, and in China, before it appeared in Europe. The earliest European example is an English engraving of 1794; it was unknown in France before the Restoration, and in Germany before 1840. Since the year 1880 the revelations of instantaneous photography have discredited this motive, which is gradually disappearing in art.

sense of colour. His bold, ample technique thrust aside the smooth timidities of the illuminators, and prepared the way for modern Impressionism. His critics do not belittle him when they call him a "sick Rubens" and a "restless Veronese," for his malady and his unrest were the diseases of his century, more human

FIG. 555.—THE DERBY.
TH. GÉRICAULT.
(The Louvre.)

and more fecund than the optimism of his favourite exemplars.

In spite of the anathemas of Ingres, to whom Delacroix was the Devil in painting, academic austerity could not resist the onslaught of the Romanticists. This austerity was opposed to the national genius, which always triumphs in the long run. An eclectic school sprang up, in which the poetry of Romanticism, its somewhat mystic sympathy with mediæval legend, a touch of Greuze's sentimentality, and even souvenirs of Boucher, blended with the tradition of classic design and the somewhat empty idealism of the Davidians. The masters of this school painted anecdotes on a grand scale, and sought to rouse emotion by choice of subject and the grace of feminine and infantine types, rather than by the intrinsic qualities of their art. Among these painters

FIG. 556.—THE MASSACRE OF SCIO.
EUGÈNE DELACROIX.
(The Louvre.)

we may mention Delaroche, a combination of Girodet and Ingres, the author of *The Princess in the Tower* (Fig. 561) and the

Hemicycle in the Ecole des Beaux-Arts; Ary Scheffer, a Dutchman naturalised in France, the gentle painter of Marguerites and Ophelias; Couture, the author of the *Romans of the Decadence*, a theatrical simulacrum of an orgy; Gleyre, Flandrin, Cogniet, Cabanel, Bouguereau, and many others. I shall not presume to judge these men in a few lines, and sum up the various qualities that will

FIG. 557.—DANTE'S BOAT.
EUGÈNE DELACROIX.
(The Louvre.)

keep their memories green. In Gleyre and Flandrin, Ingres' favourite pupil, the mystic tendency predominates; in Cabanel and Bouguereau the sensual element is stronger, but theirs is not the primitive sensuality of Rubens. Cabanel's carnations are woolly, and Bouguereau's a trifle glassy. Bouguereau's European reputation has been won mainly by religious pictures, of a smooth and sentimental kind, akin to the works of Carlo Dolci, though much superior to these in mastery of composition and drawing (Fig. 559).

Delaunay, a sincere and virile artist; Hébert, graceful, tender, and delicate, yet never insipid (Fig. 558); J. P. Laurens, the fervid chronicler of the dramas of history; Merson, Cormon, Maignan, and Duez, may perhaps be included in the same group, as painters who have devoted their talents to the same class of subjects. Many others, such as Fantin-Latour (d. 1904) and Agache, are more easily praised than classified.

FIG. 558.—MALARIA.
HÉBERT.
(Musée du Luxembourg, Paris.)

In the seventeenth and eighteenth centuries, battle-painting, represented principally by the Flemish immigrant Van der Meulen, had produced nothing in France but mediocre and pompous works chronicles of the dubious doughty deeds of certain princes. The soldier was mere food for powder and counted for nothing. Gros' *Napoleon at Eylau* was the first military picture in which the soul of a period found utterance, in which we feel the heart-beats of an artist and a kindly man. Gros placed the surgeon Percy in the foreground; the misery of the wounded, the melancholy of the morrow of carnage, filled his mind, rather than the glory of victorious leaders. His example was not thrown away, though many military painters of the nineteenth century, notably the too prolific Horace Vernet, continued to treat the episodes of war from the point of view of the patriotic illustrator, rather than of the thinker. This cannot be said of Charlet (1792-1845) and of Raffet (1804-1860), lithographers trained in Gros' studio, who

FIG. 559.—THE VIRGIN AS CONSOLER.
BOUGUEREAU.
(Musée du Luxembourg, Paris.)
(Photo. by Neurdein.)

chronicled the campaigns of the Revolution and the Empire with a sentiment at once dramatic and democratic, whose sympathies were with the obscure and heroic soldier, and who made his sufferings and his enthusiasm the central motive of their compositions (Fig. 563). Léon Cogniet's most distinguished pupil, Meissonier (1813-1891), and the pupils or imitators of the latter, Neuville and Detaille, are allied, in their treatment of military subjects, to Charlet and Raffet (Figs. 562-565).

FIG. 560.—THE BIRTH OF VENUS.
A. CABANEL.
(Musée de Luxembourg, Paris.)

A picture such as Meissonier's "1814," to give one example, is one of the glories of the French School of the nineteenth century;

there is nothing to equal it in this special branch in the art of Holland or Italy. Meissonier also painted anecdotic subjects of the

FIG. 561.—THE PRINCES IN THE TOWER.
PAUL DELAROCHE.
(The Louvre.)

eighteenth century with amazing minuteness and dexterity, and with a knowledge of form superior even to that of the Dutch masters (Fig. 566). But the most perfect of his little pictures pales beside a De Hoogh or a Vermeer, for Meissonier was too insistent a draughtsman; he coloured rather than painted, and was never able to envelop form in a luminous, caressing atmosphere.

Delacroix made Eastern subjects fashionable. The Greek war of independence, the conquest of Algiers, the increasing activity of French relations with Constantinople, Syria, and Egypt, offered a field to painters whose gifts lay in the direction of colour and picturesqueness, a field they worked with great skill. The best of these Orientalists were Decamps (Fig. 572), Marilhat, and Fromentin. Decamps was a remarkable colourist, perhaps the best France has produced so far, as we may see in his fine pictures at Chantilly. Fromentin, conscientious and a little timid,

FIG. 562.—1814.
MEISSONIER.
(Chauchard Collection, Paris.)

painted an East and Arabs marked by an artificial elegance, but with a palette full of delicate gradations. His best title to fame, however, is his literary achievement, *Les Maîtres d'Autrefois*, not only the finest, the sole masterpiece of art-criticism produced by France in the nineteenth century.

The little masters of the eighteenth century loved the country rather than Nature; those fervid worshippers of Nature, J. J. Rousseau and Bernardin de St. Pierre, had no influence upon the art of their day. The revelation of true Nature, with her frank verdure and her atmospheric transparencies, was made to France by Englishmen, Bonington and Constable (Fig. 544), who sent some of their works to the

FIG. 563.—"THEY GRUMBLED."
RAFFET.
(Lithograph.)

Salons of the Restoration period. A group of French artists established themselves at Barbizon, in the Forest of Fontainebleau, face to face with trees and rocks and pools, and produced faithful and impassioned portraits of their native land, such as French art had never yet known. The classicists accused them of representing "arid landscapes devoid of all charm, the lines of which are poor and the vegetation dry and stunted," because they took their subjects from France, not from Italy, and renounced the "adjusted landscape" with a ruined temple in the foreground. These heretics, at least, have triumphed; the Italian landscape is no more!

Théodore Rousseau (1812–1867), Daubigny (1817–1878), Dupré (1812–1889) and Diaz (1808–1876) were the masters of the new school; the animal-painter Troyon (1810–1865) may be grouped with them. Other gifted animal-painters, such as Mlle. Rosa Bonheur (1822–1899) and Brascassat (1804–1867), remained more faithful to the methods of the Dutch masters, notably Paul Potter, a somewhat dry and dangerous model. The landscape-painter Corot (1796–1875) holds a place apart; in the course of his long

FIG. 564.—SOLFERINO.
MEISSONIER.
(Musée du Luxembourg, Paris.)

career he passed from classicism to the confines of Impressionism. He was a classicist by education, and he never ceased to people his landscape with

FIG. 565.—THE DREAM.
DETAILLE.
(Musée du Luxembourg, Paris.)

nymphs and satyrs; but this superficial fidelity to tradition was without prejudice to his independence as a poet painter, a lyric master of exquisite refinement, a worshipper of Nature in her more tranquil moods, the incomparable limner of the freshness of morning and the silvery mists of evening (Figs. 567, 569).

If French landscape found its greatest interpreters in the nineteenth century, the sturdy French peasant also found his in Millet (1814–1875). He was, if I may be allowed the phrase, an idyllic realist, akin to Chardin in his technique and choice of subjects, while the tender and fraternal sentiment that breathes from his canvases reveals that sympathy with the poor and humble which has been the honour and the torment of the nineteenth century (Figs. 568, 570).

Corot and Millet have had successors worthy of them. At each annual Salon, landscape is represented by fine achievements. Français and Harpignies, Cazin and Pointelin, to name but four, are secure of a place in the Louvre. Jules Breton, a painter of peasants, like Millet, but less rugged, strove to reconcile

FIG. 566.—THE CONNOISSEURS.
MEISSONIER.
(Musée Condé, Chantilly.)

poetry and realism, without sacrificing beauty and grace to truth.

About the year 1855, the frigid calligraphy of the classicists and the exhaustion of Romanticism brought about a reaction in favour of realism and naturalism. Courbet (1819–1877) and Manet (1833–1884) were its perfervid apostles. Yet both at the outset of their careers had sought inspiration from the Spanish painters, Velasquez and Goya, rather than from Nature. Courbet's large landscapes lack atmosphere and his figures are often painted with soot; but the

FIG. 567.—LANDSCAPE, MORNING.
COROT.
(The Louvre.)

boldness of his execution and the contrast it afforded to Delaroche's smooth technique set a good example (Fig. 574). Manet's *Olympia* was even more revolutionary than Courbet's *Bathers;* it was a protest against those nude goddesses or mortals, with contours of impossible elegance, and bloodless, transparent carnations, so abundantly produced by the academicism of the nineteenth century. But this clamorous demonstration created a scandal and failed to create a school. Manet's technique was imitated more than his somewhat grotesque conception of form. Two tendencies, which, from the year 1875 onwards, developed into veritable systems, Impressionism and *Pleinairisme* (the painting of pictures in the open air), owe their origin to his technique, the leading principle of which was the juxtaposition of pure colours — for, said he, the principal person in a picture

FIG. 568.—THE GLEANERS.
MILLET.
(The Louvre.)

is the light. Impressionism[1] is a sort of pictorial stenography,

[1] The term is derived from a picture exhibited by the landscape-painter Monet, in 1863, at the Salon des Refusés. It represented a sunset and was entitled: *An Impression.*

FIG. 569.—THE BATHERS OF BELLINZONA.
CAMILLE COROT
(Cuvelier Collection, Paris.)

disdainful of details which rapid and synthetic vision cannot seize. It is also a reaction against symbolism, intellectualism, and all those elements in a picture which lie outside the true domain of art. *Pleinairisme* was a revolt against painting done in the studio, with the black shadows that are never seen in the open air. A painter may be an Impressionist without being a *Pleinairiste*, and *vice versa;* among these artists who broke with schools there were almost as many schools as individuals.

The most remarkable of the painters of figures in the open air was Bastien-Lepage (1848–1884), who died young, but whose influence outlived him. *Pleinairisme* was especially seductive to landscape painters—Monet, Pissarro, Sisley, Cézanne, who were also Impressionists in technique. Renoir and Henri Martin, although they occasionally paint landscape, are better known as painters of figures, which, when looked at closely, seem mere patches of colour, but seen from the right distance become a delight to the eye. " Impressionism," it has been said, " renews landscape by a loving and intelligent treatment of light, and, in its desire for intensity, discovers the new technique which decomposes tone in order to reinforce it." [1]

FIG. 570.—THE VIGIL.
MILLET.
(Formerly in the Tabourier Collection, Paris.)
Gazette des Beaux-Arts.

[1] Séailles, *Gazette des Beaux-Arts*, 1903, i. p. 80. The following lines are also noteworthy : " *Pointillisme* [*i.e.* applying colour in small flakes or dots] is the logical consequence of the doctrine of the Impressionists, which was, roughly speaking, that of the decomposition of rays of light. The

One of the masters of Impressionism, Degas, is a most refined artist, a draughtsman as subtle as Ingres, but deliberately vulgar or extravagant in his conceptions. Another, Besnard, seeks to convey an intense suggestion of life from the harmonious juxtaposition of the most brilliant tints, and seems to attempt to exaggerate the splendour of sunlight. A third, Carrière (d. 1905), in a spirit of reaction against *Pleinairisme*, carries his preoccupation with the fluidity of atmosphere to an extreme, and drowns his figures in the diffused glow of

FIG. 571.—PORTRAIT OF GENERAL PRIM.
H. REGNAULT.
(The Louvre.)

a twilight which emphasises their melancholy. It may be said that in general Impressionists and *Pleinairistes* have abused the function of light, making abstractions of solid realities, which nevertheless exist and claim their rights.

FIG. 572.—A STREET IN SMYRNA.
DECAMPS.
(The Louvre.)
(Photo. by Neurdein.)

FIG. 573.—THE SISTERS.
TH. CHASSÉRIAU.
(A. Chassériau Collection.)
Gazette des Beaux-Arts.

Under the influence of Millet and Courbet, reinforced by a growing sympathy with the working classes, art has greatly enlarged

academic school had known only an artificial distribution of light, a studio light, in fact. The Impressionists set themselves to analyse light, to isolate the elements, and so to increase the vibration " (Cochin, *Gazette des Beaux-Arts*, 1903, i. p. 455).

its range of subjects. It deals with the labours of towns and fields, scenes of the street, the village, the sea, the factory, not only as in the case of the Dutch masters, from a taste for picturesque observation, but in the tender and fraternal spirit of Millet. Among the painters who have contributed to this transformation, this exaltation of the genre-picture, I may mention Ulysse Butin, Lhermitte, Roll, and Steinlen. How far we are with them from " the golden shades of Watteau's parks " and " the companies who whisper of love to the rustle of satins!" [1]

FIG. 574.—THE WINNOWERS.
COURBET.
(Museum, Nantes.)
Gazette des Beaux-Arts.

The naturalism of Courbet and Manet provoked an idealist reaction, symbolistic rather than academic. The influence of the English Pre-Raphaelites played its part here; the chief representatives of this refined and aristocratic tendency in France were Gustave Moreau and Paul Baudry (Figs. 575, 576).

In the works of Puvis de Chavannes (1824–1898) we find *pleinairisme*, symbolism, and idealism, but, above all, poetry and a lofty logic. He was the greatest decorative painter of the nineteenth century, the only one who was able to paint a vast composition on a wall without making holes in it by importunate shadows.

FIG. 576.—FORTUNE.
BAUDRY.
(Musée du Luxembourg,
Paris.)

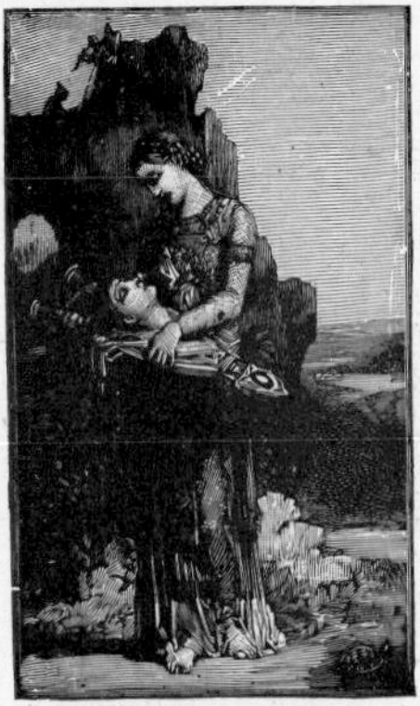

FIG. 575.—ORPHEUS.
G. MOREAU.
(Musée du Luxembourg,
Paris.)

His great works are in the Sorbonne (Fig. 580), the Pantheon, the Museums of Amiens, Lyons, Marseilles,

[1] In the words of Anatole France.

FIG. 577.—THE LADY WITH THE
CRESCENT.
BONNAT.
(E. Kann Collection, Paris.)

FIG. 578.—PORTRAIT OF ERNEST RENAN.
BONNAT.
(Psichari Collection.)
(Photo. by Braun, Clement and Co.)

580), the Pantheon, the Museums of Amiens, Lyons, Marseilles, and Boston. The contemporaries with whom he had most in common were the Lyonnais, Chenavard, a thinker rather than a painter, and Chassériau (Fig. 573), an original artist who died young (1819-1856). Puvis resembled Giotto not only in the simplicity of his attitudes and movements, but also in a deliberate lack of finish and even incorrectness in his draughtsmanship. This somewhat puerile archaism was the aberration of a man of great talent who was unsurpassed in the dexterity with which he grouped figures against heroic or idyllic landscape, but who rarely deigned to represent life in motion.

The study of the great masters of the past, who have become so accessible in the museums of Europe, is an important factor in modern art; the work of many distinguished French painters gives a sort of synthesis of a uniform academic

FIG. 579.—THE LADY WITH
THE GLOVE.
CAROLUS DURAN.
(Musée du Luxembourg,
Paris.)

education, and of the influence of some genius of a former age, to whom the artist is drawn by individual temperament. Thus, Bon-

FIG. 580.—THE SACRED GROVE.
PUVIS DE CHAVANNES.
(Hemicycle of the Sorbonne, Paris.)

nat's vigorous art (Figs. 577, 578) was nourished on that of Ribera and Velasquez; Ricard was educated by Titian and Rembrandt;

FIG. 581.—CONSCRIPTS.
DAGNAN-BOUVERET.
(Palais Bourbon, Paris.)

FIG. 582.—ST. SEBASTIAN.
HENNER.
(Musée du Luxembourg, Paris.)

Henri Regnault (Fig. 571) by Goya; Velasquez inspired Carolus Duran in his best canvases (the *Lady with the Glove,* Fig. 579);

Correggio and Prudhon meet in Henner, the painter of silvery carnations (Fig. 582); Roybet swears by Frans Hals, H. Lévy by Rubens, Bail by Vermeer; Bauffry and Benjamin Constant are Venetians; Bastien-Lepage and Dagnan-Bouveret (Fig. 581) love Holbein. It must be understood that in all these cases the posthumous lesson has been freely sought and assimilated, and that the disciple has not produced mere

FIG. 583.—CLEOPATRA ON THE CYDNUS.
MAKART.
(Museum, Stuttgart.)
Kunstgeschichte in Bildern. (Seemann, Leipzig.)

pasticci, which modern taste would not tolerate—in France at least. Schools of plagiarists such as those founded on Leonardo and Raphael in the sixteenth century would be denounced by public opinion, and even Raphael himself would be called to account for the indiscretion of his borrowings.

The schools of painting in Holland and Belgium (Israels, Wauters, Leys, and Gallait) owe something alike to David, to the French Romanticists, to the great Flemish and Dutch painters of the seventeenth century. They have produced a whole series of solid works strong in conception and design; but, strange to say, of artists bred in the lands of Rubens and of Rembrandt, there has been no true colourist among them except Braekelaer. In Holland, modern landscape has found distinguished interpreters in the brothers Maris and the marine painter Mesdag.

FIG. 584.—FIELD-MARSHAL VON MOLTKE.
LENBACH.
(Mr. S. Whitman, London.)

In Germany, the Romantic tendency was at first incarnated in a fantastic Viennese, Moritz von Schwind, who painted historical episodes and mediæval legends with a touch of deliberate archaism. But the dominant school was that of the so-called Nazarenes, whose centre of activity was Rome, and whose chief tenet was the imitation of the fifteenth century Italian. The masters of this school, Overbeck (1789-1869), Führich, and Schnorr, are now almost forgotten, as are also Cornelius and his pupil Kaülbach, who sought inspiration from Dürer; they painted as badly as Ingres, drew very

FIG. 585.—THE NEREIDS
BÖCKLIN.
(Museum, Basle.)

FIG. 586.—FREDERICK THE GREAT.
RAUCH.
(Berlin.)

feebly, and had a predilection for vast symbolic compositions, which are very wearisome and require a commentary. Historic and anecdotic painting had its Meissonier in Menzel, who made Frederick the Great and his Court live again in his works with much intelligence and great dexterity of handling. A neo-Venetian School sprang up in Vienna under Hans Makart (1840-1884), a brilliant colourist of mediocre intelligence (Fig. 583). Titian, Van Dyck, and the English portraitists were the educators of Lenbach (d. 1904), whose admirable portraits of Bismarck, Moltke, and William I. are more striking than refined (Fig. 584).

FIG. 587.—THE FIGHTING TÉMÉRAIRE.
TURNER.
(National Gallery, London.)

French realism found adherents in Uhde and Liebermann, the former inclining to mysticism, the second more directly inspired by Millet.

ART IN THE NINETEENTH CENTURY

Finally, German Switzerland produced a colourist whose extravagance was not free from affectation in Böcklin (1827–1900), at once a realist and a romanticist, a painter and a thinker, whose art suffered from his desire to dazzle and to propound riddles (Fig. 585). The Saxon Max Klinger (b. 1857) is the heir of Böcklin. Painter, engraver, and sculptor, he, too, shows a kind of deliberate eccentricity, but he is a more cultivated artist and has a more robust talent. At the present time, the influence of the French art of the last generation seems to have become dominant in Germany, which has several clever artists, but no national style.

FIG. 588.—HOPE.
WATTS.
(Tate Gallery, London.)
(Photo. by Hollyer.)

Italy has produced a *plein-airiste* landscape-painter, the portrayer of Alpine summits, Segantini (Fig. 589), who has exercised a very considerable influence upon the French School. Another Italian, Boldini, a strange compound of Baudry and Manet, should perhaps be classed among the Parisians of the Decadent School; but there are rare manipulative qualities in his elegant and neurotic portraits.

FIG. 589.—THE DRINKING TROUGH.
G. SEGANTINI.
(Società per le Belle Arti, Milan.)

Since about the middle of the nineteenth century, the French School has given the tone in art to continental Europe; England alone forms an independent province, in which, however, artists of original talent have become rare of late. In the first half of the century, the greatest of the English artists was Turner (1775–1851), a painter who worshipped light with a kind of frenzy, a romantic

321

Claude Lorrain, feverish, and sometimes theatrical (Fig. 587). [His contemporary, Constable, as I have said, deserves the credit of creating modern landscape, for he was the first to accept the literal facts of Nature as the bases for the most consummate works of art. His influence has been profound and universal. During the first half of the century, one of those local schools which have been commoner in the United Kingdom than elsewhere, at least in modern times, grew up in the cathedral town of Norwich. It produced a few landscape-painters worthy to rank with the best of other schools in Crome (1769–1821), Cotman (1782–1842), Vincent (1796–1831), and Stark (1794–1859).] Under the influence of Lawrence (d. 1830), the great school of English portrait-painters of the eighteenth century had already fallen into academicism, and English painting generally went through a phase of triviality and insignificance. From this it was rescued in 1848 by three friends, Hunt, Rossetti, and Millais, who founded the " Pre-Raphaelite Brotherhood." Millais gradually abandoned

FIG. 590.—THE YEOMAN OF THE GUARD.
MILLAIS.
(National Gallery.)

the stricter principles of the Brotherhood, and became a first-rate painter on traditional lines (Fig. 590) ; but Rossetti had a brilliant disciple in Burne-Jones, while G. F. Watts, though his development was independent, was inspired by similar ideas. Violently attacked by the academic majority, the Pre-Raphaelites were eloquently defended by the æsthete John Ruskin [a writer whose exquisite mastery of English prose was perhaps a stronger factor in the extraordinary influence he exercised on æsthetics than his dogmatic and irresponsible criticism].

FIG. 591.—LE CHANT D'AMOUR.
BURNE-JONES.
(Ismay Collection, Dawpool.)

The Pre-Raphaelites saw in Raphael an apostate from the ideal and a high-priest of academicism. They modelled themselves on Botticelli and Mantegna. But they were no vulgar imitators. The most salient characteristic of their school is intellectualism, a contempt for the doctrine of "art for art's sake." They desired to narrate and to teach, to touch the hearts of the crowd, to go to the people and convert them to new ideas of beauty. Nevertheless, they did not make

FIG. 592.—PORTRAIT OF THE ARTIST'S MOTHER.
WHISTLER.
(Musée du Luxembourg, Paris.)

their appeal through homely anecdote, after the manner of Hogarth. Antiquity and Celtic mediævalism furnished them with legends in

FIG. 593.—THE LITTLE BLUE BONNET.
WHISTLER.
(Mr. William Heinemann, London.)

which they discovered and sought to make others discover symbols. Though some of them, as early as 1848, forestalled the French School in the practice of *plein-airisme* and *pointillisme* [1] (see note on p. 314), they were not Impressionists; they had a horror of loose and hasty handling; their own method, which is minute and pedantic in touch, juxtaposed crude and violent colours without attempting to harmonise them.

This dry and artificial manner, though subservient to a high ideal, could not fail to provoke weariness and revolt. An American painter - etcher, Whistler (Figs. 592-593), who, like Manet, took

[1] Monet and Pissarro went to London in 1870, and there came under the influence of the English artists, more especially that of Turner, who had died twenty years before, and whose last works were Impressionistic.

Velasquez for his exemplar, but was less aggressive in the expression of his preferences, appeared in London exhibitions with some

FIG. 594.—PORTRAIT OF MISS LA PRIMAUDAYE.
GEORGE HENRY.
(Mr. Peacock.)

Impressionist portraits of a delicate grey tonality, and certain slightly executed landscapes " in the French manner," one of which in particular, a *Nocturne in black and gold*, created a sensation. Ruskin attacked Whistler, denouncing him as " a coxcomb who had flung a paint-pot in the face of the public." Whistler brought an action against Ruskin (1878); he obtained a verdict with *one farthing* damages, and the action, in which Burne-Jones appeared as a witness to testify against the new art, seemed to ratify the triumph of Pre-Raphaelism, which had conquered public taste and meant to maintain its position. As a fact, it was the beginning of its decline. Whistler died in 1903, acclaimed and imitated; the school of Rossetti and of Burne-Jones is almost defunct, and French art, in its most recent development, finds many adherents north of the Channel.

The æsthetics of the Pre-Raphaelite Brotherhood never held undisputed sway in contemporary England. A painter of Dutch origin, Alma Tadema, has achieved distinction by his pictures of classic life, minutely finished, but not without dignity. [Leighton, the late President of the Royal Academy (d. 1896), was a painter on the same lines, but of less virility, whose art had much in common with that of Bouguereau. Portraiture has been brilliantly represented by Orchardson (who is also famous as a

FIG. 595.—NAPOLEON ON BOARD THE BELLEROPHON.
W. Q. ORCHARDSON.
(Tate Gallery, London)

most refined painter of history and genre), by Herkomer, Ouless Shannon, Lavery (Fig. 596), the late Charles Furse, &c.; and the

English tradition in landscape has been worthily maintained by Hook, Alfred East, Adrian Stokes, Lathangue, Aumonier, &c., while Swan holds a place somewhat apart from all the rest, primarily as a painter and sculptor of animals of great originality and power.

Various local centres have arisen and contributed in their turn to the interest and originality of English Art. The most important of these is the Scottish school, which has exercised a considerable influence on British Art for the last forty years. Its chief members are Orchardson, the late John Pettie, MacWhirter, Peter Graham, Macbeth, and Murray. During the last ten or fourteen years, the most original section of this school has been that associated with Glasgow, from which city many painters of European

FIG. 596.—SPRING.

LAVERY.

reputation have issued — Lavery (Fig. 596), Guthrie, George Henry (Fig. 594), Roche, and others. Another local centre is the one founded at Newlyn, in Cornwall, some five and twenty years ago. It includes many excellent painters, whose methods are more akin to those favoured in Paris than to the traditional methods of English painting. The most able members of this *coterie* are Stanhope Forbes and his wife, formerly Miss Elizabeth Armstrong. Another group is that formed by the New English Art Club, a secession from the *queue* waiting for admission to the Royal Academy. Here the ruling spirit is that of Impressionism, in its more realistic and less sketchy form. The Club has many gifted artists among

FIG. 597.—LA MARSEILLAISE.
RUDE.
(Arc de Triomphe de l'Étoile, Paris.)

FIG. 598.—THE FIRST BURIAL.
E. L. BARRIAS.
(Petit Palais, Paris.)

its members, such as Steer, Orpin, Rothenstein, and Brabazon.]

Sculpture was but slightly affected by the Romantic movement. Down to the middle of the nineteenth century it sought inspiration mainly from antiquity, from Canova, and from Thorwaldsen. But in France, the tradition of Puget and Houdon survived; it even expanded in the hands of the Burgundian Rude (1784-1855), a vigorous artist who touched the sublime in his *Marseillaise* on the Arc de Triomphe (Fig. 597). The Salon of 1833 revealed the genius of Barye (1796-1875), an incomparable sculptor of animals, who may be called the Michelangelo of wild beasts (Fig. 621.) Cain and Gardet followed in his footsteps. In Germany also were the great sculptors Rauch and Rietschel (Fig. 586), in whom lived again, though mitigated by a Canovesque influence, something of the rugged Germanic Renaissance.

Between 1850 and about 1865, the imitation of the Italian sculpture of the Renaissance was grafted on to neo-classicism; the result was a very distinguished eclecticism, still represented by men such as Chapu, Mercié, Dubois (Figs. 599, 600, 601), Bartholdy, Guillaume, and Barrias (Fig. 598). But the tradition of Rude, revivified by a passionate study of nature, was maintained by Carpeaux (1827-1875), whose group of *Dancing* (Fig. 603) for the façade of the Opera House created not only a scandal but a school. When it was unveiled in 1869, some unknown fanatic bespattered it during the night with a bottle of ink. It was Tartuffe's handkerchief tendered to women of flesh and blood, quivering with vitality

FIG. 599.—JOAN OF ARC.
CHAPU.
(Musée du Luxembourg, Paris.)

FIG. 600.—DAVID
MERCIÉ
(Musée du Luxembourg, Paris.)

FIG. 601.—THE FLORENTINE
SINGER.
DUBOIS.
(Musée du Luxembourg, Paris.)

FIG. 602.—GENIUS GUARDING THE
SECRET OF THE TOMB.
SAINT-MARCEAUX.
(Musée du Luxembourg, Paris.)

FIG. 603.—DANCING.
CARPEAUX.
(Façade of the Opera House,
Paris.)

FIG. 604.—JOAN OF ARC.
FRÉMIET.
(Formerly Place des Pyramides,
Paris.)

and emotion, creatures to which the eye had become unaccustomed. Several contemporary masters of sculpture, Frémiet (the nephew of Rude), Dalou, Falguière, Bartholomé, and Injalbert, seem more or less akin to Carpeaux. But this school is realistic rather than naturalistic; the influence of great examples is still evident in the slenderness and elegance of the forms (Figs. 600, 601.) Integral naturalism, which had had no prophets in sculpture since the time of Donatello, has found two in our time: Rodin in France, and Constantin Meunier in Belgium. Meunier is the Millet of sculpture, a Millet who gives us true images, not of peasants, but of miners and artisans (Fig. 608). Rodin, the more varied and poetical spirit, is also the less temperate and more aggressive of the two. In addition to admirable portraits, to single figures that Donatello might have signed, and groups full of feep feeling and vibrant passion, he has expressed in marble all the visions of a heated fancy, often tending towards the monstrous and abnormal. But even when he errs, this extraordinary artist is never feeble; his forms are still living and palpitating; the clay or the marble shares the hyperæsthesia of the sculptor (Figs. 609, 610).

Florentine influences have laid their impress on the work of a

FIG. 605.—FOUNTAIN OF THE FOUR QUARTERS OF THE WORLD.
CARPEAUX AND FRÉMIET.
(Allée de l'Observatoire, Paris.)

refined artist, famous as an engraver of coins and medallions, Roty; but he is neither Greek nor Florentine; in his aristocratic elegance, he rather recalls the first French transformation of Italian art, the School of Fontainebleau and Jean Goujon. A competitor with Roty, but older than he, Chaplain, adheres more closely to classic tradition and to that of the great French medallists of the seventeenth century, Dupré and Warin.

FIG. 606.—CHRISTIAN MARTYR.
FALGUIÈRE.
(Musée du Luxembourg, Paris.)

[In England, where, for various reasons, sculpture has never flourished since those distant days when the Gothic cathedrals afforded it a shelter, one of the greatest sculptors of modern times arose about the middle of the nineteenth century. This was Alfred Stevens (1818-1875), whose monument to Wellington in St. Paul's (Fig. 612), and sketch for a memorial of the 1851 Exhibition in the Victoria and Albert Museum, are magnificent conceptions. Another good sculptor of the time was Foley (1818-1874), an Irishman. During the last twenty years this branch has shown considerable vitality in the United Kingdom, producing excellent masters in Ford, Thornycroft, Brock, Drury, Frampton, Colton, John, Leighton, who showed a keener sense of reality in marble than on canvas, and a man of real genius in Alfred Gilbert, the sculptor of the Tomb of the Duke of Clarence at Windsor (Fig. 613).]

FIG. 607.—GLORIA VICTIS.
A. MERCIÉ.
(Hôtel de Ville, Paris.)

Since about 1890 the expressive resources of sculpture have been enriched by a revival of polychromy, which increases daily in popularity. Polychromy was only banished from sculpture in the grand style in the days of Michelangelo, because a great number of antique statues were then discovered which had been washed white by rain. In classic and mediæval times sculptors coloured their marbles, and examples of polychromy, still frequent in the first half of the sixteenth century, have persisted in Spain down to our own times. We may even say that it has never been abandoned in popular sculpture and religious imagery. In this return to painted sculpture, which will perhaps be exclusively adopted in the near future, the part of initiator has fallen to a French artist, Gérôme, who was both painter and sculptor, though he shows greater original-

FIG. 608.—INDUSTRY.

C. MEUNIER.

(Musée du Luxembourg, Paris.)

ity in statuary. A typical work by him is the polychrome figure in the Luxembourg personifying the Necropolis of Tanagra (Fig. 611). Barrias in France and Klinger in Germany have successfully followed in his footsteps.

In dealing with the French art of the nineteenth century, we have noted the influence exercised by various elements from without and from the past, inspiration derived from England, Spain, Holland, Germany, Venice, Florence, and Rome. I have still a few words to say as to an influence which manifested itself in the industrial arts as early as the middle of the eighteenth century, the influence of the Far East. Chinese motives of decoration play an important part in the furniture and ceramics of the reign of Louis XV. The manufacture of Chi-

FIG. 609.—BUST OF A WOMAN.

RODIN.

(Musée du Luxembourg, Paris.)

nese porcelain began about the period of Charlemagne; traders brought specimens to Europe from the thirteenth century onward; in the eighteenth century, decoration borrowed motives from these, and Watteau amused himself by painting *Chinoiseries.*

But Chinese art had given birth to a child more gifted than itself, the art of Japan, which delights in all the subtleties of line, all the brilliant caprices of colour, disdains, symmetry by virtue of a kind of glorified strabism, and paints and carves animals with a realism still unrivalled in Europe. The golden age of this art was the eighteenth century. Europe discovered it in the second half of the nineteenth century. The lessons that had travelled so far were first assimilated by decorative art; they gave it instruction in the treatment of lacquers and enamels, but, above all, they helped it to throw off the trammels of tradition. The century that had produced so many artists had not been able to create a style; after the so-called Empire style, which dates from the closing years of Louis XV., there had been nothing but a puerile eclecticism, varied by servile imitations of antique styles. Japan gave Europe the opportunity to discover what she was seeking. It was not the parent, but the godfather, of the Modern Style.

The evolution of this style is still in its initial stage, and it is difficult to define it. It is easier to say what it is not than what it is. Of all the styles hitherto known, it is the first which has conscientiously pursued novelty, and has turned away resolutely from the beaten track. From this tendency, there is but a step to the exaggerated and the grotesque; but we must not judge by a few isolated extravagances. Inspired, as its English name suggests, by the teaching of Ruskin, who preached the worship of simplicity, of expressive line and colour, and endowed with its first masterpieces by William Morris, in connection with the Pre-Raphaelite movement, it found timely inspiration in the art of Japan, emancipation from the bondage of symmetry and of the Greek orders, an admirable comprehension of flora and fauna as decorative elements. But it looked to Japan for lessons rather than for models. It prides itself on imitating nothing, on turning away alike from classic and Gothic tradition, on substituting individual expression, the materialisation of thought, to the schematism of transmitted and conventional forms. It does not find beauty in elegance, but solely in the fitness, the eloquence of the line, the gentle or the imperious suggestion of colour. Before acclaiming or condemning this movement, we must give its as yet green fruits time to ripen.[1]

FIG. 613.—TOMB OF THE DUKE OF CLARENCE.
ALFRED GILBERT.
(Windsor.)
(Photo. by King.)

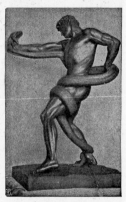

FIG. 614.—ATHLETE AND
PYTHON.
LEIGHTON.

May we be permitted to forecast the

[1] " The time has come," wrote M. H. Cochin recently, " when we may sing *De Profundis* over the so-called Modern Style " (*Gazette des Beaux-Arts*, 1903, ii., p. 44). This pronouncement seems to me very premature.

future after this rapid survey of the past? What will be the fate of art in this twentieth century upon which we have entered?

We may, I think, predict the extinction of local schools. Rapidity and facility of com-

FIG. 615.—THE MISSES HUNTER.
JOHN SARGENT.
(Mrs. Hunter.)

munication will make it impossible that rival schools should spring up a few leagues apart, like those of Athens and Argos, Florence and Perugia, Bruges and Tournai. In the eighteenth century, schools became national: we had the French School, the English School, the Spanish School. In the second half of the nineteenth century, the French school became supreme on the Continent and tended to give the tone to all the rest; but at the same time, the unity of this school disappeared; we find it embracing Classicists, Romanticists, Realists, Idealists, Impressionists. Thus, everything points to the assumption that schools will henceforth no longer bear the names of cities or of nations; there will no longer be rivalries of countries, but of principles.

How the field of our studies has expanded and at the same time gained in simplicity! In the nineteenth cen-

FIG. 616.—THE DUCHESS OF
PORTLAND.
JOHN SARGENT.
(Mrs. Meynell, *The Work of John S. Sargent*, Heinemann, London.)

FIG. 617.—COUNT TOLSTOI.
PRINCE TROUBETZKOI.
(J Reinach Collection, Paris)

tury, for the first time in history, modern art, the child of the Renaissance, had representatives in every country in Europe: the sculptor Thorwaldsen, the painters Thaulow and Edelfeldt, in the Scandinavian countries; the sculptors Antokolsky and Troubetzkoi, the painters Verestchagin, Rjepin, and Serow, in Russia; the Hungarian Munkacsy, the Galician Matejko, the Czech Brozik, the Greek Rallis, the Turk Hamdi-Bey. The United States have entered the lists brilliantly with a sculptor like St.-Gaudens (Fig. 619), and painters such as Whistler, Alexander, and Sargent. These and many others, educated in Paris, in Rome, or in Germany, have founded schools in their own countries, which are not national, but which draw vigour and inspiration from those great currents which make up European art.

Will the art of the future be primarily realistic? I think not. One of the great discoveries of the nineteenth century, photography, has made reality more familiar to us than to our forefathers. What artist, were he as gifted as a Van Eyck, would wish to compete with a sensitive plate?[1] What we demand above all things from art is what photography, even polychromatic photography, cannot give — the suggestive beauty of form and movement, the radiance, the intensity, the mystery of colour— in a word, the equivalent, in

FIG 618.—INTERIOR, IN THE "MODERN STYLE," ARRANGED BY BARBÉDIENNE-DUMAS, PARIS.

[1] " How foolish it is to think of copying nature. We need only to parallel it." (Puvis de Chavannes.)

334

art, of poetry in literature. The art of the twentieth century will be, I am convinced, idealistic and poetical, as well as popular; it will translate the eternal aspiration of man, of all men, towards that which is lacking in daily life, and that which completes it, those elements of superfluity and luxury which our sensibility craves and which no mere utilitarian progress can supplant.

Far from believing that the social mission of art is at an end, or drawing near that end, I think it will play a greater part in the twentieth century than ever. And I think—or at least hope—that greater importance than ever will be attached to the study of art as a branch of culture. This study is one which no civilised man, whatever his profession, should ignore in these days. It is in this belief that I have prepared this brief survey, which I hope may serve the educative purposes of art.

BIBLIOGRAPHY OF CHAPTER XXV.

D. S. MacColl and T. D. Gibson Carmichel, *Nineteenth Century Art*, Glasgow, 1902; J. Meier-Graefe, *Entwicklungsgeschichte der modernen Kunst*, Stuttgart, 1904; (cf. *Gazette des Beaux-Arts*, 1906, i., p. 347); M. Schmidt, *Kunstgeschichte des XIXten Jahrhundert*, vol. i–ii, Leipzig, 1904–1906; R. Muther, *Geschichte der Malerei im XIXten Jahrhundert*, 3 vols., Munich, 1893–1894 (English trans., London, 1896); H. Marcel, *La Peinture française au XIXe siècle*, Paris, 1905; K. Schmidt, *Französische Malerei*, 1800–1900, Leipzig, 1903; *Französische Plastik und Architektur*, Leipzig, 1904; E. and J. de Goncourt, *Etudes d'Art*, Paris, 1893 (cf. *Gazette des Beaux-Arts*, 1893, ii., p. 507); F. Benoit, *L'Art français sous la Révolution et l'Empire*, Paris, 1897; L. Rosenthal, *La Peinture romantique française*, 1815–1830, Dijon, 1900; A. Michel, *Notes sur l'Art moderne (Painting)*, Paris, 1896; R. Marx, *Etudes sur l'Ecole française*, Paris, 1902; L. Bénédite, *La Peinture au XIXe siècle*, Paris, 1909; C. Mauclair, *The Great French Painters, 1830 to the present day*, London, 1903; G. Lafenestre, *La Peinture française du XIXe siècle* (Baudry, Cabanel, Delaunay, Hébert), Paris, 1898; *La Collection Tome-Thiéry au Louvre* (*Gazette des Beaux-Arts*, 1902, i., p. 177); *La Tradition dans la Peinture française*, Paris, 1898; A. Michel, *L'Exposition centennale de Peinture française* (*Gazette des Beaux-Arts*, 1900, ii., p. 284); R. de la Sizeranne, *Le Miroir de la Vie, essai sur l'évolution de l'esthétique*, Paris, 1903; E. Pottier, *Le Salon de 1892* (*Gazette des Beaux-Arts*, 1892, i., p. 441; modern Art in the light of antique Art).

Ch. Ephrussi, *Gérard* (*Gazette des Beaux-Arts*, 1890, ii., p. 449); E. de Goncourt, *Prudhon*, Paris, 1876; E. Bricon, *Prudhon*, Paris, 1907; Ch. Blanc, *Les trois Vernet*, Paris, 1898; A. Dayot, *Les Vernet*, Paris, 1898; Ch. Blanc, *Ingres* (*Gazette des Beaux-Arts*, 1867, i., p. 415); H. Lapauze, *Ingres*, Paris, 1911; Yves Scantrel, *Ingres* (*Grande Revue*, June 25, 1911); J. Schnerb, *Paul Flandrin* (*ibid.*, 1902, ii., p. 114); L. Flandrin, *Hippolyte Flandrin*, Paris, 1903; M. Tourneaux, *Delacroix*, Paris, 1903; A. Alexandre, *Histoire de la Peinture militaire*, Paris, 1890; Lhomme, *Raffet*, Paris, 1892; H. Béraldi, *Raffet* (*Gazette des Beaux-Arts*, 1892, i., p. 353); H. Béraldi, *Charlet* (*ibid.*, 1893, ii., p. 46);

FIG. 619.—MOURNING.

SAINT-GAUDENS.

(Monument executed for Mrs. Adams in a cemetery near Washington.)

O. Gréard, *Meissonier*, Paris, 1897, English trans., London, 1897; M. Vachon, *Detaille*, Paris, 1896.

D. C. Thomson, *Millet and the Barbizon School*, London, 1903; E. Michel, *Les Maîtres du paysage*, Paris, 1906; W. Gensel, *Millet und Rousseau*, Bielefeld, 1902; H. Marcel, *Millet*, Paris, 1903; R. Rolland, *Millet*, London, 1903; G. Riat, *Courbet*, Paris, 1906; Moreau-Nélaton, *Corot*, Paris, 1905

B. Prost, *Tassaert* (*Gazette des Beaux-Arts*, 1886, i., p. 28); G. Larroumet, *H. Regnault*, Paris, 1890;

GENERAL BIBLIOGRAPHY.

To keep the bibliographies of this book up to date, it will suffice to take notes from the *Archäologischer Anzeiger* (antique art) and the *Repertorium für Kunstwissenschaft* (Christian, modern, and Oriental art). This latter has discontinued its bibliographies since 1904. We must resort to the *Monatshefte für Kunstwissenschaft* (Leipzig) and to the *Répertoire d'Art et d'Archéologie* (Paris from 1910).

Reproductions of many famous works of art will be found in the following works, which should form part of every art library:

Seroux d'Agincourt, *Histoire de l'Art par les Monuments* (fourth to sixteenth century), Paris, 6 vols., 1823, 325 plates, various editions and translations; F. Winter and G. Dehio, *Kunstgeschichte in Bilden*, 5 vols. (to the eighteenth century), Leipzig, 1899–1900; Reber and Bayersdorfer, *Klassichter Bilderschatz*, 12 vols., Munich, 1888–1900 (1,800 reproductions of pictures, from fourteenth to eighteenth century); the same, *Klassischer Skulpturenschatz*, 4 vols., Munich, 1896–1900 (ancient and modern sculpture); P. Vitry and G. Brière, *Documents de Sculpture française du Moyen Age*, Paris, 1904 (940 photographs); G. Hirt, *Kulturgeschichtliches Bilderbuch*, 6 vols., Munich 1887–1893 (3,500 reproductions, sixteenth to eighteenth century); S. Reinach, *Répertoires des Peintures du Moyen Age et de la Renaissance*, 4 vols., Paris, 1904 (1,100 reproductions of pictures, fourteenth to sixteenth century).

Every art library should possess also the *Dictionnaires des Artistes* of Thieme and Becker (Leipzig, 1907, *et seq.*) and of Bénézet (Paris, 1911, *et seq.*), as well as A. Michel's *l'Histoire de l'Art* and others (Paris, 1905, *et seq.*); *La Storia dell' arte*, by G. Rizzo and P. Loesca (Turin, 1913, *et seq.*), and the *Ars Una Series*.

INDEX

INDEX

INDEX

Basalt head (Louvre), 24.
Basilica of Constantine, 89
Basilicas, 98, 99.
Bassorah, 22.
Bastien-Lepage, 314, 319.
Bathers, 296, 313.
Battles of Alexander, Le Brun, 277.
Baudry, Paul, 316, 319.
Beau Dieu d'Amiens, 125.
Beaune, hospital of, 224.
Beauneveu, André, 127.
Beauvais, 116.
Beechey, William, 300.
Belle Jardinière, Raphael, 198.
Bellini, Giovanni, 168, 172; Gentile, 168, 171; Jacopo, 168.
Beltraffio, 189.
Bernardin de St. Pierre, 311.
Bernay, treasure of, 75.
Berenson, B., 165, 197
Berlin Museum, 70.
Bernini, 134, 251.
Besnard, 315.
Betti: see Pintoricchio.
Bevilacqua, Palazzo, 136.
Bianchi, 213.
Bibliothèque Nationale, 143; Ste. Geneviève, 143.
Bilbao, 257.
Birth of the Virgin, A. del Sarto, 205.
Bismarck, portrait, 320.
Boccador, Il, 136.
Böcklin, 321.
Bœotia, 80.
Boileau, 305.
Boldini, 321.
Bologna, Giovanni da, 212.
Bonheur, Mlle. Rosa, 311.
Bonington, 311.
Bonnat, 253n., 255, 257, 318.
Book of Hours, by the Limbourgs, Condé Museum, Chantilly, 218, 221; of Etienne Chevalier, by Fouquet, *do.*, 228.
Bordeaux Cathedral, 124, 126.
Borgognone, Ambrogio, 189.
Bosch, Jerome, 227.
Boscoreale, 76.
Botta, 24.
Botticelli, 156, 203, 323.
Boucher, 290, 291, 294.
Bouguereau, 308.
Boulle, 283.
Bourbonnais, school of, 229.
Bouts, Thierry, 221, 223, 234.
Brabazon, 326.

Bramante, 89, 134, 143, 199.
Brancacci Chapel, 155.
Branchidæ, 38.
Brandt, Isabella, 270.
Brascassat, 311.
Braekelaer, 319.
Brescia, school of, 181.
Breton, Jules, 312.
Breughel, 227.
Brock, 329.
Broederlam, Melchior, 217.
Broken Pitcher, Greuze, 294.
Bronze age, the, 11–12; doors of Baptistery, Florence, 159.
Bronzino, 206.
Brouwer, Adriaen, 262.
Brozik, 334.
Bruges, school of, 333.
Brunellesco, 132, 143.
Brussels, 146.
Bruyn, Barthel, 244.
Bryaxis, 40.
Brygos, 78.
Bugatto, Zanetto, 220n.
Burgkmair, 238.
Burgundy, Dukes of, 216–219; school of, 112, 128, 216.
Burlington, Lord, 145.
Burne-Jones, 299, 324.
Burning Bush, the, Froment, 228.
Butin, Ulysse, 316.
Buttresses, flying, 113.
Byzantine art, 98–104.

C.

Cabanel, 308.
Cabinet des Estampes, 267; des Médailles, 75, 82, 101.
Caffieri, 283.
Cain, 326.
Cairo Museum, 14; mosques, 102.
Caliari, Paolo: see Veronese.
Callicrates, 47.
Callot, Jacques, 275.
Calvaert, Denis, 248.
Calvary by Sluter, 218.
Cambio, Arnolfo di, 132.
Cambrai, League of, 179.
Cameos, 82.
Camondo clock, the, 296.
Campin, Robert, 224.
Campo Santo of Pisa, 153.
Canaletto, 180.
Cano, Alonzo, 255.

Canon Van de Paele, J. Van Eyck, 20, 222.
Canova, 91, 165, 297, 303, 326.
Canterbury Cathedral, 112, 116.
Caracalla, bust of, 92.
Caravaggio, 250.
Carolus-Duran, 318.
Carmine, 155, 203.
Carnac, 10.
Carpaccio, 174.
Carpeaux, 326.
Carracci, Lodovico, 248; Annibale and Agostino, 248; school of the, 248, 250.
Carrière, 315.
Carrousel, Louvre, 139, 143.
Caryæ, 51.
Caryatides in architecture, 51.
Casa Trivulzio, at Milan, 170.
Casino Rospigliosi, the, 93.
Castagno, Andrea del, 155, 205.
Castiglione, Balthazar, portrait, Raphael, 201.
Catacombs, the, 95, 96.
Caumont, Arcisse de, 106.
Cavallini, Pietro, 152.
Cazin, 312.
Cellini, Benvenuto, 212.
Celts, flint instruments, 9; art of the, 107.
Centaurs and Lapithæ, battle of, 43.
Cephisodotus, 56, 57.
Ceramicus of Athens, 65.
Certosa, the, at Pavia, 133.
Cézanne, 314.
Chaldean art, 22–28.
Chambiges, Pierre, 136.
Champaigne, Philippe de, 275.
Champmol, Carthusian Monastery, 218.
Chantilly, 136, 218, 221.
Chaplain, 329.
Chapu, 326.
Chardin, Simon, 294.
Charlet, 309.
Chartres Cathedral, 116, 121, 123.
Chassériau, 317.
Chasseur Officer, Géricault, 306.
Chenavard, 317.
Chénier, André, 304.
Chevalier, Etienne, 228.
Chian sculptures, the, 40.
Chinese art, 28, 330.
Chinoiseries, 331.
Chios, 39–40.
Chippendale, 145.
Choisy, M., 111.

INDEX

343

INDEX

INDEX

INDEX

INDEX

THE END